Everyman's Database Primer

Featuring dBASE IV® 1.1

Robert A. Byers
Cary N. Prague

SAMS
A Division of Macmillan Computer Publishing
11711 North College, Carmel, Indiana 46032 USA

FIRST EDITION
SECOND PRINTING—1991

International Standard Book Number: 0-672-22839-4

Library of Congress Catalog Card Number: 91-60315

Development Editor: *Dan Derrick*

Editors: *Jodi Jensen* and *Cheri Clark*

Technical Reviewer: *Jeb Long*

Cover Design: *Dan Armstrong*

Production: *Jeff Baker, Brad Chinn, Scott Cook, Sandy Grieshop, Tami Hughes, Bob LaRoche, Michelle Laseau, Lisa Naddy, Cindy L. Phipps, Tad Ringo, Dennis Sheehan, Bruce Steed, Suzanne Tully*

Indexers: *Jeanne Clark* and *Susan VandeWalle*

Printed in the United States of America

Trademarks

All terms mentioned in this book that are known to be trademarks or service marks are listed below. In addition, terms suspected of being trademarks or service marks have been appropriately capitalized. SAMS cannot attest to the accuracy of this information. Use of a term in this book should not be regarded as affecting the validity of any trademark or service mark.

MultiMate and Framework II are registered trademarks of Ashton-Tate Corporation.

1-2-3 is a registered trademark of Lotus Development Corporation.

dBASE IV and RapidFile are registered trademarks of Ashton-Tate Corporation.

Q&A is a registered trademark of Symantec Corporation.

PFS:FILE is a registered trademark of Software Publishing Corporation.

*This book is dedicated to my wife, Karen,
and to my three sons, David, Jeffrey, and Alex,
who make my life worth living.*

Overview

Section Four Introduction to Programming and Applications 359

Contents

Section Two Working with Your Data 107

Section Three Database Features 225

Section Four Introduction to Programming and Applications 359

Acknowledgments

This is the fourth major revision of *Everyman's Database Primer*. Over the years, many people have contributed, all adding a little of themselves. The book was born in George Tate's garage at the beginning of dBASE II and Ashton-Tate. With the help and encouragement of George Tate and the author of dBASE, Wayne Ratliff, an idea became a manuscript. The skillful editing of Virginia Bare transformed the manuscript into a book. And then, the enthusiasm and support of the entire Ashton-Tate family turned the book into a success.

The first major revision of the *Primer* was caused by the introduction of dBASE III, the big brother of dBASE II. Again, the Ashton-Tate Publications group—particularly Monet Thomson and Robert Hoffman—transformed that manuscript into another successful book. When dBASE III evolved to become dBASE III PLUS, there was yet another major revision to the *Primer*. Preparation of most of the screens and much of the technical review was accomplished by Anton Byers of Softwords. Brenda Johnson-Grau polished this manuscript with unusual skill and a wry style.

The first dBASE IV edition of *Everyman's Database Primer* was made possible through the persistent and persuasive negotiations of Larry Colker,

Larry Benicasa, and Bill Jordan of the Ashton-Tate publishing group. We want to thank David Rose for his constant editing ideas and for keeping us honest while we worked.

There are other people who provided a great deal of creativity along the way: our first editor, Sara Garcia-Grant; Lisa Holstein who created the original index; Jim Payant; and editor Denise Weatherwax.

We want to thank Fred Crownover, Karen Artan, and the dBASE IV product manager, Dave Micek, for their support, testing, and final dBASE IV diskettes. Our thanks also to Michael Cuthbertson of Symsoft for providing us with an incredible screen dump utility—HOTSHOT Graphics.

A sincere thanks to Macmillan Computer Publishing for having the fortitude to see this book through, and a special thanks to Macmillan Development Editor, Dan Derrick. He has yet to learn what he's gotten himself into. . . .

A final thanks to Diana Smith for her work on every page of this book as we made the change from dBASE IV 1.0 to 1.1.

Introduction

Who This Book Is For

Everyman's Database Primer featuring dBASE IV 1.1 is designed for the beginner who has never used a relational database management software package or dBASE IV. This may be your first experience with any software package, or you may be an experienced veteran of a word processing package like MultiMate. You might even be well versed in spreadsheets like Lotus 1-2-3 and have used the "database" features of the spreadsheet. Even if you're an expert with a flat-file manager like RapidFile, Q&A, or PFS:FILE, this book is for you.

This is the fifth edition of *Everyman's Database Primer*, the all-time best-seller of database management books featuring the dBASE family of products or any other microcomputer database package. We have carefully rewritten most of the book for dBASE IV and updated it for dBASE IV 1.1, but we have left in place the original concepts that made this book so successful.

This book is as much a learning tool as it is an easy-to-read book. *Everyman's Database Primer* is not a manual. Every discussion in this book starts at a basic level, assuming that the reader knows nothing about the subject, and gradually builds into a complete exploration of each topic. You sometimes will find yourself wanting to turn several pages at once as each topic unfolds, but please try to resist temptation because each chapter uses its topics as building blocks for the discussions in the next chapter.

When you are through with this book you will no longer be a novice. You will be an accomplished user of dBASE IV capable of extracting information from raw data and helping others do the same.

What You Will Learn in This Book

In this edition of *Everyman's Database Primer*, you will learn a great deal about databases and particularly dBASE IV 1.1. The twenty-one chapters of this book cover many topics including:

- What are databases, files, records, and fields
- Planning a database
- Creating a database
- Entering, changing, and deleting data
- Sorting data
- The Control Center
- The dot prompt
- BROWSE and EDIT screens
- Queries—extracting information
- Reports
- Labels
- Forms for data entry
- Using multiple databases
- The Applications Generator
- Importing and exporting data from other programs

Working with several sample databases, you will build a respectable inventory system for the Parrot Stereo Company that will satisfy some of the company's information needs.

Using a Database System

The primary considerations in any database system are how to

- Get data into the system
- Get information out of the system

Both of these topics will be thoroughly discussed. You will be able to create any type of database with an unlimited array of fields. You will work with character, numeric, date, logical, and even memo fields, and you will learn the intricacies of each of these. You will learn how to create both simple and complex data entry forms and how to check for data that is valid and meets your own criteria when it is entered. You will ask complex questions about your data; then you'll receive your answers in the form of simple data tables or well-dressed reports. You'll even learn how to create mailing labels and mail-merge documents. Finally, you will build an application to learn how the dBASE IV Applications Generator can help you create turnkey systems that even a novice operator can use.

It takes months of hard work to become a true expert in dBASE IV. However, by using this guide, you probably will master many of the features of dBASE IV. With this knowledge, you will be able to satisfy many of your present and future information needs.

How This Book Is Organized

The twenty-one chapters of this book are organized into four sections:

- Getting Started
- Working with Your Data
- Database Features
- Introduction to Programming and Applications

The first section, "Getting Started," explains the concepts and terminology of a relational database management system and takes you through your first database file exercise, a personal phone book system. You also learn about the Control Center, the way dBASE IV makes it easy for you to do your work. After you learn about the different menus, various work surfaces, and keys, you plan a new database file and put that knowledge to use as you create the basic Parrot Stereo database file system.

You also learn about changing your file and how to add, change, and delete your data. You'll put the records into more meaningful order by sorting and indexing them.

In section two, "Working with Your Data," you begin to use different tools available in dBASE IV. First you learn about another way to communicate with dBASE IV—the dot prompt. This is the command mode in which you type in commands directly to get your work done. Though it requires a lot of memorizing (or at least a good cheat sheet), the dot prompt mode can increase your productivity once you gain an understanding of its advantages. This section also teaches logic and operators, and the concepts of Queries and QBE (Query-By-Example) are discussed. Here you learn to extract data from your database and turn it into information. This also is when you begin to learn about some of the more exotic data types, including logical, date, and the memo field. Finally in this section, you learn to use several database files at once to create very useful database views.

Section three of this book, "Database Features," is all about reports and also offers other general information. dBASE IV features a report writer that can make the most difficult reports easy to create. The report writer handles column reports, form reports, and even mail merging. You will also create and produce mailing labels. This section includes a complete discussion of the forms generator, where you learn how to create several different data entry forms for many different uses. You'll add data entry rules to your input so only accurate data gets into your system.

This section continues with a discussion of directories. You learn more about some of the utilities of dBASE IV and DOS, and about the Control Center Tools menu. The Tools menu contains utilities that let you create keystroke macros, interface with DOS from a menu-driven system, and even password-protect your files. This section ends with a chapter on retrieving data from non-dBASE files and copying dBASE data to non-dBASE files. You learn how to import and export data from and to other software packages, including other database packages, spreadsheets, and word processors.

The last section, "Introduction to Programming and Applications," covers some rudiments of programming. You learn the difference between applications and programs and how to create a complete menu-driven system using the Applications Generator.

As you read this book, keep in mind that though there is much to learn, the material in each chapter begins at an easy level and builds gradually. Every chapter starts at the same level as the end of the one you just read. Each chapter builds on the knowledge you gained from the previous chapter to help you learn more and more. After you read the entire book and have used dBASE IV for a while, go back and read the last few pages of each chapter. All of it will make sense.

Conventions Used in This Book

The following conventions have been used to increase the readability of this book:

- All keyboard keys and combinations of keys are enclosed in angle brackets and appear in **bold** type, such as **<F2>**, **<Shift>-<Tab>**, and **<Alt>-L**. When two keys are connected by a hyphen, you should press the first key, and while it is depressed, press the second key.
- Text that is displayed on your screen appears in `monospace` type.
- Characters that you are asked to type appear in blue.
- New terms that are being introduced appear in *italics*.

[illegible]

Conventions Used in This Book

[illegible]

Section One

Getting Started

chapter 1

The Database

Database is computer jargon for a familiar and essential item in our everyday lives. A database is a collection of information organized and presented to serve a specific purpose.

One of the more familiar database examples is the telephone directory. This common printed database contains the names, addresses, and telephone numbers of individuals, businesses, and governmental agencies. The addresses and telephone numbers have little value by themselves. They are useful only when they are related to a name.

The number of databases in common use is astonishing. Some common databases are a dictionary, a cookbook, a mail-order catalog, an encyclopedia, a library's card catalog, your checkbook, and so on. Other familiar databases are stock market reports in the newspaper, an accounts receivable ledger, and a personnel file.

Why are these examples databases? Why isn't the newspaper or a nonfiction book considered a database? After all, these also contain information. The reason is specific. In each of the database examples given above, information is presented in a manner that makes it easy for you to locate some particular piece of information.

In the telephone directory, the telephone numbers and addresses are related to the name. The names are presented in alphabetical order so you can find them easily. Find the name and you find both the address and the phone number. The name is the key to using the phone book. A dictionary works similarly: There is a word and a definition. The words are listed alphabetically so that they can be found, and the definition is related to the word. The key to using the dictionary is the word.

The common element in all of the examples is organized information presented in a way that makes it easy to find by the use of a key. In other words, any information that can be presented as tables (rows and columns) can be a database. Some examples of column headings in tables that could be considered databases are shown in Figure 1.1.

Examples	Column Headings				
PHONE BOOK:	NAME	ADDRESS	PHONE NUMBER		
DICTIONARY:	WORD	DEFINITION			
CATALOG:	ITEM	DESCRIPTION	SIZE	PRT NO.	COST
STOCK REPORT:	STOCK	SHARES TRADED	HIGH	LOW	

Figure 1.1. *What's a database?*

By now, you should have a general concept of a database, and you might be asking, "OK, but what's a computer database? What can I do with it that I can't do without it?" The computer database can't do anything you can't do yourself from a printed database. However, many things are just more practical to do with a computer than without a computer.

We all have found a scrap of paper with a phone number on it—no name, just a number. If we want to discover the name that belongs to the number, the telephone book isn't much help. If, however, the telephone directory is a computer database file, we can ask the computer to check the phone number, and the name will promptly appear.

Suppose you want the phone number of someone named Smith who lives on Santa Monica Boulevard in Los Angeles. You can ask the computer's Los Angeles phone book file (perhaps called LAPHONE) for the names, addresses, and phone numbers of all the Smiths on Santa Monica Boulevard. The file may not give you a single name and number, but it will surely narrow down the search.

The computer is no panacea. It can't do anything you can't. But it can help you do the things you want to do quickly and easily. It is a tool to help you accomplish things that are simply not practical without it.

Using a personal phone book as an example, a simple database might resemble the one shown in Figure 1.2.

NAME	ADDRESS	PHONE NUMBER
Byers, Robert A Sr.	9999 Glencrest, Standale	555-9242
Byers, Robert A Jr.	48 N. Catalina, Pasedena	555-9540
Cassidy, Butch	4800 Rimrock Ct. Sunland	555-1121
Goose, Sil E.	21809 Cottage Ln., Montecito	555-8667
Prague, Burton	67343 301 Trail N., Boca Del	555-4665
Prague, Cary	60 Crosskey, Windsor	555-6887
Zeus, Thor T.	25 Lightning Lane, Greece	555-6878

Figure 1.2. *A simple database*

Of course, a real database file can contain many, many more items of information than this simple database file contains. In fact, this database is much better kept in a small notebook than in a computer. You can carry the notebook around with you and make notes in it, and it's a lot cheaper. To get value from a computer, you need to have a lot of information—in general, so much information that you can't efficiently use it without the computer.

Conceptually, a computer database file is just like one that you could create from paper and pencil. Because both a paper database and a computer database exist to be used, an appropriate question is: What do you actually do with your phone book?

You write in new acquaintances, perhaps change the addresses or phone numbers of people who move or get a new phone. Maybe you cross some people out (or erase them, if you've had enough foresight to keep your records in pencil). When you want to use the information stored there, you may be trying to make a call, going to a party, or mailing a letter. Thus, your phone book—if you keep it up-to-date—reflects a process of change and, at any given time, will supply you with the information you're looking for. The same is true of a computer database file. You can easily add, remove, or change the information in a computer database file. Likewise, you can easily view information from your database file.

In your everyday activities, you are always adding and subtracting from information at hand, changing it, selecting what you want to see, and ignoring what you don't want to see. This activity is basic to the thinking process. But you are going to put all this information that you're so accustomed to having strewn about—where you can see it and touch it—into a computer database file.

Now, there will be something holding this information—something between you and the data. Once you begin to use the computer, you need to become comfortable with the idea that the data is inside the "blinking box." Even though you can no longer "touch" the information, it is there when you need it. After you become comfortable with this knowledge, you'll be amazed at how many ways a computer database file can fulfill your information needs.

Using your computer will become as easy as using your phone book. It will take some thought, some planning, and some how-to knowledge. You need to know how to create, how to use, and how to change your store of information. In the learning process, you won't have to reinvent the wheel. You are only learning a new function—a new set of mechanics for a new machine—designed to support your efforts to perceive and process information already familiar to you.

The Purpose of This Book

It is our intention in this book to teach you about databases and how to use them. To make your learning manageable, we'll use very small database files for our examples. The same database file principles apply to both large and small databases. Exactly the same principles apply to the personal phone book example as to the white pages for Los Angeles County. The only difference is that the white pages contains many more entries. To better acquaint you with computer databases—that is, how to plan them, how to make them, how to use them, and how to change them—we are going to have you build some computer database files from a few simple examples. To help you do this, we'll use the popular database management system dBASE IV. A database management system is software that takes care of all the details involved with a database and lets you use, manipulate, and change the file contents.

Why Use dBASE IV?

dBASE IV is the successor to the most powerful relational database management software available today. It contains every tool you need as a database user.

dBASE IV allows you to quickly and easily create the structure of your database file. When you finish this, dBASE IV instantly provides you with a simple on-screen data entry form you just fill in to enter your data for each record. You can create fancy custom data entry forms in just a few minutes using the screen form generator contained in dBASE IV. After your data is in the file, you can begin to turn data into information by sorting the data or by asking questions through a feature known as query-by-example. You will find that asking to see all your customers who have owed you money for more than 60 days can be an instantly sobering experience. Besides asking questions and receiving answers, you can get completely customized reports. dBASE IV has a report writer that can create any report you can think of without any programming. You also can produce mailing labels and mail-merge documents.

Finally, for those of you who want to create a menu-driven system but are afraid to program, your fears are over. dBASE IV features a powerful, yet easy-to-use, Applications Generator that lets you start with your existing database files, screens, and reports to quickly develop menu systems that will ease data entry for the most novice computer operators, even if they haven't used dBASE IV previously.

Relational Database Management Systems

dBASE IV is a relational database manager, which means it can link several files together to make them work like one file. dBASE IV can relate your customer file, your invoice file, and your inventory file to give you the ability to work with all the data as if it were in one file. How often do you need to cross-reference information that is in many different places? With a relational database management system, you just tell the system the invoice number or the customer's name or number, and it can retrieve the customer's address and other pertinent information automatically. When customers change their addresses, you don't have to update every invoice record. Because the invoice record contains the customer's *key*, which might be a name or a number, dBASE IV automatically recognizes and affects the related files when the customer record is changed.

Flat file managers such as RapidFile, Q&A, or PFS:FILE don't have these abilities. They are incapable of performing any tasks involving more than one database file, or they require that each record contain all the information needed for the system. There is no way to look up another record in a flat file.

Today's demand for constantly changing information requires a relational database management for even the simplest systems. dBASE IV gives you all the power of a real database with the ease of use traditionally associated with a small file manager.

How a Database Management System Works for You

Take a look at an example that illustrates the concepts behind a database management system. Suppose you need to replace a part in your car. You go to an auto parts store and tell the clerk which part you need. The clerk looks up the part in a set of parts catalogs.

- The first book gives the clerk an identifying number for the part.
- The clerk then looks up this part number in another book. This book shows where the part is located within the store.
- After locating the part, the clerk again uses the number to find the cost of the part from a price list.

In this example, the actual automotive parts correspond to the data items in the database. The clerk, catalogs, lists, and storage bins correspond to the database management system. To use this automotive parts management system, you tell the clerk what you want in a language that you both understand (English) and with terminology related to cars. "I need a carburetor for a '76 Belchfire Eight," you say. The clerk takes care of all the business of getting the parts, keeping the books current, knowing how to use the books, and so forth. All you need to have is a reasonable idea of what you want. The clerk, the books, and the catalogs take care of the rest.

The same is true for the computer database management system (DBMS). As soon as a DBMS is installed on a computer, the computer becomes an expert at all the details involved in storing, cataloging, and retrieving data. All you need to do is have a reasonable idea of what you want and know a little computer terminology. This book provides you with the computer terminology you need. The computer and the database management system take care of the rest.

Another example of a database management system is a large library. In many large libraries, particularly university research libraries, you are not usually allowed access to the shelves where the books are stored. To acquire a book, you must consult the card catalog, copy information from the index card onto a slip of paper, and hand the paper to a librarian. Then, unseen by you, a librarian's assistant searches through dense book stacks to retrieve the book and then delivers it to the librarian, who in turn gives it to you.

When you return the book, much of this process is reversed. The librarian gives the book to an assistant, who returns the book to its original location. Again, the card catalog, the librarian, the assistant, and the storage facilities correspond to the computer database management system. The book corresponds to the data item. All that is required of you is a little knowledge of how to use this system; the system does all the work.

Components of a Computer Database File

A personal phone book makes a good basis for your first computer database file. You'll design that file in the next chapter. You will use it as an example, and as you proceed, you'll see that the process isn't much different from putting the information on a sheet of paper with an ordinary typewriter.

If you were going to type this information on a piece of paper, you might:

- Type a page title
- Determine how wide to make the column (how many spaces)
- Type column headings such as name, address, and phone number

With a computer database file, these activities are not optional; you must:

- Give the database file a title
- Determine the size of each column
- Assign each column a column title

Additionally, you must tell the database system what kind of information will be stored in each column and what order the information will be in.

Database Terminology

The personal phone book in Figure 1.2 is arranged as a table of rows and columns. The rows are called *records* and the columns are called *fields*. The column titles are *field names*. The kind of information stored in a field is its *field type*. The database title is the *filename*.

The Record

This entry is a record: Prague, Cary N. Windsor CT 555-5891.

Pieces of information that make up a RECORD are seen horizontally, displayed in rows across the page. Our phone book will have six rows—six records—six sets of name + address + phone number.

The Field

If you were to draw vertical lines between the names and addresses and between the addresses and phone numbers, you would isolate columns of similar information. There are four separate groups of vertically arranged data—a column of names, a column of cities, a column of states, and a column of phone numbers. These columns are called fields. Your phone book has four fields.

The Field Name. The column titles—Name, City, State, and Phone Number—are called field names.

The Field Type. The columns in this database all contain ordinary character data. The field type for each field is character. There are also numeric, date, logical (yes or no), and memo field types.

Summary

Let's recap what you have done so far. You have learned a little terminology, like database file, field, and record. You have learned that database files are similar to reference materials you use everyday, like the telephone book. Database files and computers can't do anything you can't do without them—if you have plenty of time.

Paper and pencil might be much faster and cheaper for making a telephone list, and you wouldn't have needed to learn any computer terminology. In a business application, however, this list could easily be 80, 800, or 8,000 names long. Examples in this book never have more than 20 records (in the interest of conserving paper and your time). Try to think of these examples as small sections of database files containing hundreds or thousands of records.

The entire process of creating a computer database file is very much like making a table with paper and pencil:

1. You must plan your layout, decide what information is to go in which columns or fields, and determine the physical size of each column.
2. You enter all the information into each record.
3. Only after you've done all this can you actually use the table (file) for its purpose: to look up information.

The nice part about all this is that you can accomplish this without knowing anything about the internal working of the computer. All you have to do is follow dBASE IV. It's a little like learning to drive an automobile with an automatic as opposed to a manual transmission.

Finally, you have nothing to worry about. While you are learning, you can't break the computer. If you aren't quite sure about something, just try a few things and see whether they work. Probably the hardest thing to learn is that there is really nothing difficult about working with the computer; it's an easy thing to master.

A Simple Database File Example

Before you actually start the design of your phone book database file, you need to learn how to get your computer started with dBASE IV. In this first exercise, you start from scratch. When the computer is first turned on, the video display should be similar to Figure 2.1. You are in your computer's operating system.

The Operating System

Your computer has an operating system that helps you control the computer. dBASE IV uses the operating system to perform routine tasks. You do not need to learn the details of the operating system to use a database management system.

The `C>` is a prompt. It is the operating system's way of telling you, "I'm ready; tell me what to do." The `C` designates the logged disk drive. In the case of the first examples in this book, the `C>` designates a fixed (or hard) disk drive.

```
Current date is Wed 04-03-1991
Enter new date (mm-dd-yy):


Current time is  7:55:44.94
Enter new time:


IBM Personal Computer DOS Version  4.01

C:\>
```

***Figure 2.1.** The disk operating system (DOS) screen*

Installing dBASE IV

dBASE IV comes on several floppy disks. There are also many sample disks and other associated files. Before you do anything else, you need to install dBASE IV. Insert the disk labeled **Installation** into the floppy disk drive and type `INSTALL` at the DOS prompt. Just follow the directions dBASE IV gives you to complete the installation.

Once you have installed dBASE IV in your computer, you are ready to use it. First tell your computer to find the subdirectory where dBASE IV is stored. Many of you will find that this is a directory called DBASE. Others may have called it DBASE4 or DBASEIV or even something entirely different. The DOS command `CD` (change directory) tells the operating system where to find dBASE IV.

Starting dBASE IV

At the `C>` prompt, type `CD` followed by a backslash (\) and the name of your directory where dBASE IV resides. For example, type:

```
C> CD\DBASE4
```

and press the **<Enter>** key. Your system is now in the dBASE4 directory. Now type `DBASE` at the `C>` or `C\DBASE>` prompt. The monitor display should be similar to Figure 2.2. Press the **<Enter>** key.

```
Current date is Wed 04-03-1991
Enter new date (mm-dd-yy):


Current time is  7:55:44.94
Enter new time:


IBM Personal Computer DOS Version  4.01

C:\>CD \DBASE4

C:\DBASE4>DBASE
```

Figure 2.2. *Getting into dBASE IV*

dBASE IV takes several seconds to load; while the program is loading, the red indicator on the disk drive lights up. First, the screen will resemble Figure 2.3. This is the dBASE IV initial screen. After this, the license screen appears. The top line on the screen tells you exactly what you have installed. dBASE IV is the name of the database management system. Version 1.0 tells you the particular edition of dBASE IV. A version number is similar to a model identifier, and usually each new version has all the features of earlier versions, plus new and/or improved features.

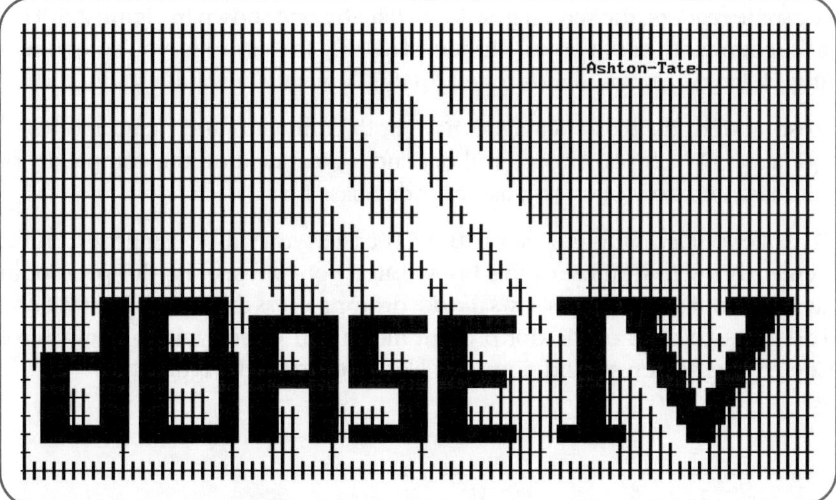

Figure 2.3. *The dBASE IV initial screen*

The dBASE Interface

What happens next depends on your version of dBASE and how it has been installed. For many readers, the screen will resemble Figure 2.4. This is the dBASE IV Control Center, a special dBASE interface that is intended to make dBASE IV easier to use for beginners and to improve productivity for experts. The Control Center lets you use the powerful dBASE command language through a system of menu options.

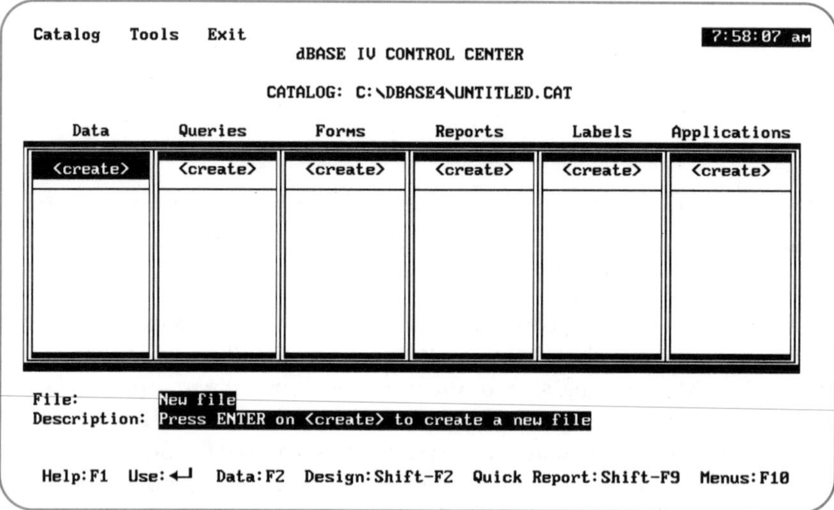

Figure 2.4. *The dBASE IV Control Center*

For some readers, the screen now looks like the one shown in Figure 2.5. This is the command, or dot prompt mode, of dBASE. In this mode, you enter direct English language commands to tell dBASE IV what you want it to do.

Most modern database managers have both command and menu modes of operation. Which you choose will depend a great deal on the complexity of your task and how often you use your database files.

To make your learning and use of dBASE IV easier, you will be using the Control Center throughout most of this book. Later, you will see the dot prompt in action. If your screen now shows the dot prompt, press the function key **<F2>**. This takes you out of the dot prompt mode and places you in the Control Center. The screen should now look like that shown in Figure 2.4.

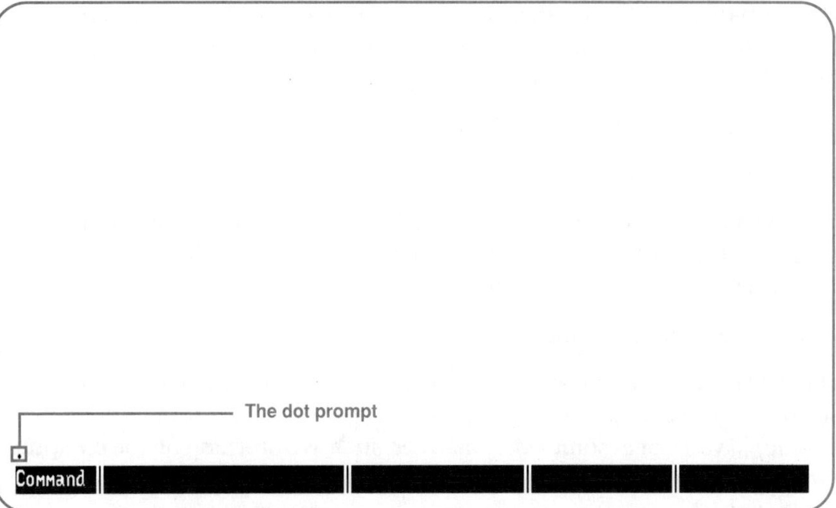

***Figure 2.5.** The dBASE IV dot prompt*

Quitting dBASE

Once you've learned how to get into a program, you need to learn how to get out of it—the right way. To get out of dBASE IV, open the menu that contains the command to exit. This is the Exit menu at the top of the Control Center. You can open all menus in dBASE IV by pressing the function key **<F10>**, or by pressing the **<Alt>** key and the first letter of the menu. From the Control Center:

1. Press **<F10>** to open the Catalog menu.
2. Press the **<Right arrow>** key twice to open the Exit menu.
3. Press the **<Down arrow>** key once to select `Quit to DOS`.
4. Press **<Enter>** to quit and return to DOS.

The computer screen will show:

```
***END RUN dBASE IV

C\DBASE4>
```

If the monitor shows the `C\DBASE4>` prompt, you have successfully exited dBASE IV.

You can quit to DOS another way: by pressing the **<Alt>** key and the initial letter of a menu name, and then typing the initial letter of a menu option. If you are still in the Control Center:

1. Press **<Alt>-E** to open the Exit menu.
2. Type to select `Quit to DOS.`

This also will take you out of dBASE IV. After using dBASE IV or any package that uses pull-down menus, you will find that using the **<Alt>-letter** combination really saves you time and keystrokes.

You are now back to your computer's operating system.

IMPORTANT: Any time you want to leave dBASE, you must use the Exit menu or the QUIT command (which you will learn about later for the dot prompt mode). If you exit in some other manner, such as by turning off the computer, you can lose data.

A Few Database File Concepts

You are almost ready to start building your computerized version of a personal phone book. Before proceeding, read these concepts and rules for database file construction.

- You must give the database file a title, its *filename* (eight characters maximum—no spaces).
- Rows are *records*, automatically numbered by dBASE.
- Columns are *fields*. For each field in the file structure, you must indicate a *field name*, a *field type*, and a *field width*.

Field Names

You need to assign column headings, *field names*, to each of the columns (fields) in the database file. Field names have rules similar to those for filenames. A field name must:

- Have no more than ten letters and numbers
- Contain no blank spaces
- Begin with a letter

Additionally, only the underscore (_) can be used as a special character, or symbol, within a field name. Your simple phone list has four column headings (that is, three field names): Name, City, State, and Phone Number. The first three (Name, City, and State) can be used as field names, but Phone Number cannot. It has more than ten letters and contains a blank space. So you have to give this column a name such as FONENUMBER, PHONE, or PHONE_NO to conform to the rules.

Field Types

Because dBASE IV handles different kinds of data in different ways, you need to tell it which kind of data is contained in each column. This is called the *field type* or *data type*. Each field can be one of six types: Character, Numeric, Float, Date, Memo, and Logical.

In the phone book example, all the fields are character fields and can contain letters, numbers, spaces, and other standard typewriter symbols. Other data types—numeric, float, date, memo, and logical—will be explained fully in later examples.

Field Width

You need to tell dBASE IV how wide the column is. The width is the number of typewriter spaces, or character spaces, the field will contain.

Record Numbers

Each time you enter a record, dBASE IV automatically gives it a number. It calls the first row (which is the first record) RECORD 1, the second, RECORD 2, and so on. You could, indeed, work with databases for a long time and do some very involved work without ever using a record number. They are, however, convenient for some things, like some types of data retrieval that will be discussed in depth in this book.

Your First Database File

Now you're ready to create your first computer database file. You will be using the dBASE IV subdirectory to store any examples. If you have exited from dBASE IV, repeat the earlier directions for entering dBASE IV. You should once again find yourself in the Control Center.

Navigating in the Control Center

You can move around in the Control Center in two ways. As you have already learned, you can get to the menus at the top of the screen with the **<F10>** key. To choose files within the Control Center itself, use the arrow keys: **<Up arrow>**, **<Down arrow>**, **<Right arrow>**, and **<Left arrow>**.

Creating the File

Make sure that the highlight is on the word `<create>` in the Data column. If the highlight isn't on `<create>`, use the arrow keys to get it there. Press **<Enter>** to create your database file structure. Absolutely nothing will happen until you press **<Enter>**.

You now have told dBASE IV to create a new database file. You are transported to the Database work surface, as shown in Figure 2.6. This is one of six work surfaces that you can access from the Control Center.

Defining the File Structure

The highlight is in a position ready for you to enter your first field name. This form is used to define each of the fields in your new database file. For each field, you must enter the field name, the field type, the field width, and the number of decimals for numeric fields. The last column in the form is where you indicate whether the data is indexed by the field.

The first field in the example is going to be called NAME. Enter the characters `NAME` into the box provided for the field name. If you make a typing error, just use the arrow keys to move the cursor back to where you made the mistake, and press **<Del>** to delete any unnecessary characters.

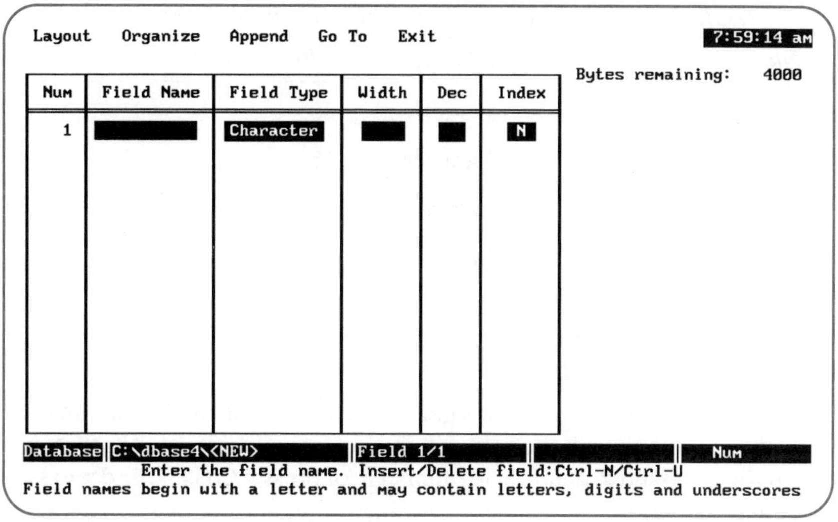

```
Layout   Organize   Append   Go To   Exit                              7:59:14 am

                                                         Bytes remaining:   4000
 Num | Field Name | Field Type | Width | Dec | Index
   1 |            | Character  |       |     |   N

Database C:\dbase4\<NEW>          Field 1/1                          Num
          Enter the field name.  Insert/Delete field:Ctrl-N/Ctrl-U
Field names begin with a letter and may contain letters, digits and underscores
```

Figure 2.6. *The Database work surface*

Press **<Enter>** to advance to the box provided for the field type. Character is the default field type. You can select another field type by typing the first letter of the desired field type (Character, Numeric, Float, Date, Memo, or Logical). dBASE IV automatically enters the rest of the characters in the field type and advances the cursor. Another way to select an alternative field type is to press the **<Spacebar>**. Each time you press the **<Spacebar>**, a different field type is displayed. When you press **<Enter>**, the cursor moves to the box for field width. Because all the field types are Character for the Phone book file, just accept the default and move on by pressing **<Enter>**.

We've arbitrarily decided that the NAME field is to be 20 spaces wide. Type `20`, then press **<Enter>**. You won't be entering any numbers for decimal places because there are no numerical fields in this file structure. Just accept the default of `N` for the Index, by pressing **<Enter>**. Indexes will be explained in greater detail in later chapters.

The field definition for NAME is complete, and dBASE IV is ready to accept the next field definition. Repeat the procedure for the other fields, as shown in Table 2.1.

Table 2.1. Enter field description into Database work surface

Num	*Field Name*	*Field Type*	*Width*	*Dec*	*Index*
1	NAME	Character	20		N
2	CITY	Character	15		N
3	STATE	Character	2		N
4	PHONE	Character	8		N
5					

This process continues until you signal that you've finished. To tell dBASE IV that you've finished with the field definition process, press the **<Enter>** key when you are asked to define field number 5, or press **<Ctrl>-<End>** to save your data and Exit.

dBASE IV will respond with `Save as:`. dBASE is asking you for the filename. Giving the file a name signals dBASE to store it in the current directory. In this example (Figure 2.7), the keyboard entry is FONEBOOK. Type `FONEBOOK` and press **<Enter>**.

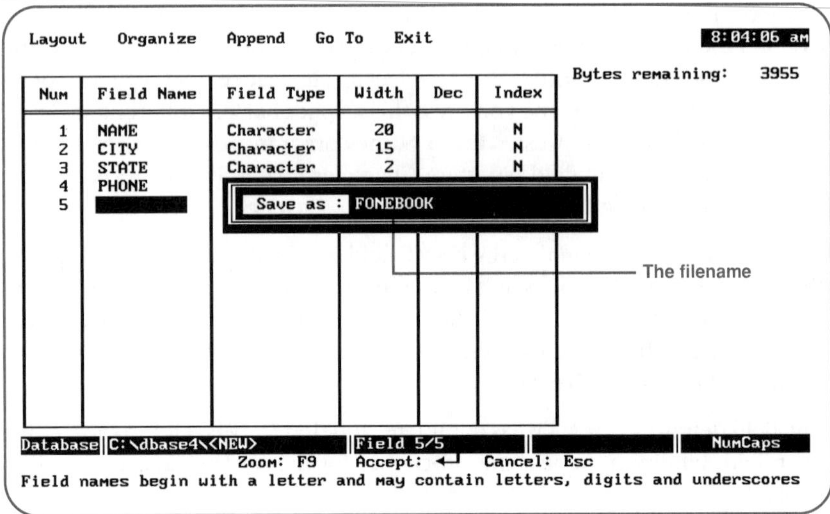

Figure 2.7. Creating the FONEBOOK database

Now that you've defined the structure of your database file, you're ready to begin entering the data.

Entering Data

dBASE IV asks if you wish to enter data now. Type a Y (for year)—but this time don't press the **<Enter>** key. dBASE IV responds directly to the Y and puts you into the data entry mode, where you are provided with an electronic data entry form (shown in Figure 2.8).

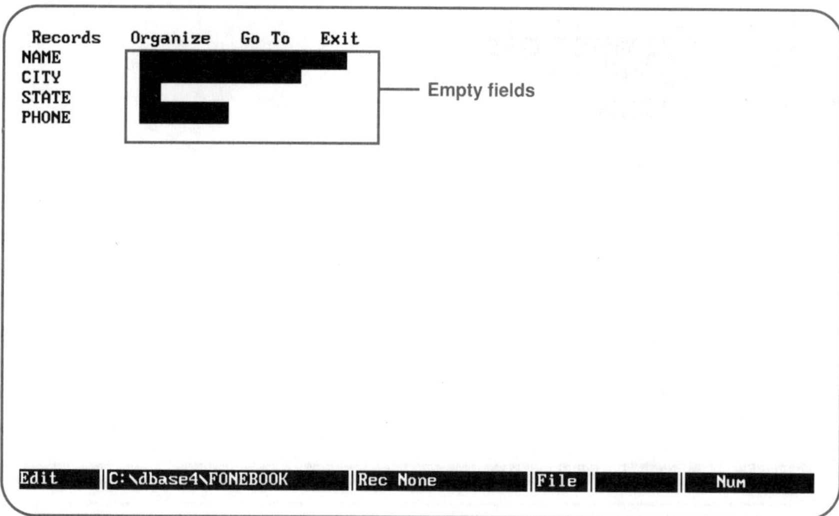

Figure 2.8. *An empty Edit screen for the FONEBOOK database*

This data entry form displays the field names and provides space for you to enter the data for each field. It's a little like having an electronic three-by-five card for each record. The cursor is in the first character position for the NAME field. As you enter data into each field, the cursor moves to the right. When you have completely entered the data for the field, press **<Enter>** to advance to the next field.

Correcting Mistakes

What happens if you make a mistake? If the mistake is in the record you are entering, use the arrow keys to back up to the mistake. Type the correct information directly over the old. Use the arrow key to move forward again. If the mistake is in an earlier record, use the **<PgUp>** key to move backward through the database to that record. Use the arrow keys to move the cursor to the mistake. Make your correction. Then use the **<PgDn>** key to move forward to where you were and continue entering data.

Entering Records

When you have entered all the data for the first record (Figure 2.9), dBASE IV clears the screen and provides you with a new, blank data-entry form for the next record. This process continues until you signal dBASE IV that you're finished.

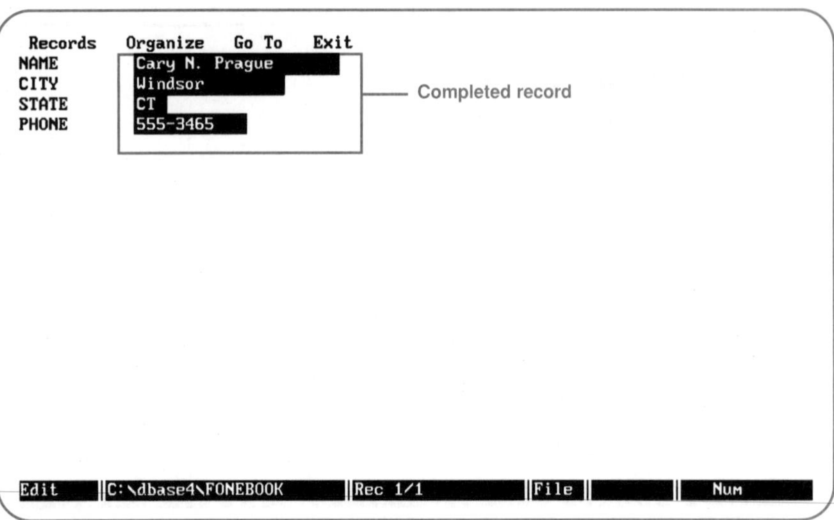

Figure 2.9. *Data entered in the Edit screen*

Make sure you have finished the first record shown in Figure 2.9 before going on. In this example, you are entering six records. Please enter each of the remaining records as shown below. Feel free to substitute your name and the names of your closest associates, but keep the city, state, and telephone information the same as shown in Table 2.2.

Table 2.2. ***Enter these records in your FONEBOOK database***

Name	*City*	*State*	*Phone*
Cary N. Prague	Windsor	CT	555-3465
Burton S. Prague	Delray Beach	FL	555-3658
Robert A. Byers, Sr.	Standale	CA	555-9242
Robert S. Byers. Jr.	Pasadena	CA	555-9548
Larry Colker	Torrance	CA	555-3662
David Rose	Torrance	CA	555-5664

BROWSEing Through Your Records

Before you tell dBASE IV that you are finished, look at one more thing—the BROWSE table. So far, you have entered your data while seeing only one record at a time. By using the **<PgUp>** and **<PgDn>** keys, you can see previous or subsequent records that you have entered. But there is also a way to see all (or a bunch) of your records at once. dBASE IV features two modes of data entry and data display, EDIT and BROWSE. You can toggle between these two modes, by pressing the **<F2> Data** key while in one mode or the other. Assuming you have entered all six of the records in the EDIT screen, you can see all your records together in the BROWSE screen.

Press **<F2> Data** to enter the BROWSE mode. Press **<PgUp>** once. Your screen should change to resemble the screen in Figure 2.10. All your fields and all your records are displayed so that you can see them together. If you had more records than will fit on the screen, you would have to use the **<PgUp>** or **<PgDn>** keys to see other groups of records. If you had more fields than will fit across the screen, you would need to use the **<Tab>** and **<Shift>-<Tab>** keys to see more fields.

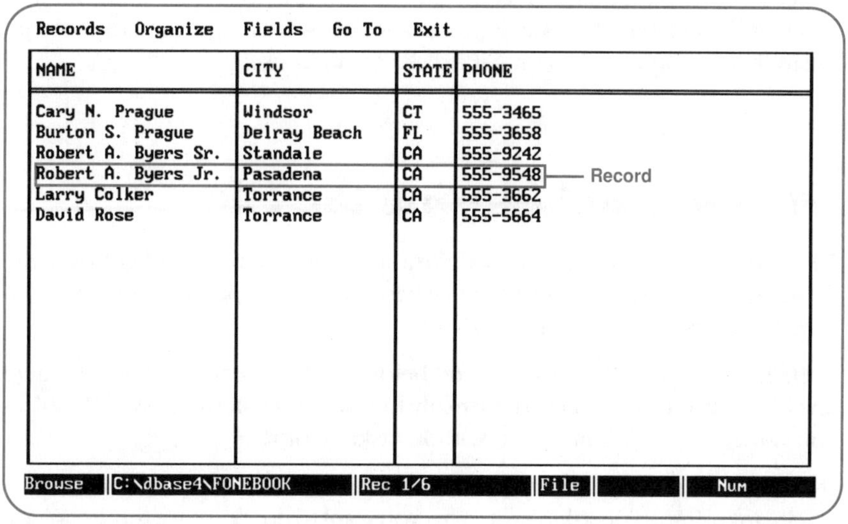

Records   Organize   Fields   Go To   Exit

NAME	CITY	STATE	PHONE
Cary N. Prague	Windsor	CT	555-3465
Burton S. Prague	Delray Beach	FL	555-3658
Robert A. Byers Sr.	Standale	CA	555-9242
Robert A. Byers Jr.	Pasadena	CA	555-9548 — Record
Larry Colker	Torrance	CA	555-3662
David Rose	Torrance	CA	555-5664

Browse | C:\dbase4\FONEBOOK | Rec 1/6 | File | | Num

Figure 2.10. *Data entered in the BROWSE screen for the FONEBOOK database*

You can press **<F2> Data** again to return to the EDIT mode. As you press **<F2> Data** you change from one mode to the other. Press **<F2>** again until you are in the EDIT mode.

Exiting the EDIT Mode

To tell dBASE IV that you're finished, press **<Ctrl>-<End>**. dBASE IV exits from the EDIT mode and displays the Control Center. **<Ctrl>-<End>** tells dBASE IV to save all your work and go back to wherever you were before the EDIT mode. Another way to leave a work surface is by pressing the **<Esc>** key. If you are still on the last record you changed, pressing **<Esc>** won't save the record. (If you move the cursor to another record, the changes will be saved.) In some work surfaces, **<Esc>** will not save anything you have done since you entered the work surface.

Using the Database File

You now have a database file. It has six records and four fields: NAME, CITY, STATE, and PHONE. Its filename is FONEBOOK, and it is on the C drive in the DBASE4 subdirectory. Notice that the FONEBOOK file now appears in the Data panel of the Control Center. It is also above the line in the Data panel. This tells you that the database file is active or in use. If it were below the line it would mean that, though it exists on your disk, it isn't in use.

Opening and Closing the File

Because the file is already in use, close it by moving the highlight over the filename and pressing **<Enter>**. What happens next depends on whether you have a certain help level on in dBASE IV.

If the file FONEBOOK simply moved below the line, then you have the help level INSTRUCT=OFF. This is normally the way you will run dBASE IV unless you want help all the time even without asking for it.

If INSTRUCT is set ON, you now see the screen shown in Figure 2.11. This is a help box. dBASE IV is asking you what you want to do. You have three choices: `Close file`, `Modify structure/order`, or `Display data`.

Make sure the highlight is on `Close file`, and press **<Enter>**.

The file is now displayed below the line indicating it is closed. You can work only with open files, so again open the file by pressing **<Enter>** with the highlight on the file FONEBOOK. If you see the message box, press **<Enter>** again to select `Use file`.

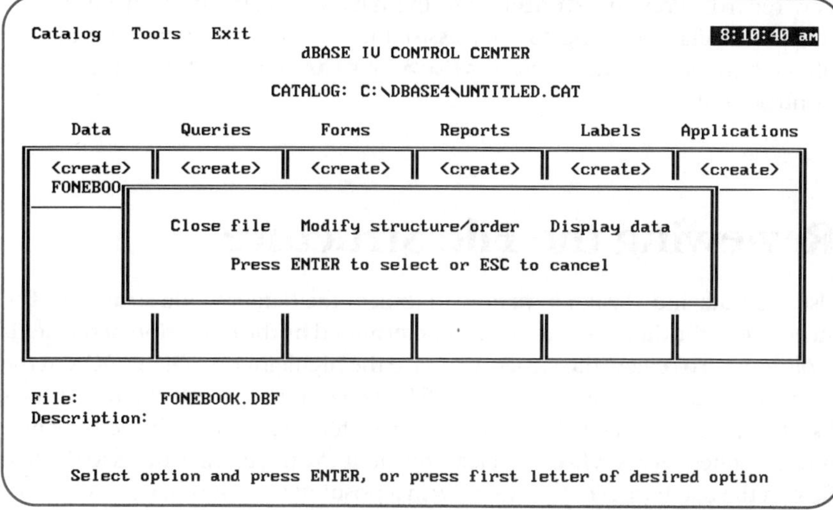

Figure 2.11. *Getting Help in the Control Center*

Moving Among Work Surfaces

Usually you do not simply open a file. Generally, you want to either display the data or redesign the database file structure. There are two key combinations that are of utmost importance in dBASE IV. In fact, knowing them will save you a lot of time and effort as you work with your data. These two keys are:

<F2>	The Data Key
<Shift>-<F2>	The Design Key

As you use dBASE IV, you will find that these keys can take you between different work surfaces quickly, without the use of the menus. If you are in the Data column of the Control Center, pressing **<F2> Data** takes you directly into EDIT or BROWSE, depending on which one you were in the last time you entered data. If you press **<Shift>-<F2> Design**, you are instantly transported into the database file structure work surface.

These shortcuts between work surfaces can be used whether or not the file is in use. If the file is not in use when you press the Data or Design keys, dBASE IV will first make the file active and then transport you to the work surface.

Move the highlight to the FONEBOOK file and press **<F2> Data**. You are instantly transported to either the EDIT or the BROWSE work surface. After you've created a database file, pressing **<F2> Data** at any time while in the Control Center moves you to the BROWSE or EDIT screens, where you can add new records. Pressing **<Enter>** on the database filename to make the file active is similar to saying to your assistant, "Chatsworth, please get me the phone book in my study." Press **<Esc>** or **<Ctrl>-<End>** to return to the Control Center.

Reviewing the File Structure

Use the Data and Design keys now to look at the database file structure. The structure of the database file is really determined by the definition of the fields (columns). To review the structure, place the highlight on FONEBOOK in the Control Center and press **<Shift>-<F2> Design**. The screen changes to look like Figure 2.12, which shows the database file structure with the Organize menu opened. Press **<Esc>** to clear the menu. Your cursor returns to the first field in the database file. You are now in a position to make changes to the file structure, if you want to. Please *don't* change the structure now. Changing the database structure lets you change the field types, sizes, and even the indexes.

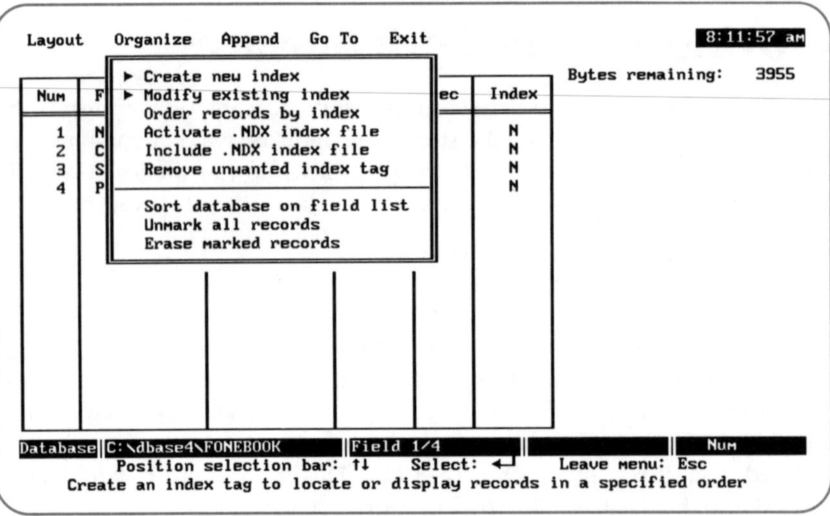

Figure 2.12. *Database work surface with the Organize menu pulled down*

Just return to the Control Center. Press **<Esc>** and type Y to confirm that you want to abandon the screen.

Selecting Records

Now you'll move on to the major use for databases—the retrieval of stored information. Perhaps you wish to retrieve some of the information you have stored so that you can look at it. One way to look at the information is to use the BROWSE mode. This will show you as many records and fields as will fit onto the screen. However, you can view and change your data using BROWSE. You can specify which fields and records you want to display through another work surface called the Query work surface.

Earlier, we talked about searching through the phone book to find the owner of a particular phone number. To demonstrate how to select records based on only a phone number, try telling dBASE to display the record containing the phone number 555-9242.

A Simple Query

First, go into the Queries panel of the Control Center. Move the highlight to the `<create>` area of the Queries panel and press **<Enter>**. This takes you to the Query work surface. The screen should now look like Figure 2.13.

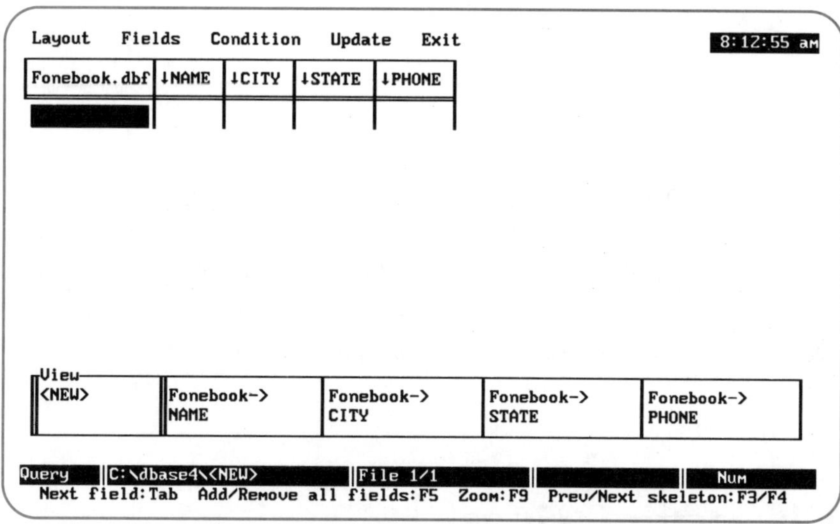

***Figure 2.13.** Empty Query work surface with the FONEBOOK database active*

Notice two areas of information on the Query screen. The top area is a list of the fields in your database file. The bottom area is a list of the FONEBOOK fields that will appear when you display the database file in BROWSE or EDIT.

Sometimes you may notice that not all of your fields are displayed on the screen. The screen can display only 80 characters, so you may have to use special keys to see the rest of your data. Right now the highlight is in what is called the *pot handle* of the query entry area. It tells you that this database file structure is for FONEBOOK.DBF. dBASE IV automatically adds the file extension DBF to all database files.

Movement in the Query screen involves several different keys. These keys are shown at the bottom of the screen. The **<Tab>** key moves the highlight from one field to the next (left to right); the key combination **<Shift>-<Tab>** moves the highlight from one field to the previous field (right to left).

Press the **<Tab>** key four times to move to the PHONE field. The highlight is now in the PHONE field. Enter `'555-9242'` in quotes, as shown in Figure 2.14.

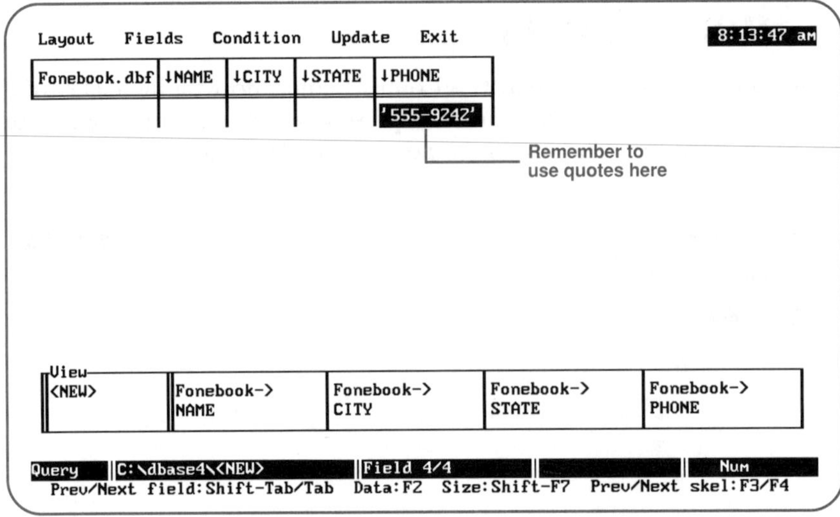

***Figure 2.14.** Selecting a phone number in the Query work surface*

Character Strings

This entry looks straightforward and it is. By typing a value, you are telling dBASE IV to display only the records whose value of PHONE is '555-9242'.

The single quotation marks (apostrophes) around the phone number in the command are called *delimiters*. They identify the beginning and the end of what is called a *character string*. The characters between the quotes are exactly—to the letter and the space—what dBASE IV is to search for. **Note:** dBASE IV also accepts double quotation marks if you choose to hold down **<Shift>** while pressing the apostrophe key.

The phone number must be identified as a character string because the phone number field (PHONE) is a character field. As mentioned earlier, dBASE IV has numeric fields. Why isn't the phone number stored in a numeric field? After all, it's made up of numbers. A good rule of thumb is to store numbers as simple characters unless they are to be used in arithmetic calculations. A host of "numeric" data is usually treated in this way—for example, phone numbers, zip codes, and Social Security numbers. You almost never use these numbers in calculations.

When you use numbers in a command, as in the preceding example, the delimiters tell dBASE to treat the number as a character string. Digits that are not enclosed by quotes are considered to be numbers: 555 is a number but '555' is a character string. All character strings—not just those containing numbers—are enclosed by quotes when used in a command.

Queries also are known as filters because you pass the data through them, and only those records that meet your criteria are selected. Once you have completed your query, you can see the selected records by pressing **<F2> Data**.

Viewing the Selected Record

Press **<F2>**. If you are in EDIT, the record with the phone number 555-9242 is showing. If you try to page up, you will find that you can't get to your other records that way. If you press the **<Down arrow>**, dBASE IV will ask you if you want to `Add new records? (Y/N)`. If you are in BROWSE, you will see only one record.

Press **<Shift>-<F2>** to enter the Query screen. Make sure the highlight is in the PHONE field, and delete the phone number by pressing the **<Del>** key ten times. Now move the highlight back to the STATE field by pressing **<Shift>-<Tab>** once. Type `'CA'` in quotes to tell dBASE to select only the records whose state value is CA. Press **<F2>** until you are in BROWSE. Again, you will see that only the records whose state value is `California` are displayed. There should be four of them.

Press **<Shift>-<F2>** to enter the Query screen. In subsequent chapters, you will learn a lot about this screen. It is the heart of database file selection and data manipulation. It is also one of the places you will sort data and join several data files together. Press **<Esc>** to return to the Control Center. You won't save this query. Just type `Y` when asked if you want to abandon operation.

Printing Records

The last thing to do before ending this whirlwind tour of the Control Center and Data Selection is to print your database file—either to the screen or to a printer, if you have one. Make sure that you have the FONEBOOK database file selected. Press **<Shift>-<F9>**. This is the Quick Report command. The screen will change to look like Figure 2.15.

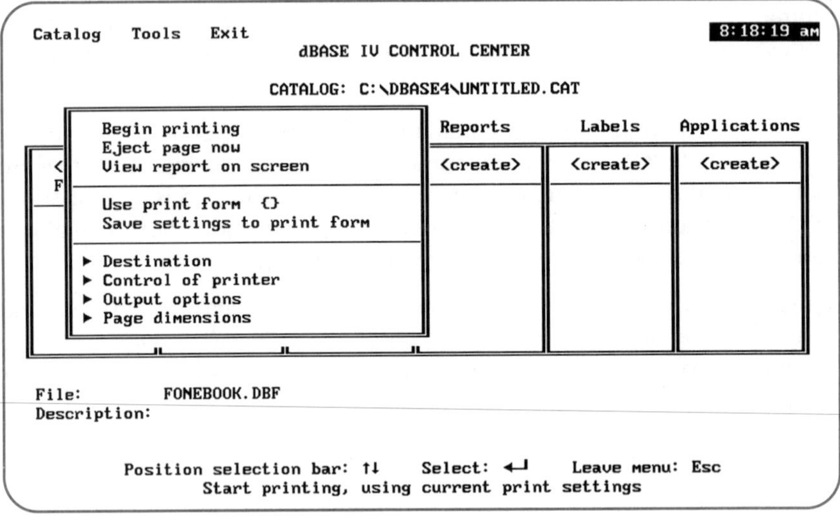

Figure 2.15. *The Quick Report screen*

dBASE IV will automatically create a report form with all your fields. It will place column titles using the field names at the top of each column. This is known as a column-oriented report and is similar to the BROWSE screen. You cannot make any changes in the Quick Report. dBASE prints all the fields and records that are in the database or query you have selected. A menu is open waiting for you to make a choice.

If you have a printer, turn it on and press **<Enter>** to select `Begin printing`. Your report will print in a few seconds. If you want to view the report on your screen, press the **<Down arrow>** twice so it is on `View report on screen` and press **<Enter>**, or simply type `V`. Remember that typing the first letter of a menu option selects it.

After your report has been printed, you return automatically to the Control Center. The printed report is shown in Figure 2.16.

Page No. 1
04/03/91

NAME	CITY	State	PHONE
Cary N. Prague	Windsor	CT	555-3465
Burton S. Prague	Delray Beach	FL	555-3658
Robert A. Byers Sr.	Strandale	CA	555-9242
Robert A. Byers Jr.	Pasadena	CA	555-9548
Larry Colker	Torrance	CA	555-3662
David Rose	Torrance	CA	555-5664

Figure 2.16. *The Quick Report output*

Summary

You've accomplished quite a lot in this chapter. You've learned how to start dBASE IV and how to quit dBASE IV. You know a bit about the Control Center and how to move the cursor from place to place within that screen. Most important, you've created your first dBASE IV file, filled it with data, and used dBASE IV and your file for their intended purposes: to retrieve data. The query feature in dBASE IV helped you select specific information. **<Shift>-<F9> Quick Report** gave you a report of the data in your file.

The next chapter will take you on a more complete tour of the Control Center. The rest of this section of the book will more thoroughly explain the process and planning of database creation that you just briefly experienced.

chapter

3

Gateway to the Database—The Control Center

In this chapter, you're going to get a tour of the Control Center; its menus, including Catalogs; and some of its various work surfaces. You'll also learn a bit about the dBASE IV Help system.

The Control Center

Before you go on to learn the various ways you can get dBASE IV to perform various database file operations, it is important to understand in some detail how to move around the Control Center and how to interact with the dBASE command mode. In Chapter 2, you learned how to start dBASE IV and how to enter the Control Center. Now it is time to learn more about the Control Center.

You have been operating dBASE IV by use of the menus in the Control Center. The Control Center is an interface between you and the powerful dBASE command language. It gives you a way of communicating with dBASE through a system of menus. The Control Center translates your menu choices into dBASE code or commands. At this point, there is no need for you to interact directly with dBASE commands at the dot prompt, because the Control Center makes it easier for you to learn and to use dBASE IV.

Start dBASE IV again and get into the Control Center. If you have forgotten how, turn back to Chapter 2 for a quick refresher. Figure 3.1 shows the Control Center as it appears when you first start dBASE IV. Because you created one database so far, it appears in the Data panel.

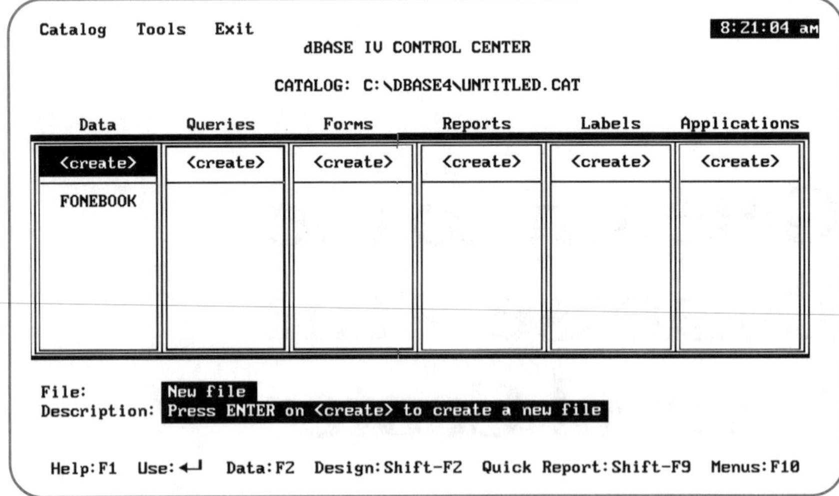

Figure 3.1. *The Control Center*

Tour of the Panels

The main area of the Control Center is divided into six columns also known as "panels." Each of these panels keeps track of the files you have created. The six panels correspond to six of the work surfaces where you can design your data. These include: Database File Design, Queries Design, Forms Design, Reports Design, Labels Design, and Applications Design.

When you create any of the above types of files and give them names, the names appear in the panel below the operation name. For example, form filenames are displayed in the Forms panel, and report filenames are displayed in the Reports panel.

Everything you create in the Control Center is linked to its original database file. You will see some files above the line in the panel and others below. When you use or activate a database file by highlighting it and pressing **<Enter>**, you will see all the files that are associated with that database file also move above the line. This helps you to know what belongs to what. A data entry form that was developed to be used with XYZ database file might be useless with ABC database file. The form was designed to view, enter, or edit the data from one database file and not the other.

You will notice that BROWSE and EDIT are not considered "work surfaces" and are not Control Center panels. This is because you use them to see or change the results of the other operations. Your data is simply displayed in either BROWSE or EDIT mode. Remember that you can always get to BROWSE or EDIT by pressing **<F2> Data**. You also can get into any work surface by pressing **<Shift>-<F2> Design**.

Remember the four keys:

- **<Enter>**
- **<F2> Data**
- **<Shift>-<F2> Design**
- **<Esc>**

Using them moves you around the Control Center and all the work surfaces without ever choosing a menu. Don't forget that you can use the **<Esc>** key to quit whatever you are doing without saving your work.

Control Center Menus

The Control Center contains two separate areas where you'll do your work. You already have learned about the six panels. The second area is where the menus are, near the top of the screen. There are three menus:

- Catalog
- Tools
- Exit

Catalogs

Catalogs are very important to dBASE IV. If you used dBASE III PLUS, you already may be familiar with catalogs. You can use the dBASE catalogs to help you remember what each database file is for, and to keep track of all the files related to each database file. Each database file can have several supporting files: queries, custom screen forms, report forms, label forms, and applications.

Once a catalog has been activated, each time you create a new dBASE IV database file or a supporting file such as a query, a screen form, or a report form, the name of the file will be added to the catalog. To help you remember what each file is for, the catalog also lets you enter a description of each file. Catalogs are always active in the Control Center. The last catalog you use reappears the next time you enter the Control Center. The first time you begin the Control Center, a catalog entitled UNTITLED.CAT is created for you. The CAT extension tells dBASE IV that it is a list of your files. There is also a master catalog, CATALOG.CAT, that keeps track of all your catalogs. Its purpose is to make sure that consistency is maintained among catalogs. The real value of the catalog lies in its ability to keep an inventory of all the supporting files that you have for each of your database files. You can create index files, report form files, format (custom screen) files, query files, and label form files from each database file you have. If you have several of these supporting files for each of your database files, the disk directory will become cluttered, and you might have difficulty remembering what each file is for and to which database file it belongs. The catalog does this remembering for you.

Using catalogs. Open the Catalog menu by pressing **<F10>** or **<Alt>-C**. The screen should look like Figure 3.2. The Catalog menu has two sections. You use the top section to interact with the catalogs. You use the bottom section to work with the various files that are in the catalogs.

When you select the first option, `Use a different catalog`, a list pops up on the right side of the screen. When you choose a catalog from the list, dBASE IV displays the names of catalogs from the master catalog, CATALOG.CAT.

The next choice is `Modify catalog name`. This choice lets you rename the catalog currently in use. It doesn't affect any of the files in the catalog; it just lets you rename the catalog.

Each catalog or file that you use in dBASE IV has a description associated with it. The last choice in the top section, `Edit description of catalog`, lets you enter or modify the description of the current catalog. You can enter any one-line description in the highlighted box that is displayed when you choose this option.

The bottom half of the Catalog menu lets you work with the files that are in the catalog. When you choose `Add file to catalog`, you can add an existing file into the catalog. The file can be part of another catalog that was created outside of the active catalog.

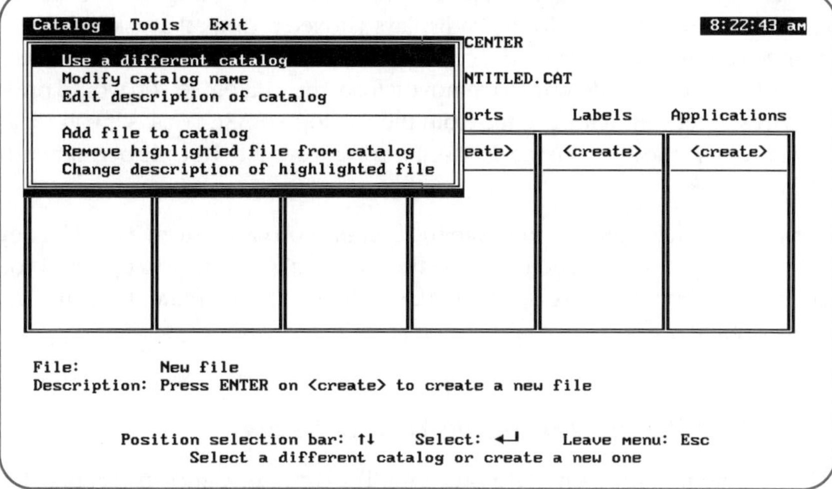

***Figure 3.2.** The Control Center Catalog menu*

The file list that appears contains only the files that are the same type as the panel in which the cursor is located. For example, if the cursor is in the Data panel, the file list contains databases (.DBF). If the cursor is in the Reports panel, the file list contains reports (.FRM).

The next option, `Remove highlighted file from catalog`, removes a selected file from the catalog and stops tracking the file. It doesn't delete the file from your disk drive—unless you ask it to when it prompts you. It merely removes the file from the catalog.

The last option in the menu, `Change description of highlighted file`, allows you to change the description of a file. Just as the catalog has a description, each file also has a description. You normally maintain these descriptions in the individual work surface where the file was created, but by choosing this option, you can change the descriptions from the Catalog menu as well.

Deleting files. dBASE IV provides a couple of ways to remove files permanently from your disk. Don't delete anything right now, while you are reading this section, but read on to learn how it's done, for later use.

You have already learned that you can remove a file from a catalog by selecting it, choosing `Remove highlighted file from catalog` from the Catalog menu, and answering yes to the first prompt. This option also deletes the file from the disk if you answer yes to the second prompt, `Do you also want to delete this file from the disk?` Another way you can remove a file from the catalog, and potentially delete it from the disk, is by highlighting the file and pressing the **<Del>** key. dBASE IV displays a boxed prompt that asks you if you want to remove the file from the catalog. If you wanted to delete the file from the disk, you also would want to remove it from the catalog, so you would press `Y` for Yes. After removing the file from the catalog, dBASE IV asks if you really want to delete the file from the disk. Answering yes deletes the file permanently from the disk.

If you accidentally delete a file from the catalog, you can restore it by selecting `Add file to catalog` and choosing the filename from the pop-up list. If you delete a file from the disk by accident, you'll need to re-create the entire file from scratch.

The Tools Menu—Changing Your Settings

The next menu in the Control Center is the Tools menu, as shown in Figure 3.3. The first option, `Macros`, is for the creation of macros, which let you record and play back your keystrokes.

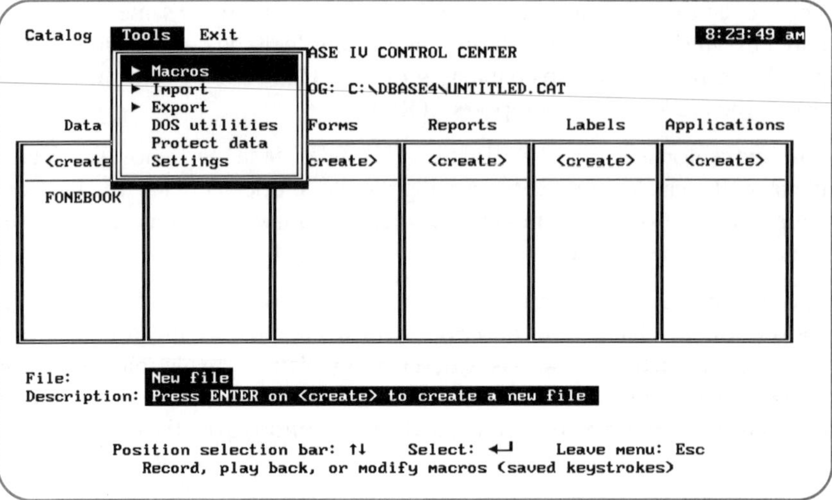

Figure 3.3. *The Control Center Tools menu*

`Import` and `Export`, the next two items, let you import and export "foreign" files. Foreign files are non-dBASE files that store their data differently than dBASE IV.

The fourth item, `DOS utilities`, gives you access to DOS directly from a menu system and lets you perform all the DOS commands without leaving dBASE.

The next selection, `Protect data`, lets you assign a password to both dBASE IV and your data. Assigning a password protects your files from access by others.

The last item in the Tools menu is `Settings`. This is where you go to view and change the various settings that affect the way dBASE runs. If you haven't already opened the Tools menu, do it now. Press **<Alt>-T** from the Control Center to open the Tools menu, then type `S` for `Settings`. The screen should look like Figure 3.4.

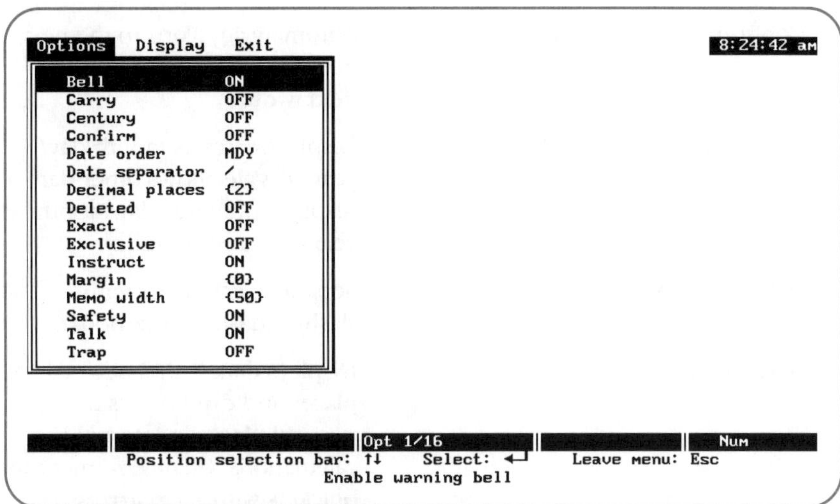

Figure 3.4. *The Settings Options submenu of the Tools menu*

The Settings Options submenu opens automatically to show 16 settings. There are also two other menus entitled Display and Exit. Display lets you select colors for the various parts of the screen if you have a color monitor. The Exit menu returns you to the Control Center.

Table 3.1 contains a brief summary of the 16 settings with their actions and their defaults. Some of these are very important because they affect some very obvious ways that dBASE IV runs. Most of the settings are toggles; that is, when you select the setting you can press **<Enter>** to change the default values.

Table 3.1. *Options in the Settings submenu of the Tools menu*

Setting	*Default*	*Description*
Bell	ON	dBASE beeps when you enter data past the field width.
Carry	OFF	Does not carry the data of the previous record to the next record when adding records.
Century	OFF	Displays dates without the century.
Confirm	OFF	Automatically skips to the next field when data entry fills the field width.
Date order	MDY	Displays dates as month/day/year. Toggle allows other date display options as day/month/year or year/month/day.
Date separator	/	Separates date parts with slashes (dashes or periods).
Decimal places	{2}	Displays data with 2 decimal places and dBASE uses 2 decimal places in internal calculations. Change number in brackets with **<Up arrow>** or **<Down arrow>** keys, or with numeric keypad. Maximum number of decimal places is 18.
Deleted	OFF	When ON, allows you to skip over records marked for deletion.
Exact	OFF	When ON, requires exact character string comparison matches.
Exclusive	OFF	Prevents shared use of a file in a network.
Instruct	ON	Enables and disables display of the panel prompt box for files at the Control Center.

Setting	*Default*	*Description*
Margin	{0}	Starts printed output {x} columns from the left. You can change the bracketed number with the **<Up arrow>** or **<Down arrow>** keys or with the numeric keypad, after pressing **<Enter>**.
Memo width	{50}	Default width for displaying memo fields.
Safety	ON	Asks for confirming message before overwriting files.
Talk	ON	When ON, displays results of commands on the screen.
Trap	OFF	Turns the debugger ON and OFF.

Make sure the setting for `Instruct` is ON, if it isn't already. Because the next section of this chapter has information about getting help, it makes sense to turn on all the options. When you are finished, use the arrow keys to select `Exit`. Press **<Enter>** and you will be returned to the Control Center.

Help

Sooner or later, most computer users will need some extra help from the software. If you don't quite know how to do something or if you make a mistake, your program can probably help you out. dBASE IV provides several kinds of help—depending on your circumstances.

Help Boxes

Help boxes appear only when you request them, by pressing **<F1> Help**. The Help boxes look like the one shown in Figure 3.5. Help boxes are context-sensitive. This means that the contents of the box that pops up depends on where in dBASE IV you are working at the time. For example, if you are in the Control Center Data panel and press **<F1> Help**, you will receive help about creating databases. Likewise, if you are in the EDIT screen, you will receive help about the EDIT screen. Press **<F1>** now, if you haven't already, to take a look at Help. Many of the screens have multiple pages. You can move forward within Help by pressing **<F4> Next**. Press **<F3> Previous** to move back a page.

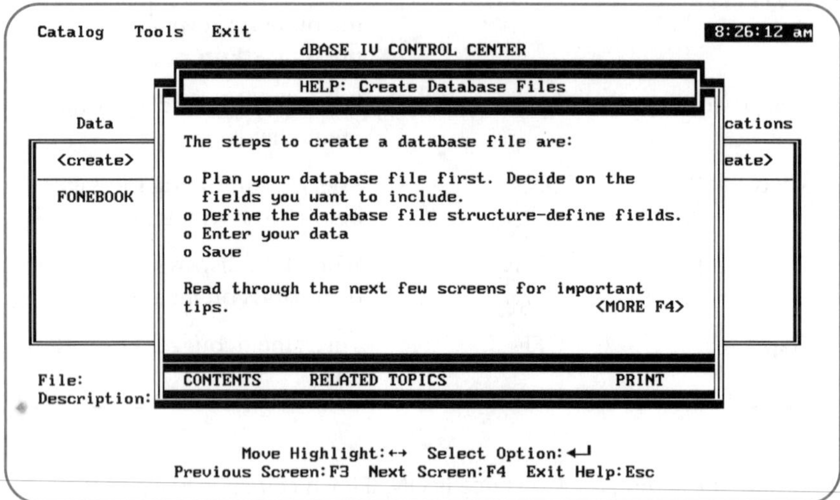
Catalog Tools Exit
8:26:12 am
dBASE IV CONTROL CENTER
HELP: Create Database Files
Data
cations
The steps to create a database file are:
<create>
eate>
o Plan your database file first. Decide on the fields you want to include.
FONEBOOK
o Define the database file structure-define fields.
o Enter your data
o Save
Read through the next few screens for important tips.
<MORE F4>
File:
Description:
CONTENTS RELATED TOPICS PRINT
Move Highlight:↔ Select Option:↵
Previous Screen:F3 Next Screen:F4 Exit Help:Esc

Figure 3.5. *The Control Center Help box*

Help Box Options

At the bottom of each Help box are several options. You can select the options by pressing the arrow keys. There are at least three choices at the bottom of each Help box. The first choice is `Contents`. Choosing this option places you in one of the table of contents screens so you can choose a new Help topic. This aspect of Help is also context-sensitive; the screen you are shown depends on where you call Help from.

The next option is `Related Topics`. When you choose this option, it displays a list of Help topics similar to the one you were just reading about and lets you choose which topic you want to view next.

The third help box option is `Print`. Choosing this causes dBASE IV to automatically print out Help screen information in a neat format. When the manual is nowhere in sight, and you find yourself constantly flipping back and forth between the Help box and actually performing the task, the print option is invaluable.

Once you begin to move around inside the Help boxes, a new option will appear between `Related Topics` and `Print`. This is the `Backup` option. This lets you trace your steps backward throughout the Help system. This option is an alternative to pressing **<F3> Previous** to back up.

You also can get Help on which key does what by looking at the Navigation line at the bottom of the screen. It provides helpful visual information as to which key is used for each operation.

Exiting Help

When you have had all the help you need, you can leave the Help system and return to where you previously had been working by pressing the **<Esc>** key.

Error Boxes

Generally, you cannot make an error in the Control Center. dBASE IV controls your movements through the menus without requiring you to enter any commands. When you are entering commands in the dot prompt, however, you may find yourself making mistakes now and then.

As you enter either commands or data, you may, upon occasion, make a typographical error. For example, suppose that you are working within the dot prompt mode and you decide to enter the Control Center. Instead of pressing **<F2> Assist**, you enter the command, ASSIST, at the dot prompt and make a typographical error. Figure 3.6 shows the error box for this situation.

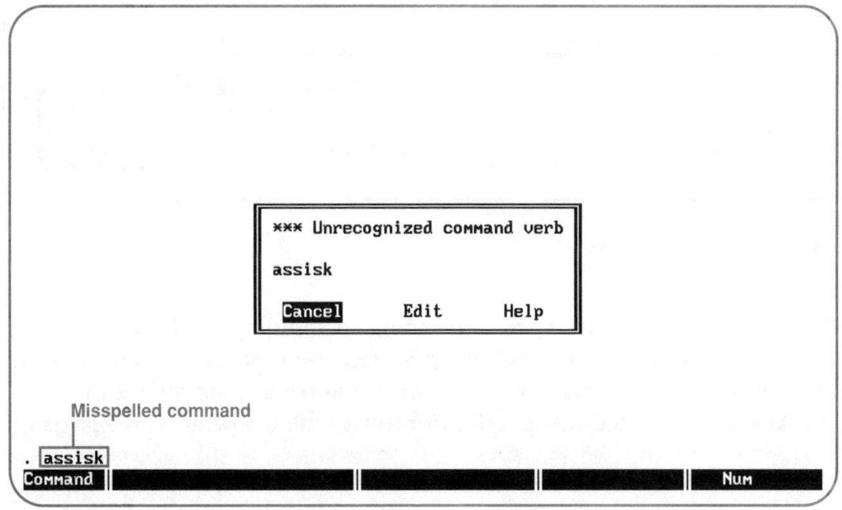

Figure 3.6. *A typical error box*

dBASE IV does not recognize this command as entered. You have three choices: cancel the command and try again, edit or fix the command, or ask for help. How much dBASE IV understands of the command will determine where in the Help library it places you. If dBASE IV hasn't an inkling of what your command is, it will place you in the Help table of contents.

The Special Keys

Your computer keyboard has a number of keys that are not on an ordinary typewriter keyboard. These special keys are indicated in the drawing of Figure 3.7. The use of these keys varies according to particular software programs. As you gain more experience using dBASE IV, you will learn how to use these keys. The diagram in Figure 3.7 shows the placement of these keys; however, depending on the type of computer you have, you may find some of these keys in different places.

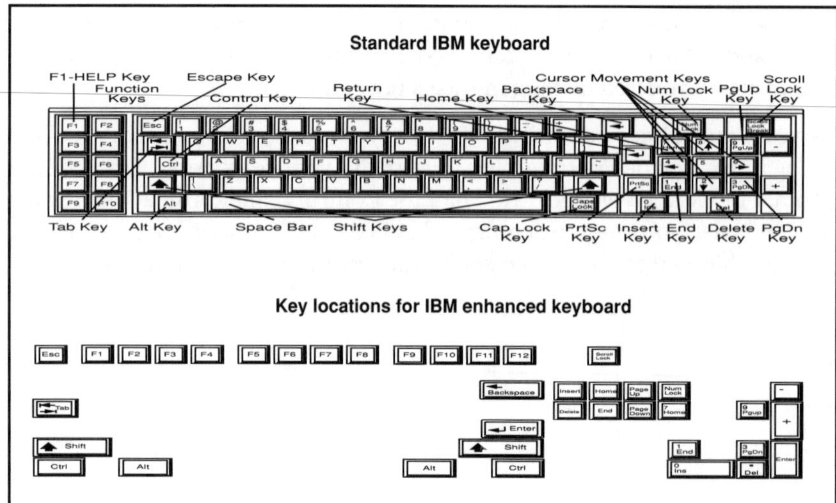

Figure 3.7. The keyboards

Many of these keys have specific meanings depending on the dBASE work surface. Keystrokes within each work surface are described when the work surface is presented. Each of these keystrokes also has some generic meaning. The keys are presented in Appendix A for you to look at now and to refer to later.

Summary

You've covered quite a variety of information in this chapter. In your tour of the Control Center you learned that there are six panels that correspond to the six work surfaces: Database File Design, Query Design, Forms Design, Reports Design, Labels Design, and Applications Design. When you create files of any of these types, the names appear in the appropriate panels. Catalogs keep track of all associated files.

There are three Control Center menus: Catalog, which helps you manage your catalogs and their files; Tools, which has options for creating and storing macros, importing and exporting files from and to other software, getting to DOS to use its commands, and adjusting dBASE settings; and Exit, which gets you to the dot prompt or out of dBASE IV and back to DOS.

dBASE IV has a context-sensitive Help system that will give you information whenever you press **<F1> Help**.

Planning a Database File

In Chapter 2, you became acquainted with database files as you went through the definition of the FONEBOOK file structure. Although you were introduced to some of the terminology associated with file structure and creation, and you have experienced some of the uses for database files, in this chapter you are going to learn the terminology in greater depth and explore an essential aspect of database file creation—planning.

Planning Your File

Planning is often considered a nuisance, particularly by the novice—not just the database novice. But if you do not plan well, you may be unhappy with your results and, of course, you might have to begin all over again.

Take the example of constructing a paper database file with a typewriter. If the typist does not plan the layout of the columns properly, the database will, most likely, "fall off" the right margin of the paper, and it will have to be redone.

The same is true of a computer database file. It is not going to fall off the paper, but if it's not properly planned, you may have to go back and start over. With a computer, though, this isn't all bad. In fact, one good approach to planning a database file is to take a shot at it expecting to have to redo it once or twice. This process is called *iterative enhancement*. One of the benefits of working with a computer database file (as opposed to a paper one) is that you can make major changes to the database file without having to reenter the data. The computer can recover most, if not all, of the data stored in the database file before the change was made.

Taking a First Cut at Your Data

The first step in planning your database file is to know what you want to accomplish with it. Before you decide what data you want to put into your database file, you must decide what you want to get out of your database file. The first step is to decide what some of your reports will look like. This will give you a good idea of what is needed for input. The next step is to make a list of the items (data) to be included in the file. Don't be concerned about perfection. Nearly any shortcoming or omission can be easily repaired or overcome.

Take a look at an example you will use throughout the rest of this book—a stereo store database file. This inventory database file is intended to indicate the stock on hand and how much it is worth. It also is intended to be used by a sales system to price the items and even determine profit or loss. To plan this file, you first make a preliminary list of the items to be included in the file, as shown in Table 4.1.

Table 4.1. *Items to include in the example database*

Type of Component	Turntable, speakers, receiver, etc.
Brand of Stereo	DIGI, HITECH, MEGASONIK, etc.
Quantity on Hand	The number of units in stock
Inventory Date	Last date an inventory was taken
Wholesale Cost	What was paid for the item
Retail Price	What the item normally sells for
On Sale?	Is the item on sale?
Features	A description for the salesman of all the features and the selling points
Vendor's Address	Address of the supplier
Discount	Discount the supplier recommends off retail

Now that you have this list describing what is to be included in your stereo store inventory, you need additional information about the working characteristics and the limitations of the database file in dBASE IV.

To set up a database on paper, you need to do two things: assign column headings for each of the columns and figure out how many spaces to use for each column. You must do both of these for a computer database file. Determining the kind of information in each column is also part of planning your computer database file.

Rules for Files and Fields

The database file and field names must conform to specific rules. Although the filename rules are based on DOS, the field name rules (and types) are specific dBASE.

Filenames

If you were to make a typewritten version of your inventory file, you might give it a title. The title could be anything you wanted it to be, like "Parrot Inventory" or "Stereo Store Inventory." The computer version of your inventory file must have a title. The title is its filename. The filename needs to:

- Contain only letters and numbers and some special characters
- Be no longer than eight characters
- Contain no blank spaces

The filename is often preceded by a symbol that identifies the disk drive in use. For example, to indicate that a certain file is located on the C drive, the disk drive is identified by a letter followed by a colon, C:.

Some possible filenames for your computerized telephone book database file are shown in Figure 4.1. You can give the database file any name you choose, as long as you follow the rules stated above.

It is a good idea to choose filenames that help you remember what is in the database file. Table 4.2 shows some examples of mnemonic (that is, intended to aid the memory) filenames.

```
            In the default drive

       TELEFONE
       FONEBOOK
       FONLST

    In the root directory of drive C:

       C:\TELEFONE
       C:\FONEBOOK
       C:\FONLST

   In the DASE4 directory of drive C:

       C:\DBASE4\TELEFONE
       C:\DBASE4\TELEFONE
       C:\DBASE4\FONLST
```

Figure 4.1. *Sample filenames*

Table 4.2. *Examples of mnemonic filenames*

CLIENTS	INVENTRY	PAYROLL
PERSONNL	QTRLYTAX	TAX1988
1988CUST	MONTH_12	

Types of Fields in dBASE IV

There are six kinds of fields used in dBASE IV:

- Character
- Numeric
- Float
- Logical
- Date
- Memo

Character Fields

Use these fields for short textual data items such as names, addresses, and phone numbers. They can be up to 254 characters long and can contain anything you can enter from your keyboard. This includes letters (both uppercase and lowercase); numbers; and special symbols, such as ?, &, <, "space," and so on. Normally you can use a character field for any purpose. In fact, you can make every field in a database file a character field.

Numeric Fields

These fields can contain only numbers. Use them when the numbers they contain are to be used for arithmetic calculations. They can contain either whole numbers (called integers) or decimal numbers. In addition to the digits, they can contain one decimal point (.) and a negative sign (–). In most database systems the positive (+) sign is understood and does not need to be entered. The negative sign and the decimal point occupy one space each and must be counted when determining the field width. A negative number such as –281.65 takes seven spaces (*bytes*) and has two decimal places. The largest number you can have is 20 digits. Numeric fields use *fixed-point* arithmetic for calculations.

Numeric fields are right-justified by dBASE IV; character fields are left-justified by dBASE IV. Examples of number columns that are right- and left-justified are shown in Figure 4.2.

LEFT JUSTIFIED	RIGHT JUSTIFIED
1	1
10	10
100	100

Figure 4.2. *Left-justified and right-justified columns*

Float Fields

This is another type of numeric field, which uses a different type of precision called *floating point*. Its greatest size is 19 digits. It is mainly used in scientific and engineering calculations, for which more precision is needed.

Logical Fields

Use this type of field when there are only two possibilities for the data (Yes/No, True/False). For example, either bills are paid or they are not. Either students attended a class or they did not attend. Either you are reading this or you are not. dBASE IV automatically assigns logical fields a width of one byte.

Date Fields

These fields, as you may have guessed, are used to store dates. dBASE IV automatically assigns Date type to a field with a width of eight bytes. Date fields accept only valid dates, which are normally entered and displayed as mm/dd/yy. The special characteristics of date fields are discussed in Chapter 11.

Memo Fields

These are special variable-length fields. You use them to store large blocks of text such as memos and short documents. dBASE IV does not store memo field data in the database file but actually stores it in a separate auxiliary file—called a *database text file*. This file has the same name as the database file and is automatically assigned a DBT file extension. The maximum size of a memo field is 64K. As data is entered into a memo field, space is automatically allocated in 512-byte increments. No space is required in the text file until data is entered into this field. A 10-byte field in the database file is used to keep track of the memo field data. Memo fields, and their special characteristics, are discussed in more detail in Chapter 11.

Unless you really need the special characteristics of logical, float, or memo fields, you can limit your field selection to character, date, and numeric fields.

Choosing a Field Name

Close on the heels of determining what type of field you want is assigning that field a field name. You know that the field name must contain ten or fewer characters. Choose field names that are descriptive—but keep them as short as possible. You will be using the field names in commands, and long names require more typing than short ones. Suppose that you need one field for each month of the year. You could name the fields JANUARY, FEBRUARY, and so forth, or you could use the shorter, and equally descriptive, JAN, FEB, and so forth.

Field Width

The size (width) of a character field is the number of "typewriter" spaces required to contain the longest entry for that field. Each letter, number, special symbol, and space counts as one character. Each character takes one byte of memory. The analogy relating the field width to space on a typewritten page also can be used as a comparison to the space in the computer's memory. Field width is always represented in bytes, and the number of bytes is the same as the number of spaces required to put the field on a typewritten page.

Although the number of spaces on a typewritten page has been compared to the number of bytes used in a field, there are differences. A typewritten page contains blank spaces used to separate the columns. Do not do this in a database file. Unused bytes are not needed to separate the fields. If, in a student roster database file, a field contains a student's age and the maximum possible age is nine, use only one byte for that field. Separating the fields when they are displayed, either on the terminal or on a printer, is achieved by other means in dBASE IV and is covered in a later chapter.

Other Considerations

In addition to file and field names, you must also consider other factors when designing your database. Some of these are based on your ideas; others result from the limitations of your computer system.

Determining the Level of Detail

Another item to consider in planning is how much information you can apply to one field name. Figure 4.3 depicts a case in which on the left there are 3 fields, and on the right, 11 fields. Your application will likely be somewhere in the middle. However, deciding whether to combine data items into a single field requires an understanding of how the data will be used. One rule of thumb is that if you are rarely (if ever) going to use the items of information separately, then combine them. Grouping items such as last name, first name, and middle initial into a single name field often allows for more efficient use of space. And it's certainly simpler to do so.

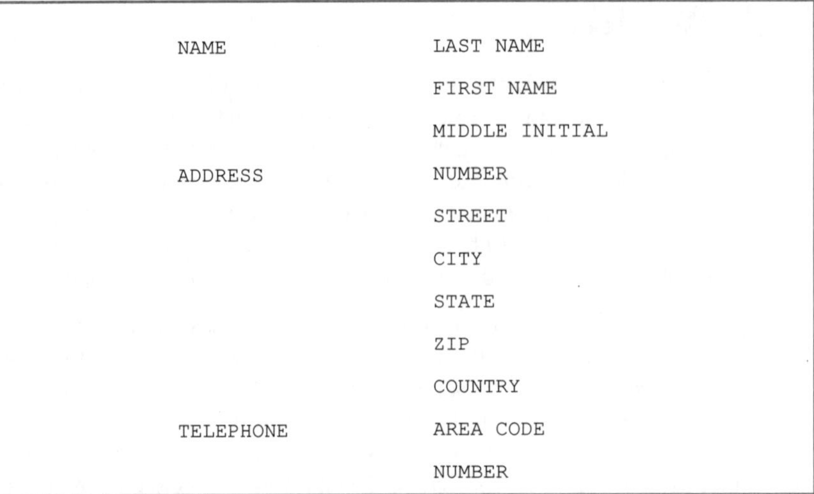

NAME	LAST NAME
	FIRST NAME
	MIDDLE INITIAL
ADDRESS	NUMBER
	STREET
	CITY
	STATE
	ZIP
	COUNTRY
TELEPHONE	AREA CODE
	NUMBER

Figure 4.3. *Grouping items like last name, first name, and middle initial into a single field*

Address is a good example of combined items and level of detail. If you think you will need the mailing address only as a single unit, you can group the street, city, state, and ZIP code. However, if you want a list of all your vendors in a certain state, you must separate your address into its normal parts—STREET, CITY, STATE, and ZIP.

Phone number is another example of detail. If you need a list of phone numbers grouped by certain area codes, you may need to split the area code and actual phone number into separate fields.

The INVENTRY File

In the next chapter you will create the database file for the stereo-store inventory database file. Call it INVENTRY. A plan for the INVENTRY database file can start with the descriptions shown in Table 4.1. However, you must assign a field name, type, and length to each description. Your plan might look something like that shown in Table 4.3. Notice that it resembles a database file structure.

Table 4.3. Creating the INVENTRY database

Field Name	*Field Type*	*Field Width*	*Decimals*
COMPONENT	C	15	
BRAND	C	10	
QUANTITY	N	3	
INVDATE	D	8	
ON_SALE	L	1	
COST	N	6	2
PRICE	N	6	2
FEATURES	M	10	
VENDADDR	C	25	

This database file has 9 fields and requires 84 bytes of memory for each record. Before you say, "Big deal—why should I go through this whole process for something I can do in my head?" remember that if you could do it in your head, you wouldn't need a computer. Each database file can contain as many as 255 fields and 4,000 bytes. Your database file could well require several hundred fields with thousands of bytes for each record. If so, you must compare your plan with the resources available to you.

Dealing with Resource Limitations

Each database management system, as well as your computer, has limitations that must be taken into account if your application is large. Computer limitations primarily involve the capacity of the disk drive(s). The disk drive must have enough capacity to store your database file. The size of the database file is approximately the size of a record times the total number of records. It is advisable to have a disk drive with enough capacity to store the database file itself plus a backup copy. The operating system also can limit your database file size. PC and MS-DOS, for example, limit file sizes to not more than 32 million bytes—that's pretty big.

The limitations imposed by the database management system are more interesting. Database system "limitations" could easily lead you off on a quest for some new and wonderful database management system that will be a panacea for your problems. The alternative to this potentially costly approach is to use your head. The resource limitations imposed by the database system are typically:

- Number of fields
- Field width
- Number of bytes in a record
- Number of records in a file

In dBASE IV, 255 fields are allowed in each database file. Each field is limited to 254 bytes, and each record is limited to 4,000 bytes. You can have only 1 billion records. The maximum size for each dBASE IV database file is 2 billion bytes. That's pretty big. It's so big that you are unlikely to encounter the limits.

To give you an idea of just how big this is, consider the following. Using a standard typewriter paper (8 1/2 by 11 inches), standard one-inch margins, and pica type, a paper database of this size would contain more than 569,000 pages. A microcomputer with a hard disk could read the database file at about 22,000 characters a second. This means that it would take the computer more than 24 hours just to read the database file. When you encounter databases that are this large, you are likely to encounter limitations in the computer hardware or in the operating system—and you probably shouldn't be using a microcomputer.

When You Need More Than One Database File

One of the most common problems in database file planning is that during the planning phase you may realize that a single database file either will not accomplish your goals for the system or will be inefficient. Generally, data is grouped together by some logical reasoning. Inventory data is kept on an inventory database file, sales data on a sales database file.

There are several reasons why database files are split up or new database files need to be created. The first is that redundant data is found in a database file. For example, the database file in Figure 4.4 has fields for the supplier's address. The supplier is assumed to be the vendor (BRAND) itself. Because there will be more than one piece of DIGI equipment, it doesn't make a lot of sense to carry the address of DIGI more than once. If you have the address in the database file more than once, you have to make sure that each time the address of a vendor changes it is changed for every record for that vendor. A more common solution is to have a separate database file for the vendor's address. You also could carry other information specific to the vendor, such as accounts payable information, or the name of the vendor's purchasing agent or his phone number. Figure 4.4 depicts this relationship.

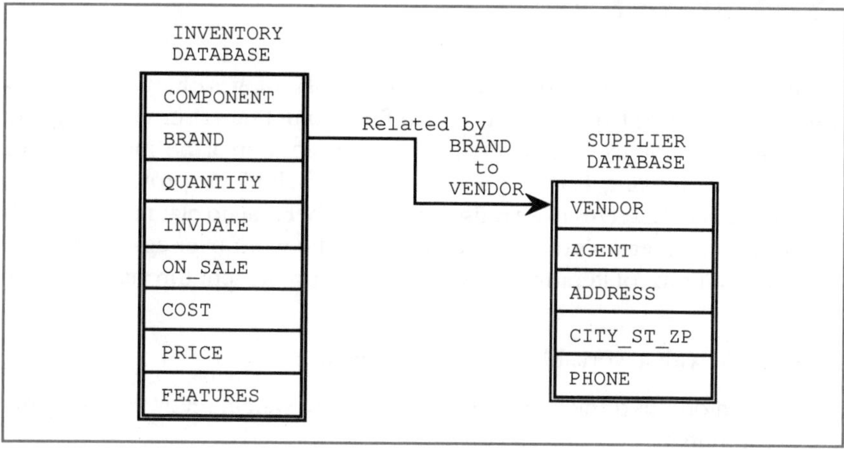

Figure 4.4. *A diagram of the inventory and supplier database files*

Relating Database Files

The two database files must have something in common to join them together in some fashion. In this case they are linked by the BRAND name, included in the second database file too.

Linking is done using a common element—some piece of data—that appears consistently across the related database files, such as an item or an invoice number. In this example the BRAND name in the INVENTORY database is common with the VENDOR name in the SUPPLIER database. Though they have different field names, their data values are the same.

This demonstrates, by the way, the definition of a relational database file system. Files can be related to each other and needless duplication can be minimized. As a matter of fact, the technical term for a database file is relation. It is usually wise to group information that is used into a single relation. It is simpler to work with one database than with two or more.

As your database gets larger, the computer takes more time to search through it. You may want to carefully consider the size of each field—and even whether you should have the field at all.

Summary

As mentioned at the beginning of this chapter, planning is often considered a nuisance. The urge to get started on your file is sometimes overwhelming. But as you gain experience, you also will gain an appreciation of the immense value of thorough planning. Planning also forces you to think the problem through before you act. If it seems like a nuisance, remember that no planning will likely result in the larger nuisance of having to do the work over again. Think of planning in terms of iterative enhancement (improvement through repeated attempts):

- Begin with a workable skeleton of a plan.
- Build on this framework until you have the system ready to put on the computer.

The most serious trap you can get caught in is to seek perfection. This can cost you time, money, and energy. Remember, you may be unfamiliar with computer database management systems, but the concept, construction, and use of computer database files are not difficult or unfamiliar. Relax and make the necessary connections from your experience. A computer database is an easy step to take into your future—not trivial, just easy.

Building Your Database File

The remaining chapters in this section examine database file usage. First discussed is how to create a good database file and then how to build, modify, order, maintain, and work with database files.

When you have finished the planning process, you are ready to begin construction of your database. First, you design the structure of the database file. You then complete the construction phase by entering all the data—a record at a time—into this structure. The most serious problem you are likely to encounter during this data entry period is to keep from being bored to death.

Prior to the development of microcomputers and database management systems, the process of creating a database file wasn't easy. It was a lengthy and expensive process involving costly hardware and the use of professional programmers. Though you could have learned to do the programming yourself, until a few years ago there was no way to avoid the use of expensive hardware. Today, with one of the available database management systems and inexpensive microcomputer hardware, you can easily do everything yourself. And, unless you are a very slow typist, it can be done quickly.

Now that you're familiar with what a computerized database file is, you are ready to move on to investigate more facets of database file capability. Although the personal telephone book exercise was a familiar example that covered the creation of a database file, it didn't offer enough material to demonstrate the full range of computer database management.

Creating the File

It is time to begin creating your database file project. The new project will use the dBASE database management system to create and use an inventory file of a retail store. We've chosen this example because most readers will be familiar with the concept of conducting an inventory. In addition, it will allow you to work with numeric as well as character fields. Your database file also will allow you to work with records that can be grouped into categories. For the chapter finale, we will prepare the report shown in Figure 5.1.

```
Page No.     1
04/03/91

COMPONENT        BRAND        QUANTITY      COST     PRICE
AMPLIFIER        DIGI               15    229.00    389.99
AMPLIFIER        ALLWOOD            10    369.00    589.99
AMPLIFIER        ONESOUND            5    529.00    899.99
COMPACT DISC     DIGI               17    389.00    625.99
COMPACT DISC     ONESOUND           26    269.00    329.99
COMPACT DISC     HITECH            125    129.00    299.99
COMPACT DISC     ALLWOOD            60    109.00    189.99
RECEIVER         ALLWOOD            30    169.00    289.00
RECEIVER         DIGI                0    299.00    529.00
SPEAKERS         MITY               22    299.00    399.00
SPEAKERS         DIGI               18     89.00    109.00
SPEAKERS         ALLWOOD           140     69.00     59.00
TURNTABLE        DIGI               15    149.00    299.99
TURNTABLE        MEGASONIK         250     39.00     69.00
TURNTABLE        HITECH              6    189.00    269.99
                                   739   3325.00   5349.91
```

Figure 5.1. *A report produced by the Quick Report feature*

The subject of the inventory is a very small stereo store. This store is so small that it carries only 15 or 20 items in stock. Nevertheless, this is more than enough to demonstrate database concepts.

To be useful, the inventory database file must contain data that will be of interest to the store owner. To begin this example, you will create the database file with some of the items planned for in Chapter 4. These include the database file shown in Table 5.1. Later, you will add the rest of the fields from your plan.

Table 5.1. *Items you will use to create your inventory database*

Field Name	*Field Type*	*Field Width*	*Decimals*
COMPONENT	C	15	
BRAND	C	10	
QUANTITY	N	3	
COST	N	7	2
PRICE	N	7	2

Defining the File Structure

The fields listed in Table 5.1 will become the columns (fields) in the new database file. Just as in the personal book example, you will use the Data panel of the Control Center to create the database file and define its structure. If you are not already in the Control Center, please get there now. Remember, if you find yourself in the dot prompt mode, just press **<F2>** to get into the Control Center.

Move the highlight to `<create>` on the Data panel of the Control Center, and press **<Enter>**. The Database work surface appears ready for you to enter your database file structure.

Next, define each of the fields for the new database file. The field definitions form the structure for the database file. Each field definition consists of a field name, a field type, and a field width. Remember that the field names must be 10 characters or fewer. When you get to the index column, just accept the default of `N` and move on. The completed field definitions are shown in Figure 5.2.

- COMPONENT is the field name for the column to contain the kind of stereo component. It is a character field 15 spaces wide.
- BRAND is the field name for the column to contain the brand names. This is a character field 10 spaces wide.
- QUANTITY is the field name for the column to contain the amount of stock on hand. This is a numeric field 3 digits wide. This field width allows values of up to 999 for each item in the inventory.
- COST and PRICE are numeric fields for unit cost and price. Unlike QUANTITY, they have decimal places. The field size is 7 bytes, to allow for the display width of the total—6 digits plus the decimal point. You need to define two decimal places to allow for prices up to 9999.99. So the final field length is 7.2 bytes.

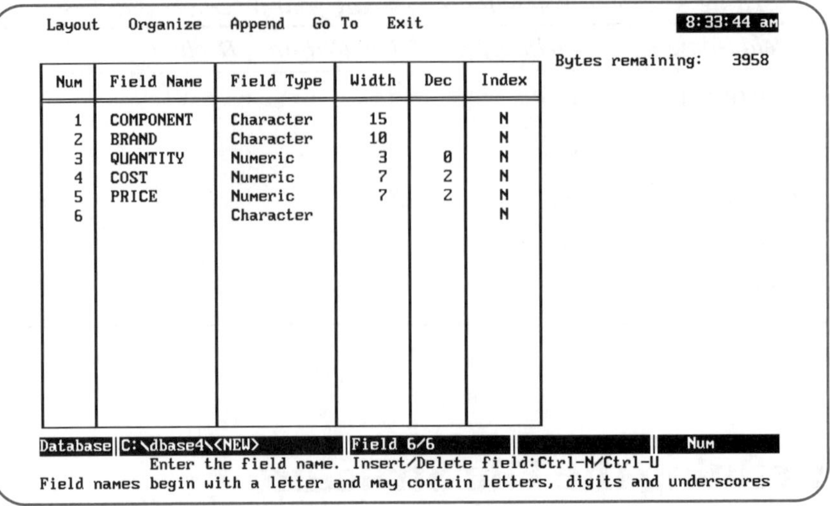

Figure 5.2. *The Inventory database structure*

When you have finished entering the data to define the INVENTRY database file, the screen will resemble Figure 5.2. To tell dBASE IV that you have finished, simply press the **<Enter>** key when prompted to enter the field name for field 6.

Assigning a Filename

The next step is to assign the new database file a name. Enter the filename INVENTRY. "Stereo Store Inventory" is too large, and it contains embedded blank spaces. INVENTRY is descriptive and is only eight characters long. Placing this database file on the hard disk drive saves the structure of the new file on the disk. dBASE IV then asks:

```
Input data records now? (Y/N)
```

With your `Y` (yes) response, you are presented with an EDIT screen "form." A representative record for this database file is shown in Figure 5.3.

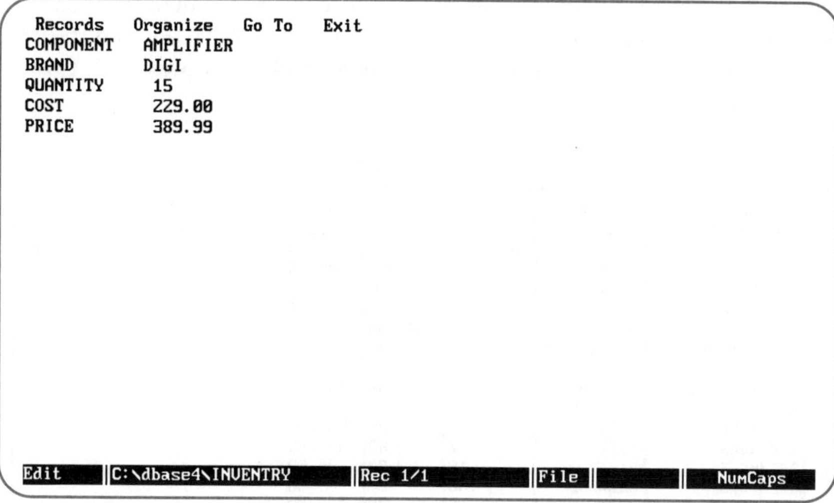

Figure 5.3. *The first INVENTRY record*

Entering Data

Data entry begins on the left of each field. If the field is a character field, the data remains at the left edge, just as it would if you were typing on a piece of paper. This is called *left justification*. Character fields are left-justified.

For numeric fields, data entry also begins at the left edge. However, when you press **<Enter>** (telling dBASE IV that you have finished entering data into the field), the number automatically moves to the right edge of the field. This is called *right justification*. Numeric fields are right-justified.

You cannot enter a letter into a numeric field. If you try to enter a letter, dBASE IV will not accept the character, and the computer will beep. The same is true for date fields. You must enter a valid date into the date field, including the numbers and slashes.

While entering data, you can use the arrow keys to move the cursor anywhere in the data entry area. You can back up to a previous character or digit and re-enter it simply by typing the new value over the old. You can back up to a previous record by pressing the **<PgUp>** key. If you do so, you can return to your new record with the **<PgDn>** key. If for any reason you exit from entering new records before you intended, you can resume adding records by pressing the **<F2> Data** key, and continue adding records beyond the last record entered.

Figure 5.4 shows a BROWSE table of all 15 records. Enter all of these records into the EDIT screen, one record at a time. After you have entered the 15th record, press **<F2>** to toggle to the BROWSE table, and press **<PgUp>** to check your work.

Records   Organize   Fields   Go To   Exit

COMPONENT	BRAND	QUANTITY	COST	PRICE
AMPLIFIER	DIGI	15	229.00	389.99
AMPLIFIER	ALLWOOD	10	369.00	589.99
AMPLIFIER	ONESOUND	5	529.00	899.99
COMPACT DISC	DIGI	17	389.00	625.99
COMPACT DISC	ONESOUND	26	269.00	329.99
COMPACT DISC	HITECH	125	129.00	229.00
COMPACT DISC	ALLWOOD	60	109.00	189.99
RECEIVER	ALLWOOD	30	169.00	289.00
RECEIVER	DIGI	0	299.00	529.00
SPEAKERS	MITY	22	299.00	399.00
SPEAKERS	DIGI	18	89.00	109.00
SPEAKERS	ALLWOOD	140	69.00	59.00
TURNTABLE	DIGI	15	149.00	299.99
TURNTABLE	MEGASONIK	250	39.00	69.00
TURNTABLE	HITECH	6	189.00	269.99

Browse | C:\dbase4\INVENTRY | Rec 1/15 | File | | NumCaps

Figure 5.4. The INVENTRY database

Notes on Data Entry

The value of a database file depends in large part on the quality of its data. You won't get far if you tell the tax auditor, "I know there are some errors, but it was really fast!" Because data entry is often dull and repetitive work, it is common practice to turn data entry over to the lowest-paid help available. This is a bad idea.

In many cases, there will be an enormous amount of data to enter into the new database file. Most real stereo stores, for example, have far more than 15 items in stock. Data entry will be, far and away, the most time-consuming part of most database file usage. Entry is done at human speed, whereas retrieval is done at computer speed.

Data entry is the part of the process most prone to error. Although entering several records may be accomplished without mistakes, error-free input for hundreds, perhaps thousands, of records is unlikely.

Data Entry Errors

When you are adding a large number of new records to a database file, such as during the initial construction, you may lose track of where you are. Or, as you are busily working, you may realize suddenly that you made an error during data entry on the last record. To correct an error or find your place, you can back up to the previous record, by pressing **<PgUp>**. Each time you press **<PgUp>**, you will move back one record in the database file. To return to adding records, press **<PgDn>** to move forward (toward the end) of the database file.

You can easily correct errors in a record by moving the cursor back to the error and typing in the correct information. Try some sample corrections. Suppose that you type in TESSTT and you want TEST. If you are not in insert mode, you can remove the final *T* by placing the cursor on the last *T* and pressing **<Spacebar>**. Remove the surplus *S* by placing the cursor on the second *S* and pressing the **<Del>** key. **<Del>** eliminates the character that the cursor is on. In insert mode, you could have just typed over the word TEST and used the **<Spacebar>** to clean up the extra two characters at the end.

Suppose that you type TET when you want TEST. You want to insert the letter *S* between the *E* and the *T*. Place the cursor on the last *T*. To insert the letter *S*, press the **<Ins>** key, type , and then press **<Ins>** again. **<Ins>** toggles the insert mode on and off. When the insert mode is on, `Ins` may be displayed either in the status bar or on the upper-right of the screen.

Perhaps you have available only part of the information necessary to complete a record, but you still want to enter what you have. Enter the information you have, and then press **<PgDn>**. This will advance you to the next record without your having to step through each of the remaining fields.

To this point the process of constructing a database file has been purely mechanical. You create a file structure according to simple rules, and then you enter data. Data entry continues until you have entered all the data. The database file is now ready to fulfill some purpose—such as providing you with the information needed to help manage a business.

If the data entry job is small, the simple mechanical approach described above is probably the best way to get the job done. It is straightforward and simple. If there is a lot of data to enter, it might be a good idea to find ways that the computer system can actually help with the entry process.

Data Entry Assistance

There are some built-in data entry aids as well as some simple procedures you can write that enable the computer to assist with or perform some of your data entry tasks for you. You can develop custom screen forms and menu systems to suit your needs with the Forms and Applications Generator work surfaces. Both the Forms and the Applications work surfaces generate dBASE IV code known as *procedures*. A procedure is an easy way of getting the computer to perform special things for you. The details of "teaching" the computer a procedure are discussed in Section 3.

You can copy the data from any field of one record to the same field of the next record. Simply place the cursor in the field next to the field from which you want to copy data and press **<Shift>-<F8>**. Instantly the data from the previous field is copied into the field where the cursor is located.

Another of these aids, the one you are going to look at in this chapter, is CARRY ON/OFF.

CARRY ON/OFF

You also can copy all the data from one record to the next. In many database files, much redundant data must be entered. In a school, for example, there are far more children than rooms and teachers, so many teacher names and room numbers are repeated. In the stereo store example, there are several brand names for each kind of component. The stock in the showroom is grouped by type of component—turntable, speakers, amplifier, and so forth—for the convenience of the customer. The various wattage sizes for a given type are usually grouped within the type.

In many cases, you can group the data in such a way as to reduce the amount of data that must be typed in. When redundancy is grouped, as in these two examples, dBASE IV can reduce the amount of typing required, by "carrying" the data forward from record to record. CARRY is turned on by resetting it in the Tools menu, under the `Settings` option.

Consider how data entry would progress if CARRY were ON. First, as you add a record, you get an initial screen display and enter the data for Record 1. The second record contains the same data as the first, and you change those fields that you didn't want to be the same. All you need do is edit those fields that are different from Record 1. When you advance, Record 3 displays exactly as Record 2 at the time of the advance. With CARRY turned OFF (the default setting), the display for Record 2 would appear blank, as would Record 3. Using CARRY ON can reduce both the amount of typing and the number of errors owing to typing mistakes.

When you have CARRY turned ON, you tell dBASE IV to carry all the data field's values to the next records. When you learn how to create custom forms, you will learn that you also can selectively control which fields CARRY data forward.

Using the Data

One of the objectives of an inventory is to find out how much money a business has tied up in inventory. When you finish an inventory in the conventional way—that is, with paper and pencil—you haul out the calculator and begin to compute the value of the inventory. The inventory value is obtained by multiplying each quantity by the corresponding cost and then adding the results. Each step in this process provides an opportunity for error. If, on the other hand, you have done the inventory with dBASE IV, you can get an error-free result immediately. With a computerized database file, your only chance for error is during data entry. With the manual method, it's possible to make a mistake every time a number is used.

Selecting Information with Queries

You can request many types of information. One of the simplest types is a total of the value at both cost and retail of your inventory. Requests of this type are handled by the Query work surface. You can use this surface for many types of data extraction. In Chapter 2 you saw how the Query screen is used to select only certain records. Now you will see how it can perform mathematical operations as well. Later, you will see the many uses of the query form, including complex data selection and grouping using multiple files.

The easiest way to get to the Query work surface from either the EDIT or the BROWSE screen is to press the **<Alt>-E** keys to get to the Exit menu. Then select `Transfer to Query Design`. This option puts you into the Query work surface, where you can define your query.

Your first request of dBASE IV is to see what a subset of your data looks like. In order to do this you must tell dBASE IV to select only certain records. Later, in Chapter 10, you will see a complete explanation of the Query Design screen. For now just make a quick selection.

Make sure the cursor is in the far left side of the INVENTRY database file *skeleton*. Press the **<Tab>** key to move the cursor under the COMPONENT field. In quotes, as shown in Figure 5.5., type:

```
'SPEAKERS'
```

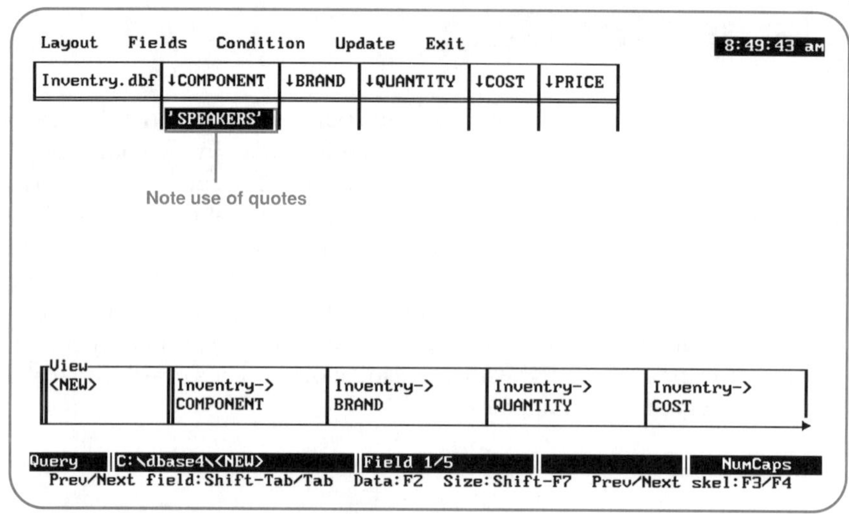

Figure 5.5. *Selecting the SPEAKERS in the Query screen*

Press **<F2>** to see the data. You are placed in either BROWSE or EDIT mode looking at your records. If you are in BROWSE mode you should see all the speakers available from the file. If you are in EDIT you should see one speaker record. Press **<F2>** again to get into BROWSE mode, where you will see all your speaker records, as shown in Figure 5.6.

Records Organize Fields Go To Exit

COMPONENT	BRAND	QUANTITY	COST	PRICE
SPEAKERS	MITY	22	299.00	399.00
SPEAKERS	DIGI	18	89.00	109.00
SPEAKERS	ALLWOOD	140	69.00	59.00

Browse C:\dbase4\<NEW> Rec 10/15 View Num

Figure 5.6. *Viewing the SPEAKERS in BROWSE*

Simple Sums

Do one more thing. Take a look at the total quantity of all the speakers in stock. To accomplish this you must use the SUM function in the QUANTITY field. Return to the Query Design screen. Press **<Alt>-E** to open the Exit menu and then type `T` to select `Transfer to Query Design`. You will be placed back in the Query screen.

Move the cursor to the right using the **<Tab>** key until you are in the QUANTITY field. Because you want the sum of the field, you must tell this to dBASE IV. In the entry area of the calculated field skeleton, enter the word SUM under the QUANTITY field. This does not go in quotes because it is an operator and not a value. Type `SUM`, as shown in Figure 5.7. The value SPEAKERS should still be in the COMPONENT field.

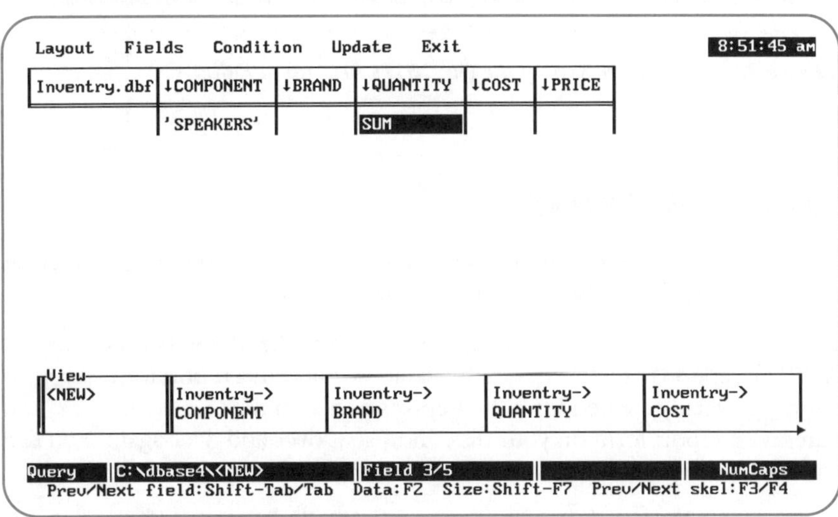

Figure 5.7. *Selecting SPEAKERS and SUMming the QUANTITY*

Now press **<F2>**. If you are not in BROWSE mode, go there by pressing **<F2>** again. You should see only one data line, which contains the sum of all the quantities of the SPEAKER records in the QUANTITY field. This is shown in Figure 5.8. You now know the total number of speaker units in your inventory.

Return to the Control Center without saving the query. Press **<Esc>** to leave BROWSE and return to the Control Center. You first need to confirm that you want to abandon the operation without saving the query.

You are now back in the Control Center. The data file, INVENTRY, should be above the line indicating that it is active. If it isn't active, make it active by highlighting it and pressing **<Enter>**.

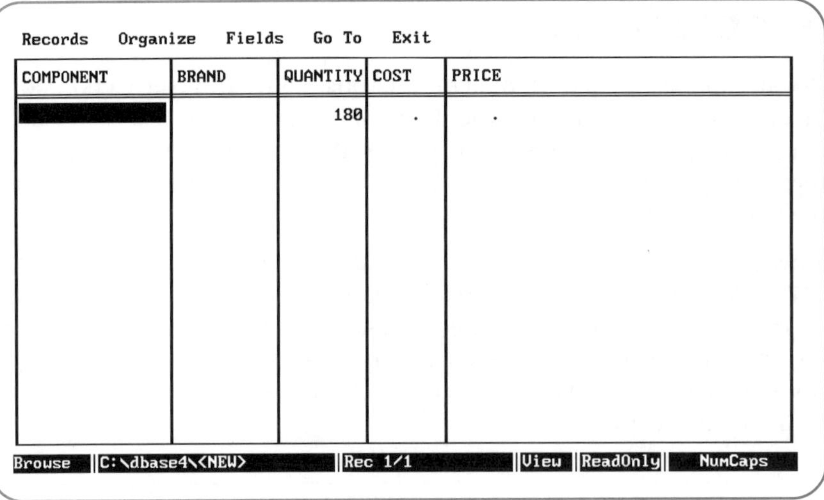

Figure 5.8. Viewing the Sum of the QUANTITY field for SPEAKERS

Quick Reports

Most database file management software systems have a built-in report writer to help you prepare reports from your database file.

Figure 5.1 is an example of a report prepared from the dBASE IV report writer. A dBASE report is prepared from the database file with a report form. A report form is normally created from the Reports panel on the Control Center. You can save a report form on your disk and use it over and over again. You can modify your report form whenever you want.

For now, use the Quick Report mode of dBASE IV. Press **<Shift>-<F9>** for a Quick Report.

dBASE IV automatically creates a report form with all your fields. It also places column titles using the field names at the top of each column. This is known as a column-oriented report and is similar to the BROWSE screen. You cannot make any changes in the Quick Report. All the fields and records that are active will be printed. If the query is still active, you also will see your new fields. A menu is opened waiting for you to make a choice about printing.

If you have a printer, turn it on and press **<Enter>** to select `Begin printing`. Your report will print in a few seconds. If you want to view the report on your screen, press the **<Down arrow>** twice so it is on `View Report on Screen` and press **<Enter>**, or simply type `V`.

After your report has been printed on paper or to the screen, you are returned to the Control Center.

Naming Your Catalog

At the top of the screen below the menus is the Catalog name. This is the name dBASE IV uses to group your files. You may have already given the catalog a name; if you did, rename it to PARROT.CAT after the name of the stereo store, Parrot Stereo. The catalog name is probably now called UNTITLED.CAT on your screen. dBASE IV automatically creates such catalog names for you when you begin. It also remembers the last catalog you used and makes that active the next time you start dBASE IV.

Press **<Alt>-C** to open the Catalog menu. Type `M` to select `Modify catalog name`. When dBASE IV asks you for a name, backspace over the old name, leaving the disk drive and subdirectory on the entry line. Enter `PARROT` for Parrot Stereo Company after the backslash (\) and press **<Enter>**. Your catalog is now named PARROT. The next time you start dBASE IV, you will see the Control Center listing the same files you last used.

Summary

You have started your stereo store database project. You have defined a file structure for the INVENTRY file, entered 15 records into the new file, and checked some inventory in the Query work surface. The Quick Report you generated gave you a printout of all your records in a format similar to the Browse screen.

To summarize, the options you have when "building" the original database range from the simple and straightforward EDIT screen to elaborate procedures for more descriptive prompts.

The next chapter will cover some methods for updating and modifying both the structure of your file and its contents.

chapter

6

Modifying a Database File

Once you have built a database file, you will inevitably make changes to it. Besides changing the contents of fields like QUANTITY and PRICE, you'll have to add some records and delete others. Evolving government regulations may require the addition of new fields to a database file. This everyday activity—changing the database file—is called *updating*.

Updating a database file takes time because it is a manual operation. Routine reports and other output products are usually accomplished automatically at computer speeds and require relatively little time.

The frequency with which the database file is updated depends, in large part, on your needs. Some updating tasks must be done daily. Others can be done weekly or even monthly. Still others are done only as necessary. Parrot Stereo, for example, might update an inventory database file as each new shipment is received. Employee hours might be updated either daily or weekly. The magnitude of the updating tasks depends on the particular application.

This chapter will tell you what changes to a database file you can make and how to make them. Changes to a database file usually fall into one or more of these four categories:

- Changing the database file structure
- Adding records
- Removing records
- Changing the contents of records

Changing the Structure of a Database File

The structure of a database file is not changed very often. Structural changes are usually in response to some change in the business environment—such as a new government regulation. Changing the structure should be undertaken with some care because there is always a chance, however slight, of losing data if you are not careful.

In many systems, the content of the database file is destroyed whenever the structure is changed. Users tend to find this more than annoying. DBMS designers have responded with ways to guard against the loss of data. dBASE IV, for example, automatically makes a backup copy of a database file at the time you make a change to the file structure. After a user changes the file structure, dBASE IV automatically moves data from the backup copy to the modified database file. The backup copy has the same name as the database file but has the file type .BAK. Keep in mind that there must be enough space on the disk to hold this backup copy.

You use the Database work surface to change the structure of a database file. You can use it to:

- Add fields
- Delete fields
- Change a field name
- Change a field width
- Change a field type
- Add an index tab
- Create, change, or delete an index tag

In dBASE IV, the process for modifying the structure looks just like the process for creating the structure. Try making some changes to the INVENTRY database file. First, you place the database file in use. Then, you can modify its structure.

From the Control Center, highlight INVENTRY in the Data panel and press the Design key, **<Shift>-<F2>**. When the work surface is displayed, press **<Esc>** to close the Organize menu (which automatically opens).

The dBASE IV work surface, with the present structure of the database file, is shown as Figure 6.1. This is the same screen you used to create the database file. At the top of the screen are the menus that let you work with other parts of the Database work surface.

```
 Layout   Organize   Append   Go To   Exit                          8:57:18 am

                                                     Bytes remaining:    3958
 Num   Field Name    Field Type   Width   Dec   Index

  1    COMPONENT     Character     15             N
  2    BRAND         Character     10             N
  3    QUANTITY      Numeric        3      0      N
  4    COST          Numeric        7      2      N
  5    PRICE         Numeric        7      2      N

Database C:\dbase4\INVENTRY       Field 1/5                          NumCaps
          Enter the field name.  Insert/Delete field:Ctrl-N/Ctrl-U
Field names begin with a letter and may contain letters, digits and underscores
```

Figure 6.1. *The INVENTRY Database work surface before any changes*

Adding a Field

To add a field, you move the cursor to where you want the new field and press **<Ctrl>-N**. A blank field definition is inserted above the field you were on. For example, to insert a new field between the current fields BRAND and QUANTITY, use the arrow keys to move the cursor to the QUANTITY field. The QUANTITY field definition is highlighted. Press **<Ctrl>-N**. A blank field space for a new field definition is inserted between BRAND and QUANTITY, as shown in Figure 6.2. dBASE IV then positions the cursor for you to enter the new field name.

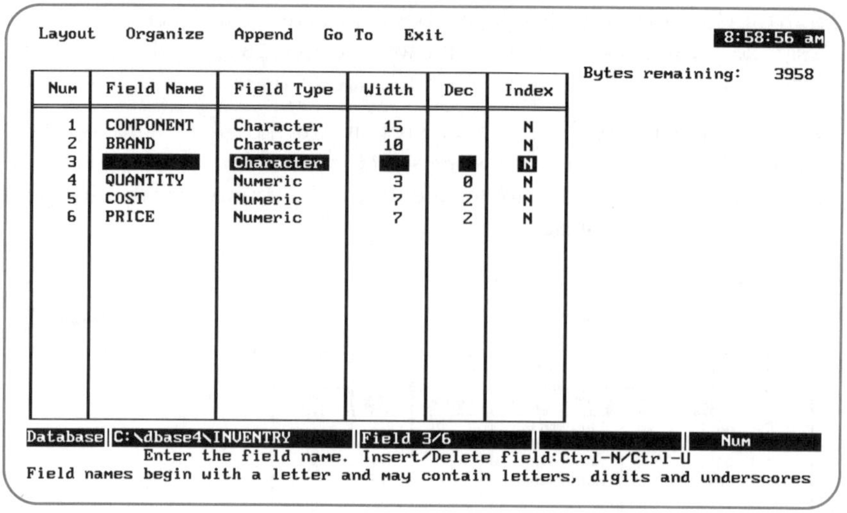

```
Layout   Organize   Append   Go To   Exit                        8:58:56 am

                                                   Bytes remaining:   3958
 Num | Field Name | Field Type | Width | Dec | Index
   1 | COMPONENT  | Character  |   15  |     |   N
   2 | BRAND      | Character  |   10  |     |   N
   3 |            | Character  |       |     |   N
   4 | QUANTITY   | Numeric    |    3  |  0  |   N
   5 | COST       | Numeric    |    7  |  2  |   N
   6 | PRICE      | Numeric    |    7  |  2  |   N

Database C:\dbase4\INVENTRY      Field 3/6                          Num
          Enter the field name.  Insert/Delete field:Ctrl-N/Ctrl-U
Field names begin with a letter and may contain letters, digits and underscores
```

Figure 6.2. *Adding a new field*

Deleting a Field

To delete a field, move the cursor to the field you want to delete. The field definition is highlighted. Press **<Ctrl>-U**. The field definition disappears—the field had been deleted. The field name and all of the data in that field are removed from the database file when the modified structure is saved. Now, delete the field you just added by pressing **<Ctrl>-U**. Your database file structure should once again look like Figure 6.1.

Changing a Field Definition

You can change any or all of the elements that make up a field definition—the field name, field type, field width, number of decimal places, or index. To make changes in the field definition, you move the cursor to highlight the field definition you want to change. Then, type in the new field information. If you change a field name, it is very important that you do not make any other change to the structure at that time. dBASE IV can save your data only if just a field name has been changed. For example, if you add a new field and at the same time you change the name of an existing field, dBASE IV has no way of knowing which field is new and which is just renamed. Do the renaming operation, and then press **<Ctrl>-<End>** to save the change (and the data). Make other changes with a subsequent use of the Database work surface.

Saving the Changes

To exit from the Database work surface and to save any changes you have made, press **<Ctrl>-<End>**. If you make any changes, you must confirm the action by pressing **<Enter>** according to the instructions that appear at the bottom of the screen. The data records that dBASE IV had saved in the backup copy are automatically reloaded into your modified database file.

New fields have no data in them. A character field that has been made smaller has its far-right characters discarded. A numeric field that has been made smaller discards its least significant digits—those to the far right—whenever a decimal number is too long to fit into the new field space. If an entire numeric entry is excluded, the field display shows an asterisk to tell you that the field display width is now too small to properly hold the value. Before erasing the backup copy, look over the contents of the database file in order to be certain that nothing has gone awry. For example, check to see that you have not made a field size too small to hold the data.

Canceling the Changes

You can change your mind about what you have done, up to a point, as long as you have not pressed **<Ctrl>-<End>** to save your changes. Press **<Esc>** to abandon any changes. This places you back at the Control Center and discards any changes you have made during that session. Even if you have already saved your changes, it still may not be too late to change your mind. Remember, dBASE IV has made a backup database file. You can erase the modified database file and rename the backup file by changing the file identifier from .BAK to .DBF. You can rename the files in DOS or through the Tools menu's `DOS tools` option in the Control Center.

Adding Records

The most common way to add new records to an established or modified file is to go to the BROWSE or EDIT screens and page down past the last record in your file. You also can get to the end of the database file easily, by using the Go To menus in the BROWSE and EDIT screens. Another way you can go directly to the bottom of a database file to add new records is through a menu in the Database work surface, which will be explained later in this book. Figure 6.3 shows the Append menu open in the Database work surface.

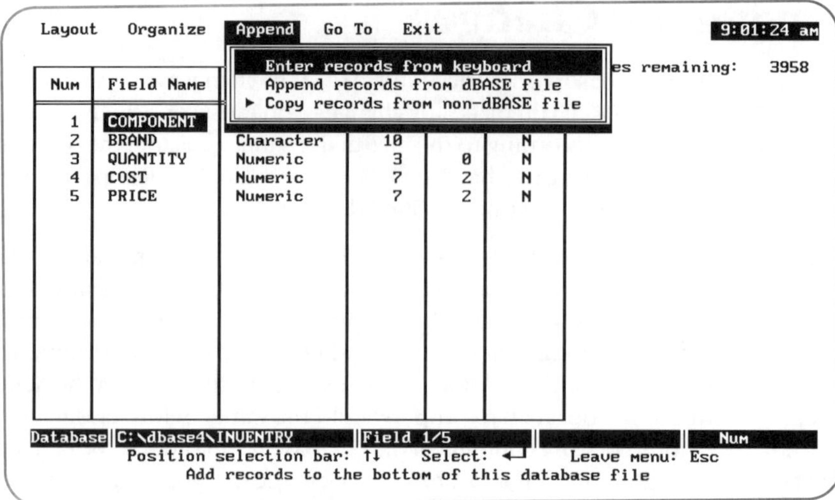

Figure 6.3. *Adding new records*

The Append menu shows you three choices. Choosing the first option, `Enter records from keyboard`, places you into the EDIT screen with a blank record displayed on the work surface. You can then enter all the records you want. The second choice in the Append menu, `Append records from dBASE file`, lets you choose another dBASE file and add all its records to your original database file. Of course, the database files must share common field names. The third choice, `Copy records from non-dBASE file`, lets you choose from some of the other database file formats and add the data from a "foreign" data file to the end of your database file.

Removing Records

You remove records using a two-step process. From the BROWSE or EDIT screens, mark the record for removal by pressing **<Ctrl>-U** while in the record. Then, remove all records that have been marked for removal with the PACKing operation. You can choose this operation, `Erase marked records`, from the Organize menu in the Database work surface. You can remove the deletion mark while in BROWSE or EDIT modes by highlighting the marked record and then pressing **<Ctrl>-U**. You can remove the marks from all marked records, by choosing `Unmark all records` from the Organize menu in the Database work surface. You must unmark the record, however, before it is erased, or PACKed, as it is technically called. Selecting `Erasing marked records` in the

Database work surface actually removes the deleted records. Once the database file is packed, those records are gone. There is NO unpack or "unerase" command.

To illustrate this process, let's remove the third record from the INVENTRY database file. Choose the INVENTRY database file and press the Data key, **<F2>**. You should now be in the EDIT screen. If you are in the BROWSE screen, press **<F2>** again to go to the EDIT screen. Using the Go To menu, go to the top record. Press the **<PgDn>** key twice to go to the third record. Press **<Ctrl>-U**. The status bar now displays `Del` on the right side. If the status bar is not displayed at the bottom of the screen, `Del` is displayed at the top of the screen. Figure 6.4 shows the record after it has been marked for deletion.

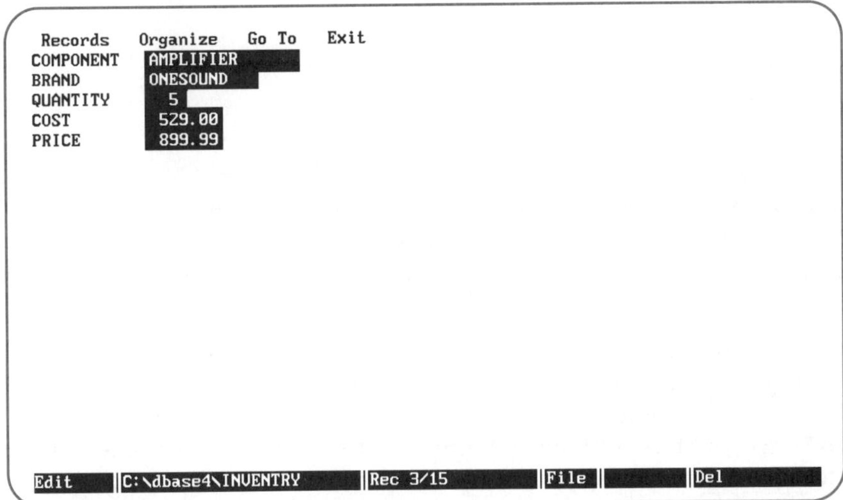

Figure 6.4. *Marking a record for deletion*

If you actually erase all the marked records, only 14 records will be in the database file. Record 4 would now be record 3, Record 11 would now be record 10, and so forth.

As long as you haven't erased the marked records, you can change your mind about records that have been marked for deletion. Remember, you can either unmark a record by pressing **<Ctrl>-U** again in the record marked for deletion, or unmark all the records by choosing the `Unmark all records` option in the Organize menu of the Database work surface.

Changing the Contents of Records

Suppose you want to make changes to the content of the inventory database file. This time you've decided to revise the prices and recount the quantity on hand. This gives you the opportunity to see two methods for changing record contents, in modes with which you are already familiar:

- EDIT
- BROWSE

EDIT

EDIT allows you to display and edit a single record at a time. You can select a single record, a group of records, or all the records for editing. You can specify records by either record number or content.

To illustrate the use of the command, edit record 6 in the stereo store inventory. Select this record by going into EDIT and either paging down to the sixth record or using the Go To menu in the EDIT screen, as shown in Figure 6.5. Notice that the record you are in appears in the status bar. In this example, the status bar should show `6/15`, indicating that you are in record 6 of 15 records. You can open the Go To menu by pressing **<Alt>-G**, or by pressing **<F10> Menu**, and then moving to the Go To menu with the arrow keys. One of the options in the Go To menu is `Record number`. When you choose `Record number`, you can enter the record number you want to go to. Choose `Record number`, type `6`, and press **<Enter>**. Record number 6 comes up on the screen, as shown in Figure 6.6.

To change the QUANTITY to 50 and the PRICE to 299.99, use either the **<Down arrow>** key or the **<Enter>** key to position the cursor in the QUANTITY field. Type `50` and press **<Enter>**. The value stored in QUANTITY changes to 50, and the cursor advances to the next field. Move the cursor to the PRICE field and type `299.99`. This changes the PRICE to 299.99 and advances to the next record, in this case, Record 7.

When you edit a record, any changes made are automatically saved when you exit from that record. You can abandon and not save changes to a record by pressing the **<Esc>** key before you leave that record. Once changes are saved, you cannot undo them with the **<Esc>** key.

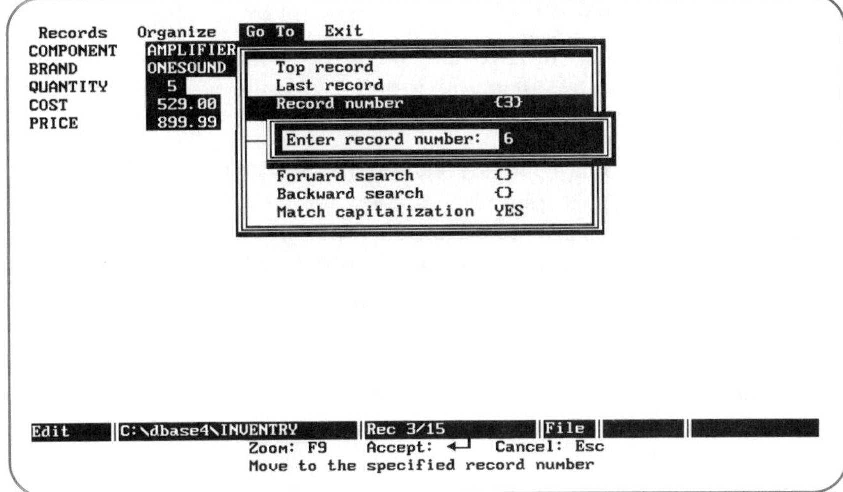

Figure 6.5. Go To a specific record number

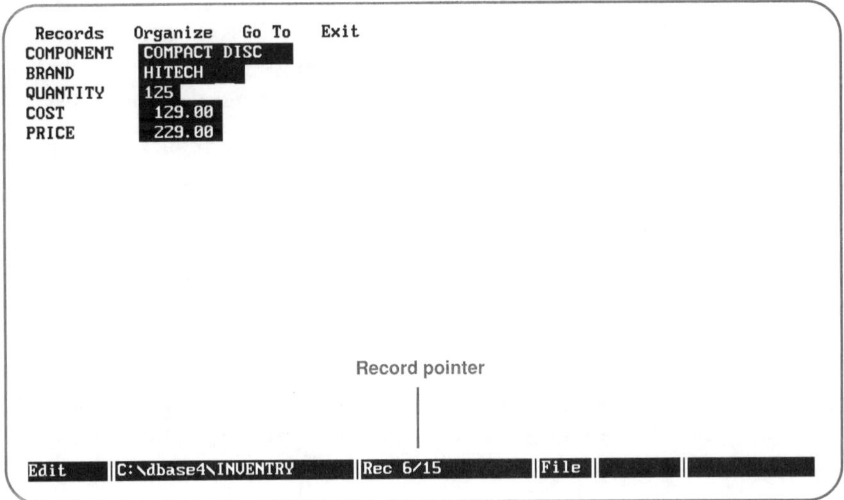

Figure 6.6. Record number 6

EDIT Screen Menu Options

The EDIT screen has several menus that contain some options for using the EDIT screen. Figure 6.5 shows the open Go To menu. As you know, this menu allows you to go directly to certain records or to leaf through the database file in certain ways.

Going Directly to Records

The Go To menu is divided into two halves. The top half has four options. The first two options let you immediately go to and display the `Top record` or the `Last record`.

The next option, as you have already learned, lets you go to a specific record by its record number. This assumes you know the record number. The last option lets you skip ahead or back a specified number of records. After you choose `Skip`, you can determine how many records to skip. A positive number placed in the entry area skips forward that many records. A negative number skips that many records backward. If you specify more records than exist when skipping forward or backward, dBASE IV will tell you that you have entered an illegal value and, of course, will not accept it.

Searching for Records

The lower half of the Go To menu contains several choices to facilitate searching through the database file. Each choice asks you to enter a string to search for. You can select the first option only when an index file is in use. After selecting `Index key search` you are prompted to `Enter search string` for the value of the index. If a record is not found, a message, `Not Found`, is displayed at the bottom of the screen, and the record pointer does not move.

The next two options, `Forward search` and `Backward search`, allow you to search for records that meet a certain criterion. First, you select the field on which you want to search, by moving the cursor to that field. When you choose either of these options, dBASE IV asks you to enter a value (specific item of data) of the field to search for. When you enter the value and press **<Enter>**, dBASE IV searches for the first occurrence of that field value either forward or backward from the present record. You can continue to search for more occurrences of that value by again choosing the search options and specifying the same search criteria. You also can use **<Shift>-<F4>** to find the next occurrence. **<Shift>-<F3>** finds the previous occurrence. Figure 6.7 displays the search criteria in the Go To menu.

The last Go To menu option, `Match capitalization`, lets you specify whether it matters if the data being searched for is capitalized.

Working with Records from the Records Menu

The first menu in the EDIT screen is the Records menu, shown opened in Figure 6.8. This menu lets you do a lot of things similar to what you can do with the keyboard, with a few differences.

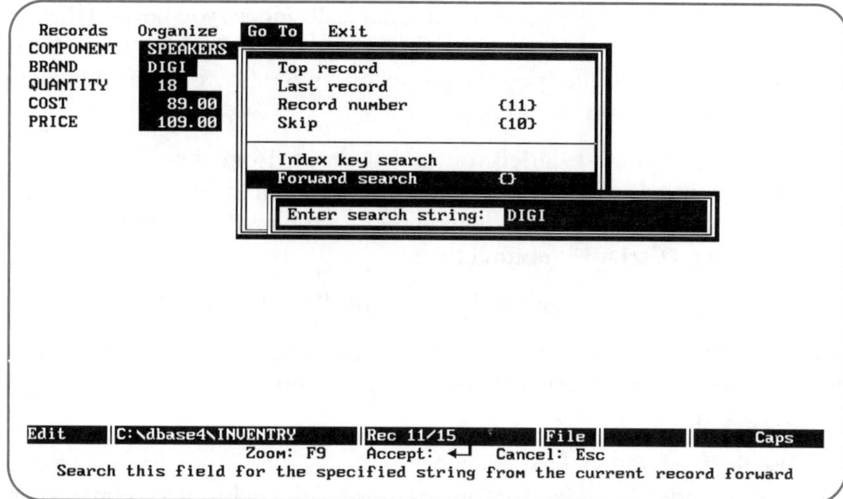

Figure 6.7. *Forward search for a DIGI brand*

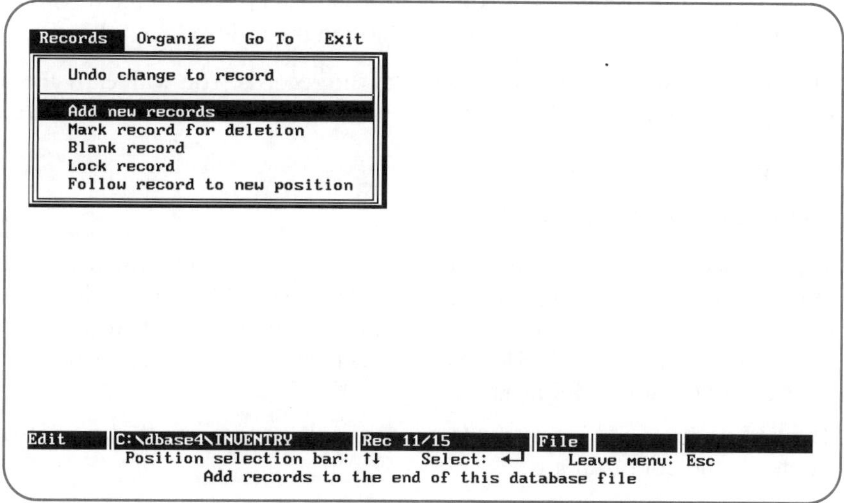

Figure 6.8. *The Records menu*

Once you make a change to a record, you can select `Undo changes to record` to reverse your change. This is almost the same as pressing the **<Esc>** key, except that you stay in the EDIT screen instead of returning to the Control Center or wherever you called the EDIT screen from. Once you leave the record, however, there is no way to undo any changes.

The next option, `Add new records`, automatically moves you beyond the last record in the file and lets you enter data into a new record. This is the same as moving the record pointer past the last record in the file yourself and telling dBASE IV that you want to add new records.

`Mark record for deletion` lets you mark the record for deletion just as if you had pressed **<Ctrl>-U**. After you select this option, it toggles to its opposite use, `Clear deletion mark`, to let you remove the mark from the record, as does pressing **<Ctrl>-U** a second time.

Choosing `Blank record` erases the values of all the fields in the record.

You use the next option, `Lock record`, to prevent someone else in a network from altering the record as you work on it. When you are done with the record it is unlocked.

You use the final option, `Follow record to new position`, when an index is in use. An index is made up of one or more of the fields of a record. When you view indexed records you look at them in their "logical," or indexed, order. If you change the value of the index key, the item will appear to change positions as it may now be either earlier or later in the logical order of the database file. Choosing this option allows you to keep track of the record by moving the record pointer to a new position in the indexed record.

The Organize menu controls the order of the records. You will learn about sorting and indexing in Chapter 7.

Exiting the EDIT Screen

The last menu is the Exit menu. There are currently three options to this menu, as shown in Figure 6.9. Depending on the place in dBASE IV from which you entered EDIT, this menu may have fewer than three options. There are three options now because the EDIT screen was called from somewhere other than the Control Center or dot prompt.

The first option, `Exit`, saves the last record and returns you to the Control Center or the dot prompt.

The second option, `Transfer to Query Design`, places you in the Query Design screen in order to let you select records and fields for your query.

The final option, `Return to Database Design`, is displayed because in this example, the EDIT screen was called from the Database work surface.

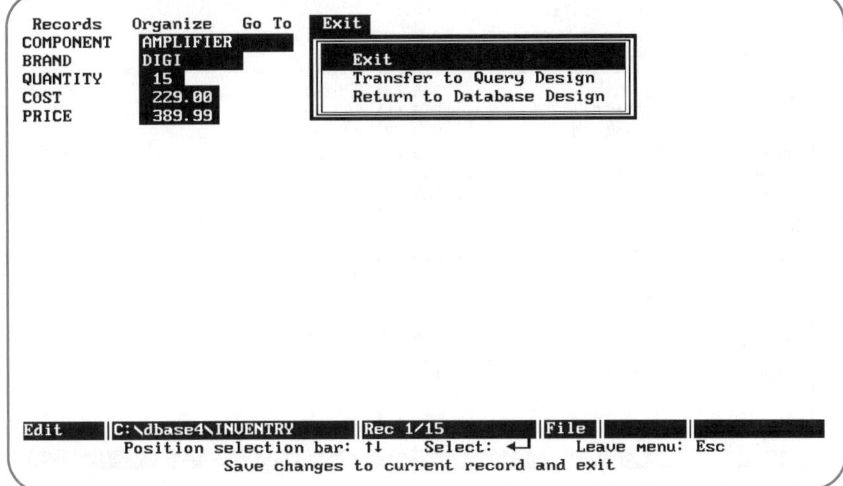

Figure 6.9. *The Exit menu*

BROWSE

Another full-screen editing command that allows viewing and changing database file contents is BROWSE. A graphic description of BROWSE is provided by cutting a section from a piece of paper. If you were to place the paper with the hole in it over this page, you could view the entire contents of the page, a portion at a time, by moving this "window" about. BROWSE provides a window onto your database file. It allows you to view one part of the database file at a time and to make changes wherever you want. A BROWSE view of your stereo store inventory is shown in Figure 6.10. You get to BROWSE from EDIT by pressing **<F2>**.

BROWSE displays each record as a single row. Only the first 80 characters of a record are displayed on the screen at one time.

The currently selected record is highlighted. Use the **<Up arrow>** and **<Down arrow>** keys to change the record selection one record at a time. Pressing the **<PgUp>** and **<PgDn>** keys scrolls the database file a screen at a time. You can edit the highlighted record simply by typing in new information.

You'll find additional features of BROWSE by looking at the menus at the top of the screen (Figure 6.10).

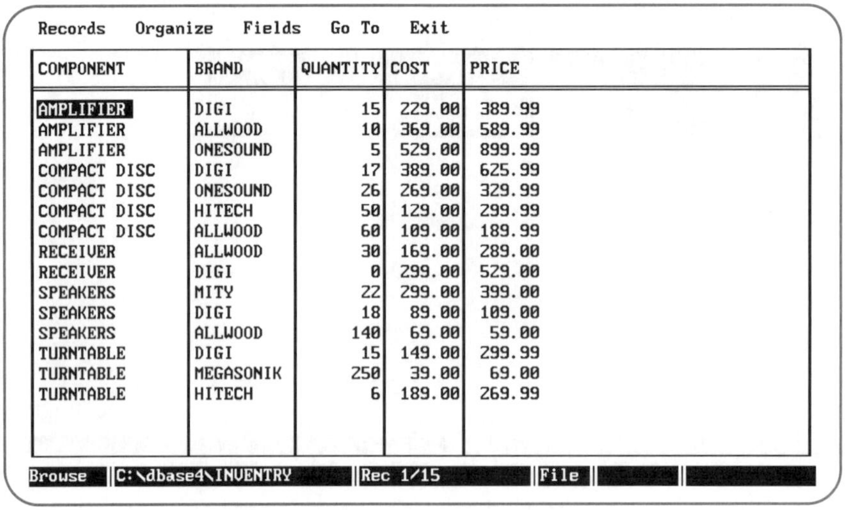

```
Records   Organize   Fields   Go To   Exit

COMPONENT       BRAND      QUANTITY COST     PRICE

AMPLIFIER       DIGI             15  229.00  389.99
AMPLIFIER       ALLWOOD          10  369.00  589.99
AMPLIFIER       ONESOUND          5  529.00  899.99
COMPACT DISC    DIGI             17  389.00  625.99
COMPACT DISC    ONESOUND         26  269.00  329.99
COMPACT DISC    HITECH           50  129.00  299.99
COMPACT DISC    ALLWOOD          60  109.00  189.99
RECEIVER        ALLWOOD          30  169.00  289.00
RECEIVER        DIGI              0  299.00  529.00
SPEAKERS        MITY             22  299.00  399.00
SPEAKERS        DIGI             18   89.00  109.00
SPEAKERS        ALLWOOD         140   69.00   59.00
TURNTABLE       DIGI             15  149.00  299.99
TURNTABLE       MEGASONIK       250   39.00   69.00
TURNTABLE       HITECH            6  189.00  269.99

Browse  C:\dbase4\INVENTRY    Rec 1/15    File
```

Figure 6.10. BROWSEing the database

BROWSE Menu Options

Four of the five BROWSE menus are exactly the same as their EDIT counterparts. BROWSE, however, contains an additional menu called Fields. The open Fields menu is depicted in Figure 6.11.

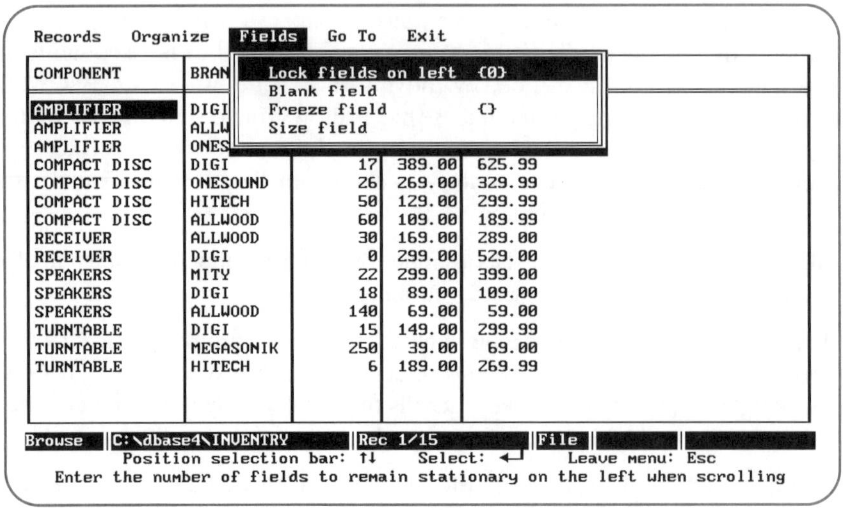

```
Records   Organize   Fields   Go To   Exit

COMPONENT       BRAN  Lock fields on left  {0}
                      Blank field
AMPLIFIER       DIGI  Freeze field         {}
AMPLIFIER       ALLW  Size field
AMPLIFIER       ONES
COMPACT DISC    DIGI             17  389.00  625.99
COMPACT DISC    ONESOUND         26  269.00  329.99
COMPACT DISC    HITECH           50  129.00  299.99
COMPACT DISC    ALLWOOD          60  109.00  189.99
RECEIVER        ALLWOOD          30  169.00  289.00
RECEIVER        DIGI              0  299.00  529.00
SPEAKERS        MITY             22  299.00  399.00
SPEAKERS        DIGI             18   89.00  109.00
SPEAKERS        ALLWOOD         140   69.00   59.00
TURNTABLE       DIGI             15  149.00  299.99
TURNTABLE       MEGASONIK       250   39.00   69.00
TURNTABLE       HITECH            6  189.00  269.99

Browse  C:\dbase4\INVENTRY    Rec 1/15    File
        Position selection bar: ↑↓   Select: ←┘   Leave menu: Esc
   Enter the number of fields to remain stationary on the left when scrolling
```

Figure 6.11. The Fields menu

The first option of the Fields menu, as you can see, is `Lock fields on left {0}`. Use this selection when panning a database file on the screen. It allows you to lock one or more of the fields on the far left of the screen. For example, you can keep a key field, such as a name, on-screen while you pan to another field that is currently off-screen. Without selecting `Lock fields on left {0}`, the name field would disappear to the left as you panned right to that other field. This is one of the reasons why it is important for you to put your identifying fields first when you create the database file.

Next is an option to erase the contents of a field called `Blank field`. Though you can erase the contents of a field by moving the cursor to the field and repeatedly pressing **<Del>**, it is quicker to use this option if the field is very long.

The third option, `Freeze field {}`, lets you edit only one field. As an example, you might want to edit only the quantity on hand when you conduct an inventory. As you press **<Enter>**, you move vertically from one record to another, but the cursor moves only into the column (field) you specify.

Finally, the last option is `Size field`. This option lets you make the display width of fields smaller or larger than their actual width. You can adjust the size in order to see more or less of a field on the screen at one time. Pressing **<Shift>-<F7>** also allows you to size a field. However, you can't make the width of a field shorter than the field name.

Maintaining a Database File

If you have a database file that consists of records on paper, there are some problems to safeguarding those paper records: a coffee spill can obscure part of a record; a piece of paper can be inadvertently thrown away. However, few things short of absolute calamity (fire, flood, or hurricane) are catastrophic to the entire paper database—this is not true with a computer database file. Accidently placing your finger on the floppy disk surface can damage it. A floppy disk is more vulnerable than a filing cabinet full of paper. All the things that work to make the database file convenient to use also work to make it susceptible to damage.

Much of the foregoing gloom can be avoided by adhering to some simple procedures. Maintain one or two backup copies of the database. This is one very good reason for having at least two disk drives on your computer system. If this is the case, you can easily copy your database file onto a floppy disk using the DOS command COPY. If your database file is too large to fit onto a floppy disk, you can use the DOS command BACKUP. This command backs up your database file onto several floppy disks.

Take some time now to make a backup copy of your INVENTRY database file, which is located on the C hard disk drive in directory DBASE4. Exit from dBASE by returning to the Control Center and choosing `Quit to Dos` from the Exit menu. When you leave dBASE IV, you are in the operating system—and you will see an operating system prompt. Insert a formatted disk into the A disk drive. Type in the COPY command as shown below:

```
C>DBASE4>COPY INVENTRY.DBF A:INVENTRY.DBF
```

One approach to backing up your files is to have two copies and to use them on alternate days. Properly used, two copies protect against loss of all except, perhaps, one day's work. If you can limit the liability to this value (barring fire, flood, or war), you have done about as well as you can do.

Summary

You have read in this chapter how to make changes to both the structure and the records of your file.

The Database work surface is where you modify file structure. Pressing **<Shift>-<F2> Design** from the Control Center gets you to your file structure so you can make changes to the number of fields, field names, field widths, and field types. Reworking the file structure also gives you an opportunity to add or change an index tag.

The BROWSE and EDIT screens provide the environment for adding records, removing records, and changing the contents of records.

Sorting and Indexing

One of the attractions of a database management system is its ability to sort data records. You can easily rearrange the records so they appear in virtually any order that is convenient for you—alphabetical, chronological, or numeric. The records in the stereo store inventory were entered alphabetically by the type of component. In effect, they were presorted by COMPONENT.

You might want to reorganize your database for a number of reasons. You might want to see the records grouped by cost or brand name, or place the stereos by their wattage size. dBASE IV provides two ways to rearrange data: sorting and indexing. This chapter covers dBASE IV sorting and indexing operations.

Differences Between Sorting and Indexing

Whether you choose to sort or index, the result when looking at the data is the same: The records are rearranged. *Sorting* physically rearranges the records and copies them to a new database file. *Indexing* creates a separate file that keeps track of which records are to be seen in what order, and shows them to you in that order.

The sort order of the records is called the *logical order*. When you sort a database file, you rearrange it so that its physical order and its logical order are the same. The order will be either alphabetical, chronological, or numeric; it will be determined automatically by the field type. Character fields are sorted alphabetically, date fields are sorted chronologically, and numeric fields are sorted numerically.

When you rearrange data, it is important to remember that each whole record, not just some of the fields, is moved. Whenever you create a record, all the field's values that belong to the record will always remain together. If you decide to sort by component, each record for the component is moved into sorted order. The component is called the *key*. Records sorted alphabetically by component would be in this order: Amplifiers, Compact discs, Receivers, Speakers, Turntables.

Indexes work the same way except that the data isn't actually rearranged; only a list of the key field is reordered. This saves valuable disk space and prevents rearranging the file each time a record is added.

You can sort and index from the Control Center by using the database file structure work surface.

Sorting

In dBASE, sorting creates a completely new copy of a database file, in addition to the original file. The records in the new file are arranged according to a sort key. As records are sorted, they are physically copied to a new database file. When the Sort menu operation finishes, you are still using the original unsorted file. To use the sorted file, you must close the original file you are using and open the new sorted file. The filename for the new database file can be anything you like, but it must conform to the rules for filenames.

Sorting a File

Create a sorted copy of your INVENTRY file. Get into the Control Center and select the INVENTRY file. Press **<F2>** to get into the BROWSE screen. Press **<Alt>-O** to open the Organize menu. You'll be spending a lot of time with the Organize menu in this chapter; it is where all sorting and indexing takes place. The Organize menu is also found in the Edit screen and the Data work surface.

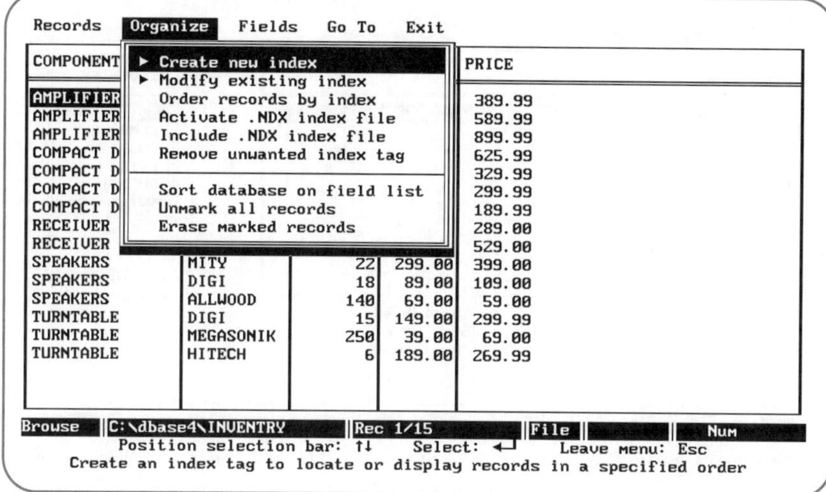

***Figure 7.1.** The work surface with the Organize menu open*

Choose `Sort database on field list` by pressing `S`. A box pops up on the screen. The box has two columns. The first column is where you enter the field name that tells how the data is to be sorted. The second column contains the type of sort. The sorting arrangement from A to Z is called an *ascending sort*. The reverse, from Z to A, is a *descending sort*. You can specify each sort key separately as ascending or descending in the sort box.

For now, use the default, `Ascending ASCII`. There are two ways to indicate the fields you want to sort on. You can type in the name of the field or fields, or you can use the Pick function key to choose from a menu of available fields. Use the Pick function by pressing **<Shift>-<F1> Pick**.

Your screen should look like Figure 7.2. The cursor is on BRAND because the field list is put in alphabetical order for you. To get to any of the other fields in the list for later sorts, you can move the cursor by pressing the **<Down arrow>** key. Because the cursor is already on BRAND, just press **<Enter>**.

The BRAND field is added to the Field order column of the sort box. If you wanted to change the type of sort, you could press **<Tab>** to move over to the second column. For this example, simply use the default.

You are finished, so press **<Ctrl>-<End>**. dBASE IV responds by asking you for a name for the file. Enter `INVBRAND`, as shown in Figure 7.3.

After you enter the file name, press **<Return>** and a new database file is created, sorted by the BRAND of the item. dBASE IV then returns you to the BROWSE screen. The original file, INVENTRY.DBF, is still the active file. You can see the data still in the original order because only a copy of the original file was made and called INVBRAND.DBF.

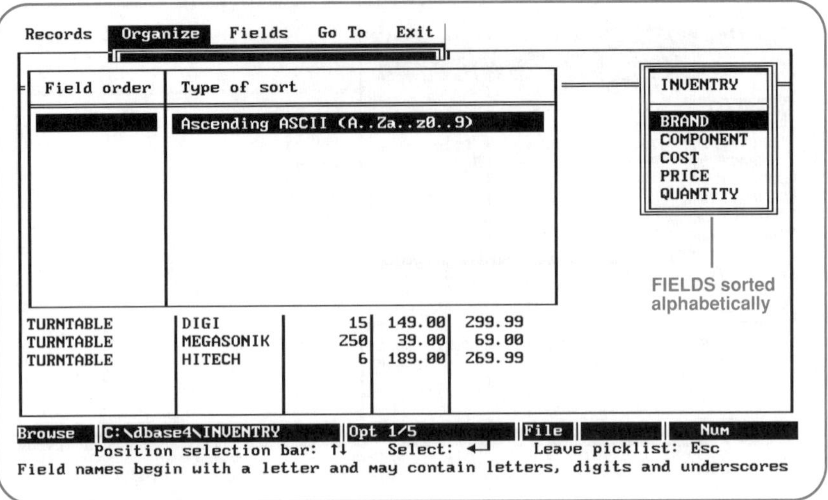

Figure 7.2. Choosing the sort order

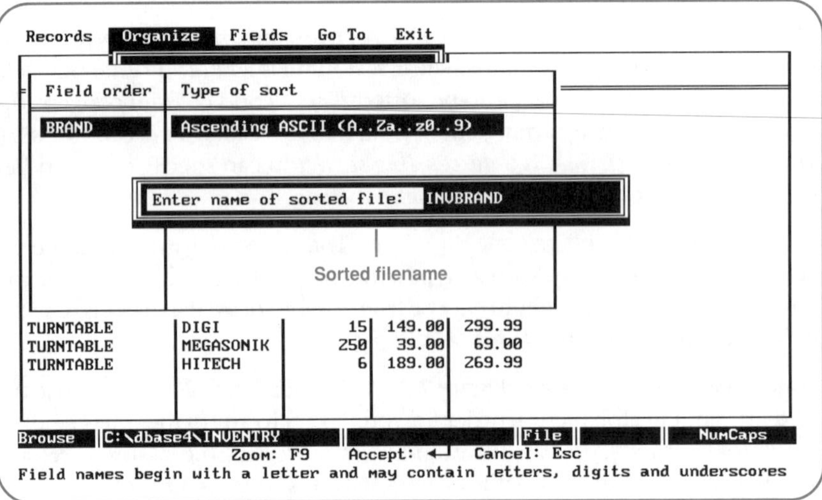

Figure 7.3. Sorting by BRAND

Press **<Ctrl>-<End>** to return to the Control Center. You will now see your new file, INVBRAND, below the line while INVENTRY is still above the line. Take a look at the data for INVBRAND. Move the cursor to INVBRAND and press **<F2> Data**. Your data is sorted by BRAND, as shown in Figure 7.4.

Records	Organize	Fields	Go To	Exit

COMPONENT	BRAND	QUANTITY	COST	PRICE
RECEIVER	ALLWOOD	30	169.00	289.00
SPEAKERS	ALLWOOD	140	69.00	59.00
AMPLIFIER	ALLWOOD	10	369.00	589.99
COMPACT DISC	ALLWOOD	60	109.00	189.99
COMPACT DISC	DIGI	17	389.00	625.99
AMPLIFIER	DIGI	15	229.00	389.99
RECEIVER	DIGI	0	299.00	529.00
SPEAKERS	DIGI	18	89.00	109.00
TURNTABLE	DIGI	15	149.00	299.99
COMPACT DISC	HITECH	50	129.00	299.99
TURNTABLE	HITECH	6	189.00	269.99
TURNTABLE	MEGASONIK	250	39.00	69.00
SPEAKERS	MITY	22	299.00	399.00
COMPACT DISC	ONESOUND	26	269.00	329.99
AMPLIFIER	ONESOUND	5	529.00	899.99

Browse | C:\dbase4\INVBRAND | Rec 1/15 | File

***Figure** 7.4. The database sorted by BRAND*

Sequences

There are two ways to sort data and two types of collating sequences. This allows up to four types of sorts:

- Ascending ASCII
- Descending ASCII
- Ascending Dictionary
- Descending Dictionary

Data can be sorted in ascending (lowest to highest) or in descending (highest to lowest) order. You have to specify whether you want to use the ASCII or dictionary collating sequence. The ASCII ascending sequence assumes that numbers are always first, then come uppercase letters, and then lowercase letters. The ASCII ascending sequence looks like this:

0123456789ABCDEFGHIJKLMNOPQRSTUVWXYZabcdefghijklmnopqrstuvwxyz

The dictionary sequence is different. It says that A's come first, regardless of case, then B's, etc. The dictionary ascending sequence looks like this:

0123456789AaBbCcDdEeFfGgHhIiJjKkLlMmNnOoPpQqRrSsTtUuVvWwXxYyZz

If you were sorting these five names, they would appear sorted as shown in Table 7.1.

***Table** 7.1. A comparison of ASCII and Dictionary sorting*

ORIGINAL ORDER	*ASCII (Ascending)*	*DICTIONARY (Ascending)*
Jones	Adams	Adams
Adams	Jones	Jones
joseph	Smith	joseph
Smith	joseph	rollins
rollins	rollins	Smith

Generally, if you use the same case for all your data, it does not make a difference in their sorted order. But when you have both lower- and uppercase letters in your sort key, you must decide in which collating sequence you want your data.

dBASE IV Sorts

You can sort the data into as many arrangements as you like. Each new sort, however, requires a separate database file. If you need to change any of the data, either you must change the records in each of the several sorted files, or you can edit the original and sort it again into its several sorted variations. This is similar to the problem a public library has with its card catalog. Each library book is listed in three separate card files: author, subject, and title. When a book is added to the library, at least three identical new cards must be added to the catalog—one for each of the three card files.

In dBASE IV, sorting creates a new database file. Some database managers allow you to sort records without creating a new file. These database products sort the data and replace the old file. This approach offers some advantage in that it can be a little faster than when creating the new file. Also, there is only one database file—which makes maintaining your database file simpler and more reliable. The disadvantage is that you must sort each time you want to use the records in a particular sort order.

Complex Sorts

If you have several keys, one can be ascending while another is descending. You can mix as many sort modes as you like.

A sort within a sort. Quite often you want to sort the database file so that you have a sort within a sort. For example, you might want to group the inventory by BRAND, and have the records belonging to each BRAND sorted by SIZE. You can do this by placing both fields as sort keys on separate lines in the sort box. This is called a *minor* key. The data is first sorted by the *major* key BRAND, and then it is sorted within groups of the same BRAND by the second or minor key, SIZE.

Multiple sorts. Keys can be made up of more than one field. When this situation exists, the data is initially sorted by the first field. Then that sorted information is grouped and resorted on the basis of the second key. For example, if you wanted to sort our stereo store by component and brand, all the records would first be sorted by component: AMPLIFIERS, COMPACT DISCS, RECEIVERS, SPEAKERS, TURNTABLES.

Within each group of components, the AMPLIFIERS, for example, the records would be sorted by brand—DIGI, HITECH, ONESOUND. Each group of the same components would also be sorted by brand. This is an example of a *multiple-key* sort.

Indexing

dBASE IV provides an attractive alternative to sorting called indexing.

Indexing creates the same effect as sorting: You can use the data in alphabetical, chronological, or numerical order. This order is created with the help of a separate index file. The index file is not a copy of the database file, but a special file that makes the original file look like it's not sorted. dBASE IV automatically creates an index if you change the `N` to a `Y` in the Index column while creating your database file structure. You can also add an index later by going back to the Data work surface and changing the `N` to a `Y` for the specified field. If you want to create complicated indexes using more than one field, use the Organize menu of the Data work surface.

Creating an Index

To illustrate, index the database file INVENTRY by PRICE. If you are not already in the Control Center, return to it and choose the INVENTRY file. Press **<Shift>-<F2>** to go to the Data work surface. The Organize menu opens. Close it by pressing **<Esc>**. Move your cursor inside the box to the PRICE field by pressing the **<Down arrow>** key. Move the cursor to the Index column using the **<Tab>** key. Type Y to tell dBASE IV you want to index the database file by the PRICE field, as shown in Figure 7.5.

```
Layout   Organize   Append   Go To   Exit                              9:59:13 am
                                                        Bytes remaining:   3958
 Num  Field Name   Field Type   Width   Dec   Index

  1   COMPONENT    Character     15             N
  2   BRAND        Character     10             N
  3   QUANTITY     Numeric        3      0      N
  4   COST         Numeric        7      2      N
  5   PRICE        Numeric        7      2      Y
           |
         Index
         field

Database C:\dbase4\INVENTRY    Field 5/5
          Enter the field name.  Insert/Delete field:Ctrl-N/Ctrl-U
Field names begin with a letter and may contain letters, digits and underscores
```

Figure 7.5. *Indexing on PRICE*

When you are finished, press **<Ctrl>-<End>** to tell dBASE IV to save the modified structure of the file. dBASE IV updates the database file and creates the index.

dBASE IV has created a file called INVENTRY.MDX. This is the multiple index file. You can create up to 47 indexes that all fit into one .MDX file. Though the file is called INVENTRY.MDX, you have created an index *tag* called PRICE. Each time you index the database file by a different key, dBASE IV creates a new tag in the .MDX file. The .MDX file is created only once—the first time you create an index for the database file. All indexes are automatically updated each time you add, change, or delete a record from the database file. The index file has the same name as the database file except for the MDX file extension.

Viewing the Indexed File

In this example, because you created a new index, the data will be processed in the index order. However, just because you create an index doesn't mean that you always see your data in the index order. In the Organize menu, shown in Figure 7.6, there is an option called `Order records by index` that allows you to view selected indexes. To see how this works, press **<F2>** to return to the BROWSE screen. Press **<Alt>-O** to open the Organize menu. Type `O` to select `Order records by index`. A Pick menu opens on the work surface. There should be only two choices, Natural Order and PRICE. Natural Order is the original order in which you entered the data. This is the equivalent of having no index active. PRICE is the only index because you have created only that index. Select PRICE and press **<Enter>** to set the order by PRICE. The data is displayed in order from lowest to highest price, as depicted in Figure 7.7.

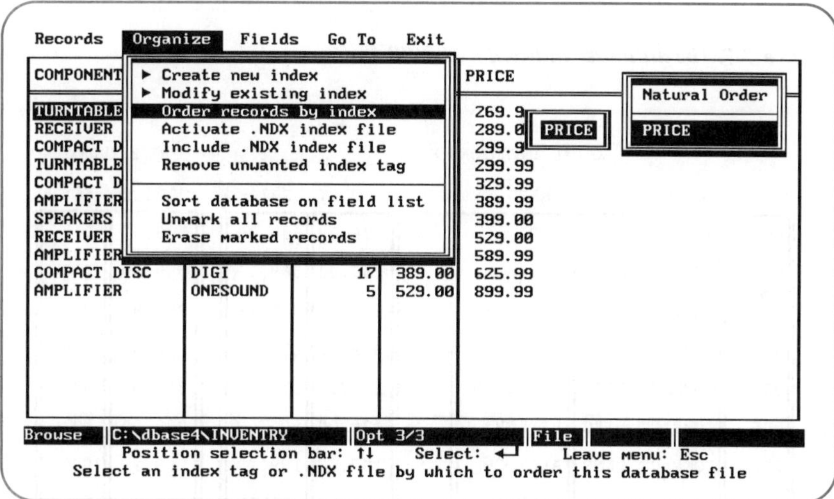

Figure 7.6. *Setting the index order*

How does dBASE IV do this? The index file is a specially designed file that holds only the contents of the key field (the index key) and corresponding record numbers. Figure 7.8 shows the conceptual view of an index file.

As long as the index file is in use, it controls the order in which the database manager accesses the database records. This makes the database file appear to be arranged according to the index key. If you were to turn off the index, the database file would appear in its original (not indexed) form. To turn the index off, close the database file and then reopen it. Remember, if a database file is open, you can select it in the Control Center and press **<Enter>** to close it. To reopen it, select it again and press **<Enter>**.

Records Organize Fields Go To Exit

COMPONENT	BRAND	QUANTITY	COST	PRICE
SPEAKERS	ALLWOOD	140	69.00	59.00
TURNTABLE	MEGASONIK	250	39.00	69.00
SPEAKERS	DIGI	18	89.00	109.00
COMPACT DISC	ALLWOOD	60	109.00	189.99
TURNTABLE	HITECH	6	189.00	269.99
RECEIVER	ALLWOOD	30	169.00	289.00
COMPACT DISC	HITECH	50	129.00	299.99
TURNTABLE	DIGI	15	149.00	299.99
COMPACT DISC	ONESOUND	26	269.00	329.99
AMPLIFIER	DIGI	15	229.00	389.99
SPEAKERS	MITY	22	299.00	399.00
RECEIVER	DIGI	0	299.00	529.00
AMPLIFIER	ALLWOOD	10	369.00	589.99
COMPACT DISC	DIGI	17	389.00	625.99
AMPLIFIER	ONESOUND	5	529.00	899.99

Browse | C:\dbase4\INVENTRY | Rec 12/15 | File

Figure 7.7. The database indexed by PRICE

ACTUAL INVENTORY FILE — PRICE INDEX

	COMPONENT	BRAND	QUANTITY	COST	PRICE	PRICE	KEY #
REC #	AMPLIFIER	DIGI	15	229.00	389.99	389.99	010
001	AMPLIFIER	ALLWOOD	10	369.00	589.99	589.99	013
002	AMPLIFIER	ONESOUND	5	529.00	899.99	899.99	015
003	COMPACT DISC	DIGI	17	389.00	625.99	625.99	014
004	COMPACT DISC	ONESOUND	26	269.00	329.99	329.99	009
005	COMPACT DISC	HITECH	125	129.00	299.99	299.99	007
006	COMPACT DISC	ALLWOOD	60	109.00	189.99	189.99	004
007	RECEIVER	ALLWOOD	30	169.00	289.00	289.00	006
008	RECEIVER	DIGI	0	299.00	529.00	529.00	012
009	SPEAKERS	MITY	22	299.00	399.00	399.00	011
010	SPEAKERS	DIGI	18	89.00	109.00	109.00	003
011	SPEAKERS	ALLWOOD	140	69.00	59.00	59.00	001
012	TURNTABLE	DIGI	15	149.00	299.99	299.99	008
013	TURNTABLE	MEGASONIK	250	39.00	69.00	69.00	002
014	TURNTABLE	HITECH	6	189.00	269.99	269.99	005
015	. . .	. . .	. .	. . .	. . .	. . .	

Figure 7.8. A conceptual view of an index file

Indexes Within Indexes

In the second example of sorting a database file, you saw how to create a sort within a sort by use of multiple sort keys. An index created in the database file structure can have only one index key—itself. You can create the equivalent of the index within an index by concatenating fields, as shown in Figure 7.9.

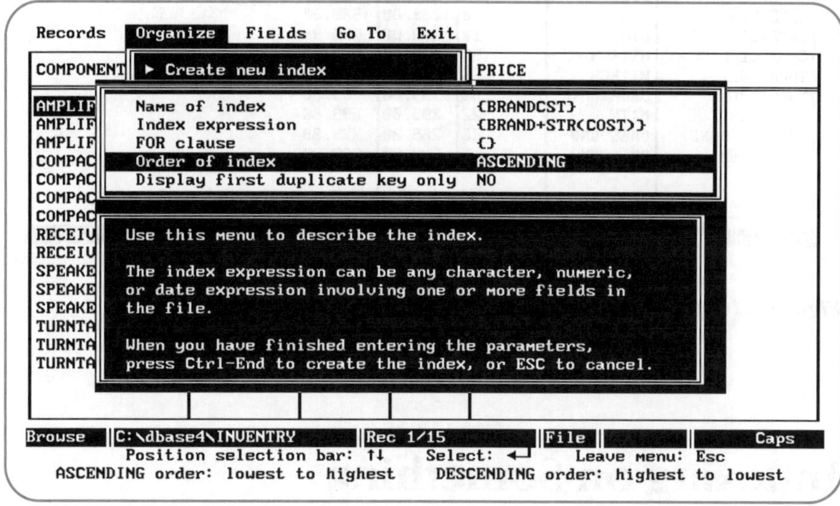

***Figure** 7.9. Indexing on more than one key—BRAND and COST*

Here you see a new index tag called "BRANDCST" made from two fields by concatenating them, or putting them together as one long key. Because one is a character string and one is a number, the number must be converted to a character string before concatenation. The STR (string) function converts a number to a character string. The plus sign (+) tells dBASE IV to put them together. If the BRAND were DIGI and the cost were $279.99, the new key would be "DIGI 279.99". This would be indexed before a more expensive DIGI such as "DIGI 899.99".

After creating the new index, select it in the `Order records by index` choice of the Organize menu. You can see the data, as shown in Figure 7.10, by pressing **<F2>** after saving the new index tag and choosing the order.

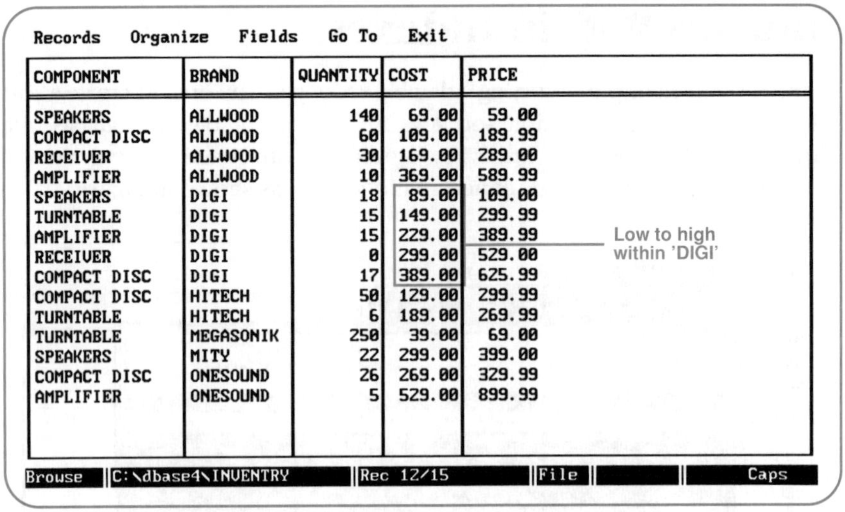

Records Organize Fields Go To Exit

COMPONENT	BRAND	QUANTITY	COST	PRICE
SPEAKERS	ALLWOOD	140	69.00	59.00
COMPACT DISC	ALLWOOD	60	109.00	189.99
RECEIVER	ALLWOOD	30	169.00	289.00
AMPLIFIER	ALLWOOD	10	369.00	589.99
SPEAKERS	DIGI	18	89.00	109.00
TURNTABLE	DIGI	15	149.00	299.99
AMPLIFIER	DIGI	15	229.00	389.99
RECEIVER	DIGI	8	299.00	529.00
COMPACT DISC	DIGI	17	389.00	625.99
COMPACT DISC	HITECH	50	129.00	299.99
TURNTABLE	HITECH	6	189.00	269.99
TURNTABLE	MEGASONIK	250	39.00	69.00
SPEAKERS	MITY	22	299.00	399.00
COMPACT DISC	ONESOUND	26	269.00	329.99
AMPLIFIER	ONESOUND	5	529.00	899.99

Browse | C:\dbase4\INVENTRY | Rec 12/15 | File | Caps

Low to high within 'DIGI'

Figure 7.10. The database indexed by both BRAND and COST

Indexing on Something That Isn't There

Although all the examples you have seen so far have used fields as the index key, you can index on some other item, as long as that item can be derived from the contents of the fields. For example, you can build an index on the value of each item in the inventory. Here, value is defined as the PRICE times the QUANTITY. An index of VALUE is shown in Figure 7.11.

When you look at your data you will not see a new column for VALUE. It is simply understood that the records are ordered as if you had created a new field that had the value of PRICE*QUANTITY.

Finding a Particular Record

Index files offer an additional bonus. You can use them to find any record almost instantly by its index key. Suppose that you have indexed your database file by the index key BRAND. BRAND has also been selected as the controlling index. Now you want to find the first record for DIGI.

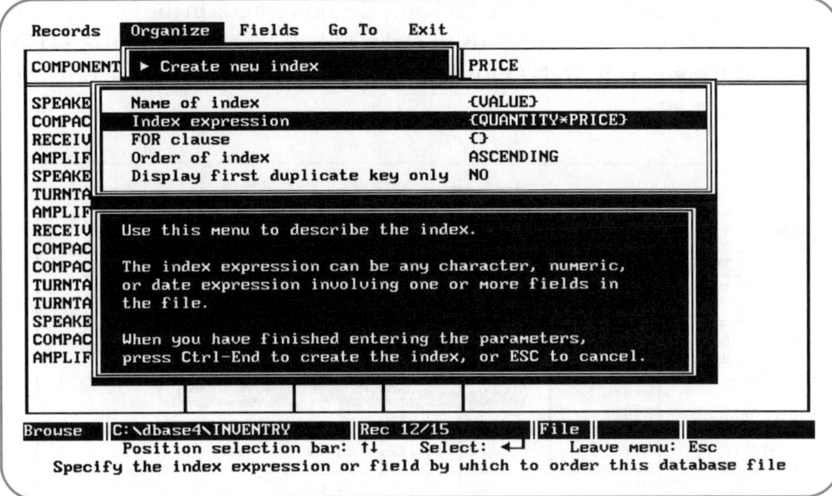

***Figure** 7.11. Indexing on a field that isn't there*

In the BROWSE or EDIT tables there are options to search for data. One of the menus is called Go To. There are several search options, as you can see in Figure 7.12. Choosing `Index Key Search` finds the record instantly. You also can find data in nonindexed files using the `Forward search` and `Backward search` options to search each record either forward (that is, toward the bottom of the file) or backward (that is, toward the top of the file) until a match is found. Whether you are using indexed or nonindexed searches, dBASE IV positions you to the desired record.

You need not enter an entire value name. You can search manually by entering just the first few letters. If, in the above example, you had entered only the letter *D*, dBASE IV would have found the first BRAND that started with *D*.

Indexed searches can locate a record quickly because dBASE IV does not search the database file itself. Instead it searches the index file for the first occurrence of the key—just as you would if you were searching a book index.

Using the Index to Select Records

You can use the `FOR clause` option of the `Create new index` option of the Organize menu to see only those records that meet the criteria entered in the `FOR clause`. To select only the compact discs, you would first open the Organize menu and select `Create new index`. As shown in Figure 7.13, you would enter a name for the index, and the selection criteria in the `FOR clause`. If you wanted to see those records in order of highest to lowest QUANTITY, you could also enter QUANTITY for the `Index expression` and DESCENDING for the `Order of index`.

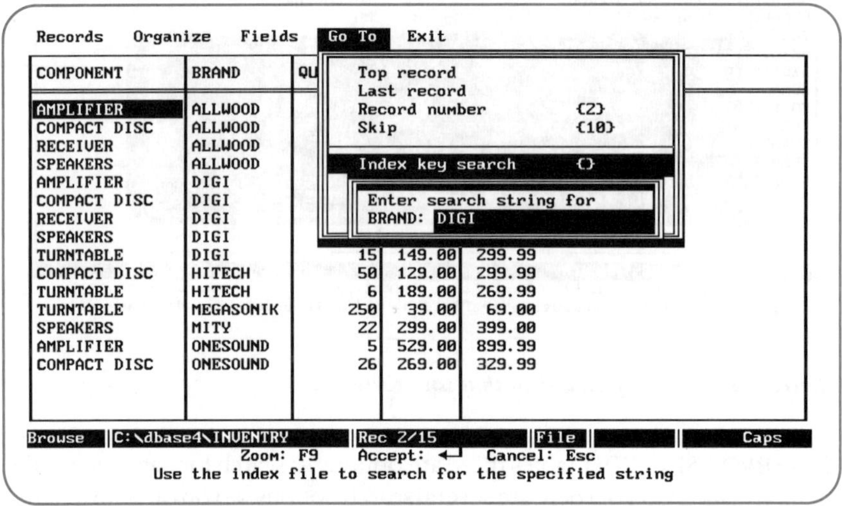

Figure 7.12. Searching the indexed database for the DIGI brand

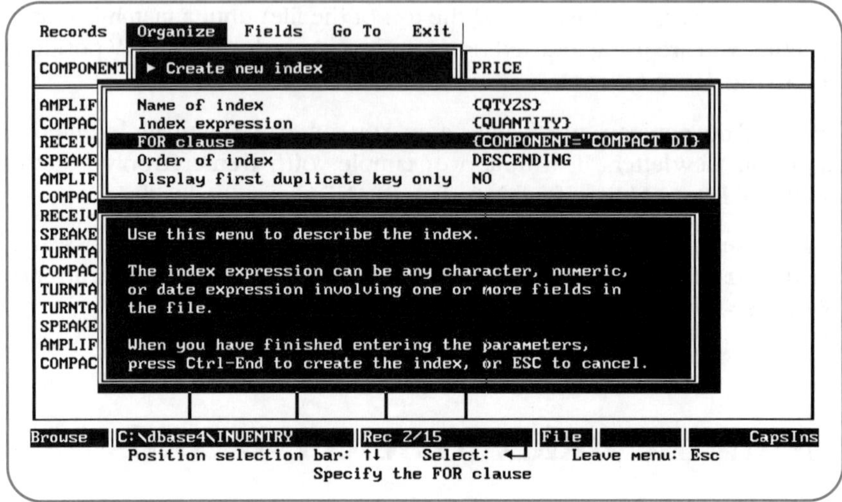

Figure 7.13. Using the index to select records

Some Index Terminology

Remember the library analogy? Imagine that the library books are data records. The card catalog comprises three index files: author, subject, and title. Each card in the card catalog represents a book that is somewhere on the shelves. Suppose that you know the title of a book. To find the book, you first find the title card in the title index. The card contains a Library of Congress number. This number points you to the location of the book in the library. In database terminology, the categories author, subject, and title are secondary keys. The Library of Congress number is the primary key. It is also a pointer to the book because it translates into a physical position in the library. The books are physical records; the cards in the card catalog are logical records.

In the INVENTRY file example, the index keys, such as BRAND, are the secondary keys. The record number is the primary key. The record number in the index file is a pointer to the actual data record. The data records in INVENTRY are the physical records; the index records are logical records.

The real purpose of the card catalog is not to sort the books into some order—but to help you find particular books. The index cards are in order to make finding the card easier than finding the book. This is exactly the same with the database file index files. Although they allow you to see data records in sorted order, their real use lies in helping you find a particular record that may be in the middle of thousands of other records in less than two seconds.

Summary

In this chapter, you have seen that you can arrange data records in alphabetical, chronological, or numerical order by either SORT or INDEX methods. Each has its advantages and disadvantages.

Sorting creates a duplicate copy of the original data records in a new database file, but in a sorted order.

Indexing creates an index file that contains the index key with pointers back to the original data records. As far as performance goes, indexing is a clear-cut winner. Depending on your needs and the number of changes to your database file, you will have to decide which is best for you.

Section Two

Working with Your Data

chapter 8

The Dot Prompt

In this section of the book, you will begin to work with the data that you have created. You will first learn about the other side of dBASE IV—the dot prompt. You will also learn about logic and how to ask questions of your data. This section also covers field types date, logic, and memo in some detail. You'll generate reports using multiple database files.

In order to use dBASE IV productively, even as a new user, you must know a little about the dot prompt. In fact, understanding how direct commands work in dBASE IV dot prompt mode will actually help you use the Control Center much better.

Up to this point, you have been operating in the dBASE IV Control Center. The Control Center is an interface—a way for you to communicate with dBASE IV. It actually sits on top of dBASE IV, and translates every menu choice you make into some dBASE IV program code or command. There has been no need, up to now, for you to understand the intricacies of these commands because the Control Center takes care of your interaction with them. This makes it easier to use dBASE IV, especially if you are just getting started.

The dot prompt mode is primarily used to program. Sometimes you use the dot prompt for tasks so simple that to perform them in the Control Center actually would take longer. You will be using some dot prompt commands in this chapter and again in future chapters as an alternative route to the Control Center menus.

Database File Commands

Begin by going to the dot prompt and taking a look at some commands that can help you work with your database file. You have already learned how to CREATE a database file, MODIFY the database file structure, USE the database file, BROWSE your records, and EDIT one record at a time. Those words in capital letters are the actual dot prompt commands and are equivalent to the same operations you learned in the Control Center.

Removing the Status Bar

First, you need to get into the dot prompt mode. If your computer is already in the dot prompt, you are all set. If you are in the Control Center, press **<Alt>-E** to exit, and type `E` to choose `Exit to dot prompt`. Your screen should look like Figure 8.1. You may have a status bar at the bottom of the screen, like the one shown in Figure 8.1. If you have, remove it by entering:

```
. SET STATUS OFF
```

at the dot prompt and press **<Enter>**.

This book uses the period (.) to indicate that you must type the command shown at the dot prompt. Don't type the period before the command. The period *is* the dot prompt!

One other thing: When you see the verb *enter* in this chapter, as in "Enter the command at the dot prompt," it means two things: Type the specified command or word *and* press the **<Enter>** key. When you are typing commands at the dot prompt, dBASE IV can't respond until you press the **<Enter>** key.

dBASE IV is not *case sensitive*. Dot prompt commands can be entered in either upper or lower case.

Now that the dot prompt is on your screen, take a look at some database commands.

Figure 8.1. *The dBASE IV dot prompt with the Status Bar*

Making a Database File Active

The first command you must learn makes your database file active. This is equivalent to highlighting a filename and pressing **<Enter>** in the Control Center, in order to bring your database file above the line. To make a database file active using the dot prompt, you USE the database file. Enter the following command:

```
. USE INVENTRY
```

After you press **<Enter>**, dBASE IV responds with another dot prompt affirming that it was able to use the INVENTRY database file. If the status bar is ON, it shows that the file is open. Try making an intentional mistake to see how dBASE IV responds. For example, USE a database file that doesn't exist. Enter:

```
. USE XYZ
```

dBASE IV Error Messages

As shown in Figure 8.2, dBASE IV responds with an error box that gives you three choices: `Cancel`, `Edit`, or `Help`.

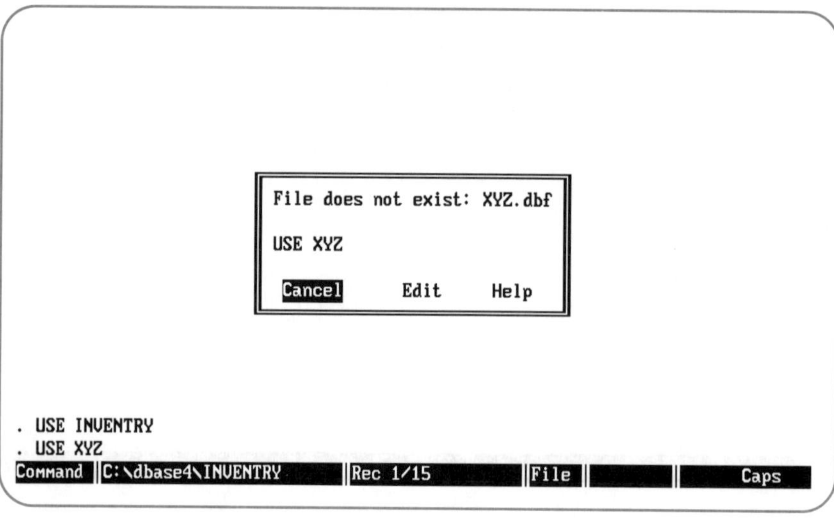

Figure 8.2. *An error box with a message*

Use the `Cancel` choice when you've made a mistake and don't want to try again with that command. The `Edit` choice places your cursor back on the command line so that you can make changes to the command you just tried to enter. `Edit` is most often used to allow corrections to a misspelled command or an incorrect filename. The third choice, `Help`, brings up a context-sensitive help screen or an index of Help topics for you to choose from.

Choose the `Cancel` option to get back to the dot prompt. Again USE the INVENTRY file; the correct way this time:

```
. USE INVENTRY
```

Whenever you USE a file, dBASE IV first closes any open files and then opens the file that you have requested. With the file open, you can display the data, see the file structure, or use any of the same work surfaces that also are available from the Control Center.

Displaying the Database File Structure

Sometimes you just need to take a look at a file's structure. To just display the structure, without changing it, enter the command:

```
. DISPLAY STRUCTURE
```

In order to use the DISPLAY STRUCTURE command, you must have a database file open. If a database file is not open, dBASE IV will ask you for the name of a database file to open. You just opened the INVENTRY database file, so now you see a list of all the INVENTRY.DBF fields, their types, lengths, decimals, and whether they are part of an index.

The total number of bytes is also displayed. If you add up the number of bytes in each field, you will notice the total shown now contains one extra. This is known as the *delete byte* and is invisible to you, but dBASE IV uses it to tell if the record has been deleted. This is one of the few displays not available from the dot prompt. However, you can get essentially the same information in the Control Center when you change the database file structure.

The LIST STRUCTURE command is an alternative to the DISPLAY STRUCTURE command. The only difference between the two is that the DISPLAY STRUCTURE command scrolls one screen of data at a time. When the screen is full, it stops and requires you to press a key to continue scrolling data. LIST STRUCTURE displays all the data, even if part of the file structure scrolls off the screen. The results of the DISPLAY STRUCTURE command are shown in Figure 8.3.

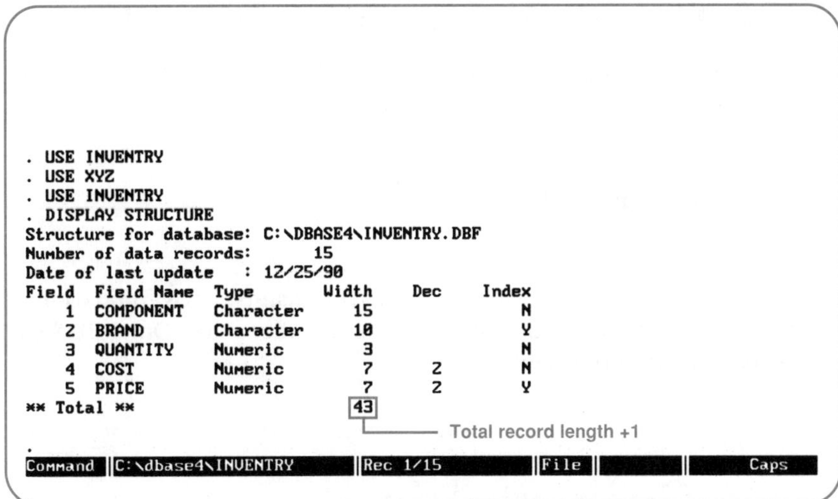

Figure 8.3. ***The structure for the INVENTRY database***

Modifying the Database File Structure

Modifying an existing structure is done with the MODIFY STRUCTURE command. This command places you in the same Database work surface that you enter from the Control Center. Just like in the Control Center, pressing **<F2>** gives you access to your data. The only difference is that when you are finished in either area, dBASE IV returns you to the dot prompt instead of to the Control Center. Enter:

```
. MODIFY STRUCTURE
```

You are placed in the Database work surface in the INVENTRY file. If there had been no file active, you would have been prompted for the name of a database file. After typing INVENTRY, the database screen would have appeared. The dot prompt offers the same options in any work surface that are available from the Control Center.

Press **<Esc>** and Y to confirm that you want to return to the dot prompt.

Abbreviating dBASE IV Commands

Any command you enter at the dot prompt can be abbreviated to its first four letters. You can enter DISPLAY STRUCTURE as

```
. DISP STRU
```

You can enter MODIFY STRUCTURE as

```
. MODI STRU
```

As you become more familiar with the various commands, you will find yourself abbreviating all of them. You cannot abbreviate filenames. Only dBASE IV commands can be abbreviated.

Data Commands

Once the database has been created and data entered, you will need to make changes, list the data, and put the data in order. You will BROWSE or EDIT, LIST or DISPLAY, and SORT or INDEX as you organize your data.

BROWSEing and EDITing the Database File

The BROWSE and EDIT commands allow you to work within the BROWSE and EDIT screens exactly as you do from the Control Center. In fact, once you enter BROWSE or EDIT, you will find that **<F2>** still toggles between the two modes.

From the dot prompt, enter:

```
. BROWSE
```

and you will see your data in the BROWSE screen. Press **<F2>** to see it in the EDIT screen. That's all there is to it. There are no real differences from the Control Center. Return to the dot prompt by pressing **<Esc>**.

There is one trick that you can do with the BROWSE screen that you cannot do from the Control Center. You can compress your titles while in BROWSE mode. This means that instead of the column titles taking up the first few lines of the screen, they are placed within the top border of the screen. This frees two more lines on the screen for data display. To see your data with the titles compressed enter.:

```
. BROWSE COMPRESS
```

Press **<Esc>** to return to the dot prompt.

DISPLAYing and LISTing Your Data

There are two other commands besides EDIT and BROWSE that show you data from your files. DISPLAY and LIST are not available in the Control Center. Like the BROWSE command, they display your data in columns; however, DISPLAY and LIST do it in a different way.

The LIST command displays all your data beginning with the first record. It moves pretty fast, and doesn't stop displaying the screens full of records until it reaches the bottom of the file.

The DISPLAY command, without any parameters, displays only the current record. When you enter the DISPLAY ALL command, it displays data like the LIST command. DISPLAY, however, stops at the end of each full screen of records and waits for you to press a key before it continues to scroll. Enter the LIST command to display all of your records:

```
. LIST
```

All your records should now appear on your screen, as shown in Figure 8.4. As you can see, the record number is displayed along with each record. If your database file were indexed, you would see the original record number. If you had more than one full screen of records, you would have been able to see only the last screen. If your data was more than 80 characters wide, it would have "wrapped" around the screen, meaning that it would have taken two or more lines to display each record. When this happens, it is best to use the BROWSE mode.

```
. LIST
Record#  COMPONENT       BRAND       QUANTITY    COST   PRICE
      1  AMPLIFIER       DIGI              15  229.00  389.99
      2  AMPLIFIER       ALLWOOD           10  369.00  589.99
      3  AMPLIFIER       ONESOUND           5  529.00  899.99
      4  COMPACT DISC    DIGI              17  389.00  625.99
      5  COMPACT DISC    ONESOUND          26  269.00  329.99
      6  COMPACT DISC    HITECH            50  129.00  299.99
      7  COMPACT DISC    ALLWOOD           60  109.00  189.99
      8  RECEIVER        ALLWOOD           30  169.00  289.00
      9  RECEIVER        DIGI               0  299.00  529.00
     10  SPEAKERS        MITY              22  299.00  399.00
     11  SPEAKERS        DIGI              18   89.00  109.00
     12  SPEAKERS        ALLWOOD          140   69.00   59.00
     13  TURNTABLE       DIGI              15  149.00  299.99
     14  TURNTABLE       MEGASONIK        250   39.00   69.00
     15  TURNTABLE       HITECH             6  189.00  269.99

.
Command ║C:\dbase4\INVENTRY     ║Rec EOF/15      ║File ║          ║         Caps
```

***Figure 8.4.** LISTing the database records*

Now try the DISPLAY command.

```
. DISPLAY
```

If you don't see anything, it's because there is no current record. When you LISTed all the records, you moved the current record pointer past the end of the file. First, return to the top of the database file and try again. The GO TOP command takes you back to the top of the database file.

```
. GO TOP

INVENTRY:   Record No      1
DISPLAY
```

This time you see the current first record. You could see all of your records by entering DISPLAY ALL. How about seeing the next 10 records? Enter

```
. DISPLAY NEXT 10
```

The next ten records, starting with the current record, are displayed.

SORTing and INDEXing

Besides being able to display records, you also can SORT and INDEX your data from the dot prompt. If you wanted to sort the INVENTRY file by the BRAND field to create a new sorted database file called INVBRAND, you would enter

```
. SORT ON BRAND TO INVBRAND
```

This is the equivalent of what you did in the sorting section of the last chapter. To index on the PRICE field, creating an index tag called PRICE in the INVENTRY.MDX file, enter

```
. INDEX ON PRICE TAG PRICE
```

Once you create an index, your data still appears in its natural order until you tell dBASE IV which index to use. Even if you only have one index in your .MDX (multiple index) file, you still must tell dBASE IV to use it. To tell dBASE IV to use an index, enter the SET ORDER TO command.

```
. SET ORDER TO TAG PRICE
Master index:  PRICE
```

Now you can access your data in PRICE order.

LOCATEing or FINDing Individual Records

You can LOCATE or FIND specific records from the dot prompt. The main difference between LOCATE and FIND is that you can LOCATE a record in any database file, but you can FIND a record only in an indexed database file, and only if what you are searching for is the key. While LOCATE searches the entire database file from the beginning, FIND uses a special searching pattern that takes no more than two seconds to find a record no matter what the database file size. Using LOCATE in a large database file may take several minutes.

The simplest form of LOCATE searches for a record with a specific condition. dBASE IV will search every record, beginning at the first record and continuing until the search is successful, or until it reaches the end of the file. Here are examples of successful and unsuccessful searches;

```
. LOCATE FOR BRAND = 'DIGI'
Record =       1
. LOCATE FOR BRAND = 'PIGI'

End of LOCATE scope
```

The FIND command requires that an indexed database file is in use. Because the index already contains the key, all you have to give dBASE IV is the value of the key that you are searching for. Once again, here are some examples of successful and unsuccessful searches:

```
. USE INVENTRY
. SET ORDER TO BRAND
. FIND DIGI
```

```
. USE INVENTRY
. SET ORDER TO BRAND
Master index:BRAND
. FIND PIGI
Find not successful
```

If the find is successful, the record pointer is positioned on the record that meets the search criteria, and you'll see another dot prompt. You still must display the record to see it. If the search is not successful, a message to that effect is displayed.

An Electronic Blackboard

The dot prompt gives you access to another dBASE IV feature not available in the Control Center: the dBASE IV blackboard. There is a simple command, called the question mark, that allows you to ask direct questions from dBASE IV and receive direct answers. A simple expression might be to add two numbers together.

```
. ?3+4
              7
```

dBASE IV returns the value 7, the sum of 3 plus 4. You also can use the electronic blackboard for any calculations with your database file. Suppose you want to know the current value of BRAND. First, go to the top of the database file. Then display the current value of BRAND.

```
. GO TOP
INVENTRY:  Record No 2
. ? BRAND
ALLWOOD
```

dBASE IV tells you the value of BRAND is ALLWOOD for the current record. How about if you wanted to see the value of the current item's QUANTITY*PRICE?

```
. ? QUANTITY*PRICE
              5899.90
```

Notice that character answers are left justified and numeric answers are right justified. There also are other operators, besides the question mark, known as *aggregate operators*. These operators automatically work with all of your data. One of these, SUM, gives you a total of an individual field, a group of fields, or even calculated fields. This example produces the sum of the quantities, and of the quantity times price.

```
. SUM QUANTITY, QUANTITY*PRICE
     15 records summed
         quantity               quantity*price
              664           112909.96
```

Summary

The concepts of commands, the dot prompt, and the electronic blackboard will all be put to good use in the next few chapters as you learn about operators, functions, and the Query work surface. While learning these new concepts, remember that you have both the Control Center and dot prompt available to you at all times.

chapter 9

Logic, Operators, and Functions

Computers and database management systems are built on the use of logic. The use of logic isn't difficult—in fact, it's kind of fun. However you feel about it, understanding computer logic allows you to get more from your computer and your database management system.

Operators and Functions

Operators and functions are tools you use when constructing commands. Even if you've never seen a computer before, you are already familiar with most of the dBASE IV operators and what they represent. Functions are provided to perform a variety of standard operations on data. SQRT is an example of a dBASE function. This function gives you the square root of a number. In this chapter, you use operators in dBASE IV to retrieve some specific data. You will wind up the chapter by using some of the dBASE functions. This chapter offers you more opportunities to work at the dot prompt in order to expand your dot prompt knowledge and expertise.

Operators

We tend to think of operators such as the plus sign (+) and the equals sign (=) as mathematical symbols. On the other hand, we frequently use these symbols with all kinds of data—not just with numbers. And this is true with dBASE IV as well as most computer languages. The plus sign is used to join items, and the equal sign is used to compare items. All the operators are grouped into four categories: mathematical, relational, logical, and string and are shown in Table 9.1.

***Table 9.1.** dBASE IV Operators*

	Mathematical
+	Addition
–	Subtraction
*	Multiplication
/	Division
**	Raise to a Power
()	Grouping
	Relational
=	Equal
# or <>	Not Equal
>	Greater Than
<	Less Than
>=	Greater Than or Equal To
<=	Less Than or Equal To
	Logical
.AND.	Logical AND
.OR.	Logical OR
.NOT.	Logical NOT
()	Grouping
	String
+	Join (concatenation)
–	Join (shift blanks)
$	Contained in

Logical Operators

There are three commonly used logical terms. These are referred to as the *logical operators*: .AND., .OR., and .NOT. These logical operators work in ways similar to their ordinary English counterparts.

The Stereo Store inventory file is the example you'll be using to learn about these operators. Make sure that your database file structure and its data match Figure 9.1. You will use this data for the next few chapters. Rather than using the concepts of .AND., .OR., and .NOT. through the Query work surface, you are going to use the DISPLAY command from the dBASE IV dot prompt. You will put these concepts to work in the next chapter by extracting data through the Query screen.

Records   Organize   Fields   Go To   Exit

COMPONENT	BRAND	QUANTITY	COST	PRICE
AMPLIFIER	DIGI	15	229.00	389.99
AMPLIFIER	ALLWOOD	10	369.00	589.99
AMPLIFIER	ONESOUND	5	529.00	899.99
COMPACT DISC	DIGI	17	389.00	625.99
COMPACT DISC	ONESOUND	26	269.00	329.99
COMPACT DISC	HITECH	50	129.00	299.99
COMPACT DISC	ALLWOOD	60	109.00	189.99
RECEIVER	ALLWOOD	30	169.00	289.00
RECEIVER	DIGI	0	299.00	529.00
SPEAKERS	MITY	22	299.00	399.00
SPEAKERS	DIGI	18	89.00	109.00
SPEAKERS	ALLWOOD	140	69.00	59.00
TURNTABLE	DIGI	15	149.00	299.99
TURNTABLE	MEGASONIK	250	39.00	69.00
TURNTABLE	HITECH	6	189.00	269.99

Browse | C:\dbase4\INVENTRY | Rec 1/15 | File | Caps

***Figure 9.1.** The Stereo Store inventory database*

Using .AND. and .OR. with =

Make sure that the INVENTRY file is active—that it is above the line in the Data panel of the Control Center. If it isn't active, select the INVENTRY file by highlighting it and pressing **<Enter>**.

Now press **<Alt>-E** to open the Exit menu, and choose `Exit to dot prompt`. After you press **<Enter>**, you will find yourself with the traditional dBASE IV dot prompt:

dBASE IV is waiting for your command. Start with a quick look at a typical DISPLAY command. Suppose you wanted to see all your records whose value of BRAND was DIGI. Enter the command:

```
. DISPLAY FOR BRAND = 'DIGI'
```

and see the results, as shown in Figure 9.2.

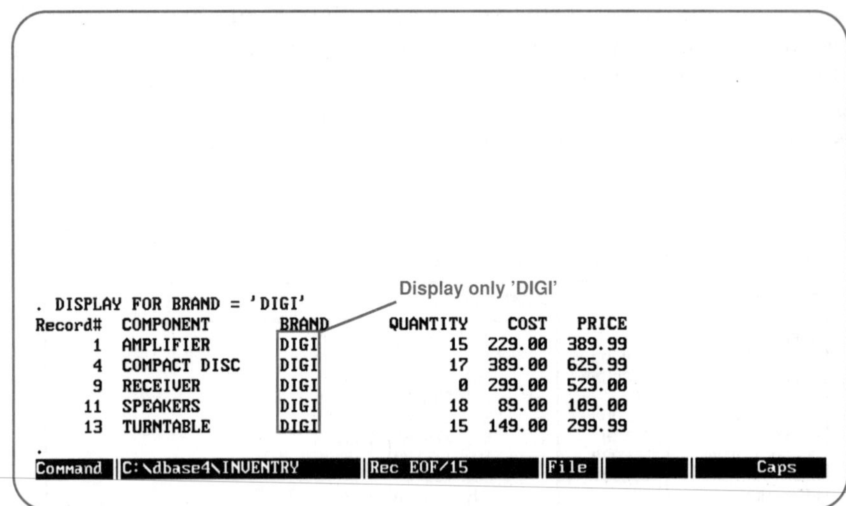

```
. DISPLAY FOR BRAND = 'DIGI'
Record#  COMPONENT       BRAND      QUANTITY     COST    PRICE
      1  AMPLIFIER       DIGI             15   229.00   389.99
      4  COMPACT DISC    DIGI             17   389.00   625.99
      9  RECEIVER        DIGI              0   299.00   529.00
     11  SPEAKERS        DIGI             18    89.00   109.00
     13  TURNTABLE       DIGI             15   149.00   299.99
.
Command ║C:\dbase4\INVENTRY   ║Rec EOF/15   ║File ║   ║   Caps
```


Figure 9.2. Displaying DIGI records

Only the components whose BRAND is DIGI are displayed. As you know, the characters DIGI, in this case, are enclosed in quotes so dBASE IV can distinguish them from field names of the same name. Single and double quotes are used interchangeably in dBASE IV as long as whatever is in front of a value has a matching counterpart in back of the value.

Suppose you wished to see all the entries for the brands of DIGI and ALLWOOD. The natural tendency would be to write the query command as:

```
. DISPLAY FOR BRAND = 'DIGI' .AND. BRAND = 'ALLWOOD'
```

Unfortunately, this command won't get you what you want. It tells dBASE IV to display all the records in which the BRAND field contains DIGI and ALLWOOD. There are none. dBASE applies the request to one record at a time—not to the entire database file.

Note that there are periods on both sides of the .AND. This is punctuation that dBASE IV needs in order to understand that these are logical operators. Remember that you need to put the periods on both sides of .AND., .OR., and .NOT.

The correct command is:

```
. DISPLAY FOR BRAND = 'DIGI' .OR. BRAND = 'ALLWOOD'
```

The section of the example database file to which this applies is shown in Figure 9.3.

Display 'DIGI' and 'ALLWOOD'

```
. DISPLAY FOR BRAND = 'DIGI' .OR. BRAND = 'ALLWOOD'
Record#  COMPONENT      BRAND      QUANTITY    COST   PRICE
      1  AMPLIFIER      DIGI             15  229.00  389.99
      2  AMPLIFIER      ALLWOOD          10  369.00  589.99
      4  COMPACT DISC   DIGI             17  389.00  625.99
      7  COMPACT DISC   ALLWOOD          60  109.00  189.99
      8  RECEIVER       ALLWOOD          30  169.00  289.00
      9  RECEIVER       DIGI              0  299.00  529.00
     11  SPEAKERS       DIGI             18   89.00  109.00
     12  SPEAKERS       ALLWOOD         140   69.00   59.00
     13  TURNTABLE      DIGI             15  149.00  299.99
.
Command ||C:\dbase4\INVENTRY        ||Rec EOF/15        ||File ||        ||      Caps
```

Figure 9.3. Displaying DIGI and ALLWOOD records

Proper use of the .AND. operator requests the common area of two groups. For example, to determine what records contain DIGI Compact Discs, the command is:

```
. DISPLAY FOR COMPONENT = 'COMPACT DISC' .AND. BRAND =
  'DIGI'
```

The order of the fields doesn't matter. The same result is obtained with the command:

```
. DISPLAY FOR BRAND = 'DIGI' .AND. COMPONENT = 'COMPACT
   DISC'
```

The result of either of these commands is shown in Figure 9.4.

Using .OR. in place of the .AND. in the last example gives an entirely different result.

```
. DISPLAY FOR BRAND = 'DIGI' .OR. COMPONENT =
  'COMPACT DISC'
```

Figure 9.5 shows the records that are displayed from this command.

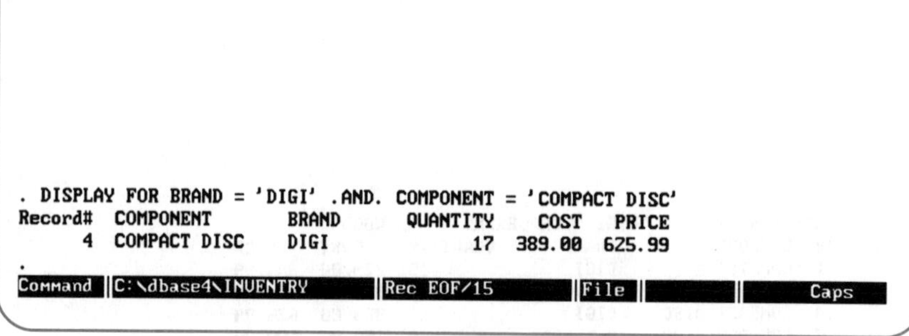

```
. DISPLAY FOR BRAND = 'DIGI' .AND. COMPONENT = 'COMPACT DISC'
Record#  COMPONENT        BRAND       QUANTITY   COST   PRICE
      4  COMPACT DISC     DIGI              17  389.00  625.99
.
Command  C:\dbase4\INVENTRY         Rec EOF/15          File            Caps
```

Figure 9.4. Displaying DIGI compact discs

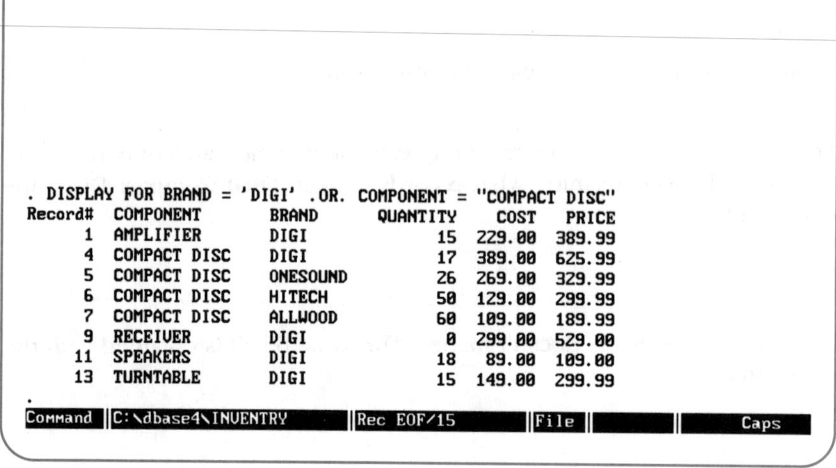

```
. DISPLAY FOR BRAND = 'DIGI' .OR. COMPONENT = "COMPACT DISC"
Record#  COMPONENT        BRAND       QUANTITY   COST   PRICE
      1  AMPLIFIER        DIGI              15  229.00  389.99
      4  COMPACT DISC     DIGI              17  389.00  625.99
      5  COMPACT DISC     ONESOUND          26  269.00  329.99
      6  COMPACT DISC     HITECH            50  129.00  299.99
      7  COMPACT DISC     ALLWOOD           60  109.00  189.99
      9  RECEIVER         DIGI               0  299.00  529.00
     11  SPEAKERS         DIGI              18   89.00  109.00
     13  TURNTABLE        DIGI              15  149.00  299.99
.
Command  C:\dbase4\INVENTRY         Rec EOF/15          File            Caps
```

Figure 9.5. Displaying all DIGI components and all compact discs

Suppose you want to extract those records whose BRAND value is ALLWOOD for either AMPLIFIER or SPEAKERS. Enter the following on one line:

```
. DISPLAY FOR BRAND = 'ALLWOOD' .AND. (COMPONENT =
  'AMPLIFIER' .OR. COMPONENT = 'SPEAKERS')
```

The records that qualify under this criteria are shown in Figure 9.6.

Suppose you inadvertently omitted the parentheses in the last example:

```
. DISPLAY FOR BRAND = 'ALLWOOD' .AND. COMPONENT =
  'AMPLIFIER' .OR. COMPONENT = 'SPEAKERS'
```

The resulting display, which is entirely different from Figure 9.6, is shown in Figure 9.7. This result occurs because the .AND. operator takes precedence over the .OR. operator. This means that because the .AND. operator is evaluated first, the resulting operation tells dBASE IV to display all ALLWOOD amplifiers along with all brands of speakers.

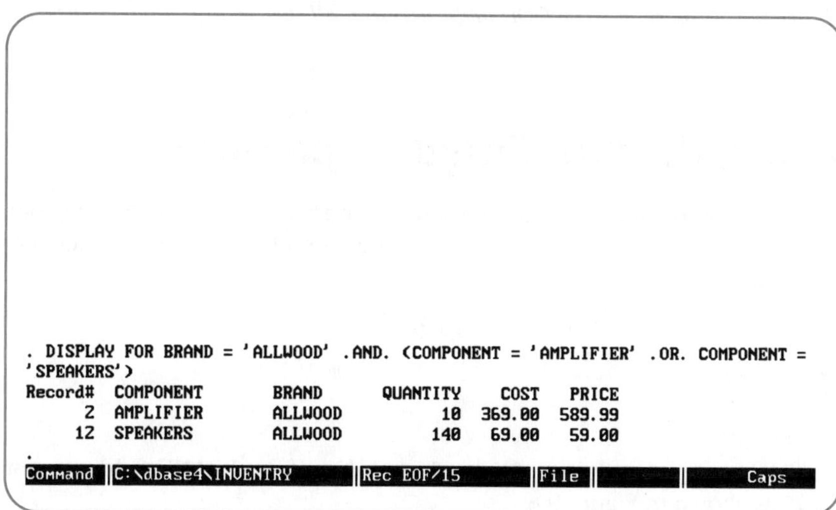

Figure 9.6. Displaying all the ALLWOOD amplifiers and speakers

```
. DISPLAY FOR BRAND = 'ALLWOOD' .AND. COMPONENT = 'AMPLIFIER' .OR. COMPONENT = '
SPEAKERS'
Record#  COMPONENT        BRAND       QUANTITY    COST   PRICE
      2  AMPLIFIER        ALLWOOD           10  369.00  589.99
     10  SPEAKERS         MITY              22  299.00  399.00
     11  SPEAKERS         DIGI              18   89.00  109.00
     12  SPEAKERS         ALLWOOD          140   69.00   59.00
.
Command  C:\dbase4\INVENTRY      Rec EOF/15       File              Caps
```

Figure 9.7. Displaying ALLWOOD amplifiers and all speakers by components

Using the Not Equals Operator

A last example dealing with the components and brands demonstrates the not equals operator. This operator has two forms: # and <>. To see all BRANDS except DIGI, enter:

```
. DISPLAY FOR BRAND # 'DIGI'
```

or

```
. DISPLAY FOR BRAND <> 'DIGI'
```

Either one displays all the records whose value of the BRAND field was not DIGI, as shown in Figure 9.8.

Greater Than and Less Than Operators

Now suppose that you want to see all the records for which cost is more than $200.00. Use the following statement.

```
. DISPLAY FOR COST > 200
```

```
. DISPLAY FOR BRAND # 'DIGI'
Record#  COMPONENT        BRAND      QUANTITY    COST   PRICE
      2  AMPLIFIER        ALLWOOD          10  369.00  589.99
      3  AMPLIFIER        ONESOUND          5  529.00  899.99
      5  COMPACT DISC     ONESOUND         26  269.00  329.99
      6  COMPACT DISC     HITECH           50  129.00  299.99
      7  COMPACT DISC     ALLWOOD          60  109.00  189.99
      8  RECEIVER         ALLWOOD          30  169.00  289.00
     10  SPEAKERS         MITY             22  299.00  399.00
     12  SPEAKERS         ALLWOOD         140   69.00   59.00
     14  TURNTABLE        MEGASONIK       250   39.00   69.00
     15  TURNTABLE        HITECH            6  189.00  269.99
.
Command  C:\dbase4\INVENTRY    Rec EOF/15    File         Caps
```

***Figure 9.8.** Displaying all BRANDs except DIGI*

Notice that the value 200 is not in quotes. This is because numbers cannot be confused with field names. Why? Because field names cannot start with a number. Figure 9.9 shows these records.

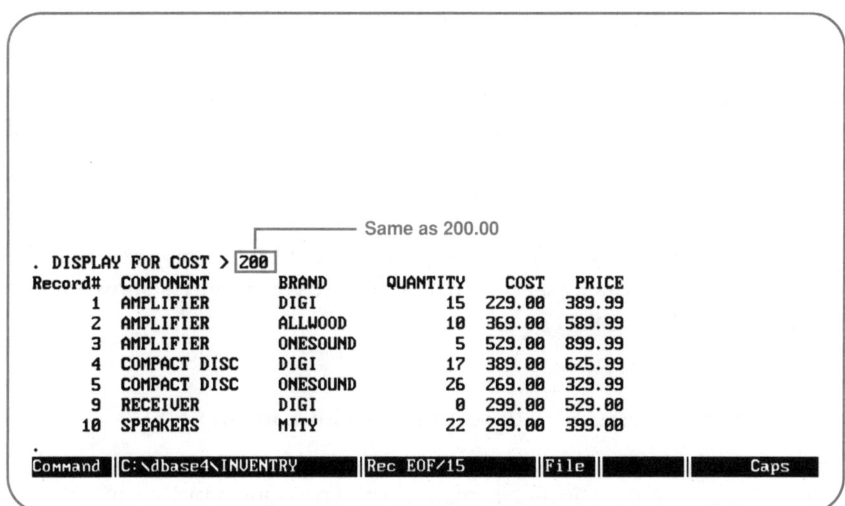


```
. DISPLAY FOR COST > 200
Record#  COMPONENT        BRAND      QUANTITY    COST   PRICE
      1  AMPLIFIER        DIGI             15  229.00  389.99
      2  AMPLIFIER        ALLWOOD          10  369.00  589.99
      3  AMPLIFIER        ONESOUND          5  529.00  899.99
      4  COMPACT DISC     DIGI             17  389.00  625.99
      5  COMPACT DISC     ONESOUND         26  269.00  329.99
      9  RECEIVER         DIGI              0  299.00  529.00
     10  SPEAKERS         MITY             22  299.00  399.00
.
Command  C:\dbase4\INVENTRY    Rec EOF/15    File         Caps
```

***Figure 9.9.** Displaying all items that cost more than $200*

You may want to get more specific by indicating a numeric range. Enter the command:

```
. DISPLAY FOR COST > 200 .AND. COST < 300
```

This limits the display, as shown in Figure 9.10.

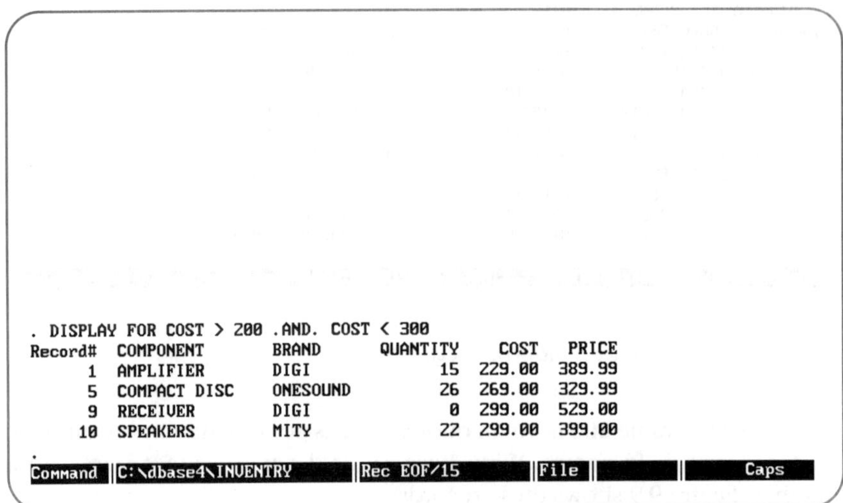

```
. DISPLAY FOR COST > 200 .AND. COST < 300
Record#  COMPONENT       BRAND        QUANTITY    COST   PRICE
      1  AMPLIFIER       DIGI               15  229.00  389.99
      5  COMPACT DISC    ONESOUND           26  269.00  329.99
      9  RECEIVER        DIGI                0  299.00  529.00
     10  SPEAKERS        MITY               22  299.00  399.00
.
Command ||C:\dbase4\INVENTRY    ||Rec EOF/15    ||File ||    ||    Caps
```

Figure 9.10. Displaying all items that cost more than $200 and less than $300

In the final example, use a calculation to determine the record selection. Suppose you wanted to see which records were sold at a margin of $100 or more. Issue the command:

```
. DISPLAY FOR PRICE-COST >= 100
```

This displays the records in the top half of Figure 9.11. You also can write the selection another way to see just the actual gross margin (as shown in the bottom half of Figure 9.11).

```
. DISPLAY FOR PRICE-COST>= 100 PRICE-COST
```

This shows only the value of the calculation PRICE minus COST.

In the next chapter, you will see how these types of queries are accomplished with the Query screen through a method known as Query by Example (QBE).

```
Record#  COMPONENT        BRAND       QUANTITY    COST   PRICE
      1  AMPLIFIER        DIGI              15  229.00  389.99
      2  AMPLIFIER        ALLWOOD           10  369.00  589.99
      3  AMPLIFIER        ONESOUND           5  529.00  899.99
      4  COMPACT DISC     DIGI              17  389.00  625.99
      6  COMPACT DISC     HITECH            50  129.00  299.99
      8  RECEIVER         ALLWOOD           30  169.00  289.00
      9  RECEIVER         DIGI               0  299.00  529.00
     10  SPEAKERS         MITY              22  299.00  399.00
     13  TURNTABLE        DIGI              15  149.00  299.99
. DISPLAY FOR PRICE-COST >=100 PRICE-COST
Record#      PRICE-COST
      1          160.99
      2          220.99
      3          370.99
      4          236.99
      6          170.99
      8          120.00
      9          230.00
     10          100.00
     13          150.99
.
Command ||C:\dbase4\INVENTRY       ||Rec EOF/15      ||File ||      ||     Caps
```

Figure 9.11. *Displaying the GROSS MARGIN (PRICE minus COST) greater than or equal to $100*

Using + and –

You can use the plus (+) and minus (–) signs with character, numeric, and date data types. Their use with date and character data is a little different than with numeric variables. The plus sign can be used to join character strings. Assume the following assignment statements performed at the dot prompt.

```
. CITY = 'HARTFORD'

Hartford

. STATE = 'CONNECTICUT'

Connecticut

. mVAR = CITY+', '+STATE

Hartford, Connecticut

. ? mVAR

Hartford, Connecticut
```

The variables CITY, STATE, and mVAR are known as memory variables. These are temporary fields that exist only in memory and not as part of any database file. The question mark tells dBASE to display the result. The numeral 2 is in quotes. This will make the memory variable TWO a character field type. Feel free to try these at the dot prompt in your system.

```
. TWO = '2'
. ? TWO+TWO
22
```

The + operator tells dBASE IV to join two character strings together.

The minus sign allows you to join two character strings and eliminate the ending blank spaces in the first of the two data items. Suppose that you have two fields, CITY and STATE. The CITY field is 30 spaces wide. Joining CITY and STATE as in the above example, except with fields, produces the following display:

```
. ? CITY + ',' + STATE

Glendale,                California
```

(which *looks* like it was done by a computer). We really want to "throw away" the blank spaces at the end of CITY. These are called *trailing blanks* because they are at the end of a field. Replace the plus sign with a minus sign.

```
. ? CITY - (',' + STATE)

Glendale, California
```

The blank spaces really aren't gone. They have simply been moved to the end of the expression; they come after California, where they are not visible. The expression containing the comma and the STATE are enclosed by parentheses, so dBASE IV treats that part of the expression as a single unit. Otherwise, the blanks would have moved between the comma and the STATE.

Adding and Subtracting from Dates

You can add (or subtract) a number from a date. When you do, dBASE IV understands that the number is a number of days. The current date is represented by the function DATE( ). To find the date that is 30 days from now, use:

```
. ? DATE() + 30
```

Conversely, to find the date 1,000 days in the past:

```
. ? DATE() - 1000
```

The result of both of these operations is a new date.

Grouping

Parentheses are used to group numbers together. dBASE IV strictly follows the order of precedence rules for arithmetic. That means multiplication and division are performed before addition or subtraction. Use the parentheses as grouping symbols if you forget which goes first or you want to modify this rule. For example, suppose you want to add two items and divide the result.

```
. ? 10 + 6 / 2

13
```

As you can see from the above example, you didn't get the answer you wanted—you got the correct result. dBASE IV divided first, then added the result of the division to the number 10. To set up this arithmetic problem properly, you put parentheses around the numbers being added.

```
. ? (10 + 6) / 2

8
```

The computer will always give you the correct answer. If the answer isn't what you expected, it's because you asked the wrong question. In these two examples, it is easy to see what's wrong. It isn't so easy when you substitute these fictitious variable names for the numbers. If the INVENTRY database is active, you can try this example. Enter:

```
. ? COST + PRICE/2
```

If you could easily pick out an error in this case, you don't need a computer. Call us—we need you.

Relational Operators

These symbols are often called the comparison operators because they are used to compare two data items. All of these operators can be used with character, date, and numeric data items. The items that are being compared, however, must be of the same data type. You cannot compare apples with oranges.

When two items are compared, the result of the comparison is either true or false. dBASE IV will return a logical true (.T.) or a logical false (.F.), depending on the result of the comparison. When the comparison is performed within a command, the result is used by dBASE IV in executing the command. For example, in the command:

```
. DISPLAY FOR COMPONENT = 'AMPLIFIER'
```

only the records in which the condition COMPONENT = 'AMPLIFIER' is evaluated as true are displayed. You can check an evaluation with the ? command in the dot prompt:

```
. ? COMPONENT = 'AMPLIFIER'
.T.
```

When you compare dates or numbers, these symbols function just as we learned in grade school. The equal sign means that two data items must be exactly equal to each other. The greater than sign (>) means that the number to the left is supposed to be greater than the number on the right (the symbol points at the smaller item).

```
. A=6
. B=5
. ?A>B        Which means, "Is A greater than B?"
.T.           Yes, it is.
```

$ (Contained In)

You can use this symbol only with character data. Use the $ to tell dBASE IV to search a field or a memory variable, to see whether a second, smaller string is contained within it. For example, suppose you have a database file of names and addresses. You want to see all the records in which the string "ONE" is contained anywhere in the BRAND field. The command looks like:

```
. DISPLAY FOR 'ONE' $ BRAND    Is ONE contained in BRAND?
```

The shorter of the two data items must (in this case) be on the left. The data item being searched must be at least as long as what you are searching for. Because "ONE" has three characters, the BRAND field needs to have three or more characters. Otherwise, ONE cannot be found because it cannot be there.

The $ (contained in) symbol causes the expression to be evaluated as if it were a comparison. You are asking if the expression is true.

Functions

Functions are tools provided to perform specific, routine tasks. dBASE IV is particularly rich in its number and range of functions. Each function performs a specific task. There are functions for dates, character strings, and numbers. Additionally, there are several functions that perform specialized tests.

Functions have names such as SQRT and DATE. Function names are always followed by parentheses. The DATE function is always DATE( ). Many functions have arguments. If a function has an argument, the argument is placed within the parentheses. For example:

```
. ? SQRT(4)

                    2.
```

In this example, the argument is the number 4. An argument can be any legitimate dBASE expression; for example:

```
. ? SQRT(COST)

. ? SQRT(COST * QUANTITY)

. ? SQRT(SQRT(4))
```

You can use functions within a dBASE expression just as you can use constants, field names, and memory variables.

Mathematical Functions

The math functions are used to perform special mathematical calculations. Some readers may not be familiar with all the calculations involved. If you are not familiar with a particular mathematical term, you probably won't need that particular function. The special mathematical functions include:

ABS	Absolute value	MIN	Minimum of two values
EXP	Exponential (ex)	MOD	Modulus
INT	Integer	ROUND	Round off
LOG	Logarithm	SQRT	Square root

dBASE displays the results of most mathematical calculations using a fixed number of decimals. Usually two decimal places are displayed. You can change this value by resetting the DECIMALS option under `Settings` in the Tools menu of the Control Center.

Character Functions

Character functions allow you to search, manipulate, and transform character data items.

UPPER and LOWER

These two useful functions are used to evaluate a data item as if it contained only uppercase or lowercase characters. dBASE treats uppercase and lowercase versions of the same letter as different characters. You can use both UPPER and LOWER to exclude the differences and force dBASE IV to treat all the characters as if they were uppercase or lowercase. For example, to search the database file ADDRESS field for HARTFORD when you're not sure whether you've been consistent when entering the character data:

```
. DISPLAY FOR 'HARTFORD' $ UPPER(ADDRESS)
. DISPLAY FOR 'hartford' $ LOWER(ADDRESS)
```

SUBSTR( )

A SUBSTRing is just a character string that is a part of another, larger character string. This function allows you to specify pieces of character strings.

```
. DISPLAY FOR SUBSTR(PHONE,7,3) = '248'
```

This command asks dBASE IV to display the records in which the seventh, eighth, and ninth characters of PHONE are 248. The function requires that you provide the FIELDNAME, the starting character position, and the number of characters in the substring.

Value Function, VAL

There are occasions when it's necessary to make a calculation using a number that has been stored as a character data. You can do this with the help of the VAL( ) function. For example, suppose you want to calculate the average value of the ZIP codes in your database file. Normally, of course, these ZIP codes have no numeric significance to anyone other than the post office. However, Snedly Economist has a new and as yet unproven theory that the average value of the ZIP codes in a customer list is directly related to profitability. We can use the AVERAGE command on the ZIP code field by adding VAL( ) to the command.

```
. AVERAGE VAL(ZIPCODE)
```

The VAL function allows us to use character data in arithmetic computations.

The STR Function

The STR (String) function allows you to convert numbers to characters when you need to combine numbers with characters in an expression, or when you need to control the width of a numeric display. You have already seen that you are not allowed to combine apples and oranges within a single expression. The STR function is the way around this rule—disguise the apples as oranges. Suppose that you have stored ZIP codes as a five-digit numeric field. You can use the STR function to convert the ZIP codes to a character string and add four blank spaces at the beginning.

```
. ? STATE + STR(ZIP,9)
```

How about decimal places? You can choose to display places or not to display them. (If there are none, you can display them anyway, and if there are some, you can ignore them.) Decimal places are displayed by simply adding the number of decimal places to the expression.

```
. ? STATE + STR(ZIP,9,2)
```

TRIM( ), LTRIM( ), and RTRIM( )

Use these functions to remove unwanted blank spaces. Suppose that you have a database file containing a 30-character CITY field and a two-character STATE field. You want to join these two fields so that the result appears natural. The CITY field contains trailing blank spaces, so the display of CITY with STATE looks like this:

```
. ? CITY + ',' + STATE

Glendale              , CA
```

In the discussion on operators, you saw that the minus sign can move these trailing blanks to the end of the expression. The TRIM( ) function allows you to make them "disappear."

```
. ? TRIM(CITY) + ',' + STATE

Glendale, CA
```

The TRIM( ) and RTRIM( ) functions are identical. They remove trailing blank spaces. The LTRIM( ) function is used to remove leading blank spaces—blank spaces that occur at the beginning of a data item. The most common use of LTRIM( ) is to remove leading blank spaces from a number that has been converted to a character string with the STR( ) function. Use this function to combine a number with the dollar sign.

```
. COST = 1.45
. ? '$' + LTRIM(STR(COST,9,2))
$1.45
```

Date Functions

The most commonly used date function is DATE( ). This function tells you the current date, according to your computer's clock calendar.

```
. ? DATE()
01/31/91
```

Summary

All of this is but a sample of the many functions available. dBASE functions are helpful, they are fun to use, and they can considerably extend what you can do with dBASE. This chapter has acquainted you with the use of dBASE operators and some functions, how they are used, and what they can be used for. Thus, you've been given a few more tools to help you begin to unlock the power of dBASE IV commands.

chapter 10

Extracting Information—Query Screens

Most database management systems, like dBASE IV, have a report writer suitable for producing a variety of standard reports. Reports are good for seeing your information in a formal way, but many times you want to see just a few records or one special record. The BROWSE screen by itself only displays your records. However, when BROWSE and reporting functions are combined with query, you are provided with some powerful tools for extracting and displaying your data. The database file provides a "central pool" of information that you can use for any purpose. With use of the dBASE IV query features, you can obtain specific information directly from your keyboard on an *ad hoc* basis, and you can use the data to prepare standard reports on a regular basis. In Chapter 2 you saw how the query language and report writer form a powerful combination to meet even your most complicated needs. In a comprehensive look at the dBASE IV query work surface, this chapter will show you many features and functions of the Query work surface, and how you can selectively retrieve data from your files.

Before you actually go about using the query to produce some answers to some questions, first take a look at how to ask questions of your data and how to receive meaningful answers.

Asking Questions

Database systems respond to user requests for information. These requests are called queries. The part of the DBMS that does this is usually called its *query language*, or as with dBASE IV, the *queries work surface*.

Planning for Queries

One of the problems facing new computer users is knowing what types of questions can be answered with the use of a DBMS like dBASE IV. You can become so bogged down in new concepts and new vocabulary that the original purpose of purchasing the computer is forgotten. This initial euphoria is lost and the work becomes drudgery, unless you plan first and stick to your plan. Remember that the computer is there to help you answer questions and to help you to solve your business problems.

There is nothing magical about the computer. Computers are tools and they can work only with the materials available to them. You cannot ask a question like "What color is the sky?" without first telling the computer the definition of color, the definition of sky, and the link between the definition of a certain color and the definition of sky. If this raw data is not available to the computer, the answer cannot be found by the computer, which has neither curiosity nor eyes.

Your own application systems will be less complicated than one that distinguishes colors, or determines what "sky" is. Your system will exist to do a certain task, like printing a mailing list, printing checks, storing payroll records or customer orders, or even keeping track of a stereo store inventory.

It is important to know what questions you will be asking about your data before you have completed your database file design. The answer either must exist in the files as a data item or must be calculated or extracted from the available data. A question like "Which employees have the following qualifications?" requires that not only the employee name be available, but also the values of each qualification. If the qualifications are as follows:

"Employee must be over 35 years of age, bilingual (Spanish), and over six feet tall."

then you must have those items available in some form. For example, if you need to know the employee's age, you can carry either the employee's age or the employee's birth date on the personnel record. It is not a good idea to carry variable information such as "age" on a database record, because you would have to adjust the value of this data item each time the employee passed a birthday. Carry the birth date instead, because the database system can calculate the age when it is needed by subtracting the birth date from the current date. To answer the above question, you would need to have these data items:

- Employee's name
- Employee's birth date
- Current date
- An indicator for "bilingual"
- Height of the employee

This example shows how some information can be calculated, such as the age from birth date and current date. Some information, like the bilingual indicator or the employee's height, must be stored as is.

The Scope of the Answer

A computer can provide answers to your business problems. Some of the answers are in the performance of repetitive tasks, such as printing mailing labels. The answer provided by the computer is that of a printing shop right on your premises. A computer produces company payroll efficiently because it can perform calculations and balancing faster.

The types of questions you can ask your database system also are limited by the data you have available. The trick is to get reliable answers from the data that you have in computer format and to recognize the limitations of the data. If you have a large amount of data available to answer your questions, not only will the answers you receive be more accurate, but also the range of questions that you ask can be broader.

For the purposes of imagining an example query system, suppose you are just starting to collect the raw data that will become your company's database file. You start by creating a list of customer names and addresses so that you can send mass mailings to the customers regularly. Using a computer to maintain the list of customers and their addresses can save time, but such a list also could be kept on typewritten paper or on file cards. The advantage to using a computer here is that you also can print mailing labels and form letters on a printer attached to the computer. You are making use of your stored data, not to mention saving the time that would normally be wasted in retyping the mailing list on labels by hand.

This limited amount of data, just the items needed to address and mail a letter, allows you to ask some questions. You can pinpoint the locations of your customers down to their street. This may not sound like much, but from this information, you can plot the locations on a map and see if there are concentrations of customers in certain areas. Depending on your business, you can use this information to redistribute your sales areas or to identify areas where your sales forces can find new customers.

Getting Answers

Summary Questions

The answers you receive from your data must be presented in a clear and logical format in such a way that you can use the answers effectively. Some questions require a detailed answer, where individual records are displayed directly from the database file. Some questions require a summary of a selected set of records, or may require a summary of the information into several groups, based on the qualifications given in the questions. The method of displaying the answers also varies; you can use either the computer monitor screen or a printer to display the answers you receive.

The general ways of displaying data are either to show the detailed data or to show a summary of the information gleaned from the data. Summary information is usually required at the higher levels of a company hierarchy; detailed data is needed at the lower levels. What information is displayed is a function of the question that is asked.

Displaying Answers

Displaying answers to your questions on the computer monitor screen has limitations that printing does not have. Most notably, the monitor screen is limited in size—display width and height—and cannot be changed easily. Printed reports, on the other hand, can be as large as the largest paper that fits into the printer. It's also possible to make a standard 8 1/2- by 11-inch report wider by putting the paper in sideways.

On the monitor screen, detailed records can be displayed either in columns or in a customized format. A columnar display is usually arranged so that one detailed record is one line on the display. This means that the data items in each record form columns down the display. A customized format usually means that one detailed record is displayed on the screen at a time. You can display more of one record this way, but only one record at once.

The amount of information that can be displayed in this fashion is limited by the width and height of the screen. Users can work around this limitation by scrolling the data up and down and panning it side to side, like a window looking in on the data. This method is awkward, however, and detailed information is best presented in printed form.

Using Queries

The Query work surface in dBASE IV is another part of the interface that helps you to communicate with, and give commands to, a very powerful data retrieval and management facility. You will use the Query screen to see how to extract specific information from your database file.

Query Languages

There are two types of query languages: *procedural* and *nonprocedural*. Procedural query languages are much like traditional computer languages, such as BASIC, FORTRAN, PL/1, and COBOL. With a procedural language, you tell the computer how to do what you want it to, step-by-step. In such languages, you tell the computer how to solve the problem, not what the problem is.

Nonprocedural languages allow you to tell the computer what information you need. The system figures out how to get the answer. There are several ways to do this in dBASE IV. One is to use the query language commands of dBASE IV from the dBASE dot prompt. Another way is to use the Structured Query Language (SQL) that is used in many mainframe environments and that is now available in dBASE IV. However, the easiest way to learn about queries is to use the Query work surface that comes with dBASE IV. As you fill in the blanks, dBASE IV creates its query commands automatically. You don't even have to know the commands yourself.

dBASE IV has features of both procedural and nonprocedural languages. Specific information can be obtained directly from the keyboard via the query language. To make effective use of the query commands, you need to know the field names and have some idea as to what is contained in the fields.

Standard Query Operations

In the rest of this chapter, you will learn many ways you can use queries to organize and manage your data. These include:

- Selecting files
- Selecting fields
- Sorting
- Selecting records (filtering)
- Creating new calculated fields
- Aggregation and totaling (SUM, MIN, MAX, AVG)
- Grouping
- Updating (many records at once)

You will see how queries are used for character and numeric data.

The Query Screen

By using the Query work surface you can ask almost any question about your data and receive meaningful information that you can look at through the BROWSE or EDIT screens, or that you can use in the creation of a report.

Take a look at a typical Query screen. Make sure the INVENTRY database file that you used in Chapter 9 is active. Check Figure 9.1 to make sure all 15 records you have are the same. If not, update the file so that it matches exactly.

Start in the Control Center. For now, whenever you begin a query, first select a database file. Activate the INVENTRY database file by pressing **<Enter>** with INVENTRY highlighted in the Data panel. If it is already active then you are all set to create your query.

Highlight the `<create>` option in the Queries panel of the Control Center and press **<Enter>**. Your screen should look like Figure 10.1. This is the Query work surface.

A Quick Tour of the Query work surface

The Query work surface has three distinct areas, just as every work surface in dBASE IV has. So far, you have learned about the Data work surface. As you can see, the Query work surface is similar.

```
Layout   Fields   Condition   Update   Exit                          10:35:18 am
Inventry.dbf|↓COMPONENT|↓BRAND|↓QUANTITY|↓COST|↓PRICE

View
<NEW>      Inventry->   Inventry->   Inventry->   Inventry->
           COMPONENT    BRAND        QUANTITY     COST

Query   C:\dbase4\<NEW>          File 1/1
 Next field:Tab  Add/Remove all fields:F5  Zoom:F9  Prev/Next skeleton:F3/F4
```

***Figure 10.1.** The Query work surface*

At the very top of the screen are the menus. You can always open the menus in dBASE IV by pressing the function key **<F10>**. This specific work surface has five menus, and each will be discussed as you use them.

The bottom area of the work surface is the status area, as you have seen in other work surfaces. The status bar keeps you informed about many things. It tells you the name of the work surface, current drive, directory, and name of the query, which, in this case, is actually unnamed, so it is called NEW. It also tells you that there is one file on the work surface. As you add more database files to the work surface, the status bar immediately updates its information. Navigation help is located below the status bar. This is where you receive messages and prompts, and usually find help with common navigating keys. In this case, four different operations are listed, including how to move from field to field, how to add or remove fields, how to zoom (or see more than the present screen size allows), and finally how to move from one file to another.

The middle of the screen, however, should interest you the most. This is where all your work takes place. This is where you place the files you want to work with to decide what information you want to extract from them.

Skeletons

Right now, both types of skeletons are displayed on the work surface: *file skeletons* and *view skeletons*. Data file skeletons are simply a list of the fields in your database file. Each file skeleton usually represents a different database file. Each field in the file skeleton occupies one position in the skeleton. Data file skeletons are used for entering the sort directions and record selections that make the Query screen work. They help you ask questions of your data. View skeletons display only the fields that will be used in your "answer." Your answer will be a temporary database file that you will use in BROWSE or EDIT screens, or in custom reports.

The first skeleton is the INVENTRY database file skeleton. This is on the top of the work area. You can see the name of the database file and as many of your fields as will fit on the screen. The area under the database file name is known as the *pothandle* because it sticks out like the handle of a pot. You use the space below the pothandle for operations that tell dBASE IV to change data values or to update the entire file. You use the area below the individual fields for operations that change the display of the file without changing the data, such as SORT and FILTER commands.

You pan left with the **<Shift>-<Tab>** key combination. You can tell that there are more fields because there is a right arrow on the far right side of the file skeleton. You can move from field to field and pan right beyond the displayed fields by pressing the **<Tab>** key. You can have as many data file skeletons as you need on the surface, but you can see only a few at a time.

The second skeleton on the work surface is known as the view skeleton. The view skeleton is always the last skeleton appearing on the work surface. This skeleton displays the fields that you will see in your query answer. Think of all the skeletons, other than the view skeleton, as questions because it is into those skeletons that you enter the sort directions and record selections. Think of the view skeleton as the answer because it lets you determine which fields you see. You can work with the data of a field in BROWSE or EDIT or custom reports only if that field is in the view skeleton.

Overview of Working with Data Queries

How do you actually work with the data? In the dBASE IV Query work surface you translate your questions into dBASE queries. You don't actually ask English-like questions or make requests like "Show me all my turntables and sort the data by BRAND." Rather, you enter dBASE query directives into the area underneath each field in the file skeletons. For example, if you wanted to see only your turntables, you would enter TURNTABLE underneath the COMPONENT field in the INVENTRY file skeleton. When you looked at your data in the BROWSE screen, you would see only turntables.

You enter selections into the data file skeleton and tell dBASE what data you want to see and how to sort your data. You can add, remove, and move fields around in the view skeleton. When you are done, you tell dBASE to save your selections. This is known as a *view* because you will be looking at just a specific portion of your data. The saved selections are stored in a query file that you can modify anytime by choosing the file in the Control Center.

You can use the view of your data several ways. You can BROWSE the data in a BROWSE table. Your data will be sorted too, if you ask dBASE to sort it. You also can see your data in the EDIT mode one record at a time. Finally, you can view your data in a custom printed report. Rather than creating a report with all your data, you can use the selected data from a view in a custom report.

Query Steps

Creating and using a query can be thought of as a step-by-step process that can be performed in almost any order.

1. Select your database file in the Control Center.
2. Create a new query.
3. Place the fields needed for the query into the view skeleton.
4. Enter sort directions in the file skeletons.
5. Enter record selections in the file skeletons.
6. Create any new calculated fields.
7. Use the query in BROWSE, EDIT, or a custom report.

Although you don't have to perform every step of this process, you may perform the steps in this order if you choose. Construct your queries one field at a time. It doesn't really matter if you sort before you select records or vice versa. But enter all your selections before saving the query and viewing your data.

Navigating in the Query Screen

There are some navigating keys you need to know when using the Query screen. A complete list appears in Table 10.1. The most important ones deserve some extra explanation. The special keys that move you from skeleton to skeleton are **<F3> Previous** and **<F4> Next**. The **<F3>** key takes you to the previous skeleton, and **<F4>** takes you to the next skeleton. Try pressing

<F4> Next. The cursor moves from the pothandle of the INVENTRY skeleton to the pothandle of the view skeleton. Move the cursor back to the INVENTRY database file skeleton by pressing **<F3> Previous**.

Table 10.1. *A summary of the keystrokes available in query-by-example*

Keystroke	*Action*
<F1>	Help.
<Shift>-<F1>	Display a pick list of field names, example variable names, functions, and operators to help build expressions in file skeletons, the Calc'd Flds skeleton, and the condition box.
<F2>	For view queries, perform query and BROWSE data. For update queries, BROWSE data of target file. **<F2>** on an update query does not perform the query.
<F3>	Go to previous object. If at first object, go to last object.
<F4>	Go to next object. If at last object, go to first object.
<F5>	When inside calculated field, file, or view skeleton, add/remove field from view.
<F6>	When inside a view skeleton, extend select one field at a time.
<F7>	When inside a view skeleton, move field.
<F9>	Zoom/Unzoom.
<F10>	Open the pull-down menu that was used last.
<Ctrl>-<End>	Save and exit.
<Ctrl>-<PgDn>	Go to last row in current column.
<Ctrl>-<PgUp>	Go to first row in current column.
<Ctrl>-<Return>	Save and continue.
<Del>	Delete one character.

Keystroke	*Action*
<Up arrow>	Go to previous line.
<Down arrow>	Go to next line.
<Left arrow>	Move one character left.
<Right arrow>	Move one character right.
<Ctrl>-<Left arrow>	Move left one word.
<Ctrl>-<Right arrow>	Move right one word.
<PgDn>	Go to next page of file skeletons.
<PgUp>	Go to previous page of file skeletons.
<Home>	Move cursor to pothandle in file skeleton or move to leftmost field in view skeleton.
<End>	Move to last column.
<Tab>	Move right one column.
<Shift>-<Tab>	Move left one column.

To move from field to field within a skeleton, use the **<Tab>** and **<Shift>-<Tab>** key combination. The **<Tab>** key takes you forward in your fields, and the **<Shift>-<Tab>** combination takes you to previous fields in your skeleton. Press the **<Tab>** key now. The cursor moves from the pothandle into the first field (COMPONENT). Press the **<Tab>** key three more times. The cursor is now in the COST field. Move the cursor back to the pothandle by pressing **<Shift>-<Tab>** four times.

An important key is **<F9> Zoom**. When you are typing in a field area and you run out of room, the area automatically pans to the left and right. There may be times when you'll want to see more characters at once than are displayed in the entry area. The **<F9>** key zooms the area into a much larger area, approximately 78 characters across by 12 lines down. This usually gives you enough space to type anything you want. Press **<F9> Zoom** to open a zoom window. Pressing **<F9> Zoom** again shrinks the area back to its original size.

The **<F10> Menu** key gives you access to the five menus at the top of the screen, as it does in all work surfaces.

Selecting Fields

You can tell if a field is in the view skeleton by looking at the field in the database file skeleton. If there is a downward-pointing arrow in the field box to the left of the field name, then the field is included in the view skeleton. Whatever is included in the view skeleton also appears in BROWSE or EDIT screens or in your reports. You can have as few as one field in the view skeleton, or as many as all the fields in the database file skeletons plus any calculated fields.

You can decide which fields will appear in the view skeleton and in what order. Right now, all the fields in the INVENTRY file appear in the view skeleton. This is the default when you create a query and have previously selected a database file. Four fields are shown in the view skeleton. There is a maximum of four fields showing in the view skeleton at one time.

Because you normally start with all fields in the view skeleton, you actually select fields by eliminating unwanted fields. To remove a field from the view skeleton, you can move the cursor to the same field in the file skeleton and press **<F5>**. You also can press **<F5>** on a field in the file skeleton to add that field to the view skeleton. For the queries you're about to design, just use the view file the way it is, with all the fields selected. At the end of this chapter, you will learn how to manipulate the view fields.

Query Sorts

So far you have selected a database file to begin your query, and you have placed fields into the view file. The next step is to decide how to display your data records. Choosing fields to be sorted determines the order in which your records will be displayed. If you already have indexes, you can use them in place of a sort. As you learned in Chapter 7, when an actual database file is sorted, dBASE IV makes a copy of the original file; the data is rearranged in that new file. In a query, dBASE IV creates a temporary database file and the data is rearranged in the temporary file. Because you save the query commands, you can recreate the database file at any time.

Forming the Question

You are about to make your first request: "Show me my data sorted by BRAND in alphabetical order." Remember, all requests or questions are formed by placing query directives in the entry areas below the field names in the file skeletons. You don't really ask an English-like question. In this example, you are working with only one skeleton, INVENTRY. Because the request asks dBASE IV to sort the data by BRAND in alphabetical order (ascending), you must tell dBASE IV to sort the data in the BRAND field.

The first step is always to move the cursor to the field you are going to work with in the file skeleton. In this case it's BRAND. So press **<Tab>** or **<Shift>-<Tab>** to move the cursor to BRAND. Because you don't know what to put in the entry area, let dBASE IV do it automatically. Make sure your cursor is in the INVENTRY skeleton in the BRAND field. Press **<Alt>-F** to open the Fields menu. This menu contains options for work with fields and data sorts. Select `Sort on this field` by typing `S`. The sort box opens on the work surface.

Depending on your data, select either ASCII or Dictionary from the sort box. Generally, if your data is character data made up of mixed case (upper and lower), choose Dictionary. Otherwise, it probably doesn't matter which you choose. Move the cursor to `Ascending Dictionary`. The screen should look like Figure 10.2. Press **<Enter>**.

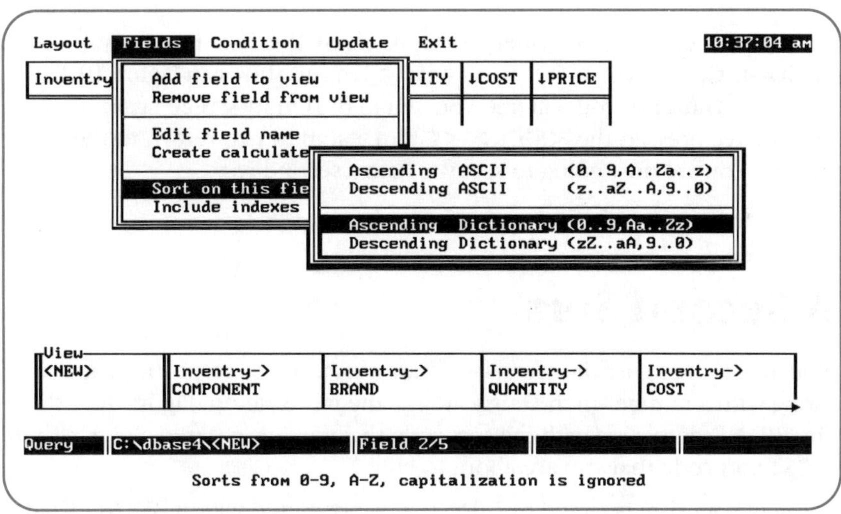

Figure 10.2. *Choosing the sort type*

When you press **<Enter>**, the code `AscDict1` appears in the BRAND box telling you that Ascending Dictionary has been selected. Press **<F2>** to see that your data has been rearranged into BRAND name order. This screen is shown in Figure 10.3.

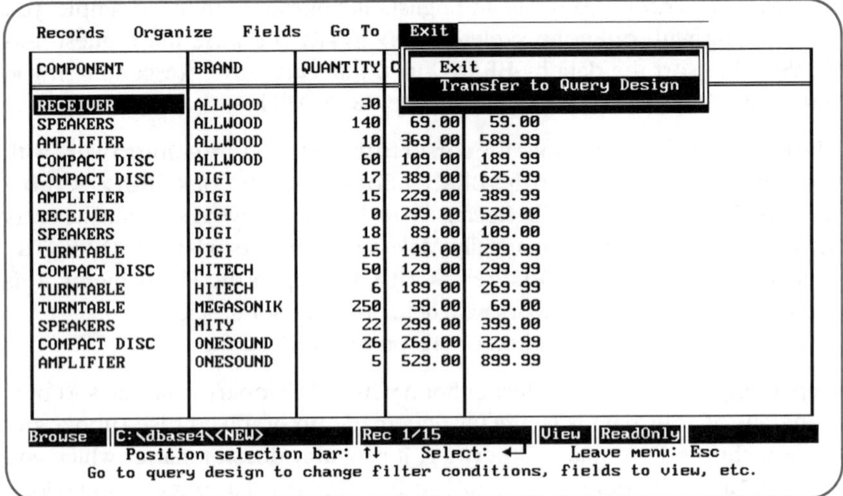

Figure 10.3. *Return to the Query work surface from BROWSE*

To transfer back to the Query Design, open the Exit menu by pressing **<Alt>-E**. Choose `Transfer to Query Design`, as shown in Figure 10.3. After pressing **<Enter>**, you will find yourself in the Query screen again. You also could have pressed the **<Shift>-<F2> Design** key to return to the Query screen. You are now going to sort the data a second way.

A Second Sort

You don't have to use the menus to create a sort. You can type the proper code along with a number in the entry area of the file skeleton. Figure 10.4 shows the BRAND entry area with the sort code that you just entered along with the COST sort code that you are about to enter.

Though your data is sorted by BRAND, it is not sorted within BRAND. That is, the DIGI equipment is in no special order. In Chapter 7 you learned about sorts within sorts. Now, sort each group of BRANDs by the highest cost. This means that you want an additional sort by COST in highest to lowest order.

Move the cursor to the COST column. Select `Sort on this field` in the Fields menu. The sort box opens up on the work surface. This time select `Descending ASCII` because it doesn't matter whether it's Dictionary or ASCII, but it does matter that it is a descending sort—you want the sequence to be highest to lowest. The characters `Dsc2` appear in the COST entry area. This tells you that it is in descending order and that it is the second sort of the query.

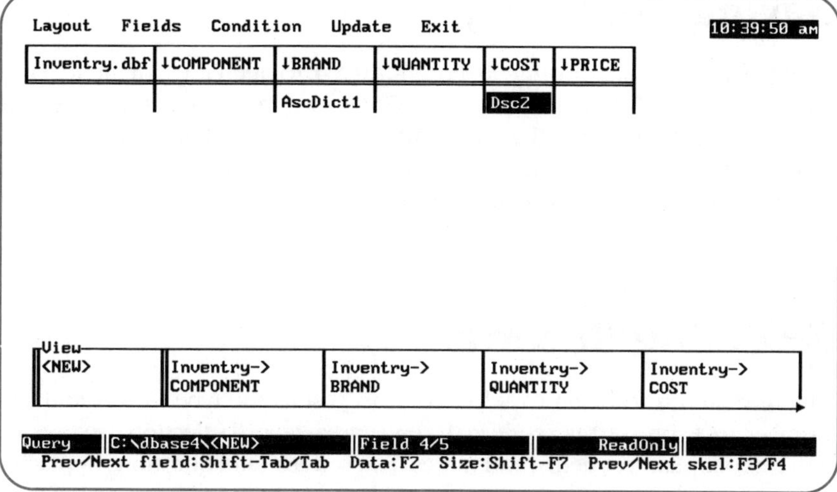

Figure 10.4. *Sorting by ascending BRAND and descending COST*

Press **<F2>** to see how the sorted data looks. Your data is now sorted by BRAND. Notice also that they are grouped from highest to lowest cost, as shown in Figure 10.5. Return once again to the Query screen by pressing **<Shift>-<F2>**.

Records Organize Fields Go To Exit

COMPONENT	BRAND	QUANTITY	COST	PRICE
AMPLIFIER	ALLWOOD	10	369.00	589.99
RECEIVER	ALLWOOD	30	169.00	289.00
COMPACT DISC	ALLWOOD	60	109.00	189.99
SPEAKERS	ALLWOOD	140	69.00	59.00
COMPACT DISC	DIGI	17	389.00	625.99
RECEIVER	DIGI	0	299.00	529.00
AMPLIFIER	DIGI	15	229.00	389.99
TURNTABLE	DIGI	15	149.00	299.99
SPEAKERS	DIGI	18	89.00	109.00
TURNTABLE	HITECH	6	189.00	269.99
COMPACT DISC	HITECH	50	129.00	299.99
TURNTABLE	MEGASONIK	250	39.00	69.00
SPEAKERS	MITY	22	299.00	399.00
AMPLIFIER	ONESOUND	5	529.00	899.99
COMPACT DISC	ONESOUND	26	269.00	329.99

Browse C:\dbase4\<NEW> Rec 1/15 View ReadOnly

Figure 10.5. *Database sorted by BRAND and COST*

Saving the Query

Save the query before moving on. Press **<Alt>-E** to open the Exit menu. Press `S` to select `Save this query and Exit`. When you are asked for the name, type `INVSORT`, for the name of the query. After the query has been saved, you are returned to the Control Center. Because you saved the query, it now appears in the Queries panel of the Control Center.

Selecting Records

The next step is to begin to select records. Just as the type of sort and sort number are expressed as a code in the entry area, record selection is expressed in terms of operators, fields, and values. You can ask valid questions by placing these in the entry areas of the database file field skeleton. Examples of valid questions that you will be asking dBASE IV in the next few pages are:

- >=300
- "TURNTABLE"
- <PRICE
- $"HARTFORD"
- Sounds like "Cary"

Whenever you select records, think of the query as a request. Although in dBASE IV you phrase requests or questions by entering selection criteria in the entry areas of the affected fields, you can think of these requests in more human terms.

In English the requests can be simple, like: "Show all the records whose list prices are over $300."

They also can be complicated requests, such as: "Show all the turntables and receivers whose gross margins are more than $125, sorted by brand name."

Queries on your data will vary depending on the data type. Numeric queries are probably the easiest because numbers can't be confused with variable names as character values can. Numeric queries can be one number, a range of numbers, or sometimes a list of numbers. When phrasing character queries, you must enclose the values in quotes to differentiate them from variables with the same name. You also will learn that there are several special operators you can use with character variables besides greater than, less than, and equal to. In the next couple of sections of this chapter, you are going to look at several different character and numeric queries.

Character Queries

As you know from previous experience in this book, character data is always enclosed in quotes to avoid conflict with variable names. With this in mind, get started right away with your first character query of this section.

Begin with a simple query. Start a new query and type `"TURNTABLE"` in the COMPONENT entry area. Make sure you enter the word TURNTABLE in quotes and uppercase letters, as shown in Figure 10.6. Press **<F2>** and you will see only your turntables listed. If the system beeps and doesn't display any turntables, dBASE IV hasn't found any records. A box showing `no records selected` will appear. Maybe you typed it wrong or forgot to put it in capital letters or in quotes. Transfer back to the Query screen when you are finished, by pressing **<Shift>-<F2>**.

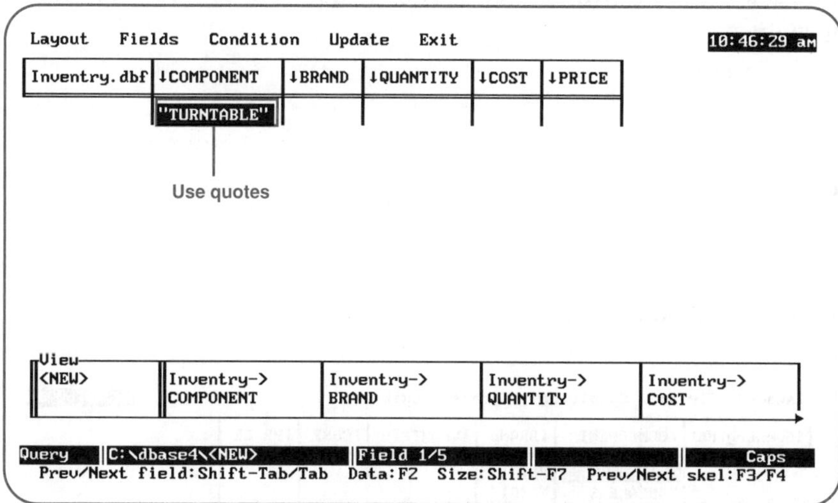

Figure 10.6. *Selecting the TURNTABLE records*

Complex Character Queries

Suppose that you want to see all the records for TURNTABLE and SPEAKERS. You can't put both values on the same line because that says: Show me all the records whose value of COMPONENT is "TURNTABLE" and "SPEAKERS".

Because each record has only one value for the COMPONENT field, you would never get any records. In numeric queries, you can request a range of values. In character queries, you request a list of values. You always join these with OR by placing them on different lines. The request is really: Show me all the records whose value of COMPONENT is "TURNTABLE" *or* "SPEAKERS".

To do this, make sure the cursor is in the component box on TURNTABLE. Press the **<Down arrow>** to open a new line, and type "SPEAKERS". If you look at your data now, you will see more records.

How about getting a little more detailed? Suppose you want to see all the TURNTABLES and SPEAKERS that were made by DIGI. With "TURNTABLE" entered on the first line of COMPONENT and "SPEAKERS" entered on the second line of COMPONENT, enter "DIGI" on both lines of BRAND. Why both lines of BRAND? Because you cannot put parentheses around queries in the QBE screen. You must somehow tell dBASE IV that you want to see the DIGI turntables and the DIGI speakers. This is equivalent to these dot prompt queries:

```
. DISPLAY ALL FOR BRAND='DIGI' .AND. COMPONENT =
  'TURNTABLE' OR BRAND='DIGI' .AND. COMPONENT =
  'SPEAKERS'
```

or

```
. DISPLAY ALL FOR BRAND= 'DIGI' .AND. (COMPONENT =
  'TURNTABLE' .OR. COMPONENT = 'SPEAKERS')
```

Figure 10.7 shows this query.

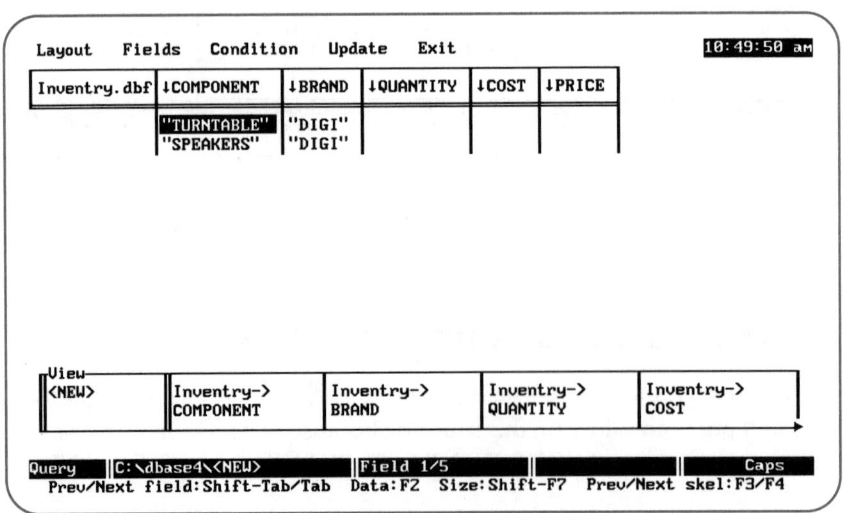

***Figure 10.7.** Selecting DIGI TURNTABLEs and SPEAKERs*

Character Operators

In character queries, you usually don't use operators such as greater than or less than, but you can use the operators shown in Table 10.2.

Table 10.2. *Operators to use in character queries*

#	Not equal to
$	Contained in
Like	Pattern match
Sounds like	Soundex match

The other operators available in character queries help you see different portions of your data.

Use the # (not equal to) or <> operators to see everything but the value you enter. For example, entering #"DIGI" in the BRAND entry area shows you everything but the DIGI equipment.

The $ (contains) operator is useful when you have a lot of data that is similar but does not match exactly. Suppose some of your COMPONENT data contains the value TURNTABLE but other items contain the word TURNTABLES. Maybe others are spelled wrong and contain TURNTABELS. Still others may be entered as RECORD TURNTABLES. You could list each of these entries on separate lines, but you would still not be assured of matching all the values. If you enter `$ "Turnt"` in the COMPONENT entry area, dBASE IV will find all the records whose COMPONENT contains the value `Turnt`. It doesn't matter where `Turnt` occurs—in the beginning, middle, or end of the value—as long as it is somewhere in the value.

Another example use of the $ is with the names of cities. If you had city data and wanted to find all the cities in Connecticut that contained *Hartford*—which would include East Hartford, West Hartford, and just plain Hartford—you could use the entry `$ "Hartford"`. As long as the characters *Hartford* were found somewhere in the value, the record would be selected.

Another variation of this is the `Like` operator. It lets you enter wildcards in an expression to find a value. In a hypothetical example, suppose you are looking for an inventory item that is identified by a code instead of its COMPONENT and BRAND. The code consists of two characters followed by three codes, like:

AB-CCA

CA-ABC

SO-AAB

You need to find all the records where the first two characters of the code are AB. You can't use the $ operator because AB is found in all of those variables. Instead, you can use the Like operator. The Like operator contains two wildcard symbols, * and ?. The ? symbol takes the place of a single character. If you were looking for the first two positions as AB, you would enter the following:

```
Like "AB-???"
```

This tells dBASE IV to select all records whose value for that field begins with AB and contains any three characters after that. You also can use the wildcard * in the following way:

```
Like "AB-*"
```

The * wildcard says anything else is acceptable for any length. Generally, you use the * to represent many characters, and you use it at the beginning or end of a search pattern.

The last character operator to learn is the `Sounds Like` operator. This operator uses a method known as SOUNDEX to see if something sounds like something else when spoken. A good example is names. If you were looking for a person named Cary in a large database of names and weren't sure how it was spelled, you could enter:

```
Sounds Like "Cary"
```

This would return such spellings as:

```
Cary

Carrie

Carry
```

Numeric Queries

Numeric queries are usually very simple because you are placing only numbers and operators in the entry area. Some of the operators that work with numbers are shown in Table 10.3.

Table 10.3. *Operators to use in number queries*

>	Greater than
<	Less than
=	Equal to
<> or #	Not equal to
<=	Less than or equal to
>=	Greater than or equal to

The first question you will ask is: "How many items do we sell whose list price is over $300.00?"

You need to place the filter, >300, in the entry area of the PRICE field in the INVENTRY skeleton. One of the easiest ways is to simply type it in.

Create a new query with the INVENTRY database file selected. All your fields should be in the view skeleton. Move the cursor to the PRICE field in the INVENTRY skeleton and type `>300`. That's all there is to it. When you press **<F2>** you will see only the data for those records whose value in the price field is over 300. How about if the amount you wanted to see was greater than or equal to 300? You would enter:

```
>=300
```

in the entry area.

Removing Old Queries

As you enter new record selections, make sure you erase old ones or you may get results you don't want. In the course of this chapter, we are showing you how to build several different queries. In reality, you would probably start each query in a new screen, unless you were looking at smaller and smaller groups of your data. Erase old queries by highlighting the query file at the Control Center and pressing the **<Del>** key a sufficient number of times or by pressing **<Ctrl>-U** once.

Complex Numeric Queries

Ranges

What would happen if you wanted to ask the question: "Show me all the records whose list prices are between 300 and 400"?

This requires entering a range in the entry area. You enter ranges for numeric variables by separating the values with a comma. Enter:

```
>300,<400
```

in the PRICE entry area. Queries placed on the same line are joined together with .AND. The above expression says: "Show me the data whose price is greater than 300 *and* less than 400." Figure 10.8 shows this request entered into the PRICE entry area.

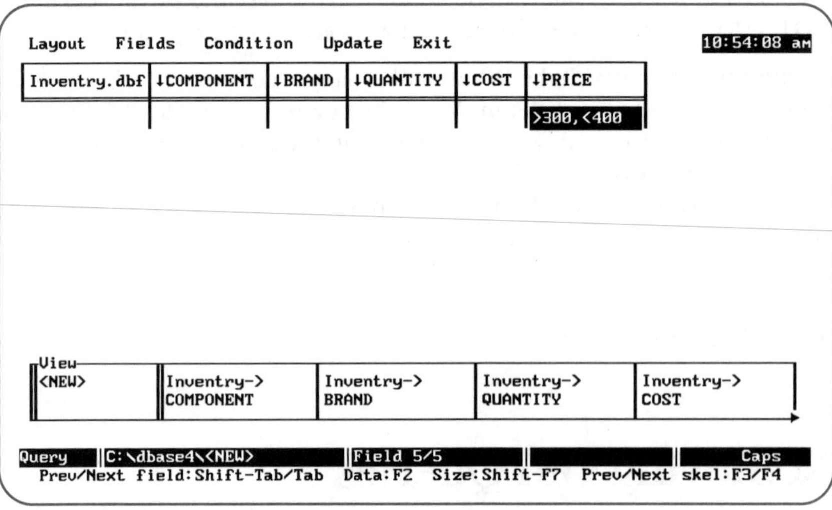

Figure 10.8. *Selecting PRICEs between $300 and $400*

Delete the query in the PRICE entry area so that you can start a new query on a clean screen.

Suppose you wanted to see which items had a COST of less than 200 and a PRICE of less then 300. You are again asking an *and* question. Enter `< 200` in the COST entry area and enter `< 300` in the PRICE entry area.

Now take a look at an OR question. If you wanted to know which items had a very low cost or a very high cost, you might ask the following question: "Show me the records where the COST is <100 or >500."

Ask OR questions by placing the ranges to be selected on separate lines in the file skeleton entry area. Try this question. Make sure that your old questions are removed or that you have started a new query. Move the cursor to the COST entry area. First enter `<100`. Next, press the **<Down arrow>**. A new line opens in the entry area. Enter `>500`. Press **<F2>** now to see your high- and low-cost items. By the way, you just asked for the equivalent of the dot prompt command:

```
. DISPLAY FOR COST < 100 .OR. > 500
```

Figure 10.9 shows an OR query, and Figure 10.10 shows the result.

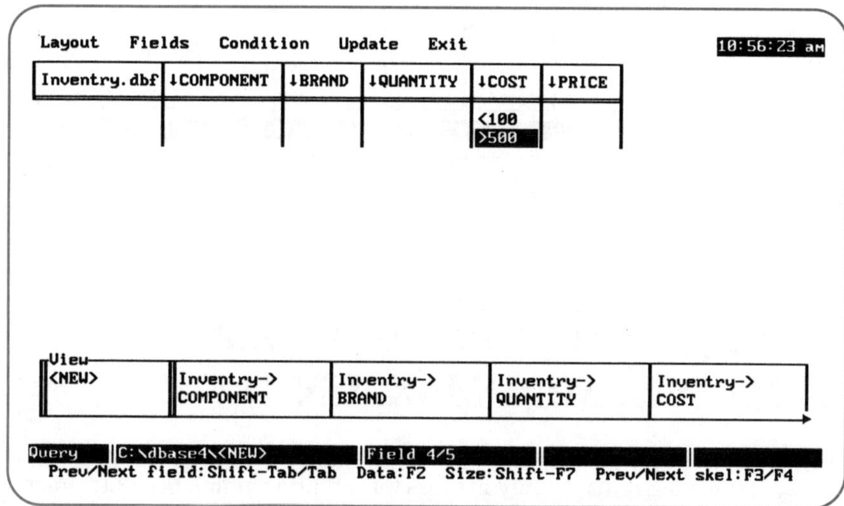

Figure 10.9. *Selecting COSTs less than $100 or greater than $500*

If you want complex queries, just remember that everything on the same line is joined together with ANDs, and entries on separate lines are joined together with ORs.

In this final example, use another variable as a value instead of a number. For example, to verify that all the records' values of COST were lower than the values of the PRICE, in order to make sure that you weren't selling any items below cost, enter the following in the COST entry area:

```
<PRICE
```

This tells dBASE to display all the records whose value of COST is lower than the value of PRICE. Of course, this shows you all the records for which this is true. You really want to see all the records for which this isn't true. Just enter:

```
>=PRICE
```

to see all the records that aren't selling at a profit.

```
Records   Organize   Fields   Go To   Exit

COMPONENT    BRAND       QUANTITY  COST     PRICE

AMPLIFIER    ONESOUND           5  529.00   899.99
SPEAKERS     DIGI              18   89.00   109.00
SPEAKERS     ALLWOOD          140   69.00    59.00
TURNTABLE    MEGASONIK        250   39.00    69.00

Browse  C:\dbase4\<NEW>    Rec 3/15    View
```

Figure 10.10. The results in BROWSE

Getting More from Your Data—SUM, AVG, MIN, MAX, CNT

In addition to sorting and selecting, there is a group of operators known as *Aggregate Operators* that allow you to ask for certain accumulations of numeric values. These include:

- SUM Totaling
- AVG Averaging
- MIN Minimum value
- MAX Maximum value
- CNT The number of records

Unlike the usual filtering, these operators work to produce a single record in the answer set that contains the requested aggregate value. Start a new query. Move your cursor to the QUANTITY field and enter `SUM` as shown in Figure 10.11. Now press **<F2>** and you will see the result of the query. The SUM of the quantities is 664. Your screen should look like Figure 10.12.

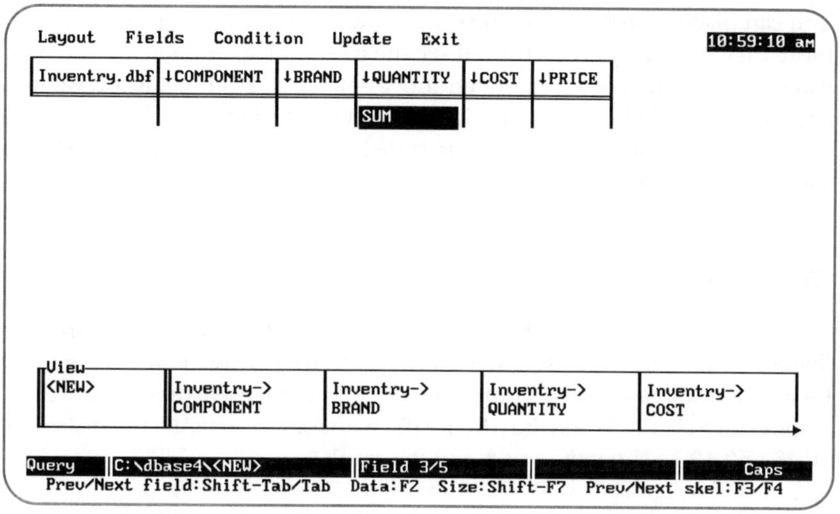

```
Layout   Fields   Condition   Update   Exit                      10:59:10 am
Inventry.dbf ↓COMPONENT ↓BRAND ↓QUANTITY ↓COST ↓PRICE
                               SUM

View
<NEW>   Inventry->   Inventry->   Inventry->   Inventry->
        COMPONENT    BRAND        QUANTITY     COST
Query  C:\dbase4\<NEW>   Field 3/5                          Caps
 Prev/Next field:Shift-Tab/Tab  Data:F2  Size:Shift-F7  Prev/Next skel:F3/F4
```

Figure 10.11. *Summing the QUANTITY*

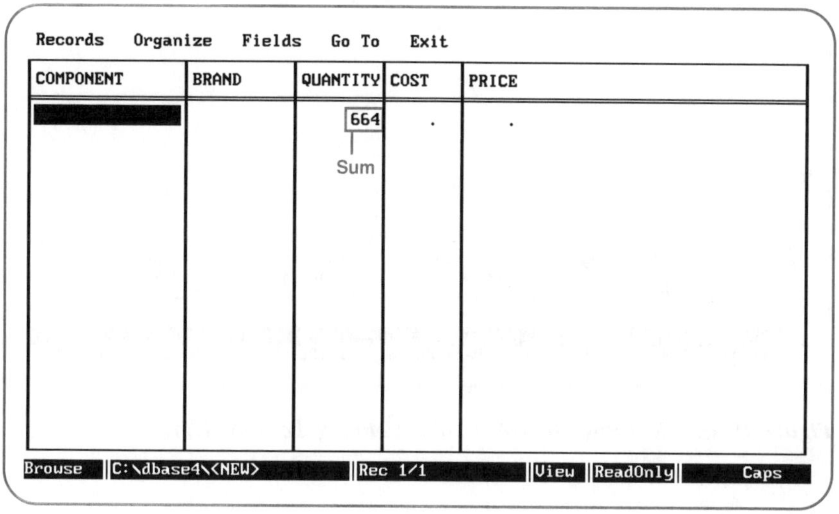

```
Records   Organize   Fields   Go To   Exit
COMPONENT   BRAND   QUANTITY COST   PRICE
                         664    .       .
                         Sum
Browse  C:\dbase4\<NEW>   Rec 1/1   View ReadOnly   Caps
```

Figure 10.12. *The results*

If you add a selection criterion to the query, you'll see the SUM for that selection. For example, enter "DIGI" in the BRAND entry area. Now press **<F2>**. You should see only the sum of the DIGI equipment.

You can place aggregate operators in any numeric field. If you have them in more than one entry area, you will see the results of all of them at once. You can have only one aggregate operator per entry area at a time. If you want to see the SUM and AVG of a numeric field, you must run two separate queries. You also can use some of the operators such as MIN and MAX in date fields to show the oldest or newest data.

Grouping

There is an operator that lets you see your information grouped by another field. For example, suppose you want to see the total of the quantities in stock for each brand regardless of component type. You can place the operator SUM in the QUANTITY field and the GROUP BY operator in the BRAND field. Figures 10.13 and 10.14 show the query and the result.

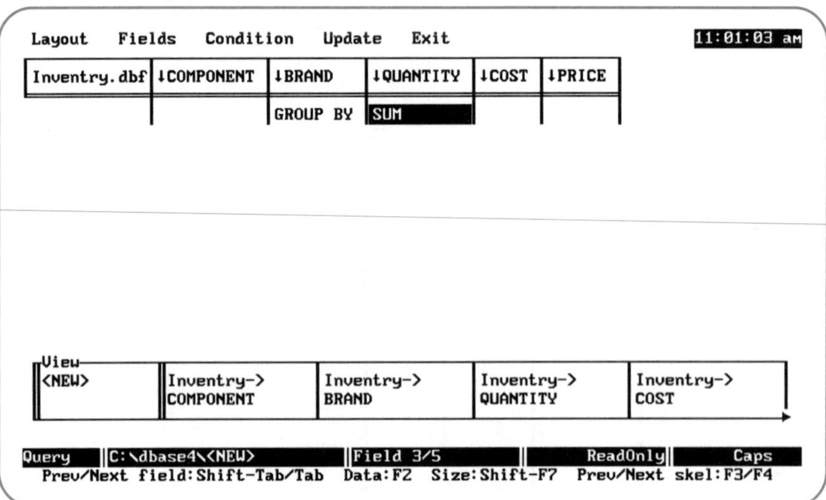

Figure 10.13. *GROUPing BY BRAND and SUMming the QUANTITYs*

GROUP BY automatically sorts your data into ascending sequence so you can see your data in the proper groups.

Calculated Fields

It is possible to look at data that doesn't exist in your database file but can be created from data contained in your database file. This requires creating new fields known as calculated fields. These fields exist only during a query, or with operations that use the query.

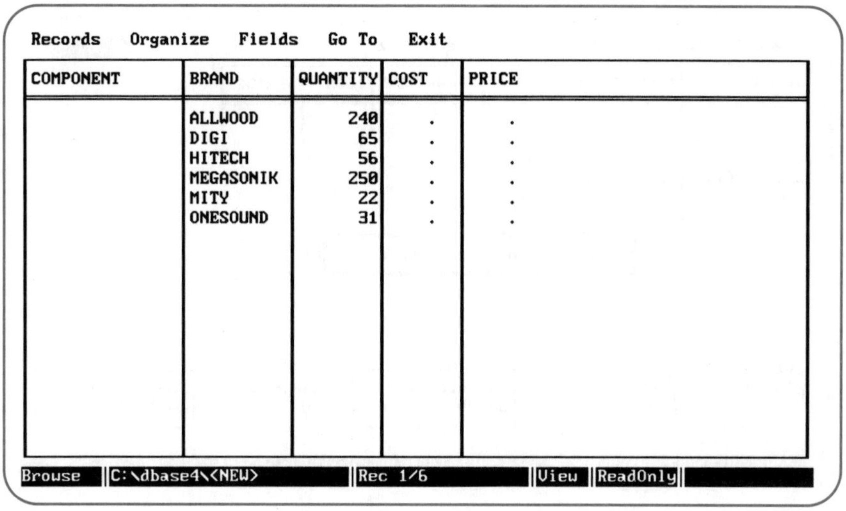

Records Organize Fields Go To Exit

COMPONENT	BRAND	QUANTITY	COST	PRICE
	ALLWOOD	240	.	.
	DIGI	65	.	.
	HITECH	56	.	.
	MEGASONIK	250	.	.
	MITY	22	.	.
	ONESOUND	31	.	.

Browse C:\dbase4\<NEW> Rec 1/6 View ReadOnly

***Figure 10.14.** The results*

Once again, start a new query with the INVENTRY file active. You will use this query later in this chapter, so be sure to start a new query and actually create the calculated field as instructed. You create calculated fields with an option on the Fields menu. Press **<Alt>-F** to open the Fields menu, and then select `Create Calculated Field`. A new file skeleton appears called `Calc'd Flds`. In this skeleton, you can use either the top or the bottom entry area. The bottom entry area is for sort and selection criteria just like the database file skeleton. You use the top entry area to give the field a name and to tell dBASE IV how to derive or calculate its value.

When you have finished creating the calculation, dBASE IV will ask you for a name. As an example, create a new field that calculates the retail inventory value of each item. The inventory value is calculated by multiplying the PRICE*QUANTITY. Assume that you want to call that variable VALUE. Enter:

```
PRICE*QUANTITY
```

in the upper entry box, as shown in Figure 10.15. Now add it to the view skeleton by pressing **<F5>**. dBASE IV asks you for the field's name. Call it VALUE. Enter `VALUE` and press **<Enter>**. It is added to the view skeleton out of sight at the far right side.

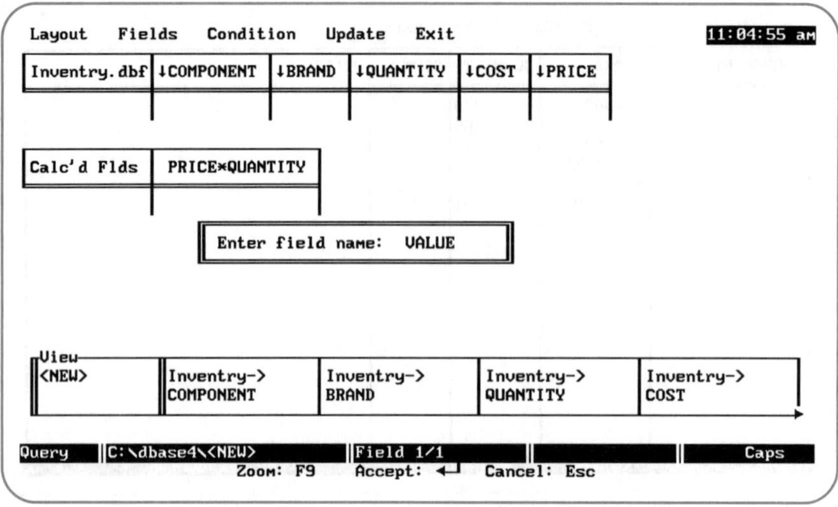

Figure 10.15. *Creating a new calculated field called VALUE*

Building Expressions with the Pick List

At some point in time, you may want to create complex calculated fields for which you'll need to use certain functions or operators that you haven't memorized. dBASE IV provides a *Pick box* to help you create your calculations and expressions.

You're going to enter COST*QUANTITY to get the inventory at cost, but you'll do it a little differently this time. You are going to use the dBASE IV expression builder to enter the rest of the expression.

If you look at the bottom of the screen, you will see a list of function keys. You are going to use the function key combination **<Shift>-<F1>**. This is known as the Pick key because it allows you to build expressions by choosing its components from menus, instead of typing out the entire expression from memory. There are several good reasons to use this method.

Suppose you have several fields and you can never remember what you called them. If you look at the INVENTRY.DBF file skeleton at the top of the screen, you will notice that only the first three fields are showing. You can get to them, as you have learned, by using the **<Tab>** key, but there is another way to find out what those field names are.

Did you call the retail price field PRICE or RETAIL? If you can't remember, you can't enter the formula to calculate total price. The Pick submenu will tell you.

Press **<Alt>-F** to open the Fields menu, and type `C` to select `Create a calculated field`. Make sure your cursor is in the upper entry box for the newly created calculated field. Press **<Shift>-<F1> Pick**. The Pick submenu should appear as in Figure 10.16.

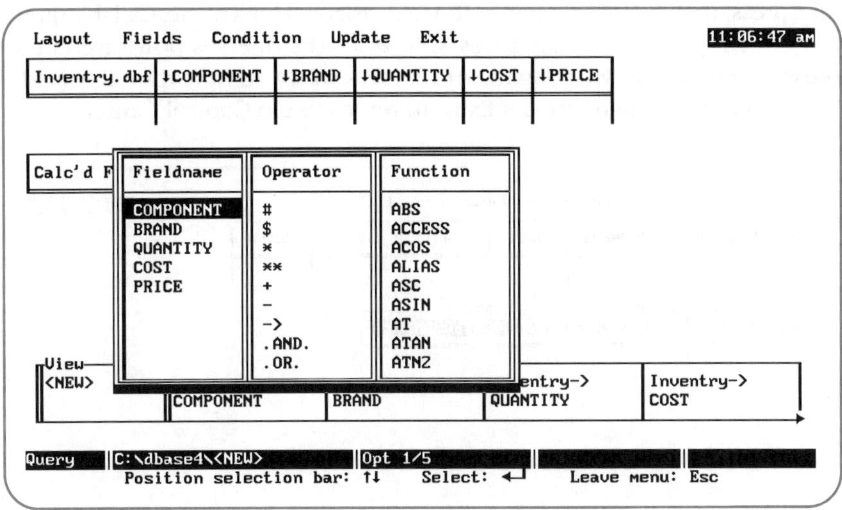

***Figure 10.16.** Using the Pick menu to create a calculated field*

The Pick submenu has three columns, labeled:

`Fieldname` `Operator` `Function`

Below each column is a list of all the possible choices. Move about in this menu box with the arrow keys. You are going to build the expression COST*QUANTITY. Move the cursor to COST in the `Fieldname` box and press **<Enter>**. The field name COST is automatically placed in the calculated field box and the pick menu goes away.

Press **<Shift>-<F1>** again to display the Pick submenu. Now move the cursor to the third choice in the `Operator` column. This is the multiplication symbol. Press **<Enter>** and again the asterisk appears in the calculated field box next to the field COST. Finally press **<Shift>-<F1>** again and choose QUANTITY in the `Fieldname` box. You have now completed the expression.

Your screen has a new calculated field that is yet unnamed. Name the field by selecting `Edit field name` from the Fields menu. Type in `COSTVAL` as the name of the field. The name appears above the calculation.

You need to add the field to the view skeleton. Whenever you create a calculated field in the Query screen, you are telling dBASE IV only that the field exists and how to calculate it. You still haven't told dBASE IV that you want to use it to view your data. Until you tell dBASE IV to place the field in the view skeleton, you will not be able to see it in an EDIT or a BROWSE screen. Press **<F5>** to place a field in the view skeleton.

Save the results before you go on. Press **<Alt>-L** to open the Layout menu, and then press `S` to `Save this query`. dBASE IV asks you for a name. Call this query `INVCOST`. Type `INVCOST` and press **<Enter>**. The query is now saved in its present form, as shown in Figure 10.17. Press **<F2>** to view your new fields. When you are through, press **<Esc>** to return to the Control Center.

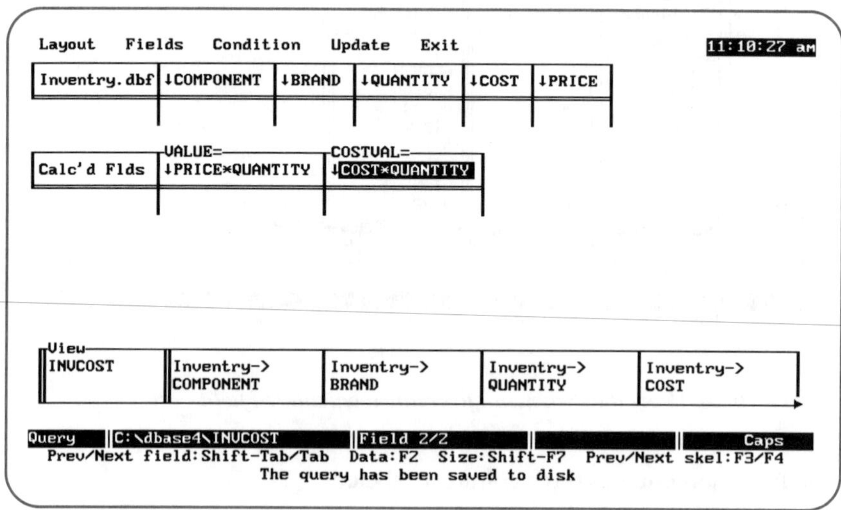

Figure 10.17. *Creating calculated fields in the Query screen*

Global Conditions

At some time, you may design a query that is extremely complicated. It may not make sense to enter selection criteria in several different fields, especially when multiple ANDs and ORs are needed. Sometimes a condition spans several database files and simply can't be accomplished by entering conditions in the field entry areas themselves. dBASE IV is the only product for personal computers on the market that features global condition boxes. They solve the problem by allowing you to create a selection criteria that affects all your database files.

Try an example of a global condition query. Continue to use the INVCOST query. Begin by pressing **<Alt>-C** to open the Condition menu. This menu has three choices. You can add the condition box, delete the condition box, or see the condition box on the screen after you have created it. Press **<Enter>** to select `Add condition box.`

You can write any type of query inside this box. For example, here is a request that combines many of the conditions you have already asked for: "Show me all the records for everything but turntables for all brands other than Hitech that have a cost of more than 200."

This query requires data from the COMPONENT, BRAND, VALUE, PRICE, and INVDATE fields. You could place each query criteria in each separate field entry area, but it may be easier to specify the whole query at once. Either by using the pick menus, or by simply typing it in, you can enter the following condition into the condition box:

```
COMPONENT # 'TURNTABLE' .AND. BRAND # 'HITECH' .AND.
   COST > 200
```

Figure 10.18 shows this condition box filled out.

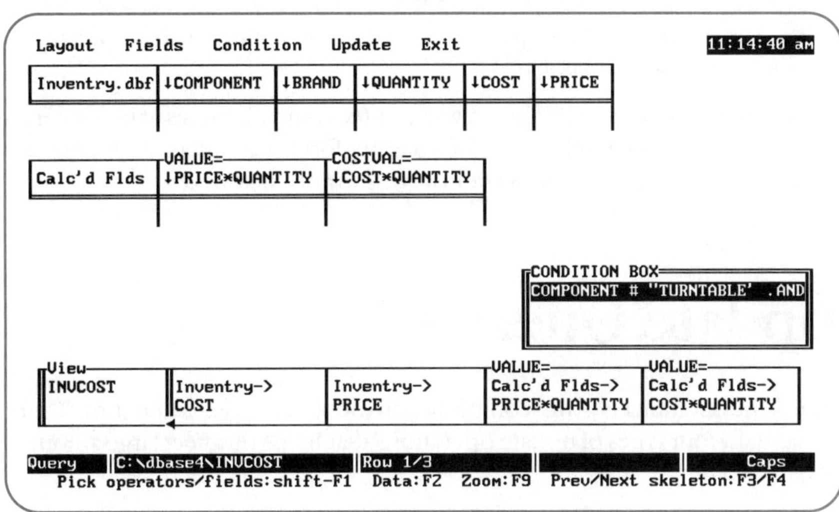

Figure 10.18. *Setting a global condition in a condition box*

This example purposely fills the condition box on three separate lines. You can zoom the condition box by pressing **<F9>**. Zooming gives you a screen 78 characters wide by 20 lines deep to handle the most complex queries possible.

Once out of zoom mode, delete the condition box by again pressing **<Alt>-C** and then pressing `D`. Your query is now in the form it was in before you added the condition box. This illustrates another reason for condition boxes. If you go to all the trouble of creating sorts, selecting fields, creating calculated fields, and setting up aggregate operators, you may want to try these formats with several record selection criteria. By using the global condition box, you can add complicated queries and then erase just the record selection portion much faster than having to go to many data fields and erasing selection criteria.

Suppose you wanted to see the sum of all the inventory valuations. You might think that you can place the aggregate operator SUM in the entry area of the calculated field VALUE. Well, you can't. In dBASE IV, only selection criteria can be placed in the entry area of the calculated field. So it is time to see the true power of queries.

Make sure you are in the Control Center. Place the cursor in the Queries panel in the entry INVCOST. If it is not active (above the line), then make it active by pressing **<Enter>**. With the cursor still on INVCOST, press **<Shift>-<F9>** to create a quick report. If you have a printer, press **<Enter>** to select `Begin printing`. All the numeric fields are automatically totaled, including the numeric calculated field. If you don't have a printer, you can view the report on the screen. The top two entries on the printing menu, which automatically pops up, give you that choice.

In the Reports chapter of this book, you will see some examples of how queries and reports interact and how even data entry forms can interact with queries to give you editing capabilities over only a portion of your data.

Update Queries

One of the last subjects of this comprehensive look at queries is updating. There are actually four types of update operations that help you affect large amounts of data at a time.

- APPEND Adds records from other files
- MARK Marks records for deletion
- REPLACE Changes data values in the database file
- UNMARK Removes marks from records

Updating takes two steps. The first step is to place the update operation in the pothandle of the file to be updated and determine which records will be affected and how. The second step is to execute the operation.

You can enter the update operation in the pothandle, or you can open the Update menu in the Query work surface to choose the update operation. Whichever way you choose, as soon as you place the update operation in the pothandle, dBASE IV tells you that the view skeleton will be deleted because the target of an update is usually the database file itself.

Creating an Update

Create a new query. Next, open the Update menu and choose `Specify update operation`. A submenu opens to let you choose the update operation. Figure 10.19 shows this menu on the work surface.

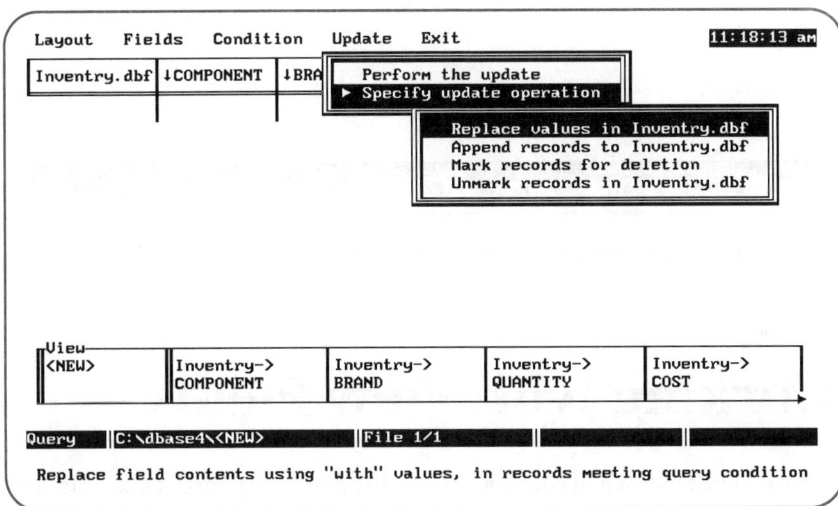

Figure 10.19. *The Update menu*

Select `Replace values in Inventry.dbf`. The word `Replace` appears in the pothandle, and dBASE IV asks you to confirm that you want to proceed with an update operation. Choose `Proceed` and you are ready to enter your criteria.

You determine the records you want to affect by entering selection criteria in exactly the same way as with record selection. Imagine that you want to raise the list price of all DIGI equipment by 15 percent. To accomplish this, enter "`DIGI`" in the COMPONENT entry area, and enter:

```
with PRICE * 1.15
```

in the PRICE entry box, as shown in Figure 10.20. When you finish, you usually would open the Update menu and choose `Perform the update`. Don't do this now, but if you had done so, you would have found that all your data for DIGI equipment would have the PRICE field increased by 15 percent.

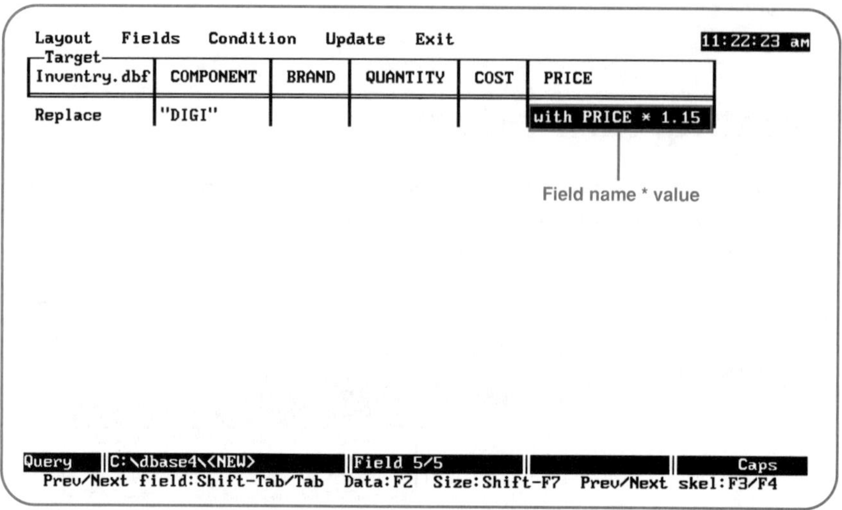

Figure 10.20. *Updating the DIGI PRICEs by 15 percent*

Working with View Fields

There may be times when you won't want all the fields in your database file. You also may want to change the order in which they appear when you use the BROWSE or EDIT modes. With the use of just a few keys, you can add, delete, or change the order of your view fields. Press **<Esc>** to get back to the Control Center, if you are not already there. Create a new query with the INVENTRY database file selected.

Adding and Deleting View Fields

Begin by removing the COST field from the view skeleton. Because all operations take place in the database file skeletons, move the cursor to the COST field in the INVENTRY skeleton. After you move the cursor to the COST field, press **<F5>** once.

The COST field in the view skeleton flashes several times and then disappears into the INVENTRY skeleton. The space from the now-missing field is closed up in the view skeleton, and the down arrow in the COST field of the INVENTRY skeleton disappears to indicate that it is no longer in the view skeleton.

Remove one more field and then add it again. Move the cursor to the BRAND field. Press **<F5>**. Again, the field disappears from the view skeleton. Add the field again by pressing **<F5>**. This time the field scoots to the right. It has been added to the end of the view skeleton, as shown in Figure 10.21.

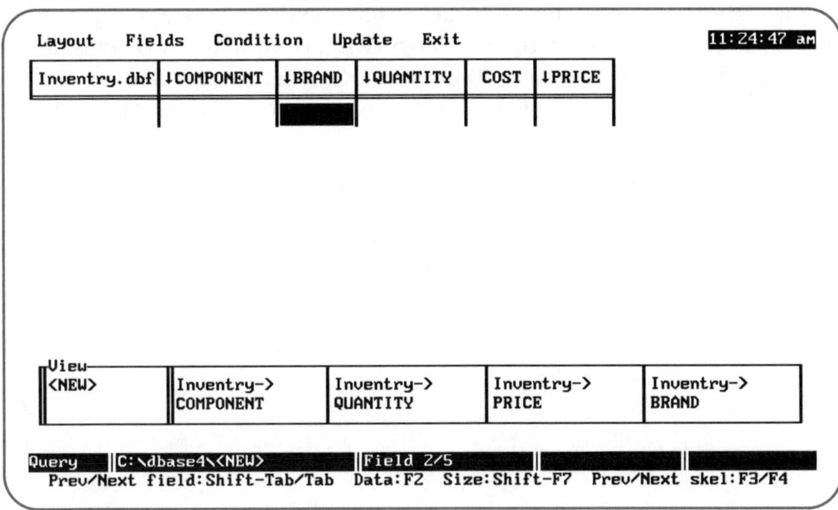

Figure 10.21. *Changing fields around in the view skeleton*

It's time to see the results of your work. Press **<F2> Data** to view the data. As you can see in the BROWSE screen, the COST field is nowhere in sight and the BRAND field is displayed last. The COST field is not gone. It is simply not displayed on the BROWSE screen. If you add a new record at this time, you will not be able to add data to the COST field. In order to transfer back to the Query Design, open the Exit menu and choose `Transfer to Query Design`. You will find yourself in the Query screen again. You also can press **<Shift>-<F2> Design** to return to the Query screen.

Changing the Order of Fields

The last thing to demonstrate is how to move fields in the view skeleton. Press **<F4>** so the cursor moves to the view skeleton. You will notice that the last line of the screen contains some navigation keys you haven't seen before. The

<F6> key selects fields. The **<F7>** key allows you to move them. Move the PRICE and BRAND fields so that they are first in the view skeleton. Place the cursor on the PRICE field in the view skeleton. In this skeleton the cursor moves along the top of the skeleton. There is no entry area in the view skeleton because it is simply a list of the fields to appear in the answer displayed with the BROWSE or EDIT screen. Press **<F6>** to begin the selection process. The field highlights. Press the **<Tab>** key to highlight the next field too. Both PRICE and BRAND should be highlighted. Press **<Enter>** to complete the selection process.

To move the fields: press the **<F7>** key to tell dBASE IV you are going to move the selected area. Press **<Shift>-<Tab>** twice, or until the two fields are in front of the COMPONENT field. Then press **<Enter>**. That's all there is to it. Press **<F2>** to again verify that your data is now in this order. Figure 10.22 shows this process in progress.

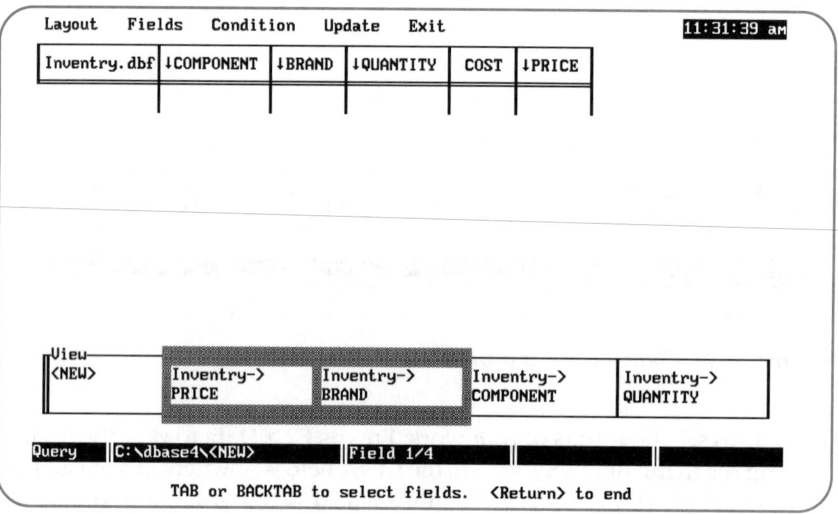

***Figure 10.22.** Moving multiple fields in the view skeleton*

Summary

In this chapter you learned many of the things that queries are used for:

- Selecting files
- Selecting fields

- Sorting
- Selecting records (filtering)
- Creating new calculated fields
- Aggregation and totaling (SUM, MIN, MAX, AVG)
- Grouping
- Updating (many records at once)

Queries can be very simple to construct and can provide you with instant information about your data. Think of each query as answering a question. Construct your queries a field at a time and first think about sorts, fields to be included in the query, and what data to look at. With this in mind, you'll soon be ready for anything.

Creating and using a query can be thought of as a step-by-step process.

1. Select your database file in the Control Center.
2. Create a new query.
3. Place the needed fields into the view skeleton.
4. Enter sort directions in the file skeletons.
5. Enter record selections in the file skeletons.
6. Create any new calculated fields.
7. Use the query in BROWSE, EDIT, or a custom report.

In this chapter you learned how queries are used for character and numeric data. In Chapter 11, you will see how date, logical, and memo fields are used. Chapter 12 will show you how queries are used for relating data from two or more database files.

chapter 11

Date, Logical, and Memo Fields

In this chapter, you will be looking at some characteristics of the special data types: date, logical, and memo fields. Date fields make it easy for you to perform data operations such as "date arithmetic" to determine the number of days between two dates, or the date when a number of days is added to an existing date. Memo fields allow you to store large amounts of text in a separate file maintained for you by dBASE IV. Logical fields are fields that can contain only one of two values—true or false. Logical fields have some special properties that make it possible to segregate data quickly and easily.

You'll create the new fields, enter data, and then use them in a variety of situations, including the dot prompt, to learn the special benefits of these three field types.

Creating Date, Logical, and Memo Fields

You'll start by adding a new field to the INVENTRY database file. Go to the Control Center and select the INVENTRY database file. Press **<Shift>-<F2> Design** to modify the database file structure. Your screen should now be showing the INVENTRY database file with the Organize menu opened. Press **<Esc>** to close the menu.

First insert a date field between the QUANTITY and COST fields. Move the cursor to the COST field and press **<Ctrl>-N** to insert a new field. Name the field INVDATE. Press **<Enter>** to move the cursor to the Field Type entry area. Press the **<Spacebar>** three times until `Date` appears in the box, or just type the letter D. Press **<Enter>** to finish entering the date field. dBASE IV automatically enters the field length of 8 for you.

Now create the logical field and place it after INVDATE. First move the cursor to the COST `Field name` area by pressing **<Enter>** as many times as necessary. Press the **<Ctrl>-N** keys to create a new field. Name this field ON_SALE. Remember to place an underscore between ON and SALE; field names cannot have any spaces. Press **<Enter>** to move to the `Field type` area. Type `L` for a logical field. Again dBASE IV automatically enters a field length. This time it's a length of 1.

The final field to enter will be called FEATURES. This memo field will be used by the store salespeople to retrieve the detailed specifications of the product. Press **<Down arrow>** to create a new field at the bottom of the screen. Name the new field FEATURES. Press **<Enter>** and then `M` for a memo field. The field length of 10 is automatically created just like the other field types.

You now have a database file that looks just like Figure 11.1. Press **<Ctrl>-<End>** to save this new database file structure. Keep the filename INVENTRY.

dBASE IV has returned you to the Control Center. You will enter data, after you read some details about these new fields.

Date Fields

Date is a special data type, designed to make working with dates as natural with a computer as without one. Although the Date type seems to be a necessary part of a database management system, not all systems offer it.

```
Layout   Organize   Append   Go To   Exit                        11:35:09 am
                                                    Bytes remaining:   3939
 Num  Field Name    Field Type   Width   Dec   Index

  1   COMPONENT     Character     15            N
  2   BRAND         Character     10            Y
  3   QUANTITY      Numeric        3      0     N
  4   INVDATE       Date           8            N
  5   ON_SALE       Logical        1            N
  6   COST          Numeric        7      2     N
  7   PRICE         Numeric        7      2     Y
  8   FEATURES      Memo          10            N

Database C:\dbase4\INVENTRY    Field 1/8                            Caps
          Enter the field name. Insert/Delete field:Ctrl-N/Ctrl-U
Field names begin with a letter and may contain letters, digits and underscores
```

Figure 11.1. *Modifying the INVENTRY database structure*

Why the fuss? Most of us are accustomed to working with dates in the more or less standard American format of MM/DD/YY. Europeans prefer a format of DD/MM/YY, whereas Japanese prefer the arrangement of YY/MM/DD. Computers favor the Japanese arrangement which, incidentally, is the standard date format proposed by the American National Standards Institute (ANSI).

Computers read from left to right. More importantly, they also make comparisons from left to right. Unless your software conforms to the ANSI standard or allows for some special adjustments, you cannot sort or compare dates and expect to get the correct result. The DATE field type solves this problem. The date is actually stored in a format that the computer prefers, but it is displayed in your preferred format. You don't even need to know that the computer has actually squirreled the information away in Urdu.

dBASE IV normally expects dates to be entered using American format of MM/DD/YY. You can, however, work with dates using the date formats of many other countries. The eleven date formats that can be specified in dBASE IV are shown in Table 11.1.

Table 11.1. *Date formats in dBASE IV*

Date type	*Format*
American	mm/dd/yy
ANSI	yy.mm.dd

continues

Table 11.1 continued

Date type	Format
British	dd/mm/yy
French	dd/mm/yy
German	dd.mm.yy
Italian	dd-mm-yy
Japan	yy/mm/dd
USA	mm-dd-yy
MDY	mm/dd/yy
DMY	dd/mm/yy
YMD	yy/mm/dd

Setting Date Formats

A special SET command allows you to choose from among these date formats. To work with dates in the French manner for example, use the command

```
. SET DATE FRENCH
```

from the dBASE IV dot prompt. You also can use the `Settings` choice of the Tools menu in the Control Center . When you select `Settings`, the Settings menu appears. You can use this menu to modify the date type. Figure 11.2 shows the Settings menu open on the desktop.

The two date choices in the panel let you select any of the possible date displays even if you don't know the names of the various types. You can just select the order of the month, day and year, and the type of separator. Separators can be a slash (/), dash (-), or period (.).

dBASE IV normally expects dates to be entered in the American manner. This is the default setting for the date format. If you always work with dates in some other specific format, include the DATE = command in the CONFIG.DB file (see appendixes).

What Century Is This?

dBASE IV assumes that you are interested in the twentieth century when you enter data. If you enter the year 01, you may be surprised to find that you have entered 1901 and not 2001. This has proved to be an annoyance to historians among others. If you need to work with dates in other than the twentieth century, you must set the CENTURY option ON.

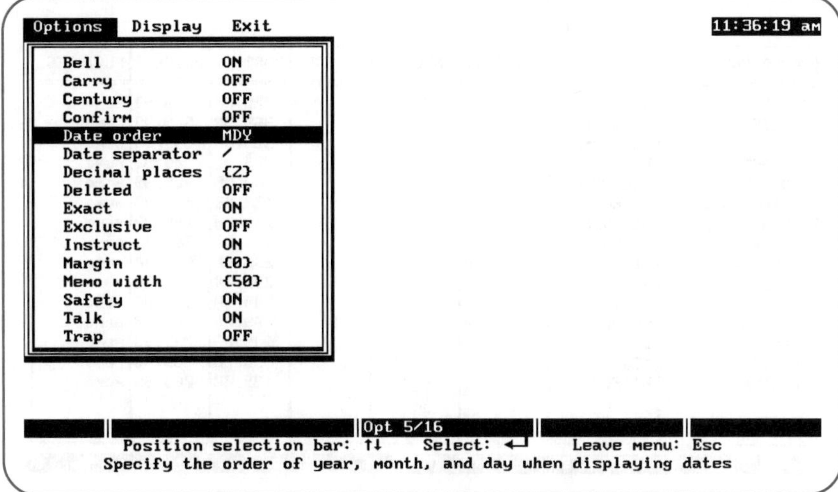

Figure 11.2. *Changing date settings*

The CENTURY option, like most other options, can be turned ON or OFF in several places. The first place is in the Tools menu of the Control Center under the Settings choice. If you look again at Figure 11.2, you will see the CENTURY setting. When the setting is OFF, you see the year displayed as two digits. When it is ON, you see all four digits of the year. Incidentally, dates are always stored in the ASCII format YYYYMMDD (the slashes are not stored). You don't have access to the first two digits of the year until you set CENTURY ON.

In the following examples, you'll use the American date format for data entry. The operations are identical to any other date format—only the appearance of the date is different. Leave the CENTURY option off to work with the two-digit century.

Date Data Entry

The BROWSE screen for this database file is shown as Figure 11.3. The date separators, the slashes, are already displayed; you do not enter them. You must, however, enter leading zeroes for single-digit date subfields.

Dates are validated upon entry. dBASE IV does not allow you to enter an invalid (nonexistent) date. An invalid date is not the same as an incorrect date. If you attempt to enter an invalid date, such as 15/27/91 (there is no fifteenth month), an error message displays on screen. You cannot move out of the date field until you enter a valid date. An important exception is the all-blanks date. You can skip over a date field without entering a value.

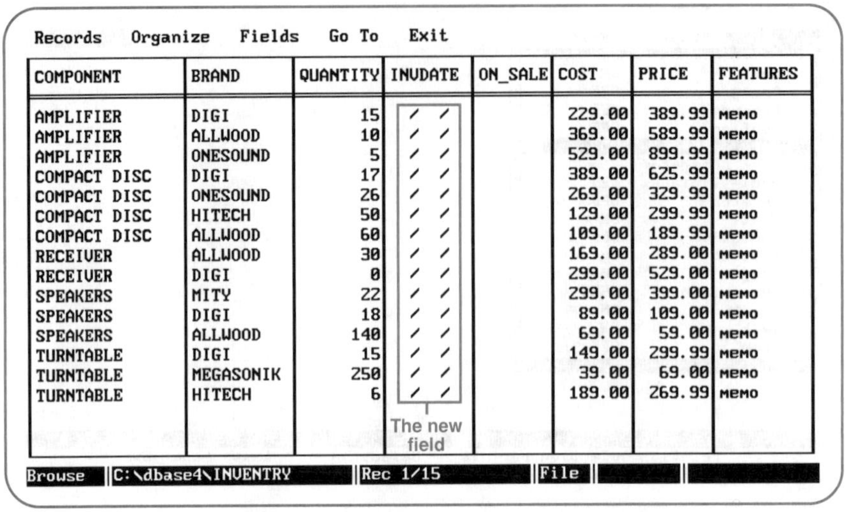

Records Organize Fields Go To Exit

COMPONENT	BRAND	QUANTITY	INVDATE	ON_SALE	COST	PRICE	FEATURES
AMPLIFIER	DIGI	15	/ /		229.00	389.99	MEMO
AMPLIFIER	ALLWOOD	10	/ /		369.00	589.99	MEMO
AMPLIFIER	ONESOUND	5	/ /		529.00	899.99	MEMO
COMPACT DISC	DIGI	17	/ /		389.00	625.99	MEMO
COMPACT DISC	ONESOUND	26	/ /		269.00	329.99	MEMO
COMPACT DISC	HITECH	50	/ /		129.00	299.99	MEMO
COMPACT DISC	ALLWOOD	60	/ /		109.00	189.99	MEMO
RECEIVER	ALLWOOD	30	/ /		169.00	289.00	MEMO
RECEIVER	DIGI	0	/ /		299.00	529.00	MEMO
SPEAKERS	MITY	22	/ /		299.00	399.00	MEMO
SPEAKERS	DIGI	18	/ /		89.00	109.00	MEMO
SPEAKERS	ALLWOOD	140	/ /		69.00	59.00	MEMO
TURNTABLE	DIGI	15	/ /		149.00	299.99	MEMO
TURNTABLE	MEGASONIK	250	/ /		39.00	69.00	MEMO
TURNTABLE	HITECH	6	/ /		189.00	269.99	MEMO

The new field

Browse | C:\dbase4\INVENTRY | Rec 1/15 | File

Figure 11.3. Empty data fields for adding date and logical data

Enter some date data, now. From the Control Center select the INVENTRY database file. Press **<F2>** to go into the data. If you find yourself in EDIT mode, press **<F2>** again to toggle into the BROWSE mode. All of your date fields are blank because you haven't entered any data yet. Enter different dates into all of them. Start with the first record and make the date 07/01/91. As you enter the date, remember that you don't have to enter the slashes. As you enter each set of numbers, the cursor automatically skips over the slashes. For each record, increase the date by half a month. That is, for the first record enter 070191, for the second, 071591, for the third, 080191, and so on, until you have placed a date in each of the records.

For now, leave the logical and memo fields blank. They are out of sight to the right anyway. You'll get to those in a little while. Right now your screen should look like Figure 11.4.

Displaying Dates

You can make calculations that directly involve dates. A date can be subtracted from another date. dBASE IV gives the answer as the number of days between the two dates. You will find this useful in the Query work surface when you need information involving date data. You also will find this useful in creating any type of calculated fields in the QBE, Form, or Report work surfaces.

```
Records   Organize   Fields   Go To   Exit
```

COMPONENT	BRAND	QUANTITY	INVDATE	ON_SALE	COST	PRICE	FEATURES
AMPLIFIER	DIGI	15	07/01/91		229.00	389.99	MEMO
AMPLIFIER	ALLWOOD	10	07/15/91		369.00	589.99	MEMO
AMPLIFIER	ONESOUND	5	08/01/91		529.00	899.99	MEMO
COMPACT DISC	DIGI	17	08/15/91		389.00	625.99	MEMO
COMPACT DISC	ONESOUND	26	09/01/91		269.00	329.99	MEMO
COMPACT DISC	HITECH	50	09/15/91		129.00	299.99	MEMO
COMPACT DISC	ALLWOOD	60	10/01/91		109.00	189.99	MEMO
RECEIVER	ALLWOOD	30	10/15/91		169.00	289.00	MEMO
RECEIVER	DIGI	0	11/01/91		299.00	529.00	MEMO
SPEAKERS	MITY	22	11/15/91		299.00	399.00	MEMO
SPEAKERS	DIGI	18	12/01/92		89.00	109.00	MEMO
SPEAKERS	ALLWOOD	140	12/15/92		69.00	59.00	MEMO
TURNTABLE	DIGI	15	01/01/92		149.00	299.99	MEMO
TURNTABLE	MEGASONIK	250	01/15/92		39.00	69.00	MEMO
TURNTABLE	HITECH	6	02/01/92		189.00	269.99	MEMO

```
Browse  C:\dbase4\INVENTRY   Rec 15/15   File
```

Figure 11.4. *Date fields with data entered*

In the present database file you have created, there is only one date field, INVDATE. Let's use that field to discuss some of the operations you can do with date fields.

Working from the Dot Prompt

Rather than spending a lot of time and energy going from the QBE screen to the BROWSE screen and back again, work at the dot prompt as you did in Chapter 9. First, get into the Control Center. Make sure the INVENTRY database file is active in the Data panel. Press **<Alt>-E** to open the Exit menu, and then press **<Enter>** to select `Exit to dot prompt.`

You should be at the dot prompt. First make sure you are at the top of your database file. At the dot prompt enter:

```
. GO TOP
```

This ensures you are at the first record of the database file. Remember that your first record contained the value 07/01/91 for the INVDATE field. Use the ? command which is a shortcut to the DISPLAY command you learned in Chapter 8. It means, "DISPLAY or 'show me' the current record in the file I am working with." Enter ? INVDATE as shown below. When you press **<Enter>**, the date displays immediately below the command you just entered.

```
. ? INVDATE
07/01/91
```

What's the Date Today?

Now do the same thing to display today's date. There is a built-in function known as DATE() which checks your system date for today's date. Type `? DATE( )` at the dot prompt. After you press **<Enter>** you see your system date, which, if you have a clock in your machine set correctly, should be today.

```
. ? DATE( )

04/03/91
```

Entering and Displaying Dates Without a Date Field

When you are comparing a date field with a date not in a date field, you must somehow tell dBASE IV that it is a date and not two numbers divided by two numbers divided by two numbers (07/01/91).

In Chapter 10, you learned how to enter character string data into the Query screen for comparison against a database field. You placed quotes around the values to differentiate them from field names. The same is true of dates. You must differentiate them from mathematical expressions by enclosing the date in braces, like this: {07/01/91}. The braces tell dBASE IV to treat what is inside as date data and not as some numbers divided by some other numbers.

Why would you want to tell dBASE IV that what you have is a date value? Suppose you wanted to see only those records that were last inventoried on October 15, 1991. You would enter:

```
{10/15/91}
```

into the INVDATE field of the Query screen. How about if you wanted to see all the records that have been inventoried before that date. You would enter:

```
< {10/15/91}
```

in the INVDATE box. The important thing is the braces. Without the braces, dBASE IV treats the date as a series of numbers.

Try these two examples using the DISPLAY command that you learned in Chapter 9. Enter the display command as shown below at the dot prompt.

```
. DISPLAY ALL FOR INVDATE = {10/15/91}
```

One record is displayed.

Now enter the following example to see all of the records that were inventoried on or before October 15, 1991:

```
. DISPLAY ALL FOR INVDATE <= {10/15/91}
```

How about records that were inventoried between August 15 and December 15, 1991?

```
. DISPLAY ALL FOR INVDATE >= {08/15/91} .AND. INVDATE
  <= {12/15/91}
```

As you will see in a few pages, when you place these entries in the Query screen, you will not use the DISPLAY ALL FOR phrase. It is used only at the dot prompt. You also will notice that because you will be using the INVDATE field entry area, dBASE IV knows that you are asking for a query about the INVDATE. In the query screen you would simply enter:

```
>= {08/15/91}, <= {12/15/91}
```

to perform the same .AND. query. As you can see from the date selection, it is no different than any other character or numeric comparisons except that the braces tell dBASE IV that it is a date value.

Date Arithmetic

You have seen some date comparisons, but how about comparing one date to another point in time? Date arithmetic will let you ask for such calculations as, "What is the date 50 days from now?" or "How many days are there between today and the inventory date?" For example, to request that dBASE IV display all records in the database file that have not been inventoried in the last 30 days, enter:

```
. GO TOP
. DISPLAY ALL FOR INVDATE <= DATE()-30
```

The expression `DATE( )-30` means 30 days ago. A date cannot be added to another date. The result is meaningless (just as it is without the computer). If you attempt to add two dates, you will receive an error message from dBASE IV. A number, however, can be added to or subtracted from a date. The number is treated as a number of days. The result of this calculation is a new date. For example, to add 18 days to the value of today's date, enter:

```
. ? DATE()

04/03/91

. ? DATE() + 18

04/21/91
```

You also can use the dBASE IV query commands, SUM and AVERAGE, with date fields in the dot prompt. However, because SUM, AVG, and any other aggregate operators cannot be used in the Query screen with calculated fields, you can accomplish this query only from the dot prompt or the report screen. For example, to determine the average of the difference between the INVDATE and today's date in the INVENTRY database file, enter:

```
. AVERAGE DATE() - INVDATE
 15 records averaged
 DATE() - INVDATE
 22.13
```

The actual answer you get depends on the current date and whether you correctly entered the dates as shown in Figure 11.4.

Date Functions

There is a long list of Date functions that are used to work with dates. Two of the most common are CTOD( ) (character-to-date) and DTOC( ) (date-to-character). The date functions are shown in Table 11.2.

***Table 11.2.** dBASE IV date functions*

Function	*Description*	*Example*
CTOD	Character To Date	
DTOC	Date To Character	
DAY	Day of Month	21
MONTH	Month of Year	10
YEAR	Year	1992
DOW	Day of Week	3
CDOW	Calendar Day of Week	Tuesday
CMONTH	Calendar Month	January
DATE	Current System Date	MM/DD/YY
DMY	Day, Month, Year format	dd/mm/yy
MDY	Month, Day, Year format	mm/dd/yy
TIME	Current System Time	hh:mm:ss

These functions make it more convenient to work with dates. CTOD( ) allows you to use a character string as a date. In dBASE IV the braces around a date string have replaced the CTOD() function from previous versions of dBASE. DTOC allows you to use a date in a character string. Remember that data types don't normally work well together. When you want to display a character field together with a number or a date, you first must convert the number or date to a character field.

Enter an example of a character and date string. First make sure you are on the first record at the top of the file.

```
. GO TOP
```

Now, place a date field inside some character text.

```
. ? 'The last inventory date for this item is '
  + DTOC(INVDATE)

    The last inventory date for this item is 07/01/91
```

The DAY, MONTH, and YEAR functions make it convenient to specify dates to be used as conditions of dBASE IV commands. The three DISPLAY commands below exemplify the use of these functions:

```
. DISPLAY FOR YEAR(INVDATE) = 1991

. DISPLAY FOR YEAR(INVDATE) = 1991
  .AND. MONTH(INVDATE) = 9

. DISPLAY FOR YEAR(INVDATE) = 1991
  .AND. MONTH(INVDATE) = 9

    .AND. DAY(INVDATE) = 15
```

The DOW (day-of-week) function returns a number code for each day of the week beginning with Sunday (1). To display all inventory dates that were Tuesdays, enter:

```
. DISPLAY FOR DOW(INVDATE) = 3
```

CDOW (calendar day of week) and CMONTH (calendar month) change dates into forms that are more convenient to use in text. As an example, use the INVDATE field from Record 1.

```
. ? INVDATE

07/01/91

. ? CDOW(INVDATE)

Friday

. ? CMONTH(INVDATE)

July
```

The system date and time, as you have already learned, gives you access to the computer's clock calendar.

```
. ? DATE()
04/03/91
. ? TIME()
11:15:03
```

dBASE IV cannot change the system date or time directly. You can change the date by entering:

```
. RUN DATE
```

You can change the time with the entry:

```
. RUN TIME
```

These commands call the operating system commands DATE and TIME. When you have entered the new date or time, you are returned to where you were previously working in dBASE IV.

Blank Dates

Normally, only date fields that have no entered data are blank. These blank fields can present some logic problems. Suppose that one of your INVDATE entries is blank. All comparisons involving this blank field with a real date will be false. There is no way to display dates that are blank using:

```
. DISPLAY FOR INVDATE = {  /  /  }
```

How, then, do you specify records that contain a blank date field? The most reliable technique is to use the year function and request those records where the year is 0. For example:

```
. DISPLAY FOR YEAR(INVDATE) = 0
```

displays any records where the date field INVDATE is blank.

Logical Fields

Logical fields are special fields that you use only when a field can have just one of two possible values. The values are usually expressed as True/False or

Yes/No. Example uses of a logic field are when you need to indicate whether or not a check has cleared the bank or whether or not an item is on sale.

Go back into the BROWSE screen and enter some logical fields. You should be at the dot prompt. At the dot prompt, enter:

```
. BROWSE
```

You are in the BROWSE screen. You need to go to the field ON_SALE which is out of sight to the right. Remember, you can press **<Tab>** to pan the screen to the right. Move the cursor into the ON_SALE field.

Enter some data into these fields. Enter T into all the fields whose COMPONENT is COMPACT DISC. It is time for all the compact discs to go on sale. Do the same for all of the DIGI equipment regardless of the COMPONENT type. When you are finished, press **<Ctrl>-<End>**.

Enter the following command at the dot prompt:

```
. DISPLAY ALL OFF FOR ON_SALE
```

The DIGI records and all the Compact Discs are displayed as shown in Figure 11.5.

```
. DISPLAY ALL OFF FOR ON_SALE
 COMPONENT       BRAND      QUANTITY INVDATE  ON_SALE     COST    PRICE FEATURES
 AMPLIFIER       DIGI             15 07/01/91 .T.       229.00   389.99 memo
 COMPACT DISC    DIGI             17 08/15/91 .T.       389.00   625.99 memo
 COMPACT DISC    ONESOUND         26 09/01/91 .T.       269.00   329.99 memo
 COMPACT DISC    HITECH           50 09/15/91 .T.       129.00   299.99 memo
 COMPACT DISC    ALLWOOD          60 10/01/91 .T.       109.00   189.99 memo
 RECEIVER        DIGI              0 11/01/91 .T.       299.00   529.00 memo
 SPEAKERS        DIGI             18 12/01/91 .T.        89.00   109.00 memo
 TURNTABLE       DIGI             15 01/01/92 .T.       149.00   299.99 memo
.
Command ║C:\dbase4\INVENTRY       ║Rec EOF/15        ║File ║      ║      Caps
```

Figure 11.5. *DISPLAYing all ON_SALE records*

The content of these fields is always entered as T or F. You can also enter Y or N, but dBASE IV will convert them to T or F. Sometimes, especially when you use them in comparisons, you delimit these values with periods (.T. , .F.). This is similar to the way character fields have quotes and date fields have braces. The periods emphasize the fact that they contain logical values. However, you should almost never have to use this delimiter because logical fields, by their general nature, do not need their values specified.

Logical field values are rarely used in comparisons. The comparison is "built-in." Suppose you use the INVENTRY database file. The field you entered data into is named ON_SALE to indicate whether or not an item is on sale. To view the items that are on sale, enter:

```
. DISPLAY FOR ON_SALE
```

And to view those that are not on sale, enter:

```
. DISPLAY FOR .NOT. ON_SALE
```

Some beginning users have a tendency to write the condition with an explicit comparison, for example, ON_SALE = .T. This isn't necessary. Logical fields are automatically false until you enter a true value during data entry. dBASE IV evaluates the field as false even though no value has been actually entered. The inventory example above shows this feature clearly; an item is not on sale until you enter T into its field.

These fields ignore the possibility of "don't know"—a condition that occurs far too often in business. Everyone is either male or female, but we may not know whether Leslie is a boy or a girl. If you need to deal with a situation where the logical value can have one of three states—Yes, No, Unknown—you'll be far better off using a character field for the data.

Memo Fields

This special data type allows you to use variable-length fields for storing text. In dBASE IV, these are called memo fields. Examples of the kind of data stored in memo fields are memoranda, abstracts, and general comments. You can designate any or all of the 255 fields in a dBASE IV file as memo fields.

You identify a field as a memo field either when you create the database file, or later, when you modify the file structure. Earlier in this chapter, you specified the FEATURES field as a memo type when you were entering field types while modifying the INVENTRY file. The field width of a memo field is automatically set to 10 bytes. This is a little misleading. A memo field can contain up to one billion bytes or 32,000 lines of text, whichever is smaller. The data is actually stored in a special auxiliary file. The 10 bytes of field width are used for pointers to tell dBASE IV the location of the field in the auxiliary file. The pointer connects information in the auxiliary file to the data record. The auxiliary file has the same name as the database file, but is given the file extension .DBT to distinguish it from the .DBF database file.

While you're entering data into the main database file, the data-entry area of a memo field displays the word `MEMO`. If the memo field contains data for a record, the word `MEMO` appears in uppercase letters. If the field is empty, the word `memo` appears in lowercase letters.

Try some memo data entry. This time work with an EDIT screen even though you can do exactly the same thing in BROWSE mode. Type EDIT at the dot prompt. Go to the DIGI Amplifier record. This is the first record in the file. Look at the status bar to find out what record you are in. Press **<PgUp>** if you are past the record, and press **<PgDn>** if the DIGI record is located later in the file. Move the cursor down to the memo marker on the FEATURES field. Figure 11.6 shows the EDIT screen and the memo marker.

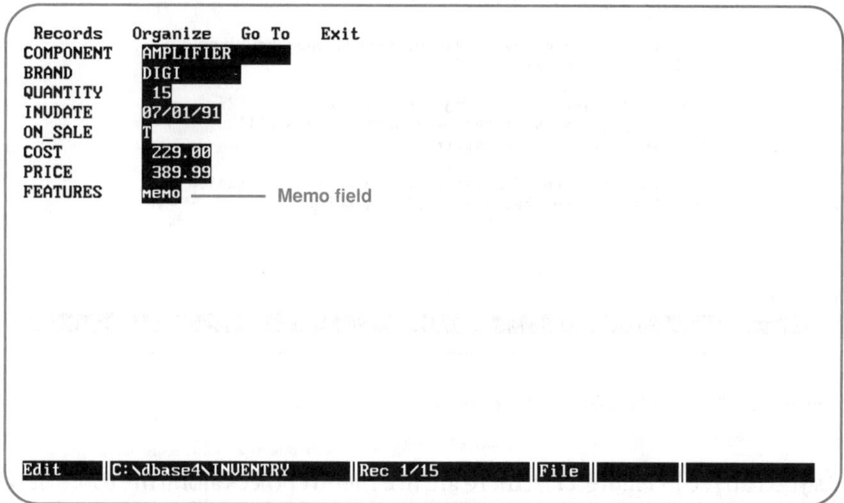

Figure 11.6. *Opening a memo marker*

Memo Field Data Entry

To enter data into a memo field, place the cursor into the memo marker. You will see that the field marker is shown in lowercase letters, indicating that no data has been entered into this field. Press **<Ctrl>-<Home>**. The screen clears and displays the current contents of the memo field. The cursor is positioned at the beginning of any text already in the field.

Enter data by simply typing in text. When you have finished entering text, press **<Ctrl>-<End>** to save it, or press **<Esc>** to abandon your entry. No space is taken in the auxiliary text file until data is actually saved in a memo field. Once data is saved, space is allocated, as needed, in 512-byte chunks. The maximum size for memo fields is virtually unlimited.

When you enter the memo field just start typing; the word processor is automatically activated. This is a fully functioning word processor. Enter a small description of the item, as shown in Figure 11.7.

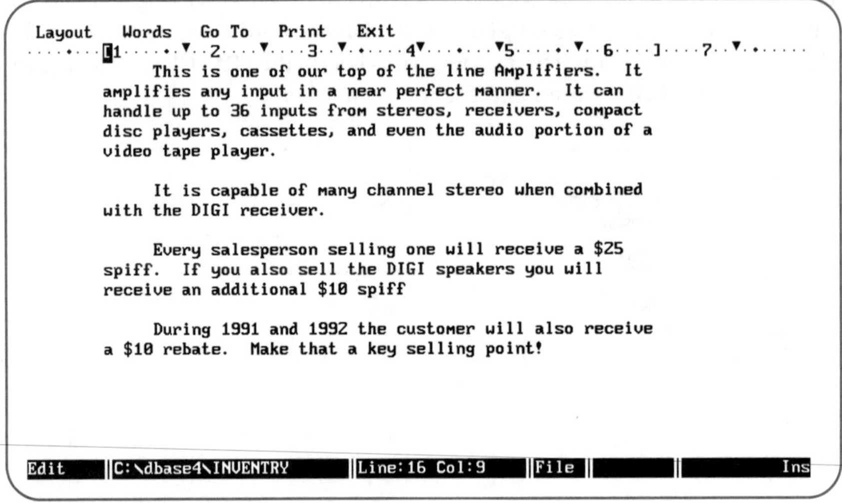

Figure 11.7. Entering data into a memo field

As you can see in Figure 11.7, there are five menu choices along the top. These choices help you perform some of the word processing chores.

You can enter the memo field only from one of the dBASE IV full-screen data entry commands, BROWSE or EDIT. When you complete your entry or edit of a memo field, dBASE IV returns you to the data entry screen from which you entered the memo field.

Memo fields give you the ability to enter, and then use, large amounts of text data that is variable in length. That is, depending on the amount of data you enter, each memo field can be from 0 to one billion bytes. In character fields, each record uses the full length of the field. No space is wasted with memo fields, even if you don't fill up the field.

Displaying the Memo Field

You can view the content of a memo field with the use of any display or reporting commands and work surfaces. You can display your memo data while varying the length of each line on the screen or report. You can control the placement of memo field data precisely on screens or reports, making the memo field an excellent way to store free form notes in your database file.

Memo field data can be imported from and exported to files other than dBASE IV files. You can even search and replace data in memo fields, as well as make selections based on the contents of the memo field.

Using the Query Screen with Special Data Types

dBASE IV has some special requirements for the date and logical field types in the QBE screen. The data must be entered in the internal format dBASE IV can use in the QBE.

Date Queries

Dates are a little different from numeric or character queries because they require that you use proper dBASE IV dates. You cannot directly enter data in the internal form of a dBASE IV date. Instead you must tell dBASE IV to convert what you enter. There are several ways to do this. When you enter data into a date field in EDIT or BROWSE, it is automatically converted to an internal date format. In order to enter date data to compare against internally stored date formats, enclose the date in braces { }. If you want to try the following examples, get into the Control Center and then the Query Design screen. Make sure the INVENTRY file is still active.

A query for a single date or a range of dates might ask the question, "What items were last inventoried on August 15, 1991?" To pose this query, enter:

```
{08/15/91}
```

in the entry area for INVDATE of the Query work surface. This tells dBASE IV to convert the characters '08/15/91' to the dBASE IV internal date format, so that it can compare them against the date value in the field INVDATE. You also can check a date range. For example, if you wanted to ask "What items were inventoried between August 15, 1991, and December 15, 1991?" you would enter:

```
> {08/15/91}, <{12/15/91}
```

This is shown in Figure 11.8 in the zoom mode of the query screen.

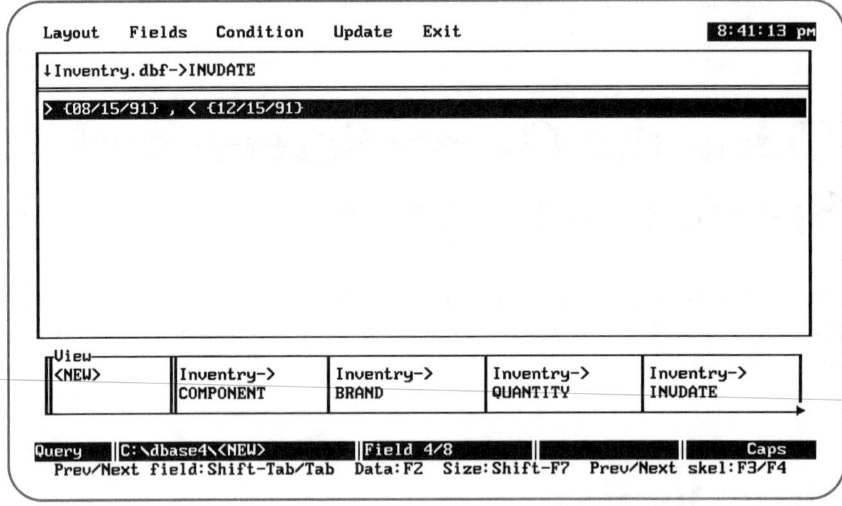

Figure 11.8. *Entering a date query in the zoomed query screen*

Another type of date query involves the system date: DATE(). Suppose you wanted to see all records that haven't been inventoried in the last 30 days. Enter:

```
< DATE() - 30
```

in the INVDATE entry box. This displays only the records where the value of INVDATE is less than 30 days ago. As you can see, the query screen makes it easier for you to enter date field queries than the dot prompt mode, but with the same result.

Logical Queries

You can query the logical data type, too. If you wanted to see all of the items that are on sale, enter:

```
.T.
```

in the ON_SALE data entry area of the Query work surface screen. When you press **<F2>**, you see only the data that is "on sale". If you want to see the data that is not on sale, then enter an `.F.` in the ON_SALE field entry area.

Creating a Quick Report

To create a quick report on all of your data, return to the Control Center. Make sure that there is no active query (above the line). If one is open, close it by selecting it and pressing **<Enter>**. Now, move the cursor to INVENTRY in the Data panel and press **<Shift>-<F9>** to create a quick report. A copy of the report is shown in Figure 11.9.

```
Page No.    1
04/03/91

COMPONENT        BRAND        QUANTITY  INVDATE   ON_SALE       COST     PRICE

AMPLIFIER        DIGI               15  07/01/91  Y           229.00    389.99
AMPLIFIER
AMPLIFIER        ONESOUND            5  08/01/91  N           529.00    899.99
COMPACT DISC     DIGI               17  08/15/91  Y           389.00    625.99
COMPACT DISC     ONESOUND           26  09/01/91  Y           269.00    329.99
COMPACT DISC     HITECH             50  09/15/91  Y           129.00    299.99
COMPACT DISC     ALLWOOD            60  10/01/91  Y           109.00    189.99
RECEIVER         ALLWOOD            30  10/15/91  N           169.00    289.00
RECEIVER         DIGI                0  11/01/91  Y           299.00    529.00
SPEAKERS         MITY               22  11/15/91  N           299.00    399.00
SPEAKERS         DIGI               18  12/01/91  Y            89.00    109.00
SPEAKERS         ALLWOOD           140  12/15/91  N            69.00     59.00
TURNTABLE        DIGI               15  01/01/92  Y           149.00    299.99
TURNTABLE        MEGASONIK         250  01/15/92  N            39.00     69.00
TURNTABLE        HITECH              6  02/01/92  N           189.00    269.99
                                   664                       3325.00   5349.91
```

Figure 11.9. *A quick report of all your data*

Summary

You have used some new data types in this chapter. You have also finalized the INVENTRY database file. You'll use the data and fields you created in this chapter to complete other chapters in this book.

Now that you have finished all there is to do with one database file, it is time to learn about using more than one database file. Though much of your future work with dBASE IV will be with only one database file, there will be times when you'll need two or more database files to complete a task or develop a system. The next chapter will address tasks involving multiple files.

chapter

12

Working with Multiple Database Files

Up to this point, you have been working with just a single database file at a time. A database management system that can work with only one file at a time is called a *file manager*. A true *database manager* can work with many database files at one time. The "database" itself is composed of all your individual database files. Up to this point, you have created and used two database files: INVENTRY and FONEBOOK. Your database consists of these two files. As you create additional files, they automatically become a part of your database, as reflected by the catalog in the Control Center. You'll be learning about multiple file relations in this chapter. You'll create a new file and relate it to your INVENTRY file. After you link the two files in the QBE screen, you will work with their data together to retrieve information. The last section of this chapter teaches you how to relate your files from the dot prompt.

Multiple-File Relationships

When a database has more than a single file, the individual database files are usually called *relations*. This distinguishes the individual files that make up a database from the database file itself. This is an important distinction in some systems, though it is relatively unimportant in dBASE IV. A physical database in dBASE IV can consist of only one file, or of any number of files. You are limited only by the number of files you can pack onto your disks.

In dBASE IV, you can think of the overall database in terms of the catalog. If a file is in your catalog, you can think of it as being part of the system. If a file is not displayed in the catalog, it is not part of the system. Of course, you can add a file to the catalog at any time.

Using a Single Database File

The simplest and most common database design is the *one-to-one relationship*. The inventory file you have been using in the last several chapters has a one-to-one database design. The term one-to-one means that for each unique identifying field, such as item number or COMPONENT and BRAND, there is another related field. In the INVENTRY database file there is a single quantity, inventory date, on-sale identifier, cost, price, and features list that is specifically identified with one COMPONENT and BRAND combination. Figure 12.1 shows the INVENTRY database file used in this book.

Why You Would Need More Than One Database File

There are several reasons why you might want more than one database file. Assume that you need some information that is not in the original file. Suppose you want to order some additional stock for the inventory. You need to know to what name and address to send the order, so you must add the vendor's name and address to the database. Figure 12.2 shows a poor way to add this information to the inventory file. The vendor's name and address appear in every inventory record. This requires a lot of extra data entry each time a new item is added to the inventory. Furthermore, because the address for a particular vendor is the same regardless of the component, you end up with a lot of redundant or duplicate information. If a vendor's address was to change, you would have to change every record.

Records Organize Fields Go To Exit

COMPONENT	BRAND	QUANTITY	INVDATE	ON_SALE	COST	PRICE	FEATURES
AMPLIFIER	DIGI	15	07/01/91	T	229.00	389.99	MEMO
AMPLIFIER	ALLWOOD	10	07/15/91	F	369.00	589.99	memo
AMPLIFIER	ONESOUND	5	08/01/91	F	529.00	899.99	memo
COMPACT DISC	DIGI	17	08/15/91	T	389.00	625.99	memo
COMPACT DISC	ONESOUND	26	09/01/91	T	269.00	329.99	memo
COMPACT DISC	HITECH	50	09/15/91	T	129.00	299.99	memo
COMPACT DISC	ALLWOOD	60	10/01/91	T	109.00	189.99	memo
RECEIVER	ALLWOOD	30	10/15/91	F	169.00	289.00	memo
RECEIVER	DIGI	0	11/01/91	T	299.00	529.00	memo
SPEAKERS	MITY	22	11/15/91	F	299.00	399.00	memo
SPEAKERS	DIGI	18	12/01/91	T	89.00	109.00	memo
SPEAKERS	ALLWOOD	140	12/15/91	F	69.00	59.00	memo
TURNTABLE	DIGI	15	01/01/92	T	149.00	299.99	memo
TURNTABLE	MEGASONIK	250	01/15/92	F	39.00	69.00	memo
TURNTABLE	HITECH	6	02/01/92	F	189.00	269.99	memo

Browse | C:\dbase4\INVENTRY | Rec 15/15 | File

***Figure 12.1.** A one-to-one relationship using the INVENTRY database*

Records Fields Go To Exit 1:06:44 pm

COMPONENT	BRAND	ADDRESS	CITY_ST_ZP	QUANTITY	COST
AMPLIFIER	DIGI	200 Disc Lane	Newport, CA 98556	15	229.00
AMPLIFIER	ALLWOOD	150 Old Trail	Omaha, NE 37754	10	369.00
AMPLIFIER	ONESOUND			5	529.00
COMPACT DISC	DIGI	200 Disc Lane	Newport, CA 98556	17	389.00
COMPACT DISC	ONESOUND			26	269.00
COMPACT DISC	HITECH	270 Shark Lane	Cape Cod, MA 84453	50	129.00
COMPACT DISC	ALLWOOD	150 Old Trail	Omaha, NE 37754	60	109.00
RECEIVER	ALLWOOD	150 Old Trail	Omaha, NE 37754	30	169.00
RECEIVER	DIGI	200 Disc Lane	Newport, CA 98556	0	299.00
SPEAKERS	MITY	212 GenMot Rd	Detroit, MI 77473	22	299.00
SPEAKERS	DIGI	200 Disc Lane	Newport, CA 98556	18	89.00
SPEAKERS	ALLWOOD	150 Old Trail	Omaha, NE 37754	140	69.00
TURNTABLE	DIGI	200 Disc Lane	Newport, CA 98556	15	149.00
TURNTABLE	MEGASONIK	42 23rd St	New York, NY 37737	250	39.00
TURNTABLE	HITECH	270 Shark Lane	Cape Cod, MA 84453	6	189.00

Repeated data

Browse | C:\dbase4\<NEW> | Rec 1/15 | View | ReadOnly

View and edit fields

***Figure 12.2.** A poorly organized database*

Using a Common Field

The solution is to create more than one database file and to use a common field to relate the two database files. This will give you a relationship known as a *table lookup*. This also is known as a *many-to-one relationship* because a record in the first file is used to look up a single value in the second file.

The inventory file example illustrates one of the most common reasons for a many-to-one relationship. This is a database file of names and addresses. Addresses change so frequently that you need to keep them stored separately with only one occurrence of a particular name and address. This way when an address changes, only one record needs to be updated. And your storage space will be greatly reduced by having only one record for each address.

Look at a conceptual diagram of the INVENTRY and VENDOR files, as shown in Figure 12.3. Each record in the first database has one (and only one) mate in the second database file. There may be many records in the first database file that will look up the same record in the second database file, but only one occurrence is found in the second database file.

Table lookup gives a database file access to data not found in the database file itself. Remember, don't just move data items from the second file into the first file. In this example you could have put the address of every vendor into the inventory database file, but then you would have to update the address in every record for that vendor every time his address changed. Also, by having the vendor database file, you have to enter only names into the inventory file. dBASE IV will then retrieve the address automatically from the VENDOR file. By having this second file, you have to update only one record and many records will be affected in the main database file.

Rules for Common Fields

The field names do not have to be the same in both database files in order to link them. The field types and sizes must be the same, however. This is the most important rule of all.

The value of the related field must be unique in the related database file; that is, there cannot be two records with the same value for the common field. Although there will be many records in the main database file with the same value, there can be only one in the related database file.

What do you do if the value of the common field is not unique? Suppose that the DIGI BRAND occurs in two different locations. You would have to use some sort of identifier, such as a vendor code, to make each unique. For example, you could use vendor DIGI-01 for the California plant and vendor DIGI-02 for the plant in Oklahoma.

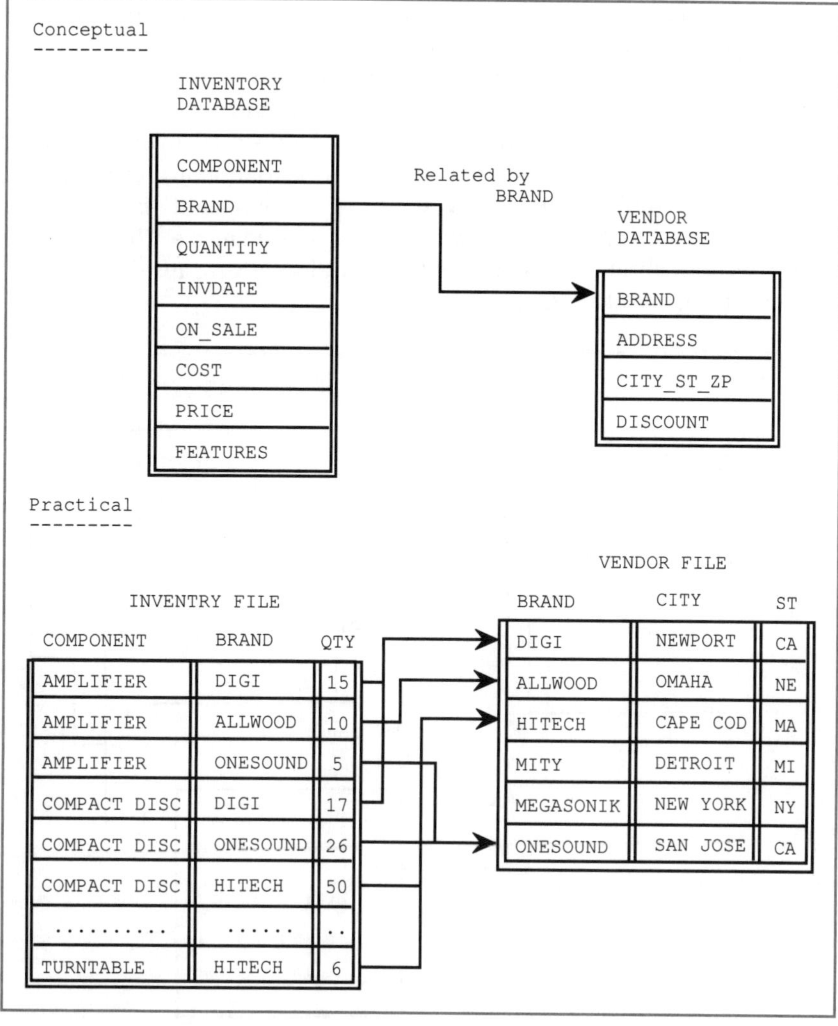

Figure 12.3. *Many-to-one relationships*

One-to-Many and Many-to-Many Relationships

Another type of related files is *one-to-many* or *many-to-many*. This means that there are multiple occurrences in a related database file of the same *key*. The key is an *identifier*—usually one field or some combination of fields—that helps you distinguish one record from another.

A good example of this is an invoice database file with several items, as shown in Figure 12.4. The first database file contains all the items occurring only once in the invoice, such as the invoice date, the invoice number, customer information, shipping information, and even the tax and discount percentage. The second database file has information for the individual invoice items that occur multiple times (unless the invoice has only one item), including the quantity, item number, description, and price. Once related, these database files can form a complete system with no data redundancies. This process is known as normalization, in database terms, and simply means that you have data occurring in only one place.

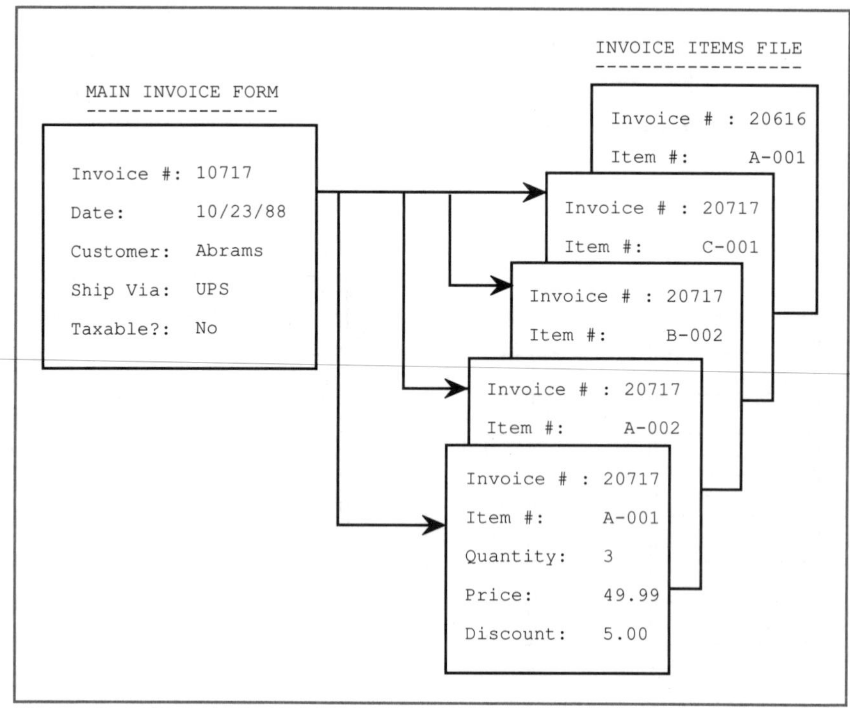

***Figure 12.4.** A one-to-many relationship*

Relation Combinations

You can have both of these types of relationships at the same time. Figure 12.5 shows an example of a file diagram for a complete sales system. There are four related files. The main file is actually the invoice file. It is related in two ways. First, by the customer number to the customer file from which customer information is retrieved. Second, by invoice number to the items file where the items on the invoice are stored. The items file is related to an inventory file from which the price at the time of purchase is retrieved. The inventory file also is checked to make sure there are enough items in stock.

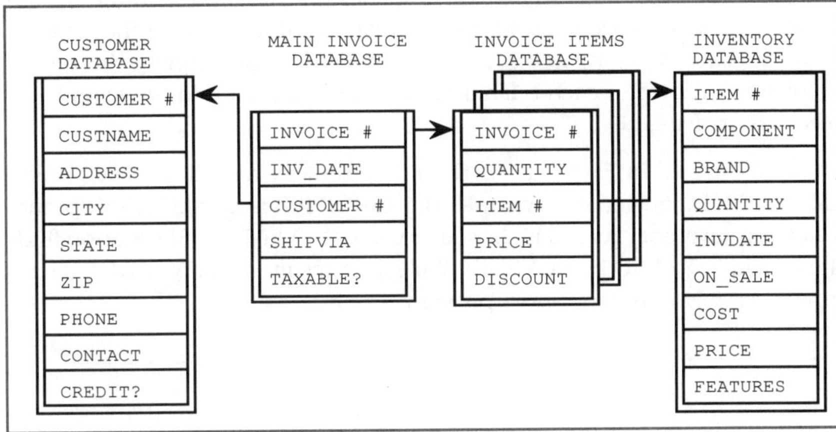

Figure 12.5. *A complete sales system example*

The relation between the invoice file and the customer file is a *many-to-one* relationship. Many invoices can use the same customer number, but there is only one customer record for each invoice. The same type of relationship exists between the invoice items file and the inventory file. There is a matching item in the inventory for each item. You can't sell an item if you don't have it in stock. The relation of the invoice file to the items file is a *one-to-many* relationship. Each invoice has many item records.

Basically, these are all the possible relationships in a database. The data of each database file that is part of a one-to-one or many-to-one relation is entered independently of others. Customer data is entered into the customer file. Inventory data is entered into the inventory file. However, when a relation is one-to-many, data entry becomes very complicated. There is no easy way to enter data in this format. Even in dBASE IV, data entry must be programmed under these circumstances. Otherwise, the data must be entered one record at a time, even though in a process like invoicing you usually enter all the records at once.

How Relations Work

When you create a relation, you are telling dBASE IV that something in the first database file also is found in another database file (or many other database files). This "something" is known as the *common field* or *key*. In the INVENTRY database example it is the BRAND name.

The main database file is where the original value is found, and the related database is the one used in the look-up or relation. dBASE IV gives the main file access to data in the related file by automatically repositioning the record pointer to a record in each related file whenever a record in the main file is accessed or changed.

This is illustrated in Figure 12.6. The first inventory record is a DIGI brand AMPLIFIER. In the second example, the AMPLIFIER is an ALLWOOD brand. When this inventory record is chosen or used, the VENDOR file relation finds the matching BRAND in the VENDOR file. As a result, all the VENDOR data is now accessible to the inventory program.

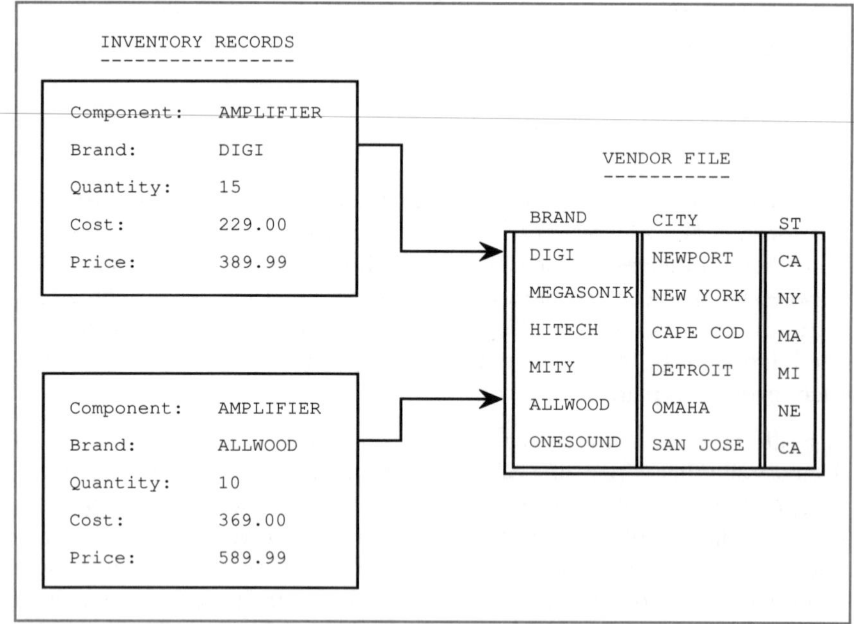

Figure 12.6. Relationships

In dBASE IV, you can have up to 10 files in use simultaneously, with multiple relations among one another. You can have up to 8 files on the Queries screen work surface at one time. This should satisfy even the most complex system you could come up with.

Setting Relations and Joining Your Files

There are several ways to establish relationships between files. The first is by setting a relation. This technique, accomplished in the dot prompt mode, requires a few simple commands to establish the relation and to determine how to view the data in the subsidiary files.

Another way to establish relations is by using the Query Design screen to specify the links between the common fields of the files. After the files are related, it will appear that two or more database files have been joined to form the view table.

Once you learn how to relate records in the Query Design screen, you will have access to many types of data you didn't have before, including records that have multiple values, like an invoice with multiple items. You can use this type of processing to create very complex reports with hardly any work.

Being able to keep the number of fields small in each database file is another advantage of relational files. In the sales example, it isn't necessary to have the customer information as part of every invoice record. Instead, you keep only the customer number or name, or whatever you have decided identifies the customer. No matter how many times that customer has purchased items from you, and no matter how many invoices for that customer you have in your file, the customer's name, address, billing information, and credit information appear only once—in the customer file. And it needs to be updated in only one place if any of the information changes.

Relating and Using Multiple Files

Once the database design has been modified to eliminate the data redundancies, the second database must be created, built, and then joined. dBASE provides specific commands to establish and use this relationship.

Creating a Second Database File

In order to see how to use two files at the same time, you'll need to create a second database file called VENDOR. This database file will contain a list of the companies that manufacture the components sold by Parrot Stereo. The file will consist of four fields. First comes the manufacturer's name—this is the same as the BRAND name in the INVENTRY file. Next will be a field where you will keep the sale discount that the manufacturer recommends you give customers during a sale. This way, when an item is on sale, you can use the file to look up the percentage off the list price. The last two fields will contain the manufacturer's address information so you can write to them whenever you need to order or have any complaints about their products.

Database Redundancies

Why not just maintain the VENDOR's address and discount information on the INVENTRY file itself? The answer is always the same: data redundancy. You never want to have the same data in two places if you can avoid it. Data redundancy leads to two problems:

- Updating data and keeping data reconciled in two places
- Extra storage for duplicate information

If you kept only the discount in the VENDOR file, you could easily argue that it's not worth the time or effort to have several database files. But when you add the address information to VENDOR, it creates lots of extra storage. Without the VENDOR file, the address information would have to be stored in the original INVENTRY file for every brand and component combination, even though several components of the same brand are sold.

At Parrot Stereo, certain components go on sale at various times. When the store is planning to have a sale, the owner of the store uses the database system to turn on the ON_SALE indicator in certain records. When a sale item is sold, the discount is retrieved from the VENDOR database file. The owner also produces a report for his salespeople of all the sale items and their sale prices. You could keep information about the sale discount for each individual component, but that would mean updating many records each time a BRAND discount changes. Whenever a customer wants to buy a sale item, the salesperson can look in the VENDOR database file for the amount of discount. The salesperson knows there is a sale because the ON_SALE field in the main INVENTRY database file is set to True for that item.

The database file you're going to create is shown in Figure 12.7. As you can see, the file has four fields and the following data: BRAND, DISCOUNT, ADDRESS, and CITY_ST_ZP. As shown in Figure 12.8, the database file has five records—one for each manufacturer.

```
Layout   Organize   Append   Go To   Exit                          12:34:08 pm
                                                  Bytes remaining:   3952
```

Num	Field Name	Field Type	Width	Dec	Index
1	BRAND	Character	10		Y
2	DISCOUNT	Numeric	5	2	N
3	ADDRESS	Character	15		N
4	CITY_ST_ZP	Character	18		N

```
Database  C:\dbase4\<NEW>          Field 1/4                    Caps
         Enter the field name. Insert/Delete field:Ctrl-N/Ctrl-U
Field names begin with a letter and may contain letters, digits and underscores
```

Figure 12.7. *The VENDOR database*

```
Records   Organize   Fields   Go To   Exit
```

BRAND	DISCOUNT	ADDRESS	CITY_ST_ZP
DIGI	0.10	200 Disc Lane	Newport, CA 98556
ALLWOOD	0.15	150 Old Trail	Omaha, NE 37754
HITECH	0.12	270 Shark Lane	Cape Cod, MA 84453
MITY	0.25	212 GenMot Rd	Detroit, MI 77473
MEGASONIK	0.08	42 23rd St.	New York, NY 77473

```
Browse  C:\DBASE4\VENDOR       Rec 1/5        File
```

Figure 12.8. *The VENDOR database records*

Database Relationships

Take a look at a conceptual diagram of the INVENTRY and VENDOR database files, as shown in Figure 12.9. Each record in the INVENTRY file has a field called

BRAND. You can relate this field to the VENDOR database file to find one or more records with the same key. The same field name is used in both database files as the key. However, this is not always true. Each database file can have different field names. The BRAND field could have been called MANUF (short for manufacturer). As long as the values of the data inside the fields match, it is not important what the fields are called.

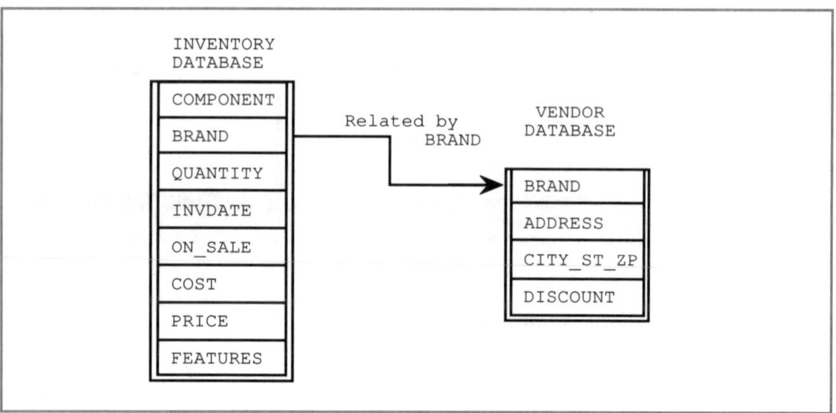

Figure 12.9. *Conceptual view of the relationships between the INVENTRY and VENDOR databases*

What type of relationship will you create between these files? Look at the files from the viewpoint of the INVENTRY file. A many-to-one relationship will exist here because there are several records in the INVENTRY file that can be related to a single record in the VENDOR file.

What data can you link in this relationship? Obviously, you can relate the records by the BRAND name. You can get the discount and address information from the vendor file for each record in the INVENTRY file. A many-to-one relationship implies that a single data record in the VENDOR file will be used many times to supply information to different records in the INVENTRY file.

However, the relationship from the VENDOR file to the INVENTRY file is a one-to-many relationship. Each single BRAND record in the VENDOR file has several corresponding BRAND records in the INVENTRY file. What can you accomplish by relating the files this way that you can't by relating the files the other way? Nothing! Generally, one relationship from one file to another can provide all the information you might need. You could argue that this arrangement provides a good means of seeing which COMPONENTS are sold by each BRAND, but you can do that without even relating the database files, because both COMPONENT and BRAND information is found in the INVENTRY database file itself.

Using the Query Screen for a Simple JOIN

First, make sure that you have created the database file as depicted in Figure 12.7, and that you have entered the data to match the sample file shown in Figure 12.8.

Looking at the Data panel in the Control Center, there should be at least two database files, INVENTRY and VENDOR. If either of the database files is active, close it now. All your database files should now be below the line in the panel. Choose `<create>` in the Queries panel to start a new query.

You need to place both the INVENTRY and VENDOR files on the Query work surface. The Layout menu opens automatically because you have no active files. Choose `Add file to query` from the Layout menu. A list of database files appears as shown in Figure 12.10. Select INVENTRY and press **<Enter>**. The file skeleton is placed on the work surface.

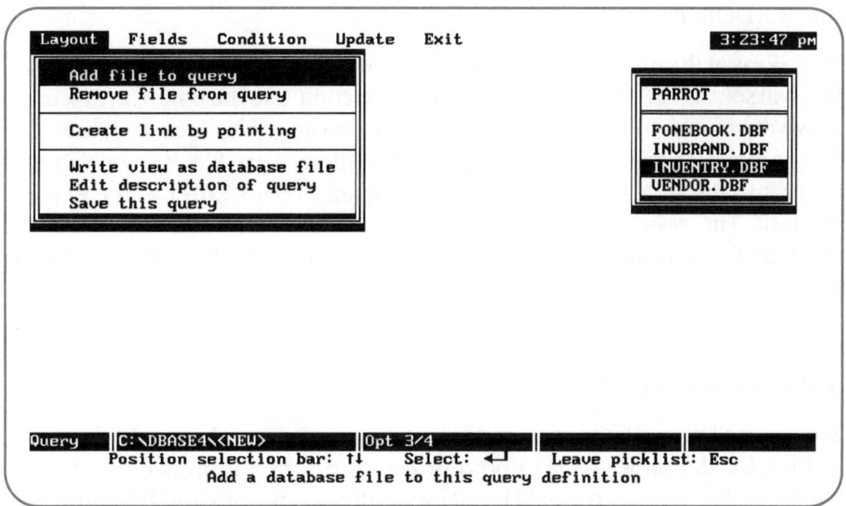

Figure 12.10. *Adding files to the Query work surface*

Next, you need to place the VENDOR skeleton on the work surface. Again press **<F10>** to open the Layout menu and again choose `Add file to query`, but this time select the VENDOR database file and press **<Enter>**. Both database files are now on the work surface.

Until you tell dBASE how these files are related, you can work with only one file at a time. Although you can select fields from each file to be placed on the VIEW skeleton, they will have no meaning until they are linked by their common key, which you know is BRAND. Therefore, the next step is to tell dBASE IV how the files are related. Because in this example the BRAND field appears in both database files, you will link the field BRAND in the INVENTRY file to the field BRAND in the VENDOR file.

The easiest way to create the link is to use the option `Create link by pointing` in the Layout menu. You can see this menu again in Figure 12.10. Before opening the Layout menu, move the cursor to the first field that you want to use in the relation. This is the BRAND field in the INVENTRY database file. Once you have the cursor in place on the BRAND entry area in the INVENTRY database file (the top skeleton), open the Layout menu by pressing **<Alt>-L**. Type `C` to select `Create link by pointing.`

After you type `C`, the menu disappears and the word LINK1 appears in the BRAND entry area. The cursor is still in this box. You are now half done. You have told dBASE IV where the link begins, but you still need to tell it what to link to. You must tell dBASE which field in the other database file contains the same value as in this database file. In this example, it is also the BRAND field in the VENDOR database file.

If you look at the message line at the bottom of the screen below the status line, you will see that dBASE IV is waiting for you to complete the link. You first must move the cursor to another file. Press **<F4>** to go to the next skeleton. The cursor moves to the pot handle of the VENDOR database file. Press **<Tab>** to move it to the BRAND field of that database file. Press **<Enter>** to complete the task. The word LINK1 also appears in the BRAND box of the VENDOR database file. You are done. You have linked the two database files, as shown in Figure 12.11.

Some Reserved Words

The word LINK1 is known as an "example variable." You have told dBASE IV to look for the same word in both places, and, when it finds it, to join the database files. The word LINK1 is not especially significant. dBASE IV automatically uses the word LINK followed by a number when it creates a link by pointing. You can just as easily move the cursor to each entry area and type any word. As long as the word is the same in two skeletons, the database files are joined. You could have used any word there, like DOG, CAT, or WINDOW, or even something like LINK1. By using the word LINK1, dBASE IV attempts to tell you it means this is used as a link.

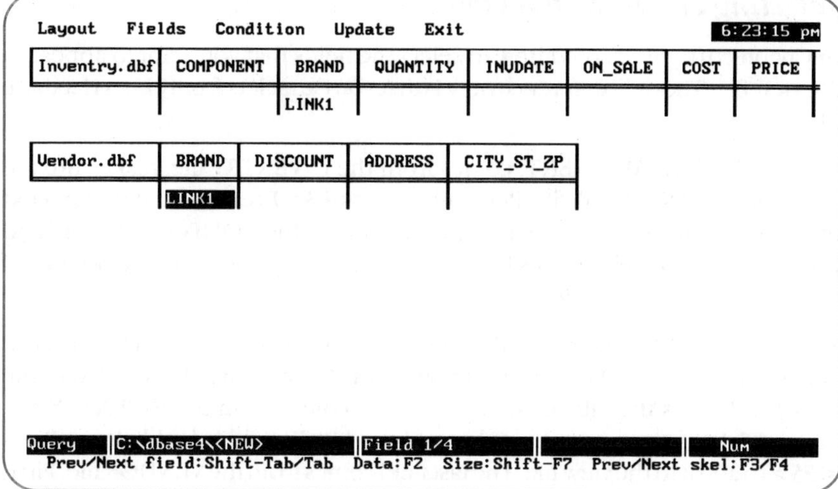

Figure 12.11. *Linking the databases by BRAND*

Don't be confused with other words you can put in the Query Design screens. Your record selections or filters that go in quotes, such as "Turntables", are placed in quotes to avoid conflict with example variables. There are also a small number of reserved words that cannot be used for LINK words. These include: GROUP BY, SUM, AVG, MIN, MAX, FIRST, and EVERY. These are all keywords that mean something in the Query screen. You have learned most of them already in Chapter 10, and you will learn about the rest in this chapter.

Retrieving Related Data

So far, you have only created the link. You haven't looked at the data yet. Create a view skeleton by selecting the fields you want in your query answer. Suppose you decide that you want the following data table:

COMPONENT

BRAND

PRICE

DISCOUNT

Selecting Fields for the View

In Chapter 10, you learned how to select the fields that you want to appear in the view file. The only difference now is that you can select from either database file.

The first field, COMPONENT, comes from the INVENTRY file. Make sure the cursor is in the INVENTRY file. Remember that **<F3> Previous** and **<F4> Next** move you from file to file. Position your cursor on the COMPONENT field and press **<F5>**. The field flashes for a second and jumps down to the bottom of the screen to begin the view file.

You can select BRAND from either file. Move one box to the right and select BRAND in the INVENTRY file. After you press **<F5>**, that field is added to the view file. Next is the PRICE field, which also comes from the INVENTRY file. Press **<Tab>** to move to the right until the PRICE field is highlighted. Press **<F5>** to add it to the view file. The last field comes from the VENDOR file. First, you must press **<F4>** to move to the VENDOR file skeleton. Next, use the **<Tab>** key to move to the DISCOUNT field. Press **<F5>** again to add that field to the file skeleton.

Notice that the filename in the view file for the DISCOUNT field tells you that it came from the VENDOR database file and not from the INVENTRY database file. Whenever you create a view skeleton, it always tells you what database file it comes from. You may not have noticed this file name before because you were working with only one file. Now it's important because it tells you which file your data came from.

Though you took three fields from the INVENTRY file and one field from the VENDOR file, you do not have to select fields in this manner. You can select fields from either database file at any time. You could now select a field from the INVENTRY file, again, and another from the VENDOR file. It doesn't matter where the fields come from, or in what order.

Displaying the Data

Your complete Query screen should look like Figure 12.12. All that's left now is to see the data. Try predicting what you will see. You have asked to see all the items in the INVENTRY database file along with their corresponding prices and discounts from the VENDOR database file. You should see all the data regardless of whether it is on sale, because you haven't told dBASE IV to figure that into the relation. All you have asked so far is to JOIN the files based on the matching BRAND fields.

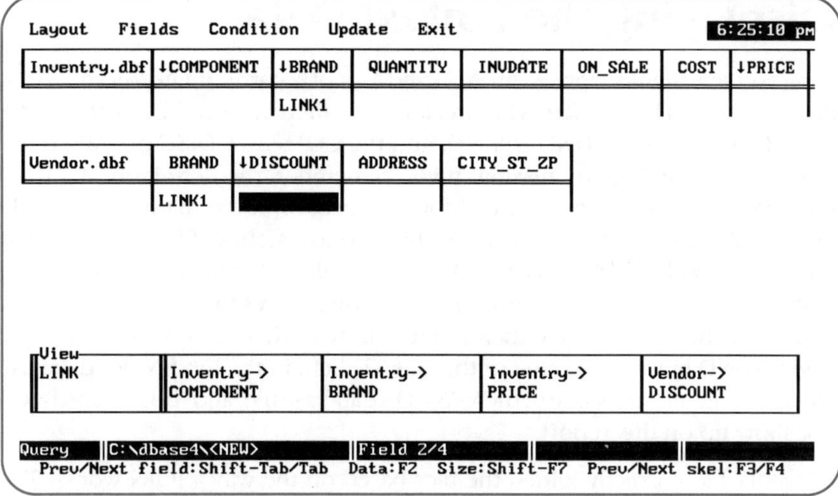

***Figure 12.12.** Selecting fields from two databases*

Take a look at the results. Get into BROWSE by pressing **<F2>**. Your data is now displayed in front of you. If you are in EDIT, press **<F2>** again to get into BROWSE. The screen should look like Figure 12.13.

Records Organize Fields Go To Exit

COMPONENT	BRAND	PRICE	DISCOUNT
AMPLIFIER	DIGI	389.99	0.10
AMPLIFIER	ALLWOOD	589.99	0.15
COMPACT DISC	DIGI	625.99	0.10
COMPACT DISC	HITECH	299.99	0.12
COMPACT DISC	ALLWOOD	189.99	0.15
RECEIVER	ALLWOOD	289.00	0.15
RECEIVER	DIGI	529.00	0.10
SPEAKERS	MITY	399.00	0.25
SPEAKERS	DIGI	109.00	0.10
SPEAKERS	ALLWOOD	59.00	0.15
TURNTABLE	DIGI	299.99	0.10
TURNTABLE	MEGASONIK	69.00	0.08
TURNTABLE	HITECH	269.99	0.12

Browse C:\dbase4\<NEW> Rec 1/15 View ReadOnly

***Figure 12.13.** Displaying the linked data*

Displaying the Linked Data

What you see might surprise you. You find a lot of records but not all your data. Remember, you had 15 items before, and now there are only 13. Where is the record for the ONESOUND BRAND, and the COMPACT DISC or AMPLIFIER COMPONENTS? They're missing! If you remember, the definition of a JOIN said that there should be a record for each record in the main database file INVENTRY that matches a record in the second database file VENDOR, and there is. If you look at the VENDOR database file in Figure 12.9, you can see that there are only five brands in the database file, yet there are six different brands in the INVENTRY database file. Because there is no match for the ONESOUND brand, the value of the BRAND field in the INVENTRY database file will never match a value in the VENDOR database file, and those records will not show up on this report.

dBASE IV has correctly joined the files based on the way a JOIN works. The linking of files to produce this type of JOIN really works only when both files have corresponding keys. You might use this type of query if you had limited the record selection to only those items whose ON_SALE indicator was true. You could then assume that there must be a sale record for the BRAND if an item for that BRAND is on sale. This type of JOIN helps locate mistakes or omissions. For now, keep the data the way it is.

Joining Every Record

Now, take a look at all the data, whether or not there is a corresponding record in the VENDOR file. Assuming you are still in BROWSE, use the `Transfer to Query Design` option of the Exit menu to change your query. You're going to modify the query slightly to see all the INVENTRY records.

Make sure you are back at the Query screen with both database files on the work surface. The LINK1 connectors should still be in the BRAND entry areas of both files. You are now going to use a keyword called EVERY to tell dBASE IV you want every record in the INVENTRY file, regardless of whether it has a match in the BRAND fields. Move the cursor into the entry area for BRAND in the INVENTRY file. Instead of creating the link by pointing, you are going to modify the link name. Change the word LINK1 in the INVENTRY file so that it reads:

```
EVERY LINK1
```

You do not need to change anything else. The LINK1 in the VENDOR database file remains the same.

If you display all the records regardless of any matching, what would display for INVENTRY records with no corresponding records in the VENDOR file? There would be one record in the view file for each of these unmatched INVENTRY records, and the field in the view file that comes from the VENDOR file, DISCOUNT, would be blank, as shown in Figure 12.14. Save this query and call it ALLITEMS. Choose `Save changes and Exit` from the Exit menu.

```
Records   Organize   Fields   Go To   Exit
```

COMPONENT	BRAND	PRICE	DISCOUNT
AMPLIFIER	DIGI	389.99	0.10
AMPLIFIER	ALLWOOD	589.99	0.15
AMPLIFIER	ONESOUND	899.99	.
COMPACT DISC	DIGI	625.99	0.10
COMPACT DISC	ONESOUND	329.99	.
COMPACT DISC	HITECH	299.99	0.12
COMPACT DISC	ALLWOOD	189.99	0.15
RECEIVER	ALLWOOD	289.00	0.15
RECEIVER	DIGI	529.00	0.10
SPEAKERS	MITY	399.00	0.25
SPEAKERS	DIGI	109.00	0.10
SPEAKERS	ALLWOOD	59.00	0.15
TURNTABLE	DIGI	299.99	0.10
TURNTABLE	MEGASONIK	69.00	0.08
TURNTABLE	HITECH	269.99	0.12

```
Browse  C:\dbase4\ALLITEMS   Rec 1/15   View ReadOnly   Caps
```

Figure 12.14. *Displaying EVERY record*

Once again you are placed in the Control Center. Move the cursor to the ALLITEMS file in the Queries panel and press **<F2>** to display the linked data now. As you can see, the rest of the INVENTRY data is showing. After examining the data, press **<Alt>-E** and `T` to select `Transfer to Query Design`.

If you had reversed the EVERY operator and had placed it in the VENDOR file instead of the INVENTRY file, the result would have been very different. First of all, if there were any records in the VENDOR file that had no corresponding records in the INVENTRY file, you would see only the VENDOR data in the record. The COMPONENT, BRAND, and PRICE would be blank. Even though there is data for the BRAND field in the VENDOR database file, the request would have been for the view file to take the BRAND data from the INVENTRY database file. Because there would be no match, the BRAND data would be blank. When using the EVERY operator, make sure that the common field is placed in the view file from the database file that contains the EVERY operator.

Also, if you were to place the EVERY operator in the VENDOR database file, the relation would become a one-to-many relation, and no data at all would show for the ONESOUND brand because there were no records in the VENDOR file for that value.

The dBASE IV QBE processor does not allow the EVERY keyword in both database files of a linked pair.

Selecting Only Certain Records

Suppose you wanted to see the data for only the items that were on sale. You would simply have to add a filter to the database file that contains the field. You can mix filters and links in your database file skeletons to further limit the displayed data. To see just the ON_SALE items, move the cursor to the ON_SALE entry area in the INVENTRY database file and type .T. in the entry area. This limits the display to only the sale items, as shown in Figure 12.15.

```
Records   Organize   Fields   Go To   Exit

COMPONENT       | BRAND     | PRICE  | DISCOUNT
AMPLIFIER       | DIGI      | 389.99 |     0.10
COMPACT DISC    | DIGI      | 625.99 |     0.10
COMPACT DISC    | ONESOUND  | 329.99 |        .
COMPACT DISC    | HITECH    | 299.99 |     0.12
COMPACT DISC    | ALLWOOD   | 189.99 |     0.15
RECEIVER        | DIGI      | 529.00 |     0.10
SPEAKERS        | DIGI      | 109.00 |     0.10
TURNTABLE       | DIGI      | 299.99 |     0.10

Browse  C:\dbase4\ALLITEMS   Rec 1/15   View  ReadOnly   Caps
```

Figure 12.15. *Limiting the display to ON_SALE items*

In the previous chapter, you entered data into all the DIGI records and all the Compact Discs to make the ON_SALE field true. This is what this filter should reveal.

Remember that you don't have to put the field ON_SALE into the view skeleton. As long as it appears in any of the file skeletons it can be used as a filter to select records.

Suppose you wanted to make the request, "Show me all the Turntable records that are on sale." To do this you merely need to add the filter "TURNTABLE" in the COMPONENT entry area of the INVENTRY database file. The .T. filter in the ON_SALE entry area remains unchanged, because you want only the items that are on sale and that are turntables. When you press <F2> to see the filtered view, you see all your turntables that are on sale. There is only one: the DIGI turntable. The present Query screen is shown in Figure 12.16.

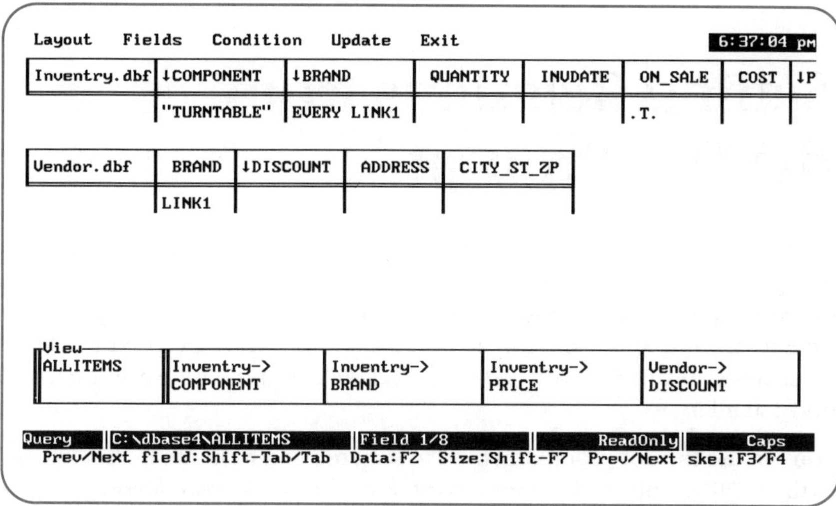

Figure 12.16. *Searching for the TURNTABLES that are ON_SALE*

Suppose you wanted to see all the records that were on sale and had discounts of less than 10 percent. All you would need to do is type `.T.` in the ON_SALE entry area of the INVENTRY database file and enter `<.10` in the DISCOUNT entry area of the VENDOR database file. The two databases are treated as one for the purpose of filtering.

Creating a New Database from the Query

One last item. Suppose you wanted to actually create a new database file consisting of just the fields COMPONENT, BRAND, PRICE, and DISCOUNT and include only the data from the query as it presently exists. dBASE IV provides the capability to actually take the present query view file, which up to now exists only in dBASE memory, and actually write it out as a database file. This option is on the Layout menu and is called `Write view as database file`. Don't try it now, but when you use this option it will allow you to take the current view of your database files—the open files and their relations, fields you have placed in the view file, sorts you have specified, and the records you have selected—to create a new database file with only the information from the current view.

This completes a long look at multiple files in the Query screen. You also can set relations in the dot prompt mode. If you want to save your query, do it now. Return to the Control Center and then exit to the dot prompt.

Setting Relations from the Dot Prompt

When you create a query in the Query work surface, dBASE IV actually interprets what you have done on the Query Design screen and generates dBASE dot prompt commands in the form of a program file. Though you never have to see this short file, it is important for you to be exposed to all the commands, just in case you see some code like it in the future and need to understand it.

You can use the dot prompt method to set a relation from the INVENTRY file to the VENDOR file. It is not important if the relation is a one-to-one, one-to-many, many-to-one, or many-to-many. This is dependent on the data, not the relation. Setting and using relations from the dot prompt are the same.

From the dot prompt, close any open files by entering:

```
. CLOSE ALL
```

This closes any database file, index, query, form, and report files. In effect, it gives you a clean slate to start with. It doesn't erase any of your data or work you've created; it just puts the files away.

Opening Databases

Now that you have cleared the environment, make the INVENTRY file active again. Enter the following:

```
. USE INVENTRY
```

This opens the INVENTRY database file without opening any indexes, and it places the file in what is known as work area 1. When you use only one database file at a time, it is not important which work area you place the database file in. The default work area is 1.

Next you must open a second work area and open your "child" database file. Work areas are opened with the SELECT command. You will select work area 2. Once this area is selected, you will open a second database file. Enter:

```
. SELECT 2
. USE VENDOR
```

Indexing the Related File

Child database files must be indexed in order to establish the relation from the parent files. When generating its code from the Query screen, dBASE IV checks to see if an index exists for the field that will be used in the child file. If it doesn't exist, dBASE IV indexes the file. When you write your own code, you also need to know whether the file is indexed. If it isn't indexed, you would enter (in this example):

```
. INDEX ON BRAND BRAND
```

However, when you created the VENDOR file, you should have automatically indexed the file on the BRAND field by placing a Y in the index column of the database file create screen. Because the database file is already indexed by BRAND, enter:

```
. SET ORDER TO TAG BRAND
```

Now you have opened both work areas and placed database files into them. Because you will establish the relation from the INVENTRY file to the VENDOR file, you have to make the INVENTRY work area active again. Currently, the VENDOR database file is active in work area 2.

Once you USE a database file, you can select its area in different ways. The first is by the original work number you gave it. The other is by its alias. An alias for a database file, just like an alias for a person, is another name by which it is known. Each database file is known automatically by an alias, which is its name, regardless of the area where it was placed. Once you establish the work area and open the database file, you can make that area active by using the database file name again, instead of the work area number.

Selecting and Relating the Files

Select the INVENTRY file by its alias. Though you know that the file is in work area 1, and you could simply enter SELECT 1, it is easier to enter the alias names when you have more than one work area in use.

```
. SELECT INVENTRY
```

This returns control to the INVENTRY database file. The VENDOR database file is still open in the second work area. Your last chore is to relate the INVENTRY database file to the VENDOR database file so that fields from both database files are available as though they were one database file. That's basically the whole concept behind relational database files. You can maintain separate database files for simplicity, and to make data entry simpler and more efficient. However, you need multiple database files to appear as one for reporting purposes. Once two database files are related, they appear as one file, and data from both can be displayed quickly and easily.

The command to relate two database files is SET RELATION. The parent database file must be selected. A relation is set from the key field in the parent database file to the indexed child file. The command:

```
SET RELATION TO BRAND INTO VENDOR
```

sets this relation between the INVENTRY file and the VENDOR file. Because the first work area where the INVENTRY database file was placed is selected, dBASE knows about that database file. The SET RELATION command assumes that you are in the parent file. The BRAND field specified in the TO clause describes the field in the parent database file that links it to the child file. The other half of the link, in the child file, is the index key. Because the VENDOR file is indexed by BRAND, there will be a valid match. The name of the fields used in the link and the index do not have to be the same. You can consider it coincidence that both files contain the field names BRAND. It isn't really necessary. The *values* of both fields must match.

The INTO clause specifies the name of the child file. Once this link is established, you can begin to see your data. Many dBASE IV commands now treat your relation as a single database file; other commands simply understand that the link makes the fields from both files available.

Remember that the type of relationship is totally dependent on your data, not on the relation you establish. Regardless of your data, you will always use the same SET RELATION command to establish the relation. Because of your data, you have established a many-to-one relationship. There is more than one record with the same value of BRAND in the INVENTRY file, but there is only one matching record in the VENDOR file, even though the record in the vendor file is used again and again. There are multiple records in the INVENTRY file for each BRAND, because Parrot Stereo sells different components of each BRAND. For example, in the DIGI brand, the store sells amplifiers, compact discs, receivers, speakers, and turntables. Because the key to the relation is only BRAND, it appears that there are many records for the BRAND.

SET SKIP TO

There is another important command to learn for setting relations. When you have a something-to-many relationship, you may want to control how many levels of duplicates are displayed. The command SET SKIP TO takes care of this. If you don't list a child file in a SET SKIP TO command, you will only see the first occurrence of a duplicate parent record.

Look back at the example of placing the EVERY operator in the VENDOR file. This could be used to show all the COMPONENTS in the INVENTRY file for each BRAND in the VENDOR file. Without the command:

```
. SET SKIP TO VENDOR
```

only the first COMPONENT of each brand would be displayed. Once the relations are set, you can use the DISPLAY, LIST, EDIT, or BROWSE commands to select your records and fields. However, there are a few more commands to understand.

Selecting the Fields

First you must decide which fields are to appear in the view file that will display the data. The SET FIELDS TO command accomplishes this task. For the example of a four field view file, the command is as follows:

```
. SET FIELDS TO INVENTRY->COMPONENT,INVENTRY->BRAND,
  INVENTRY->PRICE,VENDOR->DISCOUNT
```

Notice that the same form of selecting a field in a database file is used here as in the view file of the Query screen. The database filename is placed first. It's followed by an arrow constructed from a dash and a greater-than sign, followed by the field name itself.

Setting the Filters

Once the fields are determined, you can set any filters to indicate which records will be displayed. Filters are separately set in each work area. To filter the INVENTRY database file for the turntables that were on sale, enter:

```
. SELECT INVENTRY
. SET FILTER TO (COMPONENT = 'TURNTABLE' .AND. ON_SALE)
```

Filters have the exact same form as record selection used with the DISPLAY or LIST commands. Instead of setting a filter, you could have entered:

```
. DISPLAY ALL FOR (COMPONENT = 'TURNTABLE' .AND.
  ON_SALE)
```

All of these commands entered separately at the dot prompt create various parts of the view. The view isn't just something you create in the Query Design screen. The current view determines the open database files, indexes, and relations. It also includes the field and record selections. Whether you enter the commands from the dot prompt or use the Query screen, the result is the same. You build a "window" into your database file that "views" only what you want it to.

You can save all the dot prompt commands that create your view. To do this you enter:

```
. CREATE VIEW <filename> FROM ENVIRONMENT
```

Take a look at a QBE file that you created in this chapter. The file is shown in Figure 12.17. It contains all the commands generated by your QBE requests. Though it is produced with code that is somewhat different, it accomplishes the same tasks you have just seen.

```
* dBASE IV .QBE file
SELECT 1
USE INVENTRY.DBF NOUPDATE
USE VENDOR.DBF NOUPDATE IN 2 ORDER BRAND
SET EXACT ON
SET FILTER TO (A->COMPONENT='TURNTABLE' .AND. A->ON_SALE=.T.)
SET RELATION TO A->BRAND INTO B
SET SKIP TO B
GO TOP
SET FIELDS TO A->COMPONENT,A->BRAND,A->PRICE,B->DISCOUNT
```

***Figure 12.17.** Output of the QBE statements*

CONFIG.SYS

CONFIG.SYS is a special configuration file that you need on the root directory of the disk you use to boot your computer. This is the disk that contains your operating system, PC DOS or MS-DOS. Your operating system is always found in the root directory of the hard disk.

To create or alter CONFIG.SYS, you need to quit dBASE IV. Now your computer monitor displays a C> prompt:

```
C>
```

In the following discussion, the C> indicates the operating system prompt. At the prompt, enter:

```
CD\
```

The backslash is the symbol for the root directory. The CD is the operating system command for Change Directory. You have told the computer to go to the root directory. Next, find out if there is already a configuration file, by using the DIR (directory) command. Type:

```
C> DIR CONFIG.SYS
```

If the file is present, the operating system (DOS) displays the filename and information about the file. You need only to edit the file. If the file isn't there, you'll see the `File not found` message. The next step is to create the CONFIG.SYS file.

Creating CONFIG.SYS

You can create the file and add the appropriate statements by typing the following. Press **<Enter>** at the end of each line:

```
C> COPY CON: C:\CONFIG.SYS
FILES=99
BUFFERS=15
```

When you've finished entering the above, press function key **<F6>**. This will place a mark (`Z`) on your screen. The `Z` is called the *end-of-file* mark. Next, press the **<Enter>** key. That's all there is to it—your computer now has the needed file CONFIG.SYS on its root directory.

Editing CONFIG.SYS

If you already have a CONFIG.SYS on your root directory, be sure that it contains the following two statements. If it does not, you need to add the following two statements to the file. If you have these two statements already, make sure that the number of files is at least 99 and the number of buffers is at least 15.

```
FILES=99
BUFFERS=15
```

You can edit the file and add the above if necessary with the help of the DOS EDLIN command. Consult your DOS manual.

Why did you need to do this? Your operating system is normally set up to handle 8 files. But it immediately takes 4 back: the keyboard, screen, printer, and communications. dBASE takes 1 more, which leaves only 3 files. By placing the above statements into CONFIG.SYS, you can use a total of 15 files of all types from within dBASE IV. Ten of those 15 can be database files.

Once you have created or modified CONFIG.SYS, turn off your computer; then reboot it, that is, turn it back on. Rebooting your computer forces it to read the configuration file. Whenever the computer is booted, the operating system looks for this configuration file on the root directory. If it's there, the operating system will read it and follow the configuration instructions.

Summary

As you have seen in this chapter, the number of ways to look at your data is limited only by your imagination and good database file design. You have learned the importance of designing database files that limit redundancies. Because of your ability to set file relations, you can have your data presented any way you want.

In the next chapter you will begin to examine the printed report and how to use query files to limit the output of printed reports.

Before you move on to the next section, "Reports," take a look at something special that you need in order to use multiple files.

Section Three

Database Features

chapter 13

Reports

To get the most out of your database manager, you need to master its report generator. You use the report generator to prepare formal reports composed of the data from your files. In Chapter 2, you used the dBASE IV Quick Report Generator to prepare the report shown in Figure 2.16. In this chapter, you'll begin with a more detailed report to explore the features of the dBASE IV Report Generator in greater depth. You will produce two different types of reports—a column report and a form report—and you will learn for what applications you use each one. This chapter also covers some of the advanced features of the Report Generator, how to prepare reports using several databases, and the dBASE IV Print menu.

Designing Reports

Computer-generated reports have had the same columnar format for many years. The original data processors were accountants, and they liked to see numbers in tables and columns. They could visualize the trends of the business simply by looking at these columns of numbers. Such an ability either is an inborn talent or is learned through many years of experience.

Today, the world of computer reporting has changed so that almost any report, graph, picture, or model can be represented in any format. Graphs can be plotted with great precision and clarity; reports can be displayed on a terminal screen—and rearranged at will. A model of the business can be shown on a computer screen, with animated graphics showing the flow of goods in and out of the company.

Reports are messages from your application about the actions happening internally to the system. Reports are also the vehicle for moving business-oriented information from the computer system, where it was gleaned from data, to the manager or executive who can change that information into action.

Designing a computer report or form is a process just like other forms of design. First, the purpose of the report is defined. Then, all the people involved in producing and using the report have to agree what data items need to be shown on the report in order to produce accurate and plentiful information. Finally, the report itself is defined. Definition includes placement of all data fields and text identifiers, totals, subtotals, and even such things as the quality of the print on the page.

Types of Reports

Three types of reports commonly used in business are available through the dBASE IV Report Generator. These are:

- Column reports
- Forms reports
- Mail merging

Column reports are reports organized into rows and columns much like the BROWSE table. Each record becomes a row in the table. The only real difference from BROWSE mode is that you can create customized headers for both the page and each column, and you can have subtotals and totals on your numeric fields. Common examples of column reports include sales and inventory reports, your bank statement, and even a simple balance sheet or income statement.

Form reports, new to dBASE IV, give you unlimited control over your data. Usually created with one record or several records per page, form reports let you place data anywhere on a page and create all types of new totals and summaries. Common examples of form reports include invoices, checks, and tax forms.

Mail merging is very similar to a form report, except it is usually very heavily text-based, with data placed here and there within the text. This type of report also is known as a word wrap report because the text must be adjusted depending on the length of the data placed among the text lines. A common mail-merge report is a letter to a customer about an overdue bill. The next chapter covers mail merging and label creation.

dBASE IV handles all of these types of reports with ease, using the same report form. In fact, you use the exact same dBASE work surface and menus, whether you are creating a column, form, or mail-merge report. The only differences are how you lay out the report and what it looks like.

dBASE IV can take your data and automatically place all of it on the work surface in the form you want with just a few keystrokes. This *quick layout* acts as a starting point for you to customize your report any way you want.

WYSIWYG—from Form to Print

dBASE IV lets you create your reports by means of a what-you-see- is-what-you-get (WYSIWYG) interface. Text, including column headers, report headers, lines, and boxes, as well as fields, calculations, and summaries, is placed anywhere on the work surface that serves as a representation of the printed page. By creating a template for the report generator to follow, you can see the format of your report before it is printed. Figure 13.1 shows a complete report form. Notice how every data field and text item on the Report work surface lets you see where the data will actually be placed on the report.

This visual interface lets you place your text and fields anywhere on this work area. You can be sure that its position determines exactly where the actual printed output will go. dBASE IV uses this template to map out the data. Each record fills a part of the template, like chocolate in a mold.

Report Bands

The dBASE IV Report Generator lets you place your text and fields into horizontal report areas known as bands. There are four types of bands in dBASE IV, as shown in Figure 13.2:

- Page bands
- Report bands
- Detail bands
- Group bands

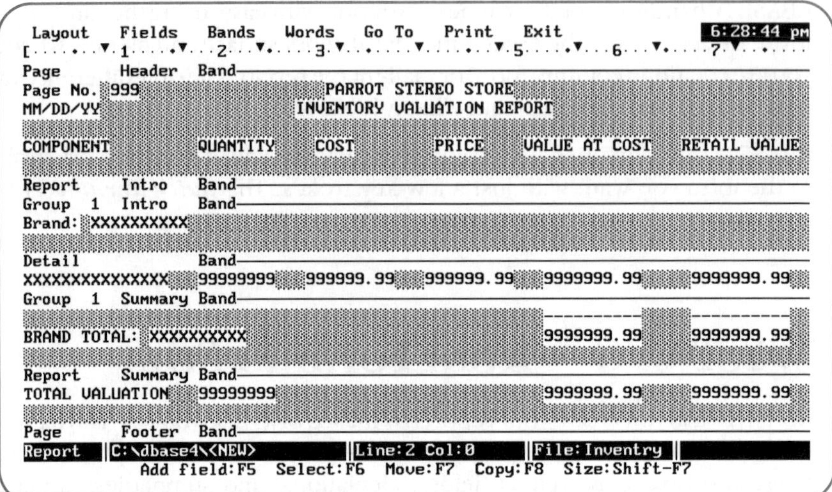

***Figure 13.1.** The WYSIWYG interface*

```
Layout   Fields   Bands   Words   Go To   Print   Exit          4:22:02 pm
Page        Header  Band
Report      Intro   Band
Group  1    Intro   Band
Detail              Band
Group  1    Summary Band
Report      Summary Band
Page        Footer  Band

Report   C:\dbase4\<NEW>   Band 1/7   File:Inventry
         Add field:F5  Select:F6  Move:F7  Copy:F8  Size:Shift-F7
```

***Figure 13.2.** The various report bands*

Page, report, and group bands come in matching sets. The header (also known as the intro) comes before the detail lines, and the footer (also known as the summary) comes after the detail lines. Headers are used primarily for identification information, such as a title, page number, date, or even a common data value. Footers are used for totals, summaries, and other statistical measures.

The Page Header comes first. Whatever appears in this band appears at the top of every page. When a new page is being produced, this band is triggered to print.

The Report Intro comes next, but appears only once in the very beginning of the report. It is often used to design a cover memo or a report title page.

For each subtotal or grouping you want on the report, you have a pair of Group bands, numbered from one to the number of groupings on your report. In the inventory example, there is just one Group band that will be grouped by BRAND. Group bands do not appear automatically as the other bands do. You must tell dBASE IV that you want a grouping and on what field or expression you want it.

The Detail band is just that. It is where the detail of the report goes. The data that makes up the report is generally found in the Detail band, one record used for each page or line, depending on the type of report.

Group Summary bands come next. You use these for subtotals of the group. You use the Report Summary band for grand totals because anything in this band appears once at the very bottom of the report. The last band is the Page Footer band. This band appears at the bottom of each page and is used for totals based on individual pages.

Column Reports

A column report has standard areas. Figure 13.3 shows these areas. These areas directly relate to the band areas that dBASE IV uses to organize its Report Generator work surface. This is the column report you will create in this chapter. This report will be an inventory valuation report.

Looking at the report, it's easy to see how the various areas of the report relate to the bands of the Report work surface where they were created. At the top of the page is the page header. Items that are placed in this area include page numbers, dates, titles, and column headings.

```
Page No.    1                PARROT STEREO STORE
04/03/91                  INVENTORY VALUATION REPORT

COMPONENT          QUANTITY    COST        PRICE    VALUE AT COST   RETAIL VALUE

Brand: ALLWOOD

AMPLIFIER                10      369.00      589.99      3690.00       5899.90
COMPACT DISC             60      109.00      189.99      6540.00      11399.40
RECEIVER                 30      169.00      289.00      5070.00       8670.00
SPEAKERS                140       69.00       59.00      9660.00       8260.00
                                                      ----------    ----------
BRAND TOTAL: ALLWOOD                                    24960.00      34229.30

Brand: DIGI

AMPLIFIER                15      229.00      389.99      3435.00       5849.85
COMPACT DISC             17      389.00      625.99      6613.00      10641.83
RECEIVER                  0      299.00      529.00         0.00          0.00
SPEAKERS                 18       89.00      109.00      1602.00       1962.00
TURNTABLE                15      149.00      299.99      2235.00       4499.85
                                                      ----------    ----------
BRAND TOTAL: DIGI                                       13885.00      22953.53

Brand: HITECH

COMPACT DISC             50      129.00      299.99      6450.00      14999.50
TURNTABLE                 6      189.00      269.99      1134.00       1619.94
                                                      ----------    ----------
BRAND TOTAL: HITECH                                      7584.00      16619.44

Brand: MEGASONIK

TURNTABLE               250       39.00       69.00      9750.00      17250.00
                                                      ----------    ----------
BRAND TOTAL: MEGASONIK                                   9750.00      17250.00

Brand: MITY

SPEAKERS                 22      299.00      399.00      6578.00       8778.00
                                                      ----------    ----------
BRAND TOTAL: MITY                                        6578.00       8778.00

Brand: ONESOUND

AMPLIFIER                 5      529.00      899.99      2645.00       4499.95
COMPACT DISC             26      269.00      329.99      6994.00       8579.74
                                                      ----------    ----------
BRAND TOTAL: ONESOUND                                    9639.00      13079.69

TOTAL VALUATION         664                             72396.00     112909.96
```

Figure 13.3. *A typical column report*

Then there is the Report Intro area. It appears only at the beginning and end of the entire report. The Report Intro is used for such items as a cover letter or just a title that appears by itself on the report. The Report Summary usually is more important because it contains grand totals for the entire report. Often a report has a Report Summary but no Report Intro. This is perfectly acceptable. Though headers and footers come in matched pairs, you do not have to use both in a report.

Likewise, page summaries are not often used. They appear at the end of each page and often contain no text or data. They are used only when some type of totals or explanation is needed on each page.

The next type of area is the group area. There is no real limit to the number of group areas a report can contain, but it often gets very confusing if there are more than three or four groupings. In Figure 13.2, only one grouping is shown for each BRAND. Each grouping has both a header and a footer. The header is used to identify the data that the group represents; the footer shows subtotals.

Last of all are the detail lines themselves. The detail lines contain the actual data from the database file that will go into the report. As the report is produced, the data appears one line at a time in the detail line area.

A Step-by-Step Design Method

Designing your reports is best done by taking a blank piece of paper and sketching out how you want the report to look. You place your titles and column headers on the page and then put all the fields from your database file in the approximate positions. Last, you add calculations and totals. Creating the report form with dBASE IV is a similar process. In this chapter, you will use the following steps to create two reports.

1. Assemble your data.
2. Choose the `Quick layouts` option or add the fields you want.
3. Delete unwanted fields and text.
4. Move fields and text into final position.
5. Create calculated and summary fields.
6. Create group bands, headers, and footers.
7. Add final column headers, text, lines, boxes, and styling.

As you create your report, you'll experience each of these steps in detail.

The dBASE IV Report Work Surface

As you saw in several chapters, reports are prepared with the help of a Report work surface. The Report work surface is where you enter the information into a screen that becomes a template for the report. It creates a disk file that contains the information to prepare the report. Because it's a disk file, you can use it over and over again and make as many copies of the report as you like. Because the database file is the source of the report data, any changes in data content are automatically reflected in the final report. You begin a report form from the Control Center Reports panel, or from the CREATE REPORT command at the dot prompt. You can modify your report design starting from the Reports panel or with the MODIFY REPORT command at the dot prompt.

Assembling Your Data

Before you create a report using the Report work surface, you must get all your data for that report into one database file or one view. If you are working with only one database file, make that database file active before you begin the report. If you need access to data from multiple database files, create a view that sets file relations and links your data.

If you are planning to ask for subtotals or groupings, make sure your data is sorted or indexed into that order. Otherwise, your groupings will turn into a big mess. Creating a Group band tells dBASE IV to produce a header and footer for each change in the group field of the database file. If the data is not sorted in group order, the data appears to dBASE IV as having many different groupings when it is really only because the data is not sequenced correctly.

To begin to create your first report, go to the Control Center and make sure that the INVENTRY file is active. Make sure that you have made the BRAND index active by going into the Database work surface and choosing `Order records by index` in the Organize menu. Move your cursor to `<create>` on the Reports panel and press **<Enter>**. The Report work surface opens so you can begin to create your report.

Using Quick Layouts

The Layout menu opens automatically because dBASE IV assumes that you will start with `Quick layouts`. Press **<Enter>** to open the `Quick layouts` option submenu. The three choices are shown in Figure 13.4. For this first example, select the `Column layout` choice.

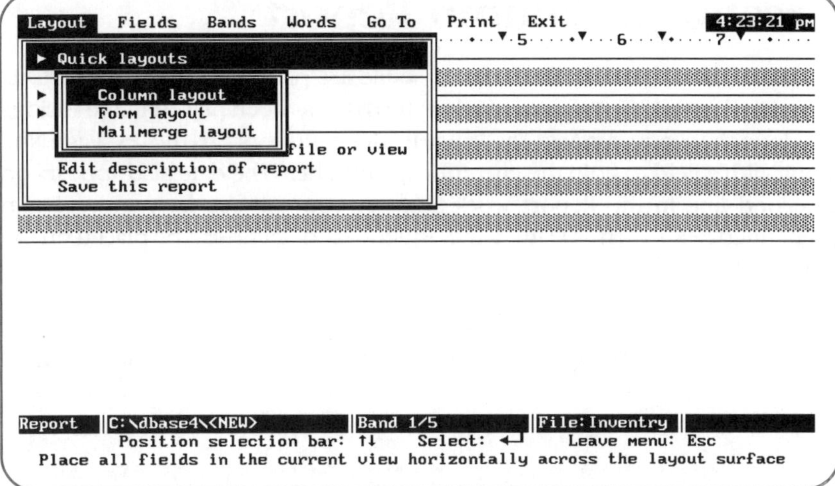

Figure 13.4. *The Layout menu on the Report work surface*

Rather than tell dBASE which fields you want to use from your database file and where to place them on the form, you can choose the option known as the `Quick layouts`. This requests that dBASE IV place all your fields in the Detail band on the form in a column, form, or mail-merge layout. It places column headings, page numbers, and the date in the Page Header. In column reports, it creates automatic totals for your numeric fields and places them in the Report Summary band.

This gives you a quick start to creating your report. In fact, this is the exact same layout used by the `Quick Report` option (**<Shift>-<F9>**) available in most work surfaces. Having all your data on the form automatically lets you begin to position it where you want it and concentrate on making the report look good.

If, however, you want only a few fields on the form, you might be better off starting with a blank form. Then you would place your fields on the form one at a time.

You'll be producing a column report as a first example, because it is the most common type of report used in business. It has many standard areas and provides great flexibility in creating an almost unlimited number of subtotals and totals. Because the detail data is usually placed in neat rows and columns, it is an easy report to understand regardless of the data or business industry.

Creating a Column Report

All the fields in the INVENTRY database file are placed on the work surface. Examine Figure 13.5. You can see that the data has been placed in the various bands on the report surface. The Page Header band contains the text Page No., along with a field to hold the current page number. The date also appears on a second line in the Report work surface. You will see later how certain predefined fields such as Date, Time, Pageno, and Recno can be placed on the work surface.

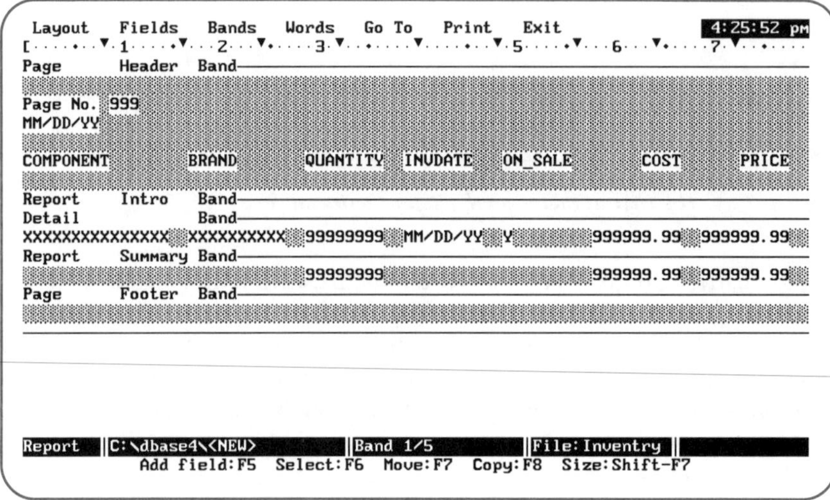

Figure 13.5. *The column Quick Report layout*

Two lines under that, but still in the Page Header band, are the column headers. These headers will be printed at the top of each page. Each band is expandable to accommodate almost any number of lines in each band. There is nothing in the Report Intro band. It appears only once at the beginning of the report, normally for a report cover or a cover letter that precedes the entire report.

After the "intros" come the detail lines. This is where your actual data is placed. If you look at Figure 13.5 you will see *X*'s where your character and memo fields are, *9*'s where your numeric fields are, *MM/DD/YY* where your date fields are, and a *Y* where the logic field is. You will see *V*'s where your memo field is. The memo field is not visible. It is off the screen to the right. You can use the arrow keys to move to the right and view the field. Once you start to work on your report and you move your cursor to one of the fields, it displays the field name below the status bar, along with the field type and length. You can remember which field is which by looking at the headers in the Page Header band.

Numeric fields are automatically totaled and placed in the Report Summary band. Because totals occur once per report, it makes sense to place grand totals in the Report Summary band. If you want totals at the end of each page as well, you can place totals (or anything else) in the Page Footer band.

Take a look at Figure 13.6. This is what this report would generate if it were printed now. Notice that there is no report title, because you haven't created one yet. There are no spaces between the last detail record and the totals. There are no explanations for the fields in the report summary. They just appear. The totals for the price fields make no sense whatsoever. The logical field is simply displayed with Y or N. Finally, the memo field is taking up several lines.

```
Page No.    1
04/03/91

COMPONENT      BRAND       QUANTITY  INVDATE  ON_SALE      COST    PRICE  FEATURES

AMPLIFIER      ALLWOOD           10  07/15/91  N         369.00   589.99  ALLWOOD AMPLIFIER:

                                                                          This is the best amplifier
                                                                          that Parrot Stereo carrys.
                                                                          It has a woofer and a tweeter
                                                                          and woofs and tweets real well.

COMPACT DISC   ALLWOOD           60  10/01/91  Y         109.00   189.99
RECEIVER       ALLWOOD           30  10/15/91  N         169.00   289.00
SPEAKERS       ALLWOOD          140  12/15/91  N          69.00    59.00
AMPLIFIER      DIGI              15  07/01/91  Y         229.00   389.99  DIGI AMPLIFIER:

                                                                          This is one of our top of the line
                                                                          Amplifiers.  However, profit margins
                                                                          are low.  Try to sell the ALLWOOD.
                                                                          It has 200 watts power.

COMPACT DISC   DIGI              17  08/15/91  Y         389.00   625.99
RECEIVER       DIGI               0  11/01/91  Y         299.00   529.00
SPEAKERS       DIGI              18  12/01/91  Y          89.00   109.00
TURNTABLE      DIGI              15  01/01/92  Y         149.00   299.99
COMPACT DISC   HITECH            50  09/15/91  Y         129.00   299.99
TURNTABLE      HITECH             6  02/01/92  N         189.00   269.99
TURNTABLE      MEGASONIK        250  01/15/92  N          39.00    69.00
SPEAKERS       MITY              22  11/15/91  N         299.00   399.00
AMPLIFIER      ONESOUND           5  08/01/91  N         529.00   899.99
COMPACT DISC   ONESOUND          26  09/01/91  Y         269.00   329.99
                                664                     3325.00  5349.91
```

***Figure 13.6.** The Quick Report output*

This is probably not the way you want your report to look. It's time to start moving the fields and designing the report the way you want it to look.

Navigating on the Work Surface

Some of the navigation keys are noted at the bottom of the screen. With them, you can add and delete fields; select one or more fields or text areas, then copy or move them; and even change the sizes of fields.

You can move within the work surface by using the normal arrow keys. The arrow keys move you one character at a time in the designated direction. The **<PgUp>**, **<PgDn>**, **<Home>**, and **<End>** keys also move you about the work surface. The **<Tab>** key can be used to move quickly from one part of the form to another.

Changing the Field Layout

Before you learn how to print the report, you need to make some changes to it so it looks like the report in Figure 13.3. The first thing you need to do is remove some of the unwanted fields and create subtotals. The COMPONENT field will remain in the detail line, but the BRAND field will be used to create subtotals. This report will be grouped by BRAND, so there is no need to have the BRAND field in the detail line. First you will delete the BRAND field and the BRAND column header. Later, you will re-create it in a Group Intro band.

Deleting Unwanted Fields and Text

When you delete fields, you also need to delete the field column headers. Deleting a field is easy. First you move the cursor to the field. When the cursor touches any part of the field, the field highlights. When it is highlighted, press **<Del>** and the field will disappear from the work surface.

Using the arrow keys, move the cursor into the Detail band. As you move through each band, the band border will highlight to tell you which band is active. Move the cursor to the *X*'s in the BRAND field. As soon as you touch any of the letters, the entire field highlights. With the BRAND field highlighted, press **<Del>**. The field disappears from the work surface.

You also need to delete the column header for BRAND. Whenever you delete a field from the Detail band, it makes sense to delete its column header as well. Move the cursor to the Page Header band and select the BRAND header. Notice that the entire text field didn't highlight. This is because it is actually *text* and not a field. Text is something you type on the work surface, and dBASE IV doesn't know where text begins and where it ends. You have to use the key **<F6> Select** to highlight more than one character in text. Once you press the **<F6>** key, everything you touch with the cursor will be selected until you press **<Enter>**.

With the cursor on the *B* in BRAND, press **<F6>**. Move the cursor four spaces to the right. The entire text, BRAND, should now be selected. Press **<Del>** and the text disappears. Delete the INVDATE, ON_SALE, and FEATURES fields and their column headers. The FEATURES field is out of sight to the right of the display. Move the cursor to the right with the arrow keys past column 80, and the FEATURES field will scroll into view.

Totaling prices makes no sense unless you are looking for averages. Delete three more fields. Move the cursor to the Report Summary band and select the COST total. Next, press **<F6>** to continue the selection, and press the **<End>** key. This selects both the COST and the PRICE total fields. You can delete both of the fields at once by pressing **<Del>**. All the fields in the Report Summary are gone, except the QUANTITY total. Your screen should look like Figure 13.7. You have just taken your first steps toward producing the report shown in Figure 13.3.

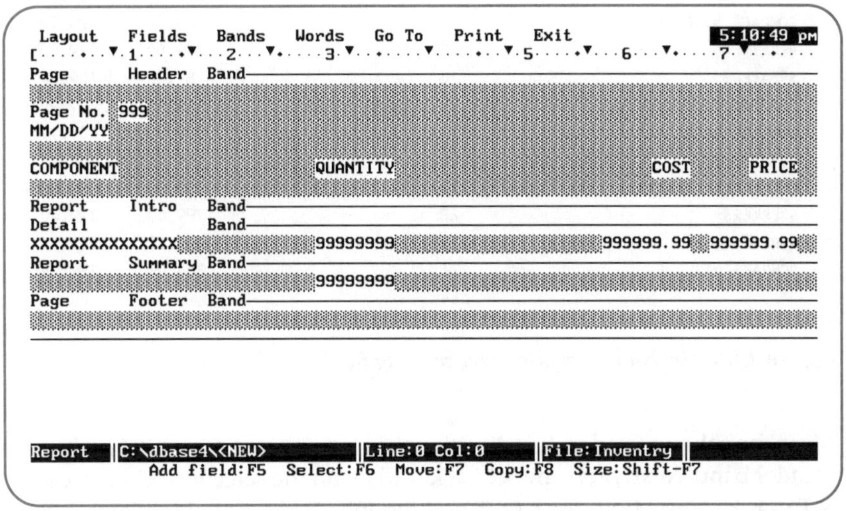

```
 Layout   Fields   Bands   Words   Go To   Print   Exit                5:10:49 pm
[·····•·▼·1····•▼···2···▼•····3·▼··•·····▼·····•··▼·5····•▼···6···▼•····7·▼·•····
Page      Header  Band──────────────────────────────────────────────────────────────

Page No. 999
MM/DD/YY

COMPONENT                     QUANTITY                          COST       PRICE

Report    Intro   Band──────────────────────────────────────────────────────────────
Detail            Band──────────────────────────────────────────────────────────────
XXXXXXXXXXXXXXX               99999999                      999999.99  999999.99
Report    Summary Band──────────────────────────────────────────────────────────────
                              99999999
Page      Footer  Band──────────────────────────────────────────────────────────────

────────────────────────────────────────────────────────────────────────────────────



Report   C:\dbase4\<NEW>            Line:0 Col:0      File:Inventry
            Add field:F5   Select:F6   Move:F7   Copy:F8   Size:Shift-F7
```

Figure 13.7. *The column report after deletions*

Once again, take a look at the result of deleting these fields on the printed report. Figure 13.8 reveals these changes. There are wide gaps in the fields, and the line spacing is as yet unchanged.

At this time, you may want to move your fields to allow room for any new fields you want to place on the work surface. In this way, you can avoid moving them twice. Each time you do one task (adding, deleting, or moving a field), you might create a few more tasks. One thing is always the same, though: the ability to continue to improve the look of the report as you develop it.

Moving Fields and Text

Your screen should look like Figure 13.7. Before you go on, close up the space left by the missing fields. The text and fields in the bands need to be adjusted. You cannot just delete blank spaces in the report screen. You must move the fields or text in order to close up the space. The cost and price data need to be moved to the left to close the gap remaining from the removal of the INVDATE field and heading.

Page No. 1
04/03/91

COMPONENT	QUANTITY	COST	PRICE
AMPLIFIER	10	369.00	589.99
COMPACT DISC	60	109.00	189.99
RECEIVER	30	169.00	289.00
SPEAKERS	140	69.00	59.00
AMPLIFIER	15	229.00	389.99
COMPACT DISC	17	389.00	625.99
RECEIVER	0	299.00	529.00
SPEAKERS	18	89.00	109.00
TURNTABLE	15	149.00	299.99
COMPACT DISC	50	129.00	299.99
TURNTABLE	6	189.00	269.99
TURNTABLE	250	39.00	69.00
SPEAKERS	22	299.00	399.00
AMPLIFIER	5	529.00	899.99
COMPACT DISC	26	269.00	329.99
	664		

Figure 13.8. *The column report after moving fields*

Move the column headers first. Position the cursor on the *C* in COST in the Page Header band. Next, press the **<F6>** key to begin the selection. Then press the **<Tab>** key until both the COST and the PRICE fields are highlighted. Press **<Enter>** to complete the selection. Once the selection is complete, it is time to move the fields. Move the cursor to the place where you want the fields to start. Press the **<F7>** key. You will see a rectangle representing the text at the new cursor position. Press **<Enter>** to finish moving the text.

The space in the Page Header line is now closed up. However, there is still space between the COMPONENT field and the QUANTITY field. This time, move all three text headers at once—QUANTITY, COST, and PRICE. Start your selection with the far-left character, the *Q* in QUANTITY, and press **<F6>**. Now press **<Tab>** to highlight all three text words. Press **<Enter>** to complete the selection. To move the selection, move the cursor to the start of the new location. Press **<F7>** and the rectangle moves a few spaces to the right of the COMPONENT text. Press **<Enter>** to complete the selection.

The message `Delete covered text and fields? (Y/N)` may appear. dBASE IV is just warning you that the original fields are being covered. Press to accept this selection.

Repeat this procedure for the fields in the Detail band and for the Quantity field in the Report Summary band. Make sure in the Detail band that you press **<F6>** before attempting to press **<F7>**. Even though you've highlighted the field, it is not selected until you press **<F6>**. Once you are finished, your screen should look like Figure 13.9. The column headers and fields are now on the left side of the page.

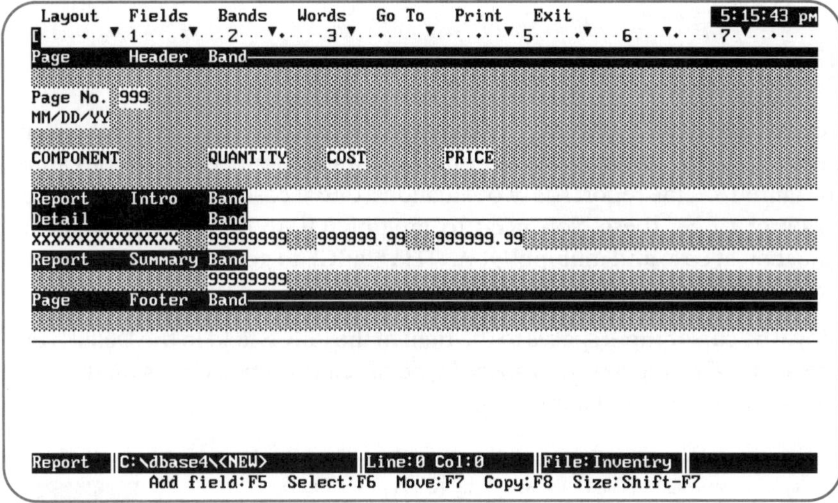

Figure 13.9. *The column report after closing gaps*

Adding Calculated Fields and Column Headers

Once you have placed all your database fields into final position, it is time to add calculated fields to the various bands. Several types of calculated fields are available. The first type is valid dBASE expressions or calculations. Calculations can be as simple as multiplying one number by another, calculating a date, changing a logical field into YES or NO, or concatenating two text fields. They also can be rather complex, including table lookup and multiple occurrences of a field. No matter what type of calculation you want to do, dBASE IV can handle it through series of menus that appear when you press **<F5>** to `Add a field` to the report form.

Another type of field is the PREDEFINED field. There are four of these fields that are automatically tracked by dBASE IV. You can use them by simply adding them to the work surface. They include:

- DATE. The current system date
- TIME. The current system time
- RECNO. The record number being printed
- PAGENO. The current page number being printed

Creating Calculated Fields

You can add fields by moving the cursor to the area where you want them and pressing **<F5>**. Begin by creating our two inventory valuations. As you can see in Figure 13.1, the report has two valuations: one at cost and one at retail price. In order to get these, you need to multiply QUANTITY*COST to get the valuation at cost, and multiply QUANTITY*PRICE to get the valuation at retail price. Start with COST.

Move the cursor three spaces to the right of the PRICE field in the Detail band. Press **<F5>** to add a field. A special type of selection box opens on the work surface, as you see in Figure 13.10.

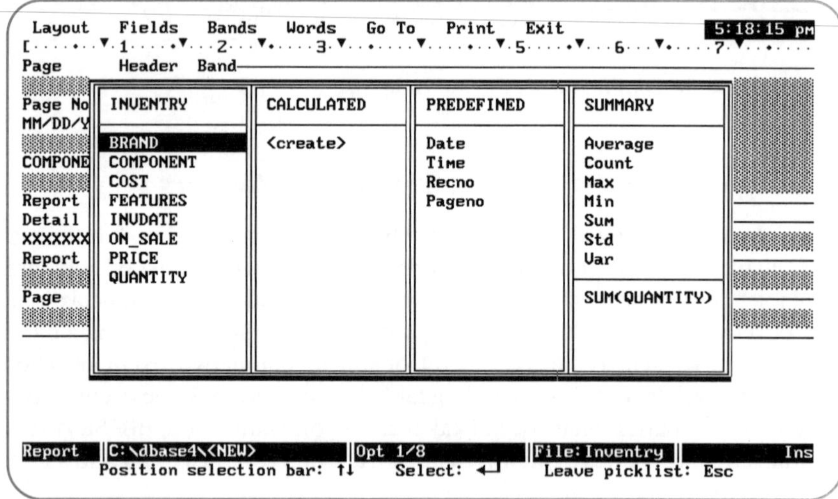

Figure 13.10. *Creating a new field*

This box lets you place fields on the work surface. The box has four columns—INVENTRY, CALCULATED, PREDEFINED, and SUMMARY. The first column shows you the name of your database file or view. Because you are using a single database file named INVENTRY, that is the title of the column. All the fields in the database file are listed. You can place any of them on the work surface by selecting one and pressing **<Enter>**. However, now you are going to create a calculated field, QUANTITY*COST.

Move the cursor to the `<create>` label in the CALCULATED column. Press **<Enter>**. Yet another menu opens and is ready for you to name and describe this field. This new menu is shown in Figure 13.11 already filled in.

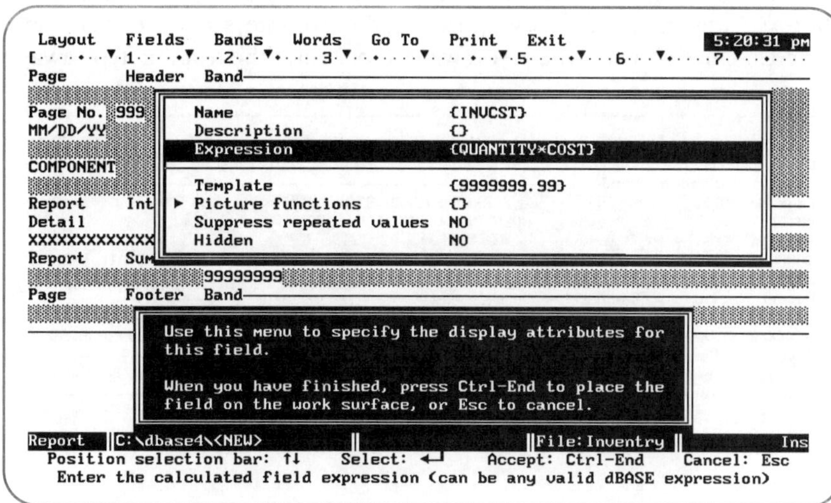

***Figure 13.11.** Creating a new calculated field*

The first entry lets you name the field. It's called INVCST. To enter it in the field, move the highlight to the `Name` option and press **<Enter>**. You can now enter the name, `INVCST`. When you are through, press **<Enter>**. The DESCRIPTION field is optional and is used only for documentation. Ignore it for now. Repeat this operation for the EXPRESSION field, and enter `QUANTITY*COST`. This creates a calculated field called INVCST whose formula is the value of QUANTITY times the value of COST. Don't worry about the lower half of the menu. It is used for changing the appearance of the field. Just accept the defaults. When you are all through, press **<Ctrl>-<End>**. This gives you a new field on the work surface, just to the right of the PRICE field. If it's not in the right place, you can use the steps you just learned to move it next to PRICE.

Create one more calculated field just to the right of this one. Follow the same steps as you just did, but this time call the field INVPRI and make the expression QUANTITY*PRICE. Make sure this field is placed on the work surface in the Detail band a few spaces to the right of the INVCST field.

Adding the Column Names

You should now have two new fields on the work surface. However, these fields need names. Though you called them INVCST and INVPRI, these names don't just appear in the Page Header area—you have to enter them. Move the cursor to the Page Header band. Place the cursor on the same line as the other headings, about four characters to the right of PRICE. Type `VALUE AT COST`, as depicted in Figure 13.12. In fact, use Figure 13.12 as a guide to change all the text in this area to match the figure. Use the arrow keys to move freely about the area. Once you are where you want to be, enter the text and type away.

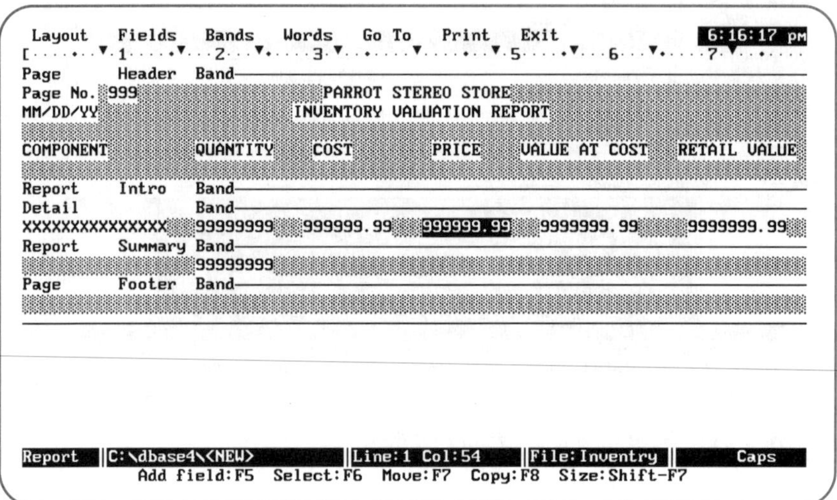

Figure 13.12. *New calculated fields added to the work surface*

There is an extra line at the top of the page. Move the cursor to the extra line and choose `Remove line` from the Words menu. The line disappears.

Add the report title as shown in Figure 13.12. The name of the company is Parrot Stereo, and this is the company's inventory valuation report.

If you use the **<Spacebar>** or the **<Backspace>** key, you may notice holes in the background. The holes are normal and are there just to let dBASE IV know where blank spaces have been entered on the form.

Once you have changed all the text, it is time to create grand totals for the inventory cost and price valuations. Your screen should now look like Figure 13.12.

Before you get to totals, take a look at what this report would look like in its present state. If you were to print the report right now, it would look like Figure 13.13. The new text appears in the Page Header band, and the calculations are complete for the Value at Cost and the Retail Value calculated fields.

```
Page No.    1                 PARROT STEREO STORE
04/03/91                  INVENTORY VALUATION REPORT

COMPONENT          QUANTITY     COST         PRICE   VALUE AT COST   RETAIL VALUE

AMPLIFIER                10   369.00        589.99        3690.00        5899.90
COMPACT DISC             60   109.00        189.99        6540.00       11399.40
RECEIVER                 30   169.00        289.00        5070.00        8670.00
SPEAKERS                140    69.00         59.00        9660.00        8260.00
AMPLIFIER                15   229.00        389.99        3435.00        5849.85
COMPACT DISC             17   389.00        625.99        6613.00       10641.83
RECEIVER                  0   299.00        529.00           0.00           0.00
SPEAKERS                 18    89.00        109.00        1602.00        1962.00
TURNTABLE                15   149.00        299.99        2235.00        4499.85
COMPACT DISC             50   129.00        299.99        6450.00       14999.50
TURNTABLE                 6   189.00        269.99        1134.00        1619.94
TURNTABLE               250    39.00         69.00        9750.00       17250.00
SPEAKERS                 22   299.00        399.00        6578.00        8778.00
AMPLIFIER                 5   529.00        899.99        2645.00        4499.95
COMPACT DISC             26   269.00        329.99        6994.00        8579.74
                        664
```

Figure 13.13. *The printed column report*

You may notice that some of the headers are off-center from the data. If your data is smaller than the field sizes, this can happen. You may want to move the headers to improve the appearance of your report.

Creating Summary Fields

After calculated and predefined fields are added to the form, you might need to add Summary records. dBASE IV is capable of creating many types of numeric summaries, including:

- **Average**. The average of a group of numbers
- **Count**. The number of records
- **Max**. The largest value
- **Min**. The smallest value
- **Sum**. The total of the numbers
- **Std**. The standard deviation of a group of numbers
- **Var**. The variance of a group of numbers

dBASE IV takes care of any accumulations and calculations to produce the desired summary. You just tell it what field to monitor, and it takes care of the rest. You can create summaries on any numeric field, whether it's calculated or in the database file.

When you choose one of these summaries, dBASE IV asks you how to break the summary. Your choice at this point is at the report or page level because you have not yet defined any group breaks. Summary fields are usually placed into the Report Summary or Page Footer bands.

There is presently one field in the Report Summary band. Create totals for the two new calculated fields. First move the cursor to the Report Summary band underneath the column for Value at Cost. Once again, press **<F5>** to add a field. The same box opens, as depicted in Figure 13.10. Notice that this time your new calculated fields are listed in the Calculated column. What you are going to do now is create a summary field. You are going to SUM the new fields INVCST and INVPRI.

Move the cursor to the SUMMARY column of the `Add field` box, and place the cursor on `Sum`. Press **<Enter>**. The screen changes to show you the Summary field entry area. As you can see in Figure 13.14, which has already been filled in, this menu lets you decide which operation to perform (in this case, SUM), which field to sum, and how often to recalculate the sum. The `Name` and `Description` fields are optional and are used only for documentation. In this case, you want to sum the INVCST field and reset the total only at the REPORT level. Later you'll see how to create a group subtotal on BRAND.

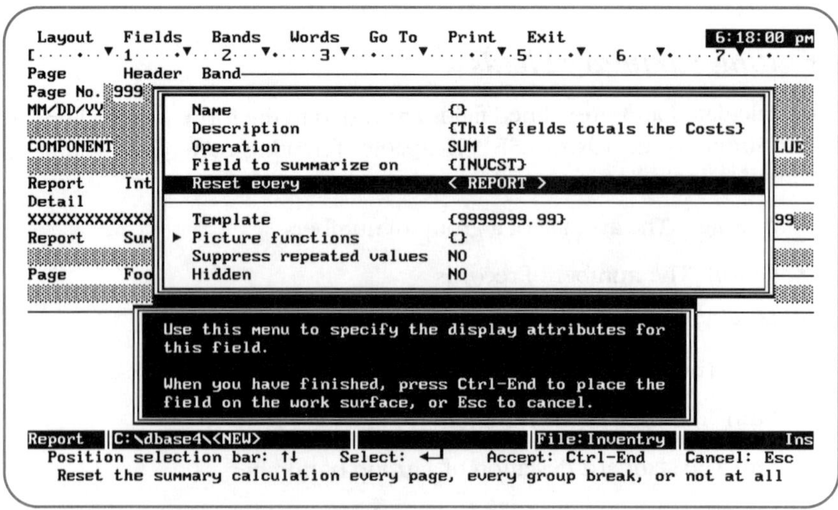

***Figure 13.14.** Creating a summary field*

Filling out this screen is a little trickier than creating a calculated field. When you created a calculated field, you entered the field NAME and the field EXPRESSION. In this box, you need to enter only the `Field to summarize on`. dBASE IV fills out the rest. The `Name` and `Description` are optional. First, explore this menu a little bit.

Move the cursor to the `Operation` line. The operation SUM is already chosen. Press **<Enter>**. A list of all the other possible operations is shown. If you wanted to, you could change your mind now and ask for a different operation. But just press **<Enter>** to close the box.

Move the cursor to `Field to summarize on`. This should be blank on your screen. This is where you tell dBASE IV which field to summarize. Press **<Enter>** and you see another menu. All your fields are listed, including the calculated fields. You want to summarize a calculated field, so move the cursor into the CALCULATED column and choose the INVCST field. Press **<Enter>** and the field is placed in the summary box. Press **<Ctrl>-<End>** to return to the Report work surface, where you'll see the new field in the Report Summary band. This should complete your work to create this first summary field.

Repeat the process for the INVPRI field, and place it next to the INVCST summary in the Report Summary band. If you examine Figure 13.15, you see that there is some text in the Report Summary band. It says TOTAL VALUATION. With your cursor still in the Report Summary band, enter this text at the beginning of the line.

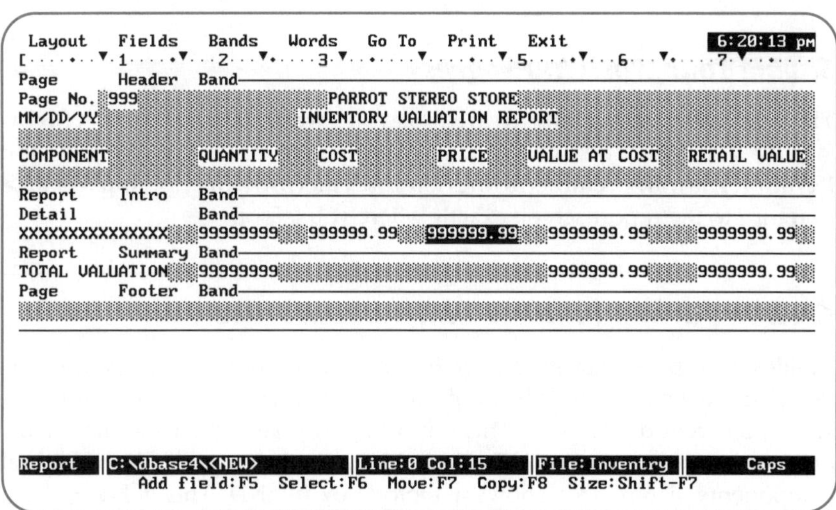

***Figure 13.15.** Report with summary fields added*

This screen in its present form and the printed report are shown in Figures 13.15 and 13.16. The Report Summary band is almost complete.

```
Page No.    1                 PARROT STEREO STORE
04/03/91                   INVENTORY VALUATION REPORT

COMPONENT           QUANTITY    COST        PRICE     VALUE AT COST   RETAIL VALUE

AMPLIFIER                 10    369.00      589.99        3690.00        5899.90
COMPACT DISC              60    109.00      189.99        6540.00       11399.40
RECEIVER                  30    169.00      289.00        5070.00        8670.00
SPEAKERS                 140     69.00       59.00        9660.00        8260.00
AMPLIFIER                 15    229.00      389.99        3435.00        5849.85
COMPACT DISC              17    389.00      625.99        6613.00       10641.83
RECEIVER                   0    299.00      529.00           0.00           0.00
SPEAKERS                  18     89.00      109.00        1602.00        1962.00
TURNTABLE                 15    149.00      299.99        2235.00        4499.85
COMPACT DISC              50    129.00      299.99        6450.00       14999.50
TURNTABLE                  6    189.00      269.99        1134.00        1619.94
TURNTABLE                250     39.00       69.00        9750.00       17250.00
SPEAKERS                  22    299.00      399.00        6578.00        8778.00
AMPLIFIER                  5    529.00      899.99        2645.00        4499.95
COMPACT DISC              26    269.00      329.99        6994.00        8579.74
TOTAL VALUATION          664                             72396.00      112909.96
```

Figure 13.16. *The printed report*

Saving Your Work in Progress

This is probably a good time to save what you have done so far. Press **<Ctrl>-<End>** and a new box will appear asking you to name the report. Call it INVRPT1. You will be returned to the Control Center. Now press **<Shift>-<F2>** to return to the report screen exactly where you left off.

Creating Group Bands, Headers, and Footers

Besides the report totals from page headers and report summaries, you may need a more detailed breakdown of your data. Perhaps you want subtotals by several different dimensions. This is most appropriate when you have many occurrences of a key like BRAND. Each BRAND in the example file has several components. Figure 13.1 shows a subtotal by BRAND. This is known as a grouping, because the data has been grouped by a field. Data can be grouped by any field or expression in the database file. The only caveat is to make sure that the data is sorted by the group expression.

When you add a Group band, dBASE IV asks you what the grouping is like. Is it an individual field, or an expression that tells dBASE when one group ends and a new one begins? Group bands, like most others, come in pairs, an intro and a summary. The Group Intro band usually contains some identifier that tells what the value of the group field is. The Group Summary is primarily used for subtotals. dBASE IV automatically takes care of resetting the totals each time a new group value occurs.

Though there is no real limit to the number of group breaks you use, it gets very complicated if you have more than a few. dBASE IV keeps track of everything for you, but it is still difficult to make good-looking reports with a lot of group breaks.

All that's left now is to group the data by BRAND. Your data should still be indexed by BRAND. If it is not, you need to go back to the Data menu in the Control Center to index the file by BRAND before you create the group bands.

Group bands let you create intros and summaries that are based on the changing of field value. Once you index or sort the database file by BRAND, you will see the data in BRAND order: first four ALLWOOD products, followed by five DIGI products, and then two HITECH products. After HITECH, a couple of brands will be listed with only one component. MEGASONIC has only a turntable; MITY produces only one set of speakers. Though in the very small stereo store file summaries of single occurrences are redundant, they are necessary only when there is more than one item in a grouping.

In this example, you want to see a subtotal for each BRAND that you carry in the inventory valuation for COST and PRICE. You have already done that for the report grand total. Now you simply want subtotals. Begin by creating a Group band.

Creating group bands. Band creation starts with the Bands menu. To add a Group band, your cursor must be in the Page Header area. Press **<Alt>-B** to open the Bands menu. This menu is shown in Figure 13.17. There are choices for adding, removing, and modifying Group bands. When you add a group, you are adding an Intro and a Summary band. You must tell dBASE IV which field you want to group on. The file must be sorted or indexed on this field, or the groupings will be a mess because the data is not in order. dBASE IV prints a new Group Intro at the beginning of each new group and a Group Summary at the end of each group.

Other options in this menu start a band on a new page, create word-wrap bands, and even change the type or quality of the printing along with the line spacing for that band. You can temporarily stop the data within a band from printing by closing the band from this menu.

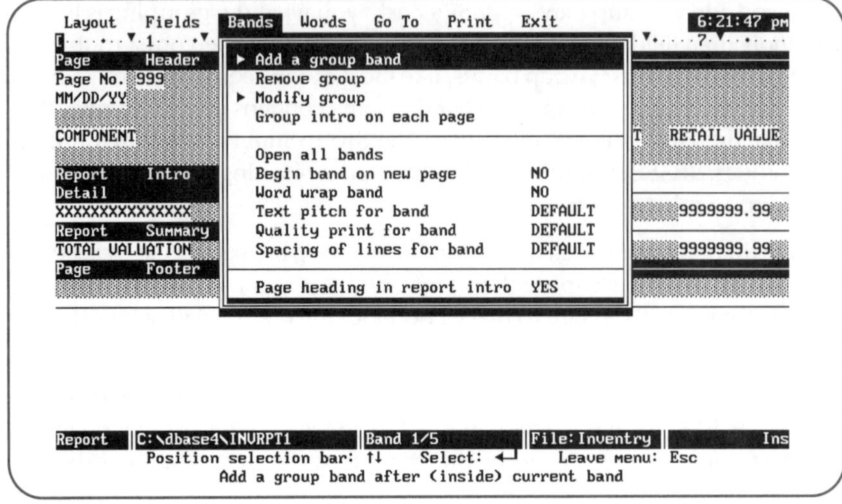

Figure 13.17. *The Bands menu*

Now, create the Group band for BRAND. Place your cursor into the Page Header band. With the Bands menu open, select `Add a group band`. Press **<Enter>**. The screen changes to ask you how to group the data. You have three choices—`Field value`, `Expression value`, or `Record count`. In this case, work with a single field. Choose `Field value` and press **<Enter>** again. The last menu in this sequence allows you to choose a field to group by. Choose the BRAND field. A new band appears on the screen ready for you to enter an intro and a summary.

Keep the intro simple. First, type the text `Brand:` into the Group 1 Intro band, as in Figure 13.18. Be sure to leave a space after the colon (:). After you complete the text, press **<F5>** to add the BRAND field to the right of the text. When you are through entering the brand label and field, press **<Enter>** to add a blank line.

To create the subtotals for INVPRI and INVCST, you need to add two more summary fields. This time you'll add them to the Group 1 Summary band. Move the cursor to the Group 1 Summary band, above the INVPRI summary in the Report Summary band. When you add these new summary fields, you must make sure you `Reset Every {BRAND}`, instead of every {Report} as you did the last time you added summary fields. Otherwise, add the summary fields by the same process as before. Review the process of creating the summary fields if you need help.

```
Layout  Fields  Bands  Words  Go To  Print  Exit                    6:25:33 pm
[····▼·1····▼···2···▼·····3·▼·········▼·········▼·5·····▼···6···▼·····7·▼······
Page      Header  Band
Page No. 999                       PARROT STEREO STORE
MM/DD/YY                         INVENTORY VALUATION REPORT

COMPONENT          QUANTITY   COST        PRICE    VALUE AT COST  RETAIL VALUE

Report    Intro   Band
Group  1  Intro   Band
Brand: XXXXXXXXXX

Detail            Band
XXXXXXXXXXXXXXX  99999999  999999.99  999999.99  9999999.99    9999999.99
Group  1  Summary Band
                                                 ----------    ----------
BRAND TOTAL: XXXXXXXXXX                          9999999.99    9999999.99

Report    Summary Band
TOTAL VALUATION  99999999                        9999999.99    9999999.99

Page      Footer  Band
Report   ||C:\dbase4\INVRPT1       ||Line:1 Col:0     ||File:Inventry ||     Caps
         Add field:F5  Select:F6  Move:F7  Copy:F8  Size:Shift-F7
```

Figure 13.18. *An almost-completed column report screen*

Don't forget to label the Group Summary band by adding the words `BRAND TOTAL:`, followed by the BRAND value. You won't track the total quantity by BRAND, so there is no need for a third summary field in the Group Summary. You also will add a blank line above and below the totals and create a pair of underlines, as shown in Figure 13.18.

Add a line after the Report Summary band. All this spacing is important when the report prints out. Without it, your detail, header, and summary lines would run together.

Adding final column headers, text, lines, boxes, and styling. It is important not to display data fields by themselves without any explanation of what the data means. Though some type of field output is readily apparent to you, it's probably foreign to the reader and, therefore, needs some clarification. Make sure that all your columns have column headers, and that all your non-column-oriented fields have labels either to the left or just above them. By labeling your fields, calculations, and summaries, you make your form much more readable.

After you've made sure that column headers are in place and that you have added page numbers and a date, take a good look at your report template. Print it out. Is it as nice as it should be? How can you improve the look further?

Text can make the report more readable, but you can make it fancier and draw attention to specific areas on the report through the use of lines and boxes. Lines help segregate parts of the form, and boxes draw attention to specific report items. It's easy to draw lines and boxes on the template. You establish one corner and then "draw" the box with the arrow keys by moving the cursor both horizontally and vertically until the box encloses the desired area.

Styling, another important feature in dBASE IV, lets you choose letter font type. You can add emphasis to particular report items or sections by choosing bold, italic, or underlined styles. Styling brings you another step closer to the perfect report.

The Layout, Fields, and Words Menus

Before you go on, take a moment to look at a few of the menu choices available in the report screen. You have already seen the Layout menu described in Figure 13.4. This menu is used to perform quick layouts and to draw lines and boxes on the work surface. In fact, you will add some lines and boxes to the Forms report you'll create later in this chapter.

The next menu is the Fields menu, shown open in Figure 13.19. The `Modify field` choice offers you the options of changing a field size or the way a field is displayed. Every field that you have defined and placed on the work surface for the INVENTRY file is listed in the Modify field submenu. The fields from the basic database file are there, along with the calculated fields you created earlier in this chapter. Even the five summary fields that you placed in the Report Summary band are shown. Because BRAND appears in two different places, it is listed twice. You can modify any of these fields. This menu lets you do some of the same things you can do with function keys, like adding and deleting fields. Choosing the `Add field` option does exactly the same thing as pressing **<F5>**. You have already learned that you can remove fields by selecting them and pressing **<Del>**. This is just an alternative method.

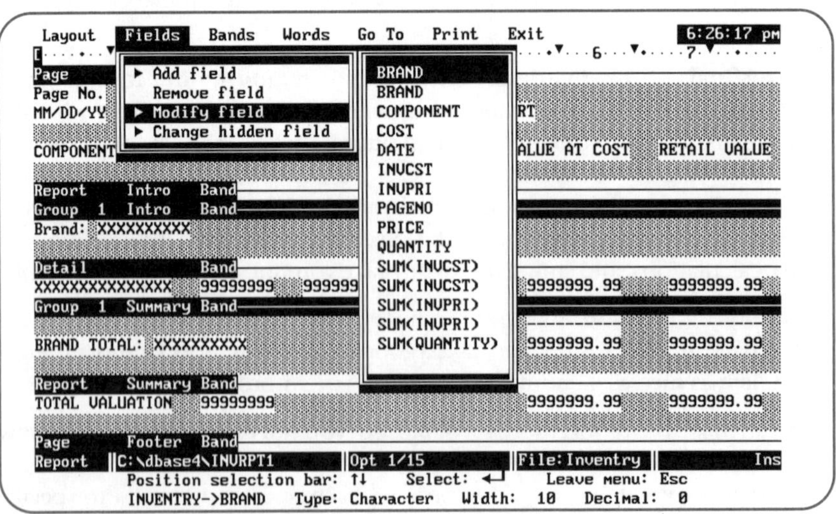

Figure 13.19. Modifying your fields

Another menu to examine is the Words menu. You will use this extensively in the Forms report. For now, take a look at some of the choices, shown in Figure 13.20.

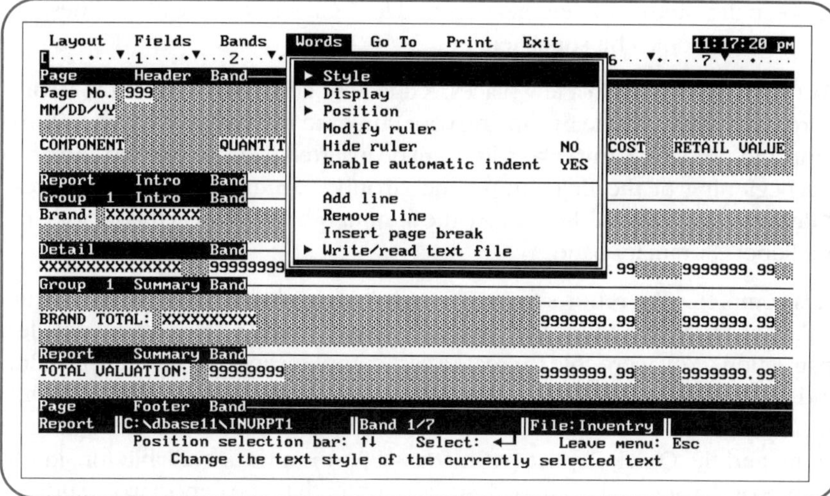

Figure 13.20. *The Words menu*

The Style menu opens to reveal print styles such as Bold, Underline, and Italic, so you can print the selected text or fields in a different letter font. The Display submenu is not available in reports. The `Position` option affects whether fields are left, right, or centered within the entry area. The two ruler options affect the settings and display of the horizontal ruler located just below the menu bar on your screen.

The bottom of the menu lets you perform some critical functions like adding and deleting blank lines in the form. You can add new blank lines another way, by pressing **<Enter>** at the end of a line. However, to remove a line, it is best to use this menu option. If you are creating forms that will span more than one page, the `Insert page break` option allows you to determine where page breaks will be.

Moving Fields and Text into Final Position

If you haven't already moved all your fields to exactly where you want them and added the appropriate column headers and text to make the form more readable, now is the time to do it.

Once you complete these tasks, your report is finished. This example report doesn't need any fancy text, lines, or boxes. You may need, however, to add some blank lines, as shown in Figure 13.18. Some strategically placed blank lines will ensure that there is adequate spacing in the printed report, particularly between data lines and their headers and footers. Without the blank lines, the layout might look a bit squashed.

You need blank lines in a few places. A line has been inserted after the Group Intro band. This is done by moving your cursor to the end of the Group Intro band and pressing **<Enter>**. A line will be inserted. Now, move the cursor to the beginning of the first line in the Group 1 Summary band, and press **<Enter>** to add a blank line before the Summary band. Repeat this process for the Report Summary band.

This completes the reports form. Though it seems like a lot of work, it really isn't. It just took some time to read this explanation and work with the detailed instructions. You were able to create a very complex report by visually selecting and placing your fields. In fact, this author created the final form from scratch in only three minutes. The `Quick layouts` option gives you a great starting point, and the Quick Report (**<Shift>-<F9>**) is always available for simple reports of all your data from work surfaces other than the Report work surface.

Printing the Report

Though the Print menu is full of all sorts of options to make printing very controllable, printing the report is easy. You will look at the Print menu in detail after you create the form report next. For now, just open the Print menu and choose `Begin`. If you don't have a printer, choose `View report on screen`. The finished report is shown in Figure 13.21.

Saving the Report

Save the report format so you can use and modify it later if you need to. Choose the `Save changes and exit` choice from the Exit menu. If you have already saved it once and given it a name, you will be returned to the Control Center. If not, when dBASE IV asks you for a name, call it INVRPT1. dBASE IV will then save the report form and return you to the Control Center.

```
Page No.     1                PARROT STEREO STORE
04/03/91                  INVENTORY VALUATION REPORT

COMPONENT            QUANTITY   COST        PRICE    VALUE AT COST   RETAIL VALUE

Brand: ALLWOOD

AMPLIFIER                  10    369.00      589.99      3690.00        5899.90
COMPACT DISC               60    109.00      189.99      6540.00       11399.40
RECEIVER                   30    169.00      289.00      5070.00        8670.00
SPEAKERS                  140     69.00       59.00      9660.00        8260.00
                                                      ----------     ----------
BRAND TOTAL: ALLWOOD                                    24960.00       34229.30

Brand: DIGI

AMPLIFIER                  15    229.00      389.99      3435.00        5849.85
COMPACT DISC               17    389.00      625.99      6613.00       10641.83
RECEIVER                    0    299.00      529.00         0.00           0.00
SPEAKERS                   18     89.00      109.00      1602.00        1962.00
TURNTABLE                  15    149.00      299.99      2235.00        4499.85
                                                      ----------     ----------
BRAND TOTAL: DIGI                                       13885.00       22953.53

Brand: HITECH

COMPACT DISC               50    129.00      299.99      6450.00       14999.50
TURNTABLE                   6    189.00      269.99      1134.00        1619.94
                                                      ----------     ----------
BRAND TOTAL: HITECH                                      7584.00       16619.44

Brand: MEGASONIK

TURNTABLE                 250     39.00       69.00      9750.00       17250.00
                                                      ----------     ----------
BRAND TOTAL: MEGASONIK                                   9750.00       17250.00

Brand: MITY

SPEAKERS                   22    299.00      399.00      6578.00        8778.00
                                                      ----------     ----------
BRAND TOTAL: MITY                                        6578.00        8778.00

Brand: ONESOUND

AMPLIFIER                   5    529.00      899.99      2645.00        4499.95
COMPACT DISC               26    269.00      329.99      6994.00        8579.74
                                                      ----------     ----------
BRAND TOTAL: ONESOUND                                    9639.00       13079.69

TOTAL VALUATION           664                           72396.00      112909.96
```

Figure 13.21. *The finished column report*

Creating Reports with Multiple Database Files

Creating reports with more than one database file is no different from creating reports with a single database. This is because when multiple database files are linked together in the Query screen, they appear as one database file to the report writer. The only real complexity occurs when there are multiple occurrences of the detail data for the same key. In this section of the chapter, you will see how to handle multiple databases in the report writer. The product will be a printed form report.

Before you move on to the next section, make sure you have a view that contains the linked databases. In the last chapter, you created a view called ALLITEMS. This consisted of placing both the INVENTRY and the VENDOR files on the screen and linking them, by entering the words EVERY LINK1 in the BRAND entry area of the INVENTRY file, and the word LINK1 in the BRAND entry area of the VENDOR file. If you no longer have a view containing all the fields of both the INVENTRY and VENDOR files named ALLITEMS, create a new view now. If you still have ALLITEMS, make sure that it contains all the fields from both database files (except BRAND from the VENDOR file) and also that it contains the links. Remember, you can select all the fields from a database file by pressing **<F5>** in the pothandle of the database file. You can call this new view REPOVIEW when you save it. When you're finished creating the view, you can skip ahead to the section in this chapter called FORM REPORTS. If you need more help creating the database view, read on from here.

Refresher on Creating a View File

If you need to re-create the view from scratch, follow the instructions in this section. You will use this view to create the form report that is discussed under the heading Form Reports and that is shown in Figure 13.23. If you don't have the INVENTRY and VENDOR database files, re-create them and then make a new view by linking the two database files as described here or in Chapter 12.

First, return to the Control Center. Select the INVENTRY database file in the Data panel and press **<Enter>** to make it active. Next, select `<create>` in the Queries panel and press **<Enter>**.

This will open the QBE work surface, ready for you to create your view. You need to place both the INVENTRY and the VENDOR files on the work surface. The INVENTRY file should already be on the work surface and all of its fields selected in the view file. Open the Layout menu by pressing **<Alt>-L**. Choose `Add file to query` from the Layout menu. A list of database files appears.

Select the VENDOR database file and press **<Enter>**. Both database files are now on the work surface. Next you have to select the fields from the VENDOR file to place in the view file. You want to place all the fields except the BRAND field from the VENDOR file into the view file. The BRAND field is already in the view file from the INVENTRY file, and you cannot enter it twice. The easiest way to accomplish this is to place each field from the VENDOR file into the view file individually, skipping the BRAND field.

The next step is to tell dBASE IV how the files are related. You know that they are related by BRAND. Because the field BRAND appears in both database files, you will link the BRAND field in the INVENTRY file to the BRAND field in the VENDOR file.

Enter the example variable LINK1 in both database files. Because all the records in both database files are needed, regardless of whether matches are found in both, you must add the keyword EVERY to the link in the INVENTRY file skeleton. This Query Design screen is shown in Figure 13.22 with the links created and the last four fields of the view skeleton displayed. Notice that the common field BRAND was selected only from the INVENTRY database file.

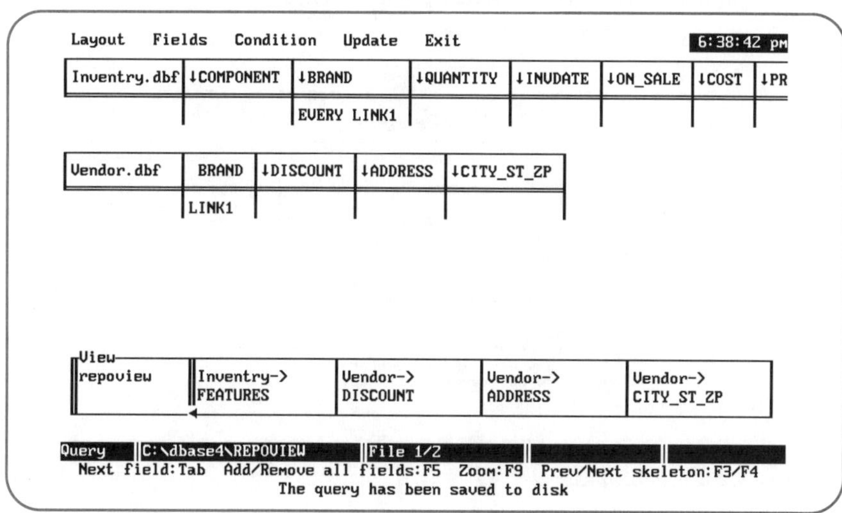

Figure 13.22. *Linking databases for the report form*

Finally, save this view by choosing `Save this query` from the Layout menu. Call it REPOVIEW. Return to the Control Center.

Figure 13.23 shows the form report that you will create in the rest of this chapter. It shows a sales report of two of the items in the inventory. Though only the first two pages are shown in this figure, there is actually one report page for each item in the inventory.

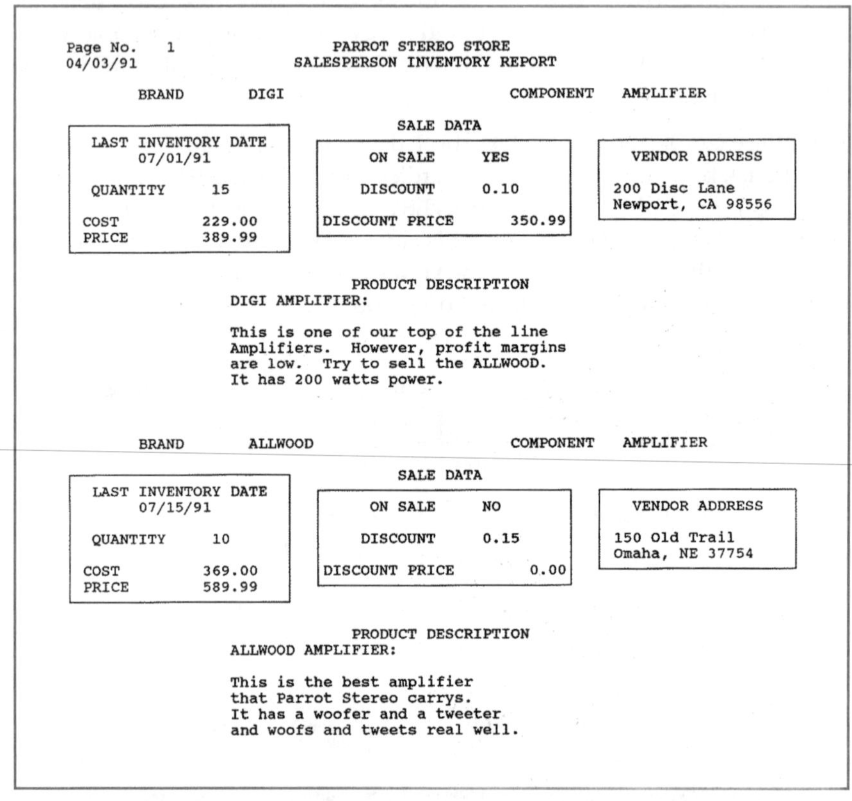

```
Page No.    1                PARROT STEREO STORE
04/03/91                SALESPERSON INVENTORY REPORT

       BRAND        DIGI                          COMPONENT   AMPLIFIER

                                     SALE DATA
  LAST INVENTORY DATE
       07/01/91                 ON SALE      YES         VENDOR ADDRESS

  QUANTITY     15               DISCOUNT     0.10       200 Disc Lane
                                                        Newport, CA 98556
 COST          229.00        DISCOUNT PRICE     350.99
 PRICE         389.99

                                 PRODUCT DESCRIPTION
                  DIGI AMPLIFIER:

                  This is one of our top of the line
                  Amplifiers.  However, profit margins
                  are low.  Try to sell the ALLWOOD.
                  It has 200 watts power.

       BRAND        ALLWOOD                       COMPONENT   AMPLIFIER

                                     SALE DATA
  LAST INVENTORY DATE
       07/15/91                 ON SALE      NO          VENDOR ADDRESS

  QUANTITY     10               DISCOUNT     0.15       150 Old Trail
                                                        Omaha, NE 37754
 COST          369.00        DISCOUNT PRICE       0.00
 PRICE         589.99

                                 PRODUCT DESCRIPTION
                  ALLWOOD AMPLIFIER:

                  This is the best amplifier
                  that Parrot Stereo carrys.
                  It has a woofer and a tweeter
                  and woofs and tweets real well.
```

Figure 13.23. *The form report*

This is known as a form report because the information is not placed into neat little rows and columns. The majority of information in a form report appears in the detail section rather than in the headers or footers. In fact, in this report, there are only two areas used, the page header and detail areas. This is typical of a form report. Even the column or data headers are part of the detail areas. You can even see some lines and boxes separating some data items from others. dBASE IV is capable of creating very sophisticated form reports, including tax forms, invoices, and checks.

How Form Reports Differ from Column Reports

Form reports are traditionally used to place data in specific locations on the printed page. Usually a form report record is spread out on the whole page, whereas column reports have as many records on a page as will fit. Form reports are usually much fancier than column reports because there is more room to work with.

Using several database files, you can create very complex form reports like invoices. Invoices are especially difficult because they combine all the features of a form and a column report. They may look like form reports because they take up an entire page, but a portion of an invoice is created like a column report. The many items in an invoice, including quantities, part numbers, descriptions, and price, are the detail portions of an invoice report and are like a column report. The page headers and footers act as a form and contain several lines including descriptions and summaries. You are about to create a simple form with all its fields in the Detail band.

Creating the Initial Form

Creating a form report is much like creating a column report. You'll spend more time making the form pretty than worrying about totals. Though a form can have totals as on an invoice, it contains other information that doesn't require totals.

Start from the Control Center. Make sure that REPOVIEW is active. If it isn't, choose it in the Queries panel of the Control Center and press **<Enter>**. Next, you'll create the form report, so move the cursor to `<create>` in the Reports panel and press **<Enter>**.

The Layout menu opens automatically because dBASE assumes that you will start with `Quick layouts`. Press **<Enter>** to open the `Quick layouts` option. The three options of this menu are listed. Rather than individually placing each of your data items on the work surface, you can automatically place all of them in one of these forms. For this example select the `Form layout` choice.

Instantly all the fields in the REPOVIEW view file are placed on the screen. Examine Figure 13.24. You can see that the data has been placed in the various bands on the report surface. The Page Header band contains the text, `Page No.`, along with a field to hold the current page number. The date appears on a third line in the Report work surface.

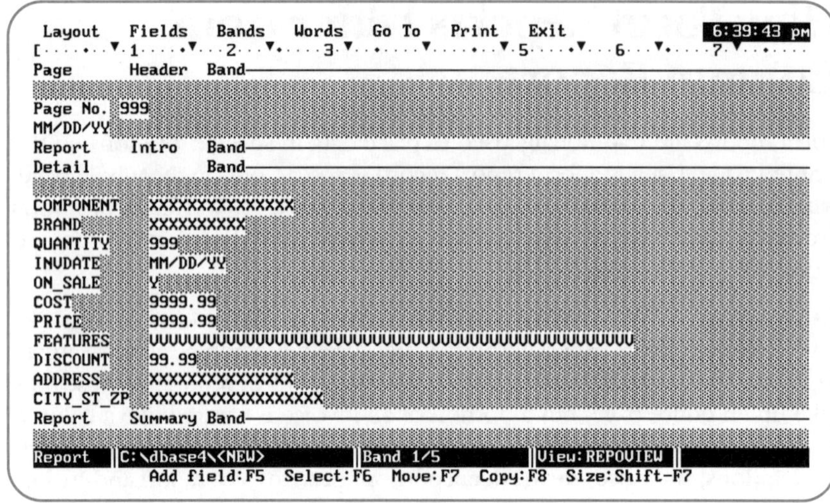

***Figure 13.24.** The Quick layout for the REPOVIEW view file*

The Detail band contains all the fields that are active in the view. Instead of being arranged in a single line across the report as in the column reports, they are arranged down the band in two columns. The first column contains the field names, and the second column contains the fields themselves. No summaries are created. In a form report, dBASE IV assumes that you are not looking for any totals and it doesn't calculate any.

Moving Text and Fields

All the data you need is on the work surface. There are no fields to delete. The next step is to move the fields about the work surface into approximate positions for the report.

Using the function keys shown on the bottom of the screen in Figure 13.24, begin to move the fields on the work surface. Remember, the goal is for the report to look like Figure 13.23. You will add details like lines and boxes later.

There is no one right way to move the fields about. An efficient method is to place all the database fields on the work surface, then add new fields, rearrange the fields again, add lines and boxes, rearrange fields again, and finish any little details. The key to designing a form report is constant rearranging.

```
 Layout   Fields   Bands   Words   Go To   Print   Exit                  6:59:46 pm
[····▼·1·····▼···2···▼·····3·▼·······▼······▼·5·····▼···6···▼·····7·▼·······
Page No. 999                      PARROT STEREO STORE
MM/DD/YY                      SALESPERSON INVENTORY REPORT
Report    Intro   Band
Detail            Band

        BRAND       XXXXXXXXXX                     COMPONENT    XXXXXXXXXXXXXXX

   LAST INVENTORY DATE
        MM/DD/YY                 ON SALE       Y          VENDOR ADDRESS

                                DISCOUNT     99.99    XXXXXXXXXXXXXXX
   QUANTITY     999                                   XXXXXXXXXXXXXXXXXX

  COST         9999.99
  PRICE        9999.99
                                PRODUCT DESCRIPTION
                  VVVVVVVVVVVVVVVVVVVVVVVVVVVVVVVVVVVVVVVVVVVVVVVVVV
Report    Summary Band

Page      Footer  Band
Report    C:\dbase4\<NEW>                Line:0 Col:0         View:REPOVIEW
                  Add field:F5   Select:F6   Move:F7   Copy:F8   Size:Shift-F7
```

Figure 13.25. *Beginning a report form*

Transforming Fields with IIF

When you place a field on the work surface, it will be displayed at that location in the printed report. However, you can change the way fields are displayed. For example, you can transform a field from one type of data to another. Logical fields provide a good example of this.

Logical fields. Logical fields pose a special challenge and a great opportunity to display their data better. A logical field exists to tell you if something is true or false. However, the values, .T. and .F., are not very attractive on a report. The IIF (Immediate IF) function transforms data from one form to another.

The first example involves the logical field ON_SALE. Create a new field that uses the logical field in a calculation. Make the value of this new field YES if the value of ON_SALE is true, and NO if it's not true. To do this, first delete the logical field ON_SALE, and then open the Fields menu by pressing **<Alt>-F** and choosing `Add field`. After the box opens up, move the cursor to the `<create>` label in the CALCULATED column. Press **<Enter>**. A submenu opens and is ready for you to name and describe this field. The submenu is shown in Figure 13.26.

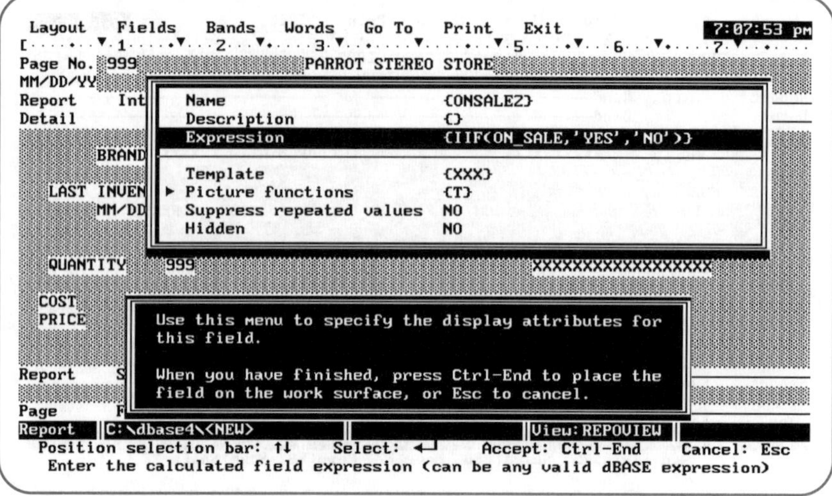

Figure 13.26. *Transforming a logical field*

The areas have been filled in. The top area names the new field ONSALE2. The calculation is shown as:

```
IIF(ON_SALE,'YES','NO')
```

This is the IIF command. It says, "If the value of the field ON_SALE is true, then set the value of ONSALE2 to YES. If it is false, then set the value of ONSALE2 to NO." The value of the logic field ON_SALE is unchanged. The value was simply used in a calculation. When the report is produced, the value YES or NO is shown in place of T or F for each record.

Calculating numeric fields. Another field is necessary for the report: the calculation of the sale price. The calculation of sale price is the retail price less the retail price times the discount rate: PRICE –(PRICE*DISCOUNT). Another way to express the calculation mathematically is price times one minus the discount: PRICE * (1–DISCOUNT).

Use the first calculation for this example. But, to go a step further, change the expression so that if the item isn't on sale, the discount price is not displayed. Again, create a new field. This time, call it DISCPRI. The expression in this case: IIF(ON_SALE,PRICE – (PRICE*DISCOUNT),0).

Only a portion of the calculation is displayed in the box in Figure 13.27. At the bottom of the screen is the entire box in zoom mode. This calculation places the discount price on the report if the item is on sale. A zero prints on the report if the item is not on sale.

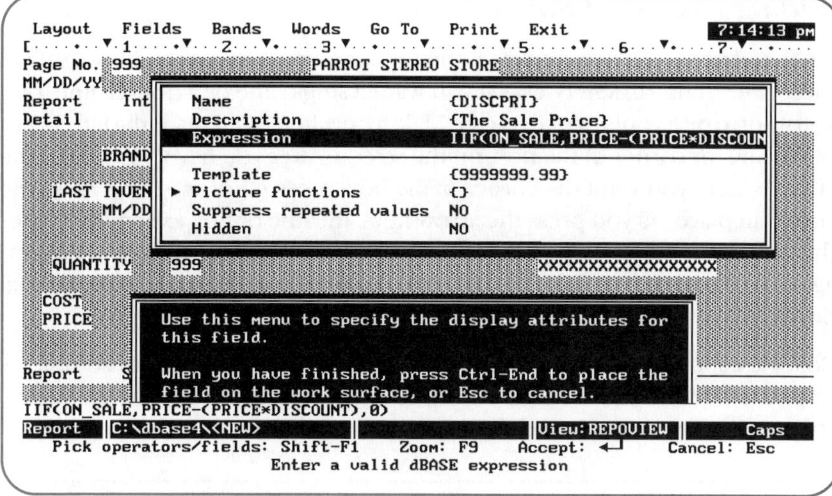

***Figure 13.27.** Adding a calculated field to calculate the discount price*

Figure 13.28 shows the form as it presently has been changed with the two new fields. You may need to make some minor changes as you add fields to make room for these new fields. Now it is time to add some boxes.

```
Layout  Fields  Bands  Words  Go To  Print  Exit                 7:20:00 pm
Page No. 999                 PARROT STEREO STORE
MM/DD/YY                SALESPERSON INVENTORY REPORT
Report   Intro   Band
Detail           Band

        BRAND        XXXXXXXXXX                 COMPONENT   XXXXXXXXXXXXXXX

   LAST INVENTORY DATE
        MM/DD/YY                  ON SALE    XXX           VENDOR ADDRESS

   QUANTITY     999              DISCOUNT    99.99       XXXXXXXXXXXXXXX
                                                         XXXXXXXXXXXXXXXXXX
  COST         9999.99     DISCOUNT PRICE  9999999.99
  PRICE        9999.99

                                PRODUCT DESCRIPTION
                 VVVVVVVVVVVVVVVVVVVVVVVVVVVVVVVVVVVVVVVVVVVVVVVVVV
Report  C:\dbase4\<NEW>         Line:2 Col:0      View:REPOVIEW
         Add field:F5  Select:F6  Move:F7  Copy:F8  Size:Shift-F7
```

***Figure 13.28.** The report form after adding calculated fields*

Adding Lines and Boxes

Lines and boxes are selected from the Layout menu. Once you choose one of these selections, dBASE IV asks if you want a single line or a double line, or if you want to pick your own character. Make your choice and place the left corner of the line, or corner of the box, on the screen. After you have positioned the cursor where you want the corner of the box, press **<Enter>**. This locks the corner in place. As you press the arrow keys, the line or box expands to cover the area to the cursor. When the box covers the desired area, press **<Enter>** again. Create each box this way. Lines are nothing more than one-dimensional boxes.

Boxes are shown entered on the work surface in Figure 13.29. This completes all entries for the form report. Again, to make room for some of the boxes, some of the fields are moved slightly.

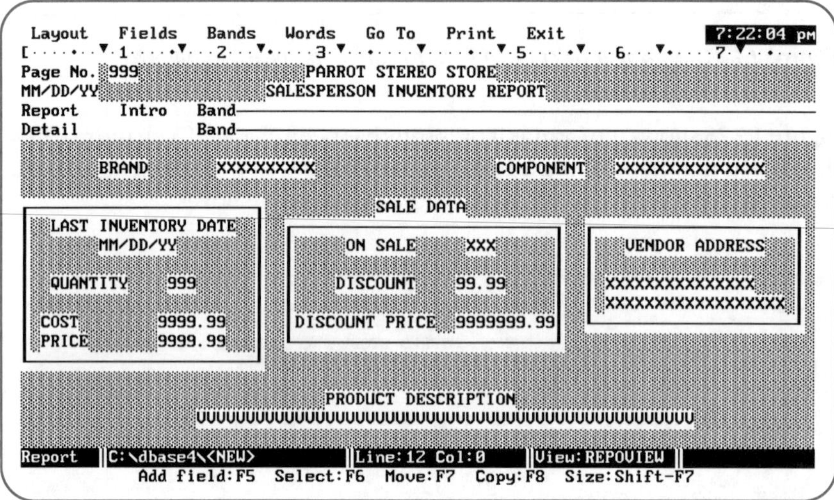

***Figure 13.29.** The report form after adding boxes*

Customizing and Styling the Data

Before you go on and print the form, there is one thing left to do. You can affect the way a field is displayed without creating new fields. If you select `Modify field` while a field is highlighted, the Validation submenu for that field will appear. If no field is highlighted, a field pick list will appear. Once you've chosen a field from the list, another submenu opens from which you can choose `Picture functions`. This option allows changes to the display of both the field size and the field appearance. This menu appears in Figure 13.30.

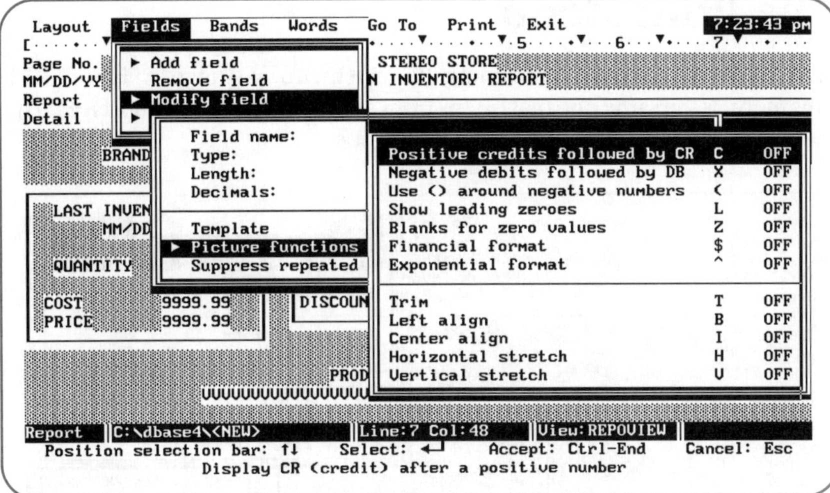

***Figure 13.30.** Changing the display appearance with pictures*

The top half of this submenu contains options for putting the debit and credit symbols around numbers, or parentheses around negative numbers. You can show leading zeroes or blanks in place of a value of zero. A financial format can be specified with dollar signs and commas. You can combine several of these functions, such as the $ and (, for more complex displays.

The bottom part of the Picture functions submenu handles numbers that exceed the lengths you have allowed for them. You can tell dBASE IV to trim a field, if it exceeds the allowed length. You also can left- or center-align the field within the display area. The last two choices let you determine how to expand a field when the field exceeds its allotted size. The default is vertical stretch. This means if a field exceeds its width, dBASE IV places the characters that exceed the field length below the field display area. If you turn on `Horizontal stretch`, dBASE IV uses the area to the right of the field. Be aware of any fields that might be in the way of a stretching field, so that there are no conflicts or collisions.

Printing Reports

You can print your finished report to the screen, the printer, or a file. There is a slew of options devoted to printing your report. Keep in mind that whatever data is active will print. You can't select a database file or view that doesn't have all the fields that your form requires, but you can filter data to select only certain records. As long as the fields are in the file structure, dBASE IV will process whatever data you give it.

The Print Menu

Start the printing process by opening the Print menu, as shown in Figure 13.31. This menu is the same one that opens from any of the other work surfaces. This menu has several options and four submenus.

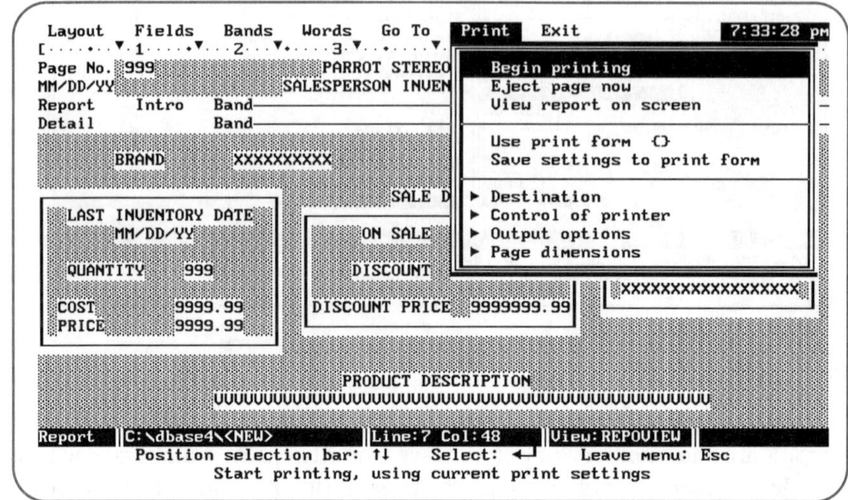

***Figure 13.31.** The Print menu*

The first option at the top of the Print menu is the `Begin printing` command. This is the GO signal for dBASE IV to start printing the active file to wherever you told it to print, using whatever print settings you told it to use. Before you print the report by selecting this option, make sure all your other print options are selected.

The next option, `Eject page now`, sends a form feed to the printer. Use it to help align the printer before starting.

The last option in the first section lets you send the output to the screen instead of the printer.

The next two options in the middle of the Print menu let you save common print settings. After you create a set of print choices that you'll use frequently, you can save those settings using the `Save settings to print form` option. You can then give the settings a name. Later, when you decide you want to activate those settings, choose the `Use print form {}` option.

Destination Submenu

The last four options in the bottom section of the Print menu bring up individual submenus that control the printing to an even finer detail. The first option is the Destination submenu shown in Figure 13.32. This menu lets you choose between the PRINTER and a DOS FILE as printing destinations. If you choose DOS FILE, you also must name that file using the second option in this submenu. The default name is the same as the object name. With the third choice on this submenu, you have the option of which printer to print to. You probably already selected this during your system setup. The last option, Echo to screen, lets you print a file to the printer or a file and see it display on the screen.

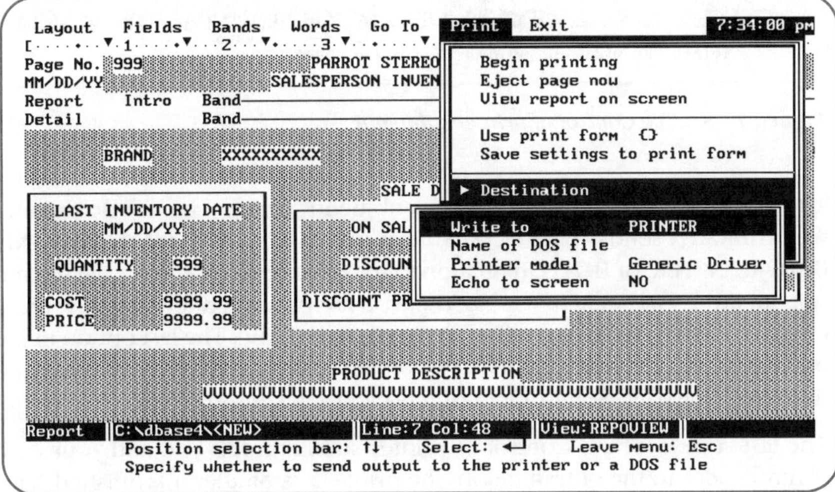

Figure 13.32. *The Destination submenu*

Control of Printer Submenu

Choose this submenu only if you are sending report output to a printer. This menu, shown in Figure 13.33, has three sections.

The first option in the top submenu section lets you choose the text pitch, such as DEFAULT, PICA, ELITE, or CONDENSED. The second option determines if letter quality is turned on for your printer.

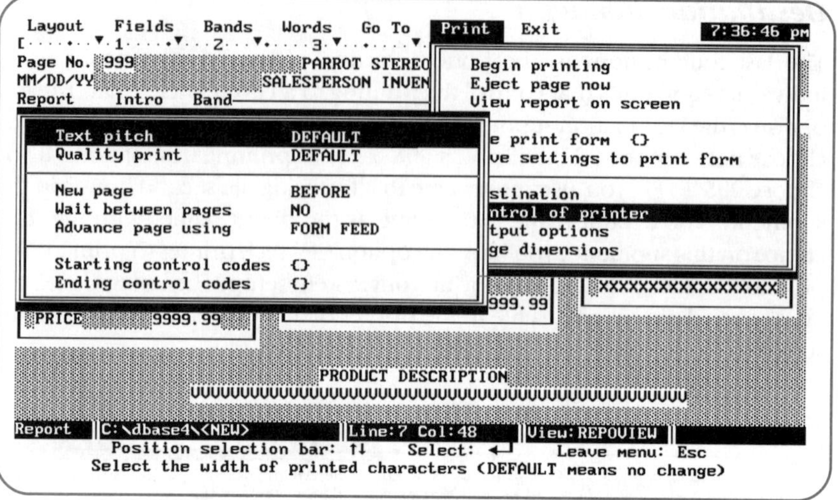

Figure 13.33. *The Control of printer submenu*

There are three options in the middle submenu section. The first determines when dBASE IV sends a page eject to the printer. It lets you choose from NONE, BEFORE, AFTER, or BOTH in relation to the page break. If you set the second option, `Wait between pages`, to YES, you are prompted to put a new piece of paper in the printer or confirm to continue printing. The last option in the middle section lets you tell dBASE IV whether to send line feeds or a form feed to advance the page. Some older printers need to take advantage of this option.

The last section of the Control of printer submenu lets you add your own control codes to the output before the print starts or after it is finished. This allows you to send control characters for complex control of both dot matrix and laser printers.

Output Options Submenu

The third submenu is shown in Figure 13.34. Its options determine how much of the report prints out. You can specify the starting and ending pages to print, but you must specify actual page numbers. You also can start the page numbering on a number other than page 1. The last submenu option lets you choose the number of copies.

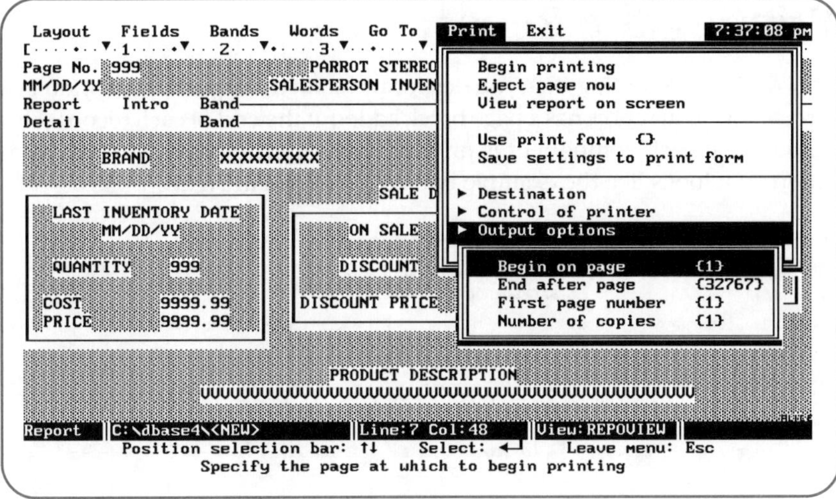

Figure 13.34. *The Output options submenu*

Page Dimensions Submenu

This submenu has three choices, as shown in Figure 13.35. It lets you select the length of the page before there is a page break. It also lets you specify the number of characters to reserve from the left for a blank margin. The last option lets you select single, double, or triple spacing.

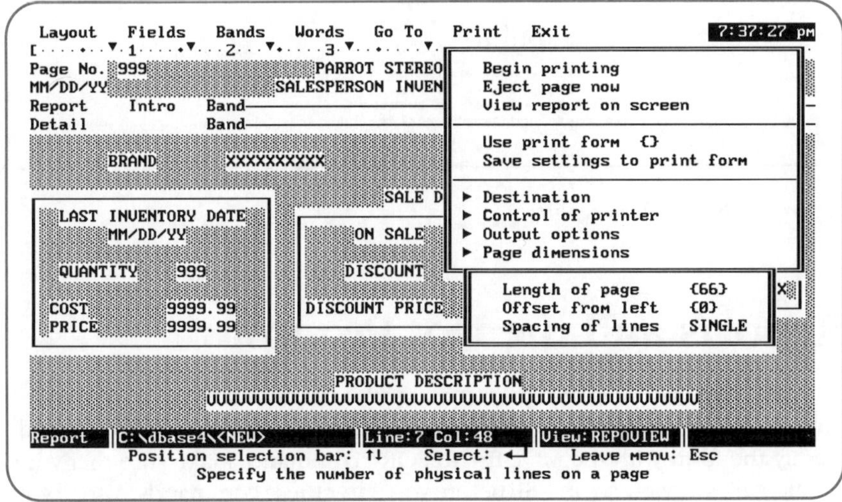

Figure 13.35. *The Page dimensions submenu*

Printing the Report

Choose the print settings that you desire, and send the report to the printer or screen. The final report has a page break added at the end of each record. This ensures that each component is printed on a separate page. Print the form report so it looks like the example two pages shown in Figure 13.36.

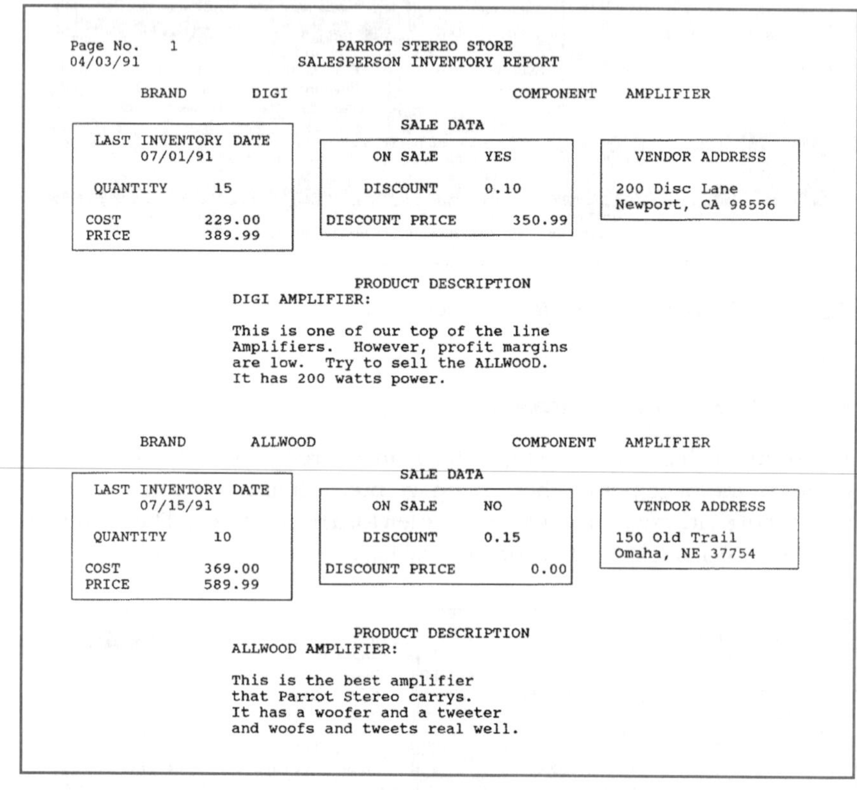

```
Page No.    1                  PARROT STEREO STORE
04/03/91                  SALESPERSON INVENTORY REPORT

      BRAND        DIGI                          COMPONENT    AMPLIFIER

                                  SALE DATA
 LAST INVENTORY DATE
       07/01/91              ON SALE      YES          VENDOR ADDRESS

 QUANTITY      15            DISCOUNT     0.10         200 Disc Lane
                                                       Newport, CA 98556
 COST           229.00     DISCOUNT PRICE       350.99
 PRICE          389.99

                                PRODUCT DESCRIPTION
                         DIGI AMPLIFIER:

                         This is one of our top of the line
                         Amplifiers.  However, profit margins
                         are low.  Try to sell the ALLWOOD.
                         It has 200 watts power.

      BRAND        ALLWOOD                       COMPONENT    AMPLIFIER

                                  SALE DATA
 LAST INVENTORY DATE
       07/15/91              ON SALE      NO           VENDOR ADDRESS

 QUANTITY      10            DISCOUNT     0.15         150 Old Trail
                                                       Omaha, NE 37754
 COST           369.00     DISCOUNT PRICE         0.00
 PRICE          589.99

                                PRODUCT DESCRIPTION
                         ALLWOOD AMPLIFIER:

                         This is the best amplifier
                         that Parrot Stereo carrys.
                         It has a woofer and a tweeter
                         and woofs and tweets real well.
```

Figure 13.36. *The form report*

Reports and the Dot Prompt

Here are some alternative report commands you can use directly at the dot prompt. You can enter the work surface with the CREATE REPORT command. Modify the form with the MODIFY REPORT command. Make sure that your database files or view are in USE before you enter these commands. Also, if you attempt to modify a report without the proper database file or view active, or with a database file whose structure has been altered, you won't be able to work with the new fields and may not even be able to get back into the form until those fields have been re-created.

You also can run the column report from the dot prompt. The command:

```
. REPORT FORM INVRPT1
```

sends the form to the screen; the command:

```
. REPORT FORM INVRPT1 TO PRINTER
```

sends the report to the printer. You can even add filter commands right in the REPORT FORM command itself. Suppose you wanted to see all the records for items with a cost exceeding $300. You would enter:

```
. REPORT FORM INVRPT1 FOR COST > 300 TO PRINTER
```

This would print the report but would only use the data with a cost field value exceeding $300.

Summary

This completes a fairly thorough look at dBASE IV column and form reports. By following the seven-step method, you can create sophisticated reports in just a few minutes. The seven suggested steps are:

1. Assemble your data.
2. Choose the `Quick layouts` option or add the fields you want.
3. Delete unwanted fields and text.
4. Move fields and text into final position.
5. Create calculated and summary fields.
6. Create group bands, headers, and footers.
7. Add final column headers, text, lines, boxes, and styling.

The next chapter covers labels and mail merging. There is little difference between reports and labels except that there are no bands and the label size is much smaller.

chapter

14

Labels and Mail Merging

This chapter covers the specialized commands that dBASE IV provides to help you prepare and print standard labels. You also will see how to create and use a mail-merge document.

Labels can take many forms, from the standard mailing labels sent out to customers, to labels that indicate the price and description of sale items. Examples of mail-merge documents include letters to vendors to order more of a product, and letters to customers about overdue bills. In a mail-merge document, data fields are placed within the text. When the report is printed, dBASE IV fills in the values for the fields. Usually, a mail-merge document contains one record per page.

You create labels using the Label work surface, which you reach through the Labels panel on the Control Center. This work surface is similar to other work surfaces except that it is very small. In fact, it looks just like a label. Mail-merge documents are created from the Report work surface.

Differences Between Reports and Labels

Theoretically, anything you can put into a label can be put into a report. Why, then, if you have a Report work surface, do you need labels too? The answer is easy. Several labels can be printed across and down a page. A record fills one label in the top-left corner of a sheet of labels. Then the second record fills a label in the top-middle of the label sheet. The third record fills the label in the top-right of the label sheet. The report form isn't set up to print that way.

Computer labels come in standard sheets of rows and columns. The total number of labels on each sheet varies according to label size and the layout of the labels on the sheet. The number of columns across a sheet of labels is called the number of labels. What kind of labels should you choose? First of all, they need to be big enough. After that, what kind to choose depends on how you are going to use the labels. If you are going to print hundreds of labels at a time, you will be happier with three or four labels across a sheet. Most printers can print multicolumn labels faster than they can print single-column labels because the printer takes time to advance for each new line. On the other hand, if you are going to print only a handful of labels, you might be happier with single-column labels.

To create and print labels, you first go to the Label work surface and create the label form. Once this is created, you can print the labels any way you want. You can make changes to your label form any time after you've created it. You also can determine at the time you print how many labels across the page to print. Various spacing widths are available to accommodate virtually any type of label.

The Label Form

Printed labels have long been a favorite of time-conscious businesspeople. Although printed labels have many uses, the most common is the old-fashioned mailing label. Use the VENDOR database file, which contains the BRAND, ADDRESS, and CITY_ST_ZP fields, to create your labels. Review the database file structure of the VENDOR database file, as shown in Figure 14.1.

Layout Organize Append Go To Exit 2:47:43 pm

Bytes remaining: 3952

Num	Field Name	Field Type	Width	Dec	Index
1	BRAND	Character	10		Y
2	DISCOUNT	Numeric	5	2	N
3	ADDRESS	Character	15		N
4	CITY_ST_ZP	Character	18		N

Database C:\dbase4\VENDOR Field 1/4 Ins

Enter the field name. Insert/Delete field:Ctrl-N/Ctrl-U

Field names begin with a letter and may contain letters, digits and underscores

Figure 14.1. *The VENDOR database used for labels*

You'll use these fields to create a simple set of labels. Because the database file has only five records, it will be easy to see the results. Start by going to the Control Center and making the VENDOR file active. Now, move the cursor to the `<create>` marker of the Labels panel and press **<Enter>**. The Label work surface appears, as shown in Figure 14.2.

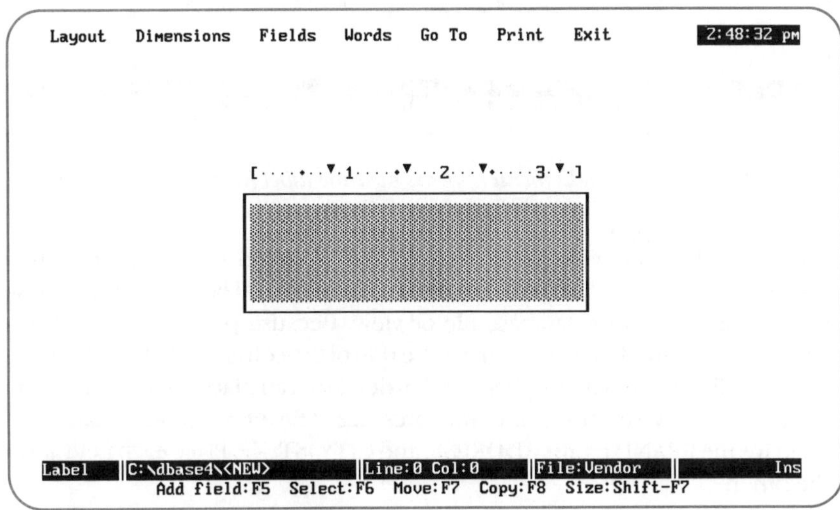

Figure 14.2. *The empty label form*

The Label work surface looks very similar to other work surfaces you have already used. The menu on top contains many similar options. Later, you will see some of the differences. Once the label form appears on the work surface, you can add the fields right away.

Adding Fields to the Label

You add fields to the label form by pressing the **<F5> Add** key. You also can select `Add Field` from the Fields menu. When you press **<F5> Add**, the menu appears over the label form, as shown in Figure 14.3.

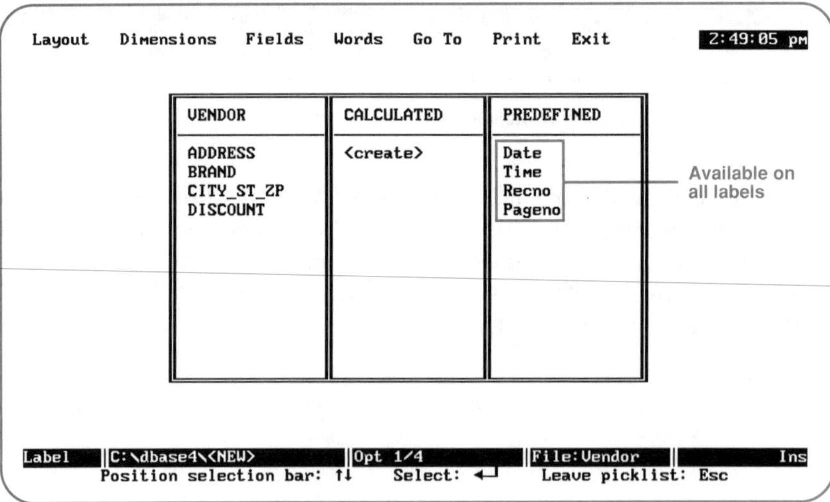

Figure 14.3. *The Add Field menu appears over the label form*

This menu box lets you place fields in the label form. The box has three columns, VENDOR, CALCULATED, and PREDEFINED. The first column shows you the name of your database file or view. Because you are using a single database file named VENDOR, that is the title of the column. All the fields in the database file are shown in alphabetical order. You can place any of them on the work surface by selecting one and pressing **<Enter>**. Create a label that contains the BRAND name, ADDRESS, and CITY_ST_ZP. Place each field above the other.

Once the fields are placed on the label, you can move them about freely. Choose BRAND first and press **<Enter>**. The standard Fields menu will be displayed completely filled in for the field. Then press **<Ctrl>-<End>**, unless you want to change the size or display characteristics. A series of *X*'s appears in the label form to show the placement of the field when the label is printed. Move the cursor under the first *X* and press **<F5>** again. Next select the ADDRESS and press **<Enter>** (and **<Ctrl>-<End>** again). Another block of *X*'s appears below the first, showing the placement of the ADDRESS field in the label form. Repeat the process for the CITY_ST_ZP field.

When you are through, the label form should look like Figure 14.4. The three blocks of *X*'s correspond to the three fields. In the figure, you can see the first group selected. You also can see at the bottom of the screen that the field information is showing, telling you the field name, type, width, and number of decimals. As you move the cursor to each field, the display changes, showing you the different field names.

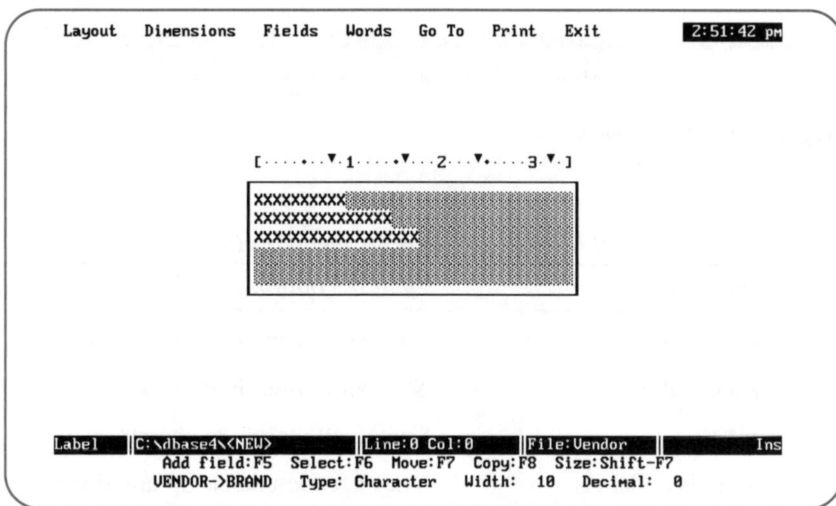

Figure 14.4. *Fields in the label form*

Once the fields are in the label form, you can add text to the label form or move the fields about by using the **<F6> Select** and **<F7> Move** keys. You can add and delete lines by using options found in the Words menu. The label can be as large as the dimensions you set for it.

Setting Label Dimensions

To set the dimensions of a label, you use the Dimensions menu, as shown in Figure 14.5. Look at the bottom half of the menu first. You can set many of the label size dimensions yourself, or you can use one of the many predefined sizes that come set up with dBASE IV.

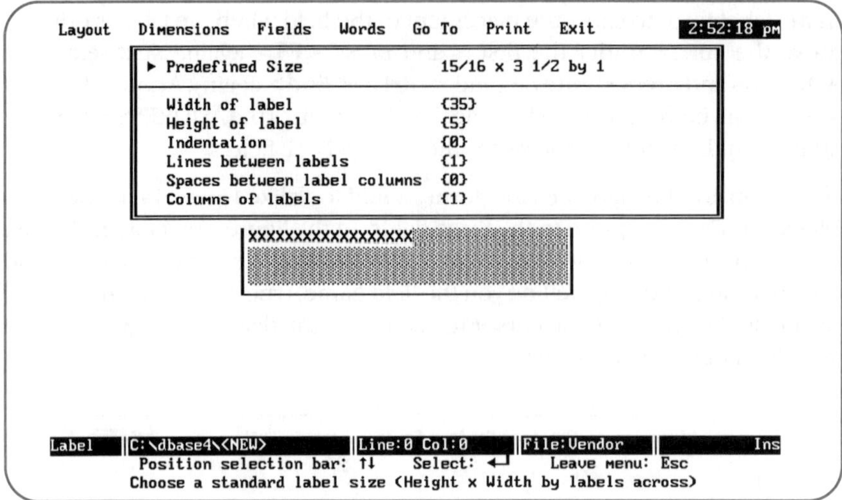

***Figure 14.5.** The Dimensions menu*

***Table 14.1.** Dimensions menu options*

Menu option	*What the option affects*
Width of Label	Number of characters across the label
Height of Label	Number of lines in each label
Indentation	Size of left margin in characters
Lines between labels	Lines between labels up and down
Spaces between label columns	Characters between labels across
Columns of labels	Number of labels across the sheet

These selections give you the ability to create labels of almost any size or dimension. Sometimes, however, you may not want to take the time to measure your label sheet. In those cases, you can use the Predefined Size submenu, as shown in Figure 14.6.

The default size is the first one in the list of sizes. To select another size from this list, press **<Enter>** to open the submenu. The Size menu appears, as shown in Figure 14.6. Use the **<Up arrow>** or **<Down arrow>** key to highlight the choice that is closest to your labels. When you choose a predefined size, the other menu options, such as `Width of label`, are automatically assigned values to match the particular selection. All the options assume that your printer is set to print 10 characters per inch (cpi) and 6 lines per inch.

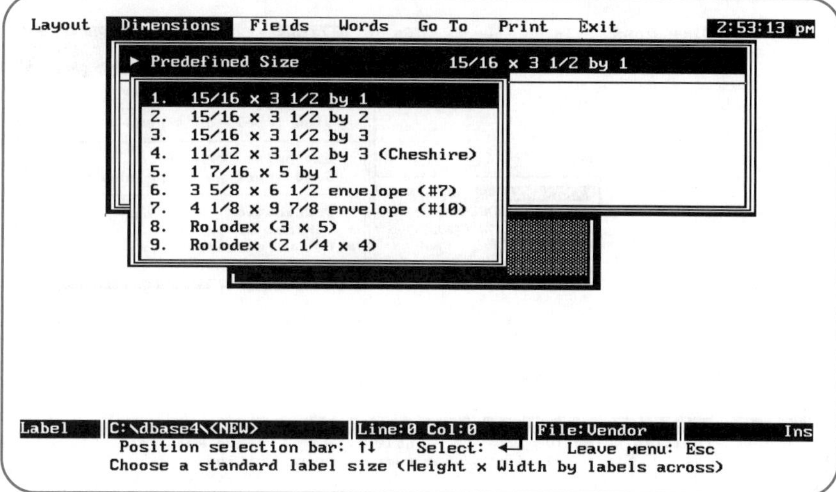

Figure 14.6. *The Predefined Size submenu*

Computer printers can print at just about any print density. The three most common are 10, 12, and 17 characters per inch (pica, elite, and compressed). If your printer is set to something other than 10 cpi and 6 lines per inch, you need to make appropriate adjustments in the options settings. The options settings need to be changed only if your printer is set to a nonstandard configuration, or if you are not using one of the dBASE IV standard label sizes.

Printing the Labels

The Print menu is shown in Figure 14.7. The print options are very similar to the options you learned about in the last chapter. The main difference is the third option, `Generate sample labels`. This option generates several sample labels from your database file. This also gives you a chance to align your paper before the final print. A print of your VENDOR file is shown in Figure 14.8.

Printing Selected Labels

Whatever data you define or select will print on the labels. You can select the data using the Query Design screen or use another form of the LABEL command from the dot prompt. The LABEL FORM dot prompt command also can be used to print selected labels using the FOR command. Suppose that you want to print labels for vendors in New York. You might enter:

```
. LABEL FORM VENDOR FOR 'NY' $ CITY_ST_ZP TO PRINT
```

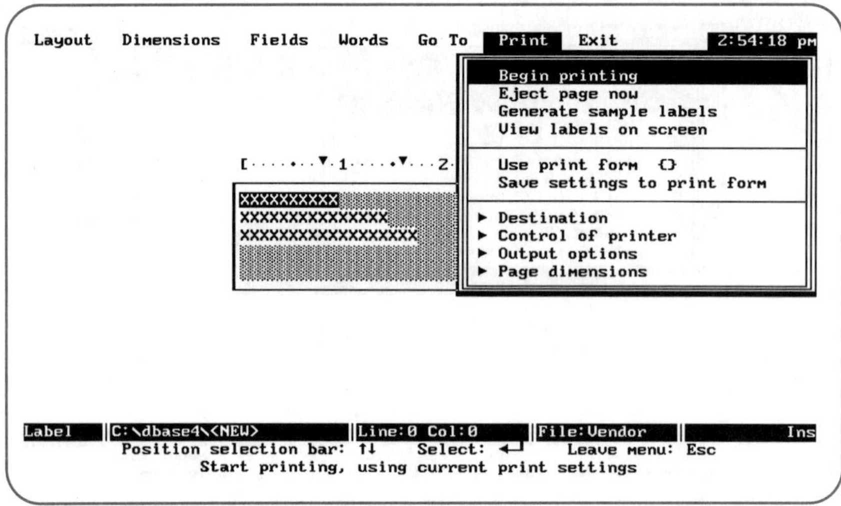

***Figure 14.7.** The Print menu*

DIGI
200 Disc Lane
Newport, CA 98556

ALLWOOD
150 Old Trail
Omaha, NE 37754

HITECH
270 Shark Lane
Cape Cod, MA 84453

MITY
212 GenMot Rd
Detroit, MI 77473

MEGASONIK
42 23rd St.
New York, NY 77473

***Figure 14.8.** The printed labels from the VENDOR file*

The output from this command would be labels for only those vendors having NY as part of the content of the CITY_ST_ZP field.

One final example shows you a label used for something other than a mailing. Suppose that you wanted to generate pricing labels for your inventory. Figure 14.9 shows you an example of a label form for this use. You can combine text, fields, and even calculated fields on labels to be used for any purpose.

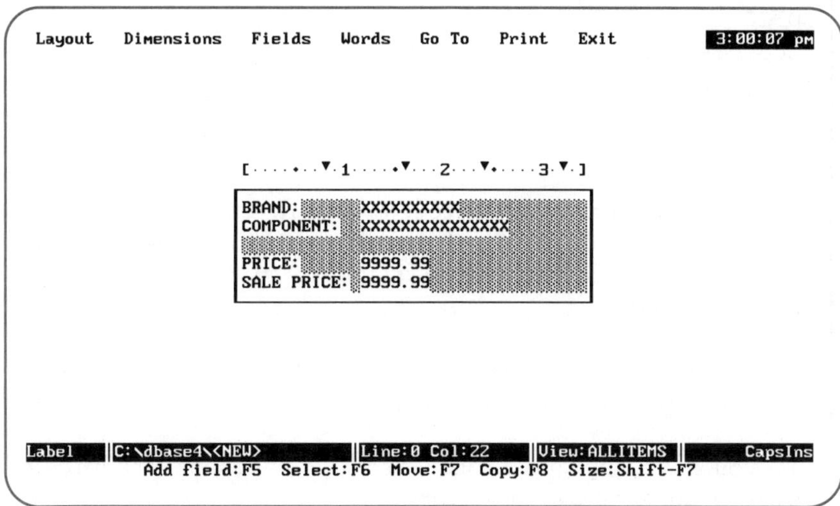

Figure 14.9. *A pricing label*

Mail-Merge Reports

A mail-merge report, a form letter for example, contains text throughout the report. You produce a mail-merge report like a standard form report except that you use a special type of band on the report form called the Word Wrap band. This band allows the text to be adjusted when fields of different lengths are inserted. It is very similar to the way a word processor works. When you type past the end of a line, the text "wraps" around to the beginning of the next line. If you add some new text in the middle of a line, all the text shifts accordingly.

Produce a mail-merge letter to your vendors. Figure 14.10 shows the letter you send out for each of the products. The letter tells the vendor some information about the store's current stock level and retail prices. In order to produce this letter as shown in Figure 14.10, you will need to use information from both the INVENTRY and the VENDOR files. In Chapter 13, you created a view called REPOVIEW. You can use this again to create your letter.

```
DIGI
200 Disc Lane
Newport, CA 98556                                    04/03/91

Dear Sirs:

We have recently completed an inventory of your
AMPLIFIER. As of 07/01/91 we have 15 in stock.  It is
our intention to maintain a quantity sufficient for our
selling needs.

Our current selling price is $389.99.  When we have a
sale we discount the price by 10.00%.

If you have any questions with our business practices
please contact me immediately.

                                                Sincerely,

                                           Ashton J. Parrot
```

Figure 14.10. *A letter to suppliers*

Creating a Mail-Merge Report

Make sure you begin in the Control Center. To make the REPOVIEW view active, choose REPOVIEW in the Queries panel and press **<Enter>**. REPOVIEW moves above the line in the Queries panel. Now select `<create>` in the Reports panel. The Reports Design screen opens. As always, the Layout menu also opens automatically. Press **<Enter>** to open the `Quick layout` option. In Chapter 13 you used `Column layout` and the `Form layout`. As you can see, there is one report type left, `Mailmerge layout`. Choose this option and press **<Enter>**.

As you can see in Figure 14.11, all you get is a relatively empty work surface. There are no fields placed on the work surface and no column headers. Why should there be? You have asked for a mail-merge report. Because there is no way of knowing which fields you might want to use, dBASE IV cannot place anything on the work surface for you. dBASE IV has, however, made some important preparations for your work.

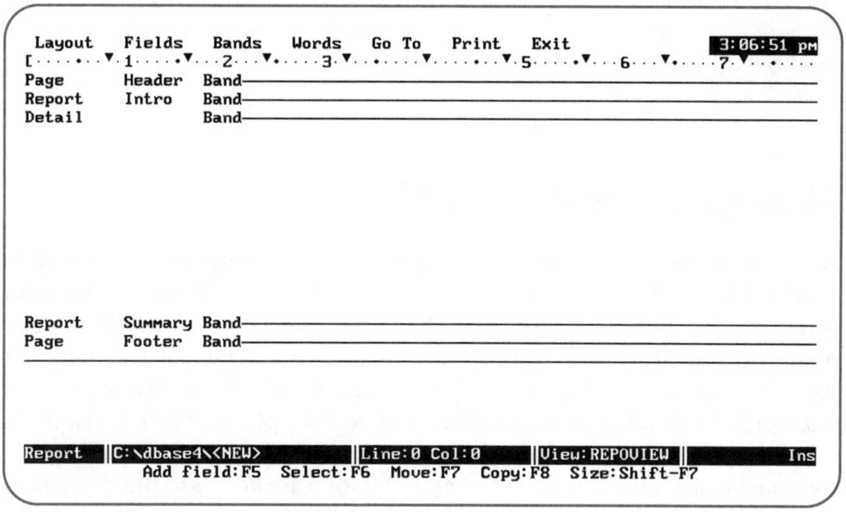

```
 Layout   Fields   Bands   Words   Go To   Print   Exit                3:06:51 pm
[·····•··▼·1·····•▼···2···▼·····3·▼·······▼·······▼·5·····▼···6···▼·····7·▼·······
Page      Header  Band────────────────────────────────────────────────────────────
Report    Intro   Band────────────────────────────────────────────────────────────
Detail            Band────────────────────────────────────────────────────────────






Report    Summary Band────────────────────────────────────────────────────────────
Page      Footer  Band────────────────────────────────────────────────────────────
──────────────────────────────────────────────────────────────────────────────────


Report   ║C:\dbase4\<NEW>        ║Line:0 Col:0    ║View:REPOVIEW ║             Ins
            Add field:F5  Select:F6  Move:F7  Copy:F8  Size:Shift-F7
```

Figure 14.11. *The mail-merge report work surface*

Word Wrapping

dBASE IV has closed all the bands except the Detail band. All the work in a mail-merge document occurs in the Detail band. Next, the options `Word wrap` and `Begin band on new page` have been turned on in the Bands menu. Because you are creating a mail-merge document, you will want your text to wrap around the data fields. This is probably the most important part of mail merging.

Look at some conceptual views of word wrapping. The text might be entered onto the work surface as follows. Each field name in capital letters represents a field placed within the text.

```
An inventory of your COMPONENT was taken last week. It appears
that we have QUANTITY in stock. Our present sales price is PRICE.
```

When the report is produced, however, it prints out like this:

```
An inventory of your speakers was taken last week. It appears that
we have 106 in stock. Our present sales price is $189.99.
```

However, if the field value happened to be large and expanded to a point that the line couldn't hold all the characters, it might look something like this:

```
An inventory of your compact disk players was taken last week.
It appears that we have 11,345 in stock. Our present sales price
is $129.89.
```

Mixing Fields with Text

When the report is produced, there will be a separate page for each record in the data file. The value for each field for a given record displays where the field was located in the text. Figure 14.12 shows two conceptual views of our mail-merge document. The top half of Figure 14.12 shows the actual field names as part of the document. This is not how you do it in dBASE IV, but this is how many word processors allow you to mix data with text. By placing the field names in the text (and usually enclosing them in brackets or some other delimiter so that they can be distinguished from the text), the software knows to put the data in place of the field name when the text is printed. The bottom half of Figure 14.12 shows how the text and fields appear when entered into the dBASE IV Report work surface.

When you enter a field in the Report work surface, the field size and type are indicated by the usual templates: *X*'s for character fields, *9*'s for numeric fields, *L* for logic fields, and MM/DD/YY for date fields. Because the mail-merge layout is really a report, it works the same way as a report. In a mail-merge report, however, you don't identify the field content with its field name, as you do in a column report.

Now, create the letter to your suppliers. You can begin by entering the text as you want it placed in the letter. Figure 14.13 shows all of this text without any of the fields. Spaces have been placed where your fields will go. Remember that as you enter the text and reach the end of a line, the words automatically wrap to the next line.

Once this is done, you can place your fields on the work surface. As you learned in Chapter 13, there are several ways to add a field. You can press **<F5>** to view a list of database file, calculated, predefined, and summary field names. You also can press **<Alt>-F** to open the Fields menu and choose `Add Field`. Either way, you choose a new field to be entered and then decide if you want to change the fields template, or picture display. Placing fields in the mail-merge layout is no different from placing them in the column or report layout.

A Conceptual View of a Mail Merge Document—Field Names

BRAND
ADDRESS
CITY_ST_ZP DATE

Dear Sirs:
We have recently completed an inventory of your COMPONENT. As of INVDATE we have QUANTITY in stock. It is our intention to maintain a quantity sufficient for our selling needs.

Our current selling price is PRICE. When we have a sale we discount the price by DISCOUNT%.

If you have any questions with our business practices, please contact me immediately.

Sincerely,

Ashton J. Parrot

A Conceptual View of a Mail Merge Document—Field Templates

XXXXXXXXXX
XXXXXXXXXXXXXXX
XXXXXXXXXXXXXXXXXXXX MM/DD/YY

Dear Sirs:
We have recently completed an inventory of your XXXXXXXXXXXXXXX. As of MM/DD/YY we have 999 in stock. It is our intention to maintain a quantity sufficient for our selling needs.

Our current selling price is $999.99. When we have a sale we discount the price by 99.99%.

If you have any questions with our business practices, please contact me immediately.

Sincerely,

Ashton J. Parrot

***Figure 14.12.** Conceptual views of mail merging*

```
 Layout   Fields   Bands   Words   Go To   Print   Exit                3:11:57 pm
0·····•··▼·1·····•▼···2···▼•·····3·[···•·····▼······•··▼·5·····•▼···6···▼•·····7·▼··•·····
Detail            Band──────────────────────────────────────────────────────────────


Dear Sirs:

We have recently completed an inventory of your            .
As of           we have       in stock.  It is our intention to
maintain a quantity sufficient for our selling needs.

Our current selling price is         .  When we have a scale we
discount the price by        .

If you have any questions with our business practices please
contact me immediately.

                                Sincerely,

                                Ashton J. Parrot

Report   ║C:\dbase4\<NEW>          ║Line:18 Col:32   ║View:REPOVIEW ║           Ins
            Add field:F5  Select:F6  Move:F7  Copy:F8  Size:Shift-F7
```

Figure 14.13. *Placing the text on the work surface*

There are nine different fields to add in this layout. Eight of the fields are database fields, and one is the PREDEFINED field `Date`. Add the first field, BRAND. Place the cursor four lines above *Dear Sirs:*. If you don't have any blank lines, make sure you have Insert on, then move the cursor to the *D* in *Dear Sirs:* and press **<Enter>** four times. This will add four blank lines into the Detail band.

With the cursor four lines above the salutation, press **<F5>**. The Fields menu opens. Choose BRAND.

Once BRAND is chosen, the Fields submenu opens on the work surface. This menu lists the field name, type, and length. It also has options to change the template or picture display. Leave this field alone. Press **<Ctrl>-<End>** to accept this field. The template (XXXXXXXXXX) is placed on the work surface four lines above the salutation. Repeat this for ADDRESS and CITY_ST_ZP on the next two lines. After these three fields are on the work surface, move the cursor to the right side of the screen on the CITY_ST_ZP line. You are going to add the PREDEFINED field `Date`. Again, press **<F5>** to open the submenu. Move the cursor to the PREDEFINED column and choose `Date`. Press **<Ctrl>-<End>** to add it to the work surface.

You have now completed all the fields for the top of the letter.

Now you can add the rest of the fields to the body of the letter. Though all of the letter is located in the Detail band, the letter contains some fields that aren't between other text. You have already completed those fields.

The first field that goes into the body of the letter is the COMPONENT field. Figure 14.12 can be used as a guide to the placement of all the fields. Whenever you create a mail-merge layout, it is a good idea to sketch out the placement of fields and text on a piece of paper, just as you would when creating a report or screen form.

Move your cursor to the first text line after the salutation, and place the cursor just to the right of the text *of your*. This is where the COMPONENT field goes. Press **<F5>** and choose the COMPONENT field from the list. Press **<Ctrl>-<End>** to place the field on the work surface. Some of the text already on the screen moves over. As the space is used by the COMPONENT field template, the text is adjusted through the word-wrapping process.

You can repeat this process for INVDATE, QUANTITY, PRICE, and DISCOUNT. When you put the PRICE field in the letter, you can select the `Financial format` picture function. This will place a dollar sign in front of the amount when it is printed. Your final screen appears in Figure 14.14.

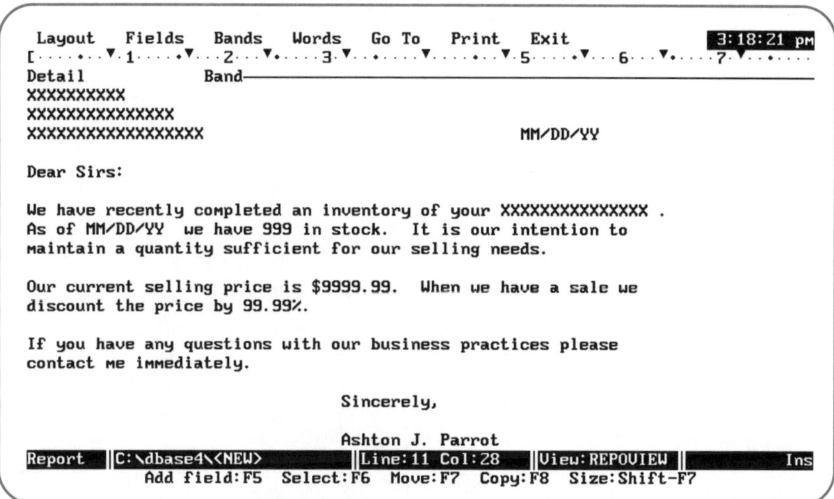

Figure 14.14. *Placing the fields on the work surface*

Printing the Letter

The last thing to do is to try out your mail-merge document. Press **<Alt>-P** to open the Print menu, and press **<Enter>** to begin printing. You should see the same output as shown in Figure 14.10.

Summary

In this chapter, you have examined the commands you can use to prepare labels for a variety of uses. You are not restricted to mailing labels. Use labels for inventory shelves, file folders, book plates—anywhere that you might otherwise use a gummed label.

Both labels and mail-merge documents can help you communicate to your customers, suppliers, and co-workers. Combining labels and mail merging with reports and the Query Design screen, you should now be able to use your data efficiently and productively.

In the next chapter, you will see how to create custom screens to make getting your data into dBASE IV as easy as getting it out.

chapter 15

Custom Screens

Creating special customized screens such as the one in Figure 15.1 was once a source of woe for computer users. Beginners couldn't do it and programmers hated doing it. The result was nearly always dull screens with terse messages. Today, dBASE IV makes it easier for anyone to create special screens.

Custom screens offer more than just a pleasing appearance. These screens allow you to make better use of the limited screen space. By adding lines and boxes you can segregate common data items and change the order in which you edit data. Most important, custom screens can provide complete edit checking of the data.

Without a custom screen you get a standard screen like the one you have seen in the EDIT mode—all the field names along the left side and the fields themselves next to each field name. This screen is adequate as a default screen. You can, however, always improve on a standard form, because you know what you want the screen to look like. This chapter will help you design custom screens that will streamline data entry. The functional design of your new screens will make data entry faster, easier, and most important, more accurate.

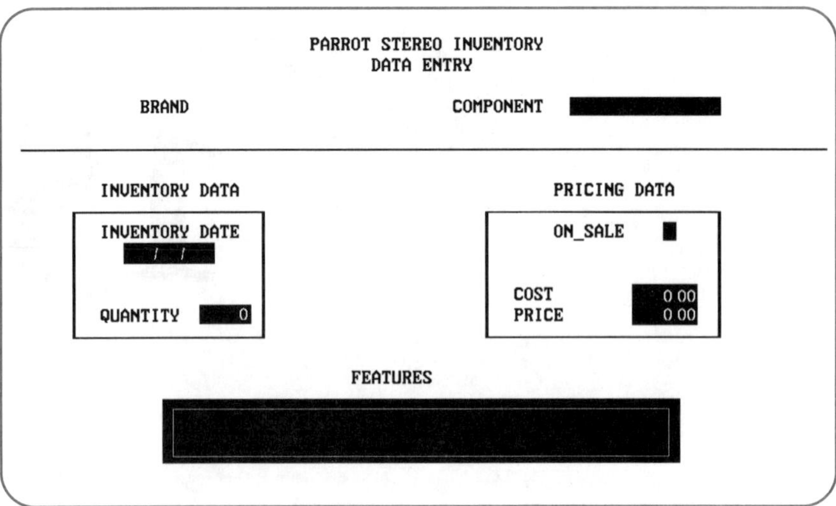

Figure 15.1. *A custom data entry screen*

Creating a Custom Screen

To get started, go to the Control Center and make the INVENTRY file active. Then, move the cursor to the `<create>` marker of the Forms panel and press **<Enter>**. The Form work surface appears, as shown in Figure 15.2.

The screen form looks very similar to other work surfaces you have already seen. The menu on top contains many options you have already used. In fact, if you have read the previous two chapters on reports and labels, you have already seen all the menus in this work surface. This form gathers the information that dBASE IV needs to produce your custom screen and to store the information in a disk file. The filename for this screen form must conform to the standard rules for disk filenames. dBASE IV automatically adds the SCR file identifier to this filename. When you have completely defined the screen, dBASE IV uses the *screen file* to produce a second file. This second file is called a *format file*. dBASE IV will automatically assign the format file the same name as the screen file, but with an FMT file identifier.

The screen-creating menu system works in the same way as in the other dBASE work surfaces. You can move around the work surface with the usual arrow keys. You can highlight text by first pressing **<F6> Select**. Then you can select as much text as you want, one character at a time, simply by moving the cursor. Once it's selected, text can be moved around the work surface freely. You select fields by moving the cursor onto any part of the field and then pressing **<F6> Select**. The entire field highlights, and then you can move the field by moving the cursor to the desired position and pressing **<F7> Move**. You also can select multiple fields and text with the **<F6> Select** key.

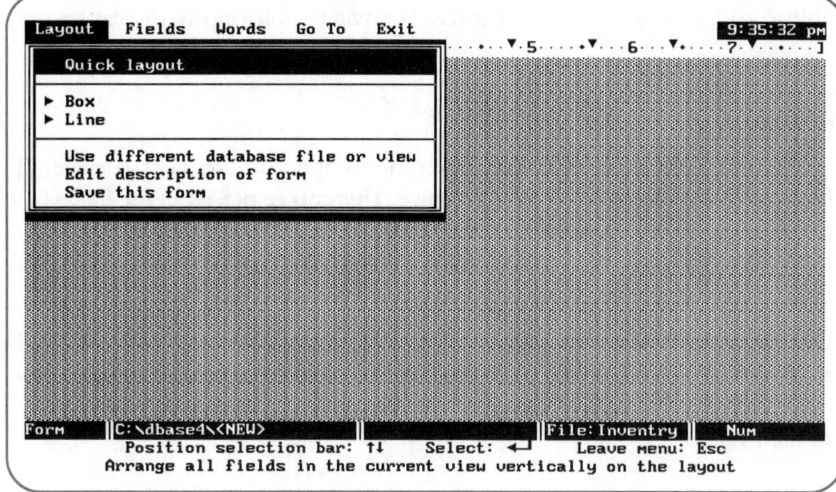

***Figure 15.2.** The Form work surface*

Process for Screen Creation

It's best if you create custom screens following a step-by-step process, much like the process you learned in the Reports chapter:

1. Select a database file
2. Choose the file fields
3. Compose the screen
4. Select templates and pictures
5. Determine edits for each field

As usual, you start with the database file.

Step 1: Select a Database File

Before you can begin to create a custom form, the database file with which the custom screen is to be used must be active. If you were not using that database file when you entered the work surface, you can choose the `Use different database file or view` choice from the Layout menu. For this example, select the INVENTRY database file.

As in the Report work surface, you can choose any database file or view. However, if you choose a view that has multiple database files, you will not be able to add, change, or delete records. You will be able only to display records.

Step 2: Choose the File Fields

In Figure 15.2 you can see the Layout menu open on the work surface. The highlight is on the `Quick layout` choice. This choice places all the fields from the database file onto the work surface. Unlike the Report work surface, which lets you work with more than one database, you can edit data in only one database file at a time.

Once you press **<Enter>** to select `Quick layout`, your data is placed on the work surface. It looks exactly like the EDIT mode's default form. As you can see in Figure 15.3, all the field names are lined up along the left side with the fields to their right.

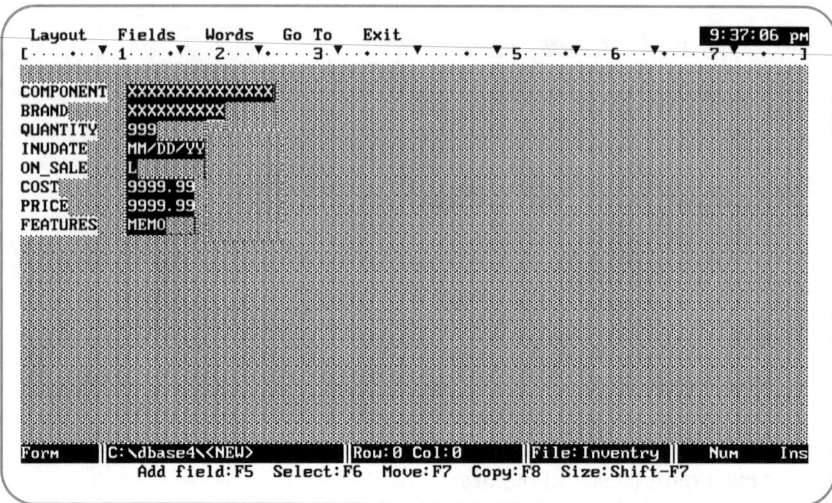

Figure 15.3. *The Form layout screen with Quick layout*

If you were to save this form right now, it would perform just like the EDIT mode screen. If you don't choose `Quick layout`, you will work with a blank work surface. The **<F5> Add Field** key lets you add fields to the work surface from the current database file. Of course, you also can open the Fields menu and choose `Add field`.

You also can delete fields by selecting them and pressing **<Del>**. Like in any other work surface, you select fields by simply moving the cursor onto any part of the field. As soon as the cursor touches the field, it highlights. You are then free to delete, change, or move the field.

Once you have loaded all the fields onto the work surface, you can begin to place them in their custom positions on the work surface.

Step 3: Compose the Screen

Compose your custom screen from the work surface. The work surface should initially resemble Figure 15.3. This is the starting point for creating the custom screen. Note that the field areas are shown in reverse video. Character fields are filled with *X*'s, numeric fields are filled with *9*'s, date fields read MM/DD/YY, logical fields are filled with *L*'s, and the memo field says MEMO.

Moving the cursor. You already know basic cursor movement with the **<Left arrow>**, **<Right arrow>**, **<Up arrow>**, and **<Down arrow>** keys. The **<Left arrow>** and **<Right arrow>** keys move the cursor one space in the direction of the arrow, and the **<Up arrow>** and **<Down arrow>** keys move the cursor one line up or down. You can move the cursor farther with the use of the **<Ctrl>** key. To move the cursor to the beginning (or the end) of the line, press the **<Home>** or **<End>** key. The status bar keeps track of the cursor position.

Adding and deleting blank lines. There are several ways to add and delete blank lines. You can add lines from the current cursor position by pressing **<Ctrl>-N**. When you add a blank line, everything below the cursor moves down one line and a blank line appears below the cursor. Delete a line using the `Remove Line` option of the Words menu.

You also can add and delete lines with the Words menu choices. The menu choices are helpful and work just as well, if you have trouble remembering the key combinations.

Entering text. To enter text on the screen, move the cursor to where you want the text and type it in. Later, if you don't like its location, you can select the text with the **<F6>** key; then move it with the **<F7>** key.

Moving fields and adding text. You can put fields anywhere on the screen—and in any order. Figure 15.4 shows the screen partly completed and with the fields moved to their approximate new locations. Note that field 1, COMPONENT, has been placed after BRAND.

To move a field, place the cursor anywhere on the field area. Then press the **<F6>** key to select the field. Then press **<F7>** to begin the move. Move the cursor to where you want the field to be. Press the **<Enter>** key. The field moves to the new position.

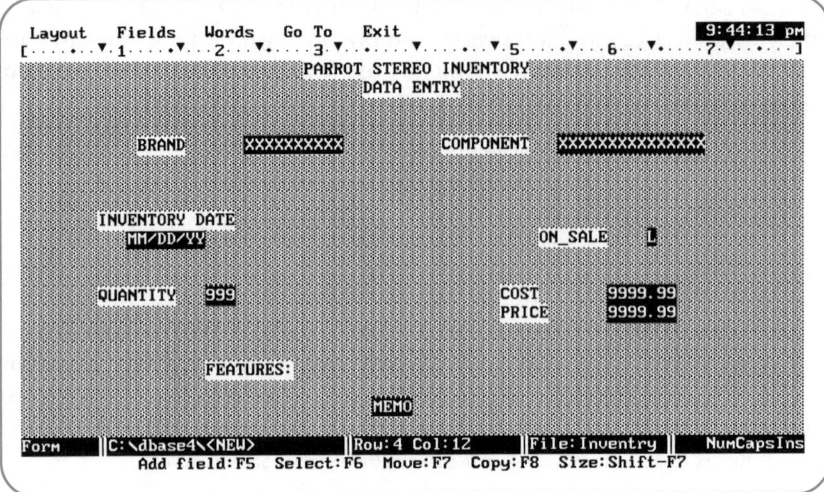

***Figure 15.4.** Adding text and moving fields around the work surface*

Notice in Figure 15.4 that some text has been added at the top of the screen and the text for the inventory data and the memo field has been changed. Changing the text in this screen does not change the actual field names on the database file. You can change field names only by going back to the Database work surface. Changed text in this screen applies only to this data entry screen.

Drawing lines and boxes. Adding lines and boxes is another step that you should consider in creating forms. You select lines and boxes from the Layout menu. Once you make one of these selections, you are asked if you want a single line or a double line.

The next step is to decide where one corner of the box is going to be. Position one corner of the box and press **<Enter>**. This "locks" the corner in place. As you press the appropriate arrow keys, the box expands to cover the area. When the box is the right size, press **<Enter>** again. You create each box this way. Lines are created the same way, except that they are one-dimensional.

Lines and boxes are shown entered on the work surface in Figure 15.5. There also is more text above the boxes to separate the Inventory data from the Pricing data. This completes most of the entry for the form.

If you need to erase a line or a box, simply select it and press **<Del>**. You can move boxes just as you move fields and text by pressing **<F7>** after the box is selected.

Composing the data entry form is an iterative process. Each time you add some text, a line, or a box, or move a field, something else probably needs to be moved as well. As you go through this process, keep in mind how you want the final screen to look.

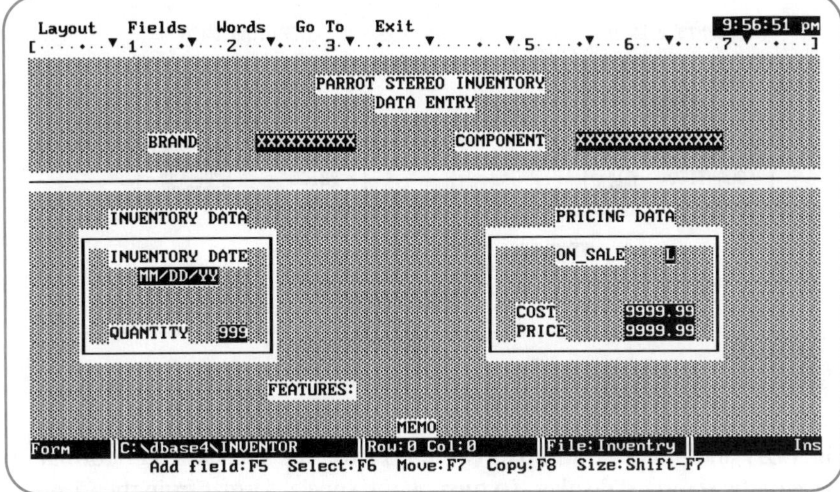

Figure 15.5. *Adding lines and boxes to make the form more readable*

Testing the Screen

Before going on to add more functionality, like picture displays and editing options, you really need to test the screen. Though you get a pretty good idea of what the screen will look like when you're creating it, there is nothing like a good test drive to make sure it works the way you expect it to. Once you are happy with the layout, you can name the screen and save it.

Press **<Alt>-E** to open the Exit menu. Choose the `Save` option. dBASE IV asks you to name the screen. Call it `INVENTOR`. When you are done, dBASE IV returns you to the Control Center. From the Control Center, place the cursor on the form name and press **<F2>**. You should be in an EDIT screen using the new form. The first record in the database file is displayed. Figure 15.6 shows this screen. Not bad for five minutes of work!

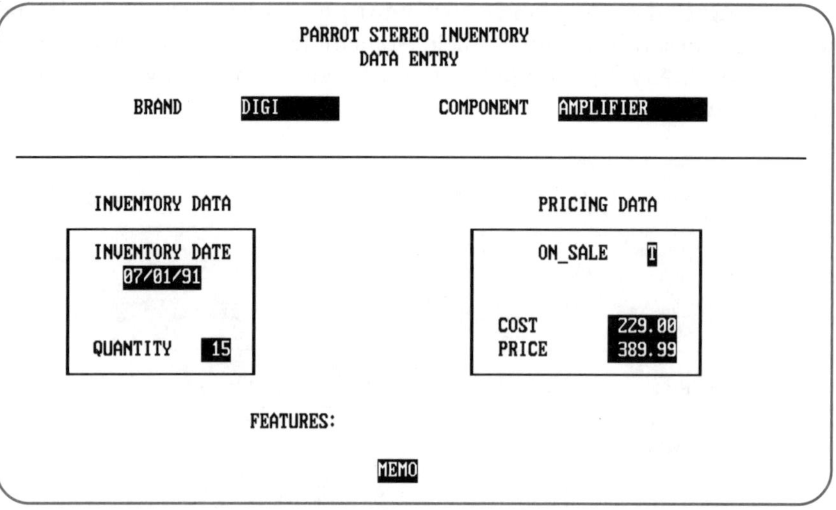

Figure 15.6. The EDIT screen with the first record

The EDIT and APPEND commands will now use the special screen format in place of the standard display. To turn off the special format from the Control Center, choose the database file or view and press **<Enter>**. This sends the form file below the line in the panel. If you close the database file you are using, the FORMAT file also automatically closes. When you reopen the database file, you must again choose the form to re-establish the custom screen.

Controlling Data Entry Display and Validation

Once you have placed all the fields on your screen, take a little time to look at each field to decide if you can enhance its capabilities to accept data input. It is in this section of the chapter that you will get to the last two steps of custom screen creation—Step 4, select templates and pictures, and Step 5, determine edits for each field.

Facilitating Data Entry

The two primary concerns of data entry are to enter the data quickly and to enter the data accurately. There is a fine balance between these two areas of concern. How you approach the balance of speed and accuracy is one of those items that determines your personal style. A system developer expects all information stored in the computer to be completely correct and accurate. However, people do the data entry, and they sometimes make errors. You will find that it is prudent to check for valid data at the time it's entered, and not allow bad or incorrect data into the system.

The data entry program checks for the accuracy of the incoming data with a process called editing. There are three types of data editing: format editing, correctness editing, and validity editing. There are two ways you can perform this editing: by using input formats on each character of the input as specified by templates and picture functions, or by using edit options to check the entire field.

Editing data begins by modifying a field on the screen. You can modify any field by selecting it and pressing **<F5>**, or by choosing the Fields menu and selecting `Modify field`. Either way, a field box appears that lets you manipulate different characteristics about the field during data entry. The field box is shown for the BRAND field in Figure 15.7.

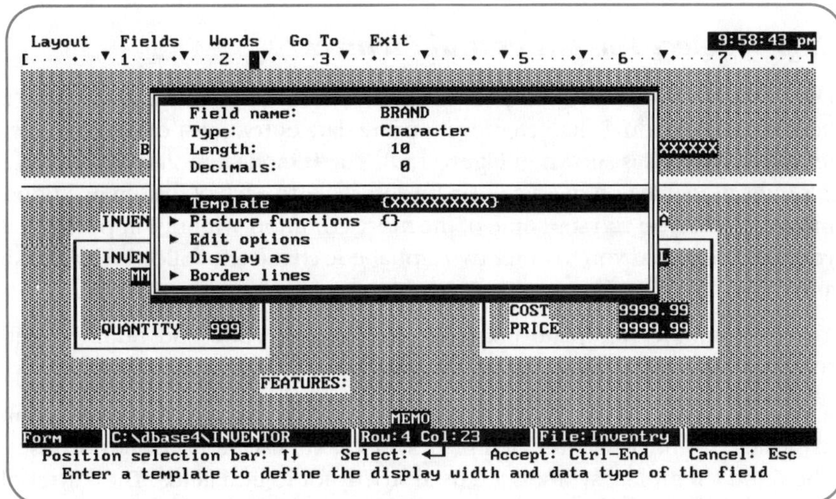

Figure 15.7. *Modifying a field's characteristics*

The top half of the box contains the field name, data type, length, and number of decimals. Because this comes from the database file structure, you cannot change any of these here.

You can add fields to the screen that are not part of the database file structure. These fields are called *memory variables* because they exist only in memory and are not part of any database file. Their primary function is to display calculations involving either a field and a value or several fields. For example, if you had the quantity and price fields in the database file (like the inventory database file), a memory variable could multiply the fields to get a total value. If you had added the field to the screen as a memory variable, you could make changes to it here.

dBASE IV naturally provides a limited measure of control to facilitate data entry. It allows you to enter only numbers into numeric fields and only valid dates into date fields. You can, however, provide a great deal more control for data entry through the custom screen. For example, you can restrict the data entry for character fields to the letters a-z, and you can force the entry to uppercase (A-Z). You also can restrict the entry of date or numeric data to a range of values. You can do this with the help of the templates, picture functions, and edit options.

In the BRAND box there are five selections at the bottom of the box. The last two selections are available only for memo fields, and they will be explained later in the chapter. The other three selections affect the way the field looks, how data is entered into a field, and whether the input is accepted as valid input.

Step 4: Select Templates and Pictures

Data entry templates. A template lets you specify what can be placed into a field at the individual character level during data entry. A list of the character template symbols is shown in Figure 15.8. The BRAND template is simply 10 *X*'s indicating that any character can be entered into each of the ten positions. In Figure 15.8 you can see some of the more common symbols. Suppose that your field required you to enter two alphabetic characters followed by a dash and three numbers. You could set up the template or *mask*: AA-999.

A phone number template that allowed the area code and number, and required the parentheses and dash, would be as follows: (999) 999-9999.

A blank space acts as a mask preventing data entry or display into that position of the field. Some of the other template symbols are used for specific purposes. The Y and L template symbols are used strictly for logical fields. The ! symbol instantly converts lowercase letters to uppercase and stores them that way.

Be aware that any symbol, other than the symbols listed in Figure 15.8, appears not only as you type in the data, but actually becomes part of the record itself. The parentheses in the phone number template are a good example of this. However, you can specify that these symbols not be part of the record by using the R picture function.

When you use any of the template symbols that allow only alpha characters, such as the A template, and you attempt to enter a number, the cursor simply does not move. Nothing is entered into the field, and the cursor just sits on the entry area.

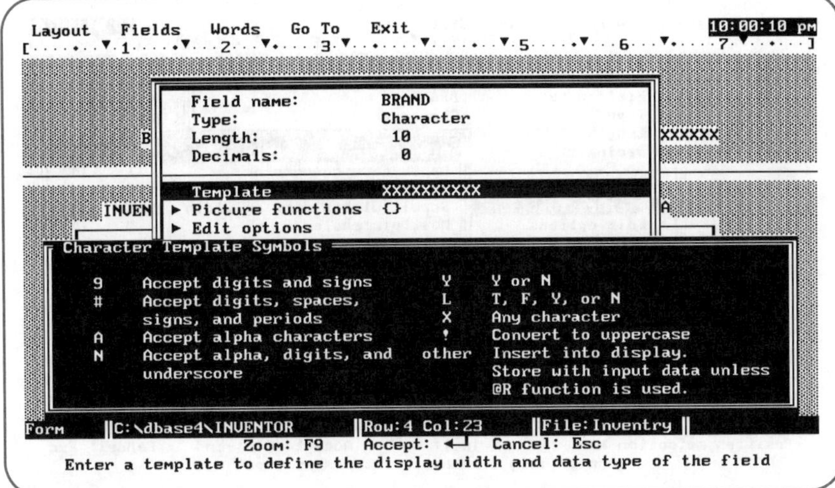

Figure 15.8. *Character templates*

When you use a symbol not on the list, like the parentheses, your cursor skips over that symbol as you enter the other template data. The phone number field looks like this when you see the blank field.

Figure 15.8 shows only the character templates. Numeric and logical fields have their own sets of templates.

You can use the $ and * characters in numeric fields of dollar figures to create a *check-protected* format. Any leading zero that is matched with an asterisk or dollar sign will be replaced by that character.

Character picture functions. Picture functions also affect the display and storage of the entire field. Figure 15.9 shows the character picture functions.

Character data can be edited and displayed using picture functions. The alphabetic functions are: `A`, `!`, `R`, `S`, and `M`. The `A` function (`Alphabetic characters only`) tells dBASE IV to accept only alphabetic characters in the input field. The `!` (`Upper-case conversion`) is a direction to change all lowercase letters to uppercase. The `R` (`Literals not part of data`) function removes the insertion characters before storing the value to a field. If you have entered template characters other than the predefined characters, these new characters, called insertion characters, are placed in the field as part of its value. The `R` function keeps this from happening.

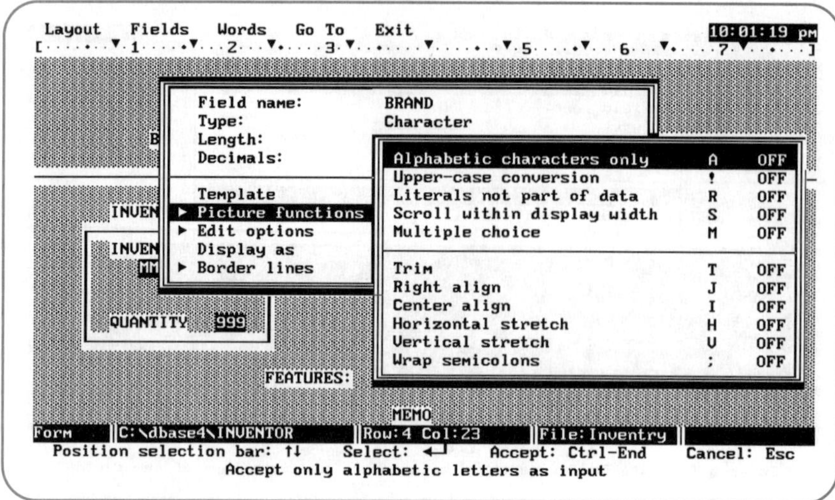

***Figure 15.9.** Character picture functions*

The `S` (`Scroll within display width`) function creates a scrollable field that is *n* characters wide. The *n* must be a positive integer. As you enter the data into an area smaller than the field width, the data will scroll, or pan, so you can enter all your data. For example, you can define an input area of 10 characters for a field that is actually 20 characters long. Only 10 characters are displayed on the screen. After the first 10 characters are entered, the field will pan out of sight to the left side of the field. The data is still in this "window" and can be changed by normal means of editing data.

The final function at the top of the box is the `M` (`Multiple choice`) picture function. This is one of the best functions available in dBASE IV. When you choose this function, dBASE IV asks you to enter allowable choices. Suppose you enter four choices for BRAND into the multiple choice entry area that appears after you turn this picture function on:

```
HITECH,ALLWOOD,DIGI,ONESOUND
```

When you use the data entry form, the first option, HITECH, appears in the BRAND entry area. With the cursor in the entry area, you press the **<Spacebar>**. Each time you press the **<Spacebar>**, a different value from the list appears. After the last value is displayed, the first one returns and the list continues. You are restricted to choosing one of the values in the list. This is an excellent way to limit data entry to allowable values.

The bottom of the box contains five functions common to both character and numeric picture functions for displayed data that won't be edited. The first is the `Trim` function. This tells dBASE IV to remove any leading or trailing blanks.

The two alignment selections align the field automatically left, right, or center within the field width, regardless of its data type. Remember that the default for character fields is left-aligned, and the default for numerics is right-aligned. The box contains the two options other than the default.

The last two selections are for stretching the data entry area. Besides the `S` function to scroll your output, there are two more options that let you enter data into a field whose display length exceeds the width of the entry area. `Horizontal stretch` expands the entry area on the same line as data is entered. `Vertical stretch` adds new lines below the original entry area. Each line is the same width as the original area.

Numeric picture functions. The numeric picture functions for display fields are `C`, `X`, `(` (left parenthesis), and `L`. The functions for both display and edit fields are `Z`, `$`, and `^`. These allow global editing on numeric data, where the whole number is affected. Numeric picture functions are shown in Figure 15.10.

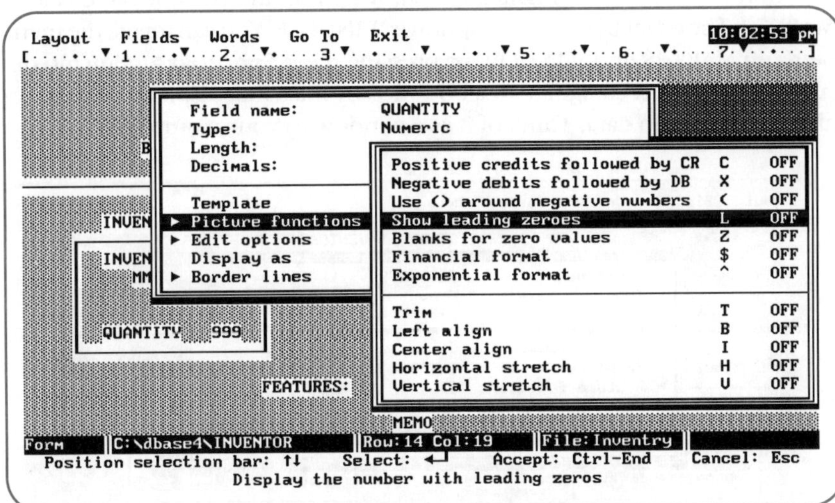

***Figure 15.10.** Numeric picture functions*

The `C` function (`Positive credits followed by CR`) displays a `CR` after positive numbers are entered. The `X` (`Negative debits followed by a DB`) function displays a `DB` after negative numbers are entered. Functions also can be used together by turning both on.

The `(` function displays negative numbers enclosed in parentheses. The `L` (`Show leading zeroes`) function displays leading zeros in a field. The `Z` (`Blanks for zero values`) function displays a blank field when the value of that field is zero.

Financial format, $, automatically places dollar signs and commas around numbers as you enter them. The Exponential format, ^, places numbers in scientific notation.

When used properly, these picture functions and templates can enhance the data entry process. You will find that most of your data entry is of the simple character or numeric variety. But when some fields need special data entry attention, these tools can help your operator do the job correctly and quickly.

Entering data into memo fields. At the bottom of the field box there are two more options that haven't been discussed. These options apply only to the memo field type and affect the display of memo fields. If you remember from Figure 15.6, the memo field is displayed as a small marker on the work surface. If the field is empty, memo appears in lowercase. If that record contains memo data, MEMO appears in uppercase.

Figure 15.11 shows the Modify field box for the FEATURES memo field. The selection Display as is highlighted showing that the current value is for a MARKER. The other Display as option is WINDOW. You can toggle the menu between MARKER and WINDOW by pressing the **<Spacebar>**. A memo display window is a rectangular area bounded by lines that display a portion (or all) of your memo data. Think of it as a window to your memo file.

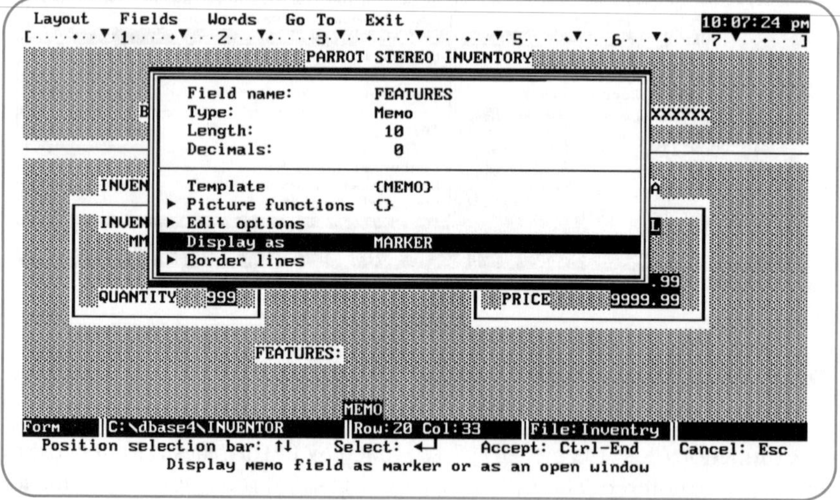

Figure 15.11. *A memo field display*

When you select WINDOW, also select the type of Border lines that will surround the window. Choices include SINGLE and DOUBLE. Once you make the WINDOW selection, a box opens on the work surface. You can manipulate this box just like any other box. You can select it with the **<F6>** key. You can then move it with **<F7>** or resize it with the **<Shift>-<F7>** keys. Figure 15.12 shows the memo window on the work surface after the FEATURES text has been moved as well.

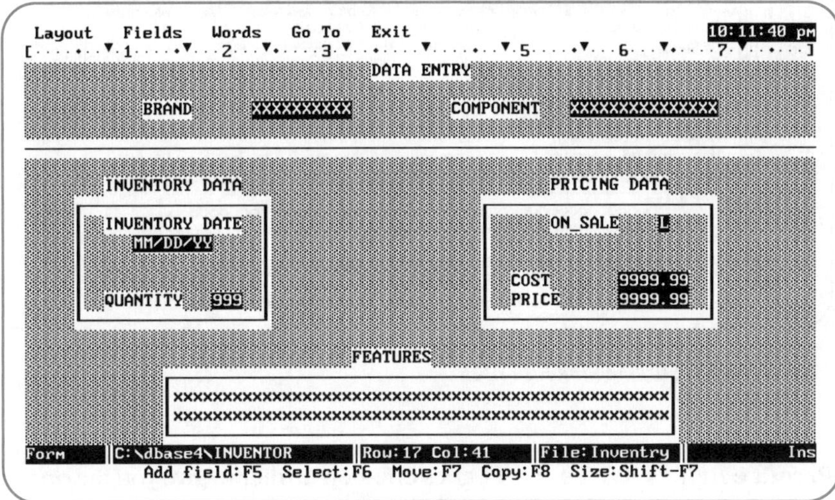

Figure 15.12. *Opening a memo window*

Once you have determined your final entry instructions, you can turn your attention to data validation at the field level.

Step 5: Determine Edits for Each Screen

Editing the entire field. There is an entire menu full of selections that make things happen when the cursor selects a field. This box is known as the `Edit options` box and is one of the selections from the field box. When you make this selection the `Edit options` box opens, as shown in Figure 15.13. There are some typical selections for the BRAND field illustrated in this figure.

Editing allowed. The first option lets you determine if this field can be changed or entered during data entry. One reason for you to decide against allowing editing might be that the data entered into this database file comes from somewhere else. Maybe the data comes from a "posting" procedure in a program, or perhaps the data is calculated for this field by a program. Whatever the reason, if this selection value is NO, the cursor will not move into the field when data entry is performed. In this example, the value is YES and the BRAND field can be entered or changed.

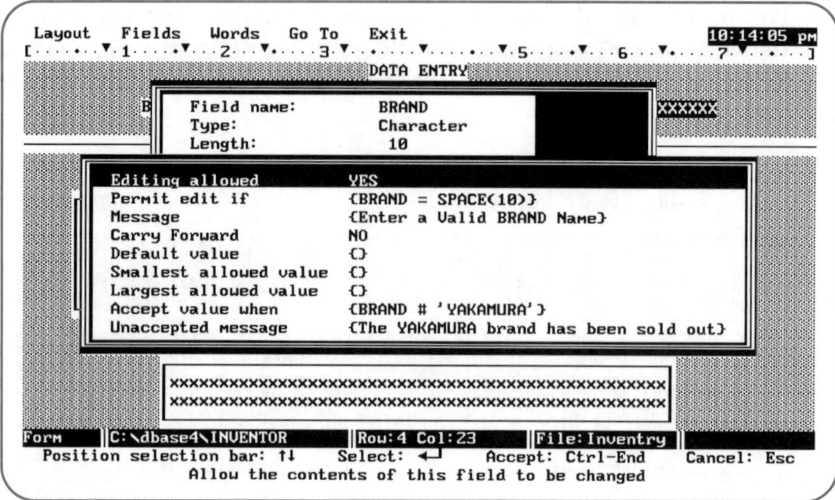

***Figure 15.13.** Entering the Edit options*

Permit edit if. `Permit edit if` goes one step further to give you the option of determining if a field can be edited at the time the record is displayed. In this example of Figure 15.13, the operator is allowed to change the value of BRAND only if BRAND = SPACE(10). This means that if the field is blank the user can change it. This also means that if the field contains something, the field can't be changed. A common example might be a Social Security form used by the government. One of the fields on the report could be a logical field called DECEASED. If the value of DECEASED is true, you wouldn't want to allow an entry except to the fields that have to do with payments due and death and survivors' benefits. This option gives you selective access to the fields that need to be edited and denies access to those for display only.

Message. The `Message` option lets you write a message that will display centered at the bottom of the screen when the cursor moves into that field on the form. In this case, the message is a prompt for the user entering data. `Enter a valid brand name` will appear below the status bar each time the cursor moves into the BRAND field.

Carry Forward. One of the options in the Settings submenu of the Tools menu is `Carry`. When `Carry` is set ON, dBASE IV copies an entire record into the next record to make it easier and faster to enter data that changes only slightly from record to record. However, keep in mind that this option copies the *entire* record. If you want only a few fields carried, you are out of luck. The `Carry Forward` setting, accessible through the `Edit options` box, is a little more specialized than the `Carry` setting.

The `Carry Forward` option allows you to select at the field level whether the value from a field in the last record entered is copied to the next record. This gives you control on a field level basis and lets you copy only parts of records to make data entry easier.

For example, you are entering all 40 invoices today for the XYZ company. To make your work a bit easier, you could design your entry form to carry forward just the date, company number, and address fields.

Default value. `Default value` lets you determine what value the entry form shows each time a new record is entered. The default value does not override a `Carry Forward`. Common default values include today's date or a system date, the most common choice from a list of choices, or any data that is repetitive among records.

Smallest allowed value and Largest allowed value. Primarily, these options are used with numeric and date fields to perform range checking. By using both options, you can check to see if a number is larger than the `Smallest allowed value`, or if that number is smaller than the `Largest allowed value`. You also can make sure that an entered date falls within one or both ranges. The next option accomplishes this task.

Accept value when. This is probably the most powerful of all the dBASE IV editing commands. With a condition specified for `Accept value when`, the user cannot leave a field until the specified data entry conditions are met. Any valid dBASE IV condition can be placed here—including range checking expressions, logical comparisons, checks for character strings, date verification, lists of choices, and so on. You can use any expression that can be added to a DISPLAY FOR command as an `Accept value when` condition.

In this example of Figure 15.13, the option contains the phrase `BRAND # 'YAKAMURA'`, indicating that any value other than YAKAMURA will be accepted. You can have the complex expressions here, including .AND.s, .OR.s, and parentheses.

This option offers the most complex error checking you can imagine at the field level. Once the cursor enters the field, it cannot leave until acceptable data has been entered. By using this option with many of the fields, you can create a nearly foolproof edit checking routine without ever writing a programming command.

Unaccepted message. This last option lets you write an error message that will display centered below the status bar to tell the user why the data is not being accepted. Entering invalid data triggers the message.

These are the various options that provide the capabilities for complete input data entry and validation. Whether you are going to be entering a few simple fields with no special data concerns, or creating a screen that will be part of a complex system in which "data integrity" must be perfect, the screen form can help you.

Looking At a Format File

When you create a custom screen, you are creating a screen and choosing options that dBASE IV saves in an SCR (screen) file. dBASE IV uses this file to re-create your screen form in case you want to change it. When you are through working with the SCR file, dBASE IV creates another file called a format file, with an FMT extension. The format file contains programming commands that are run by dBASE IV. Later on, if you write a custom program, you can actually take the format file and integrate it into your program.

Take a look at the format file that dBASE IV created from this custom screen file and a few of the options you entered, as shown in Figure 15.14. You can see pictures, templates, and edit options, as well as the positioning of the statements.

Each entry into this file is a dBASE IV command. The basic command is the @ command. It is most often used in this form:

```
@ row,column SAY 'display text' GET field
```

The various picture options, templates, and edit options are part of the @ command. The SAY and GET options can be combined on one line. When they are, the field is displayed one character space after the last character displayed with the SAY. The SAY must be before the GET. Each command can include all the editing options.

Other commands you might notice include line and box drawing commands, along with the window command for the memo field.

Before you leave this subject, take one more look at the screen generated by the format file, as shown in Figure 15.15. The memo field is shown with data entered into it, and a message is displayed at the bottom of the screen.

```
*************************************************
*— Name......: INVENTOR.FMT
*— Date......: 4-04-91
*— Version...: dBASE IV, Format 1.1
*— Notes.....: Format files use “” as delimiters!
*************************************************

*— Format file initialization code ——————
PRIVATE lc_exact, lc_talk, lc_display, lc_status

IF SET ("TALK") = "ON"
   SET TALK OFF
  lc-talk = "ON"
ELSE
  lc_talk = "OFF"
ENDIF

lc_exact = SET("EXACT")

lc_cursor = SET("CURSOR")

SET CURSOR ON

ON KEY LABEL Shift-F2 ln_temp = attsheet( "INVENTOR" )

lc_status = SET("STATUS")
*— SET STATUS was OFF when you went into the Forms Designer.
IF lc_status = "ON"
   SET STATUS OFF
ENDIF

*— Window for memo field Features.
DEFINE WINDOW wndow1 FROM 18,14 TO 21,65

*— @ SAY GETS Processing. ————————

*— Format Page: 1
@ 1,29 SAY "PARROT STEREO INVENTORY"
@ 2,35 SAY "DATA ENTRY"
@ 4,12 SAY "BRAND"
@ 4,23 GET Brand PICTURE "XXXXXXXXXX" ;
    VALID BRAND # 'YAKAMURA' ;
   ERROR "The YAKAMURA brand has been sold out" ;
    WHEN BRAND = SPACE(10) ;
    MESSAGE "Enter a Valid BRAND Name"
@ 4,43 SAY "COMPONENT"
```

Figure 15.14. The dBASE IV format file for the INVENTOR custom screen

```
@ 4,55 GET Component PICTURE "XXXXXXXXXXXXXXX"
@  6,0  SAY  "----------------------------"
@ 8,8 SAY "INVENTORY DATA"
@ 8,53 SAY "PRICING DATA"
@ 9,5 TO 15,24
@ 9,46 TO 15,69
@ 10,8 SAY "INVENTORY DATE"
@ 10,53 SAY "ON_SALE"
@ 10,64 GET On_sale PICTURE "L"
@ 11,11 GET Invdate
@ 13,49 SAY "COST"
@ 13,60 GET Cost PICTURE "9999.99"
@ 14,8 SAY "QUANTITY"
@ 14,19 GET Quantity PICTURE "999"
@ 14,49 SAY "PRICE"
@ 14,60 GET Price PICTURE "9999.99"
@ 17,33 SAY "FEATURES"
@ 18,14 GET Features OPEN WINDOW wndow1

*- Format file exit code ----------------

*- SET STATUS was OFF when you went into the Forms Designer.
IF lc_status = "ON"  && Entered form with status on
  SET STATUS ON     && Turn STATUS "ON" on the way out
ENDIF

IF lc_cursor = "OFF"
  SET CURSOR OFF
ENDIF

IF lc_exact = "OFF"
  SET EXACT OFF
ENDIF

IF lc_talk = "ON"
  SET TALK ON
ENDIF

RELEASE WINDOWS wndow1

RELEASE lc_talk, lc_fields, lc_status

*- EOP: INVENTOR.FMT
```

Figure 15.14. Continued

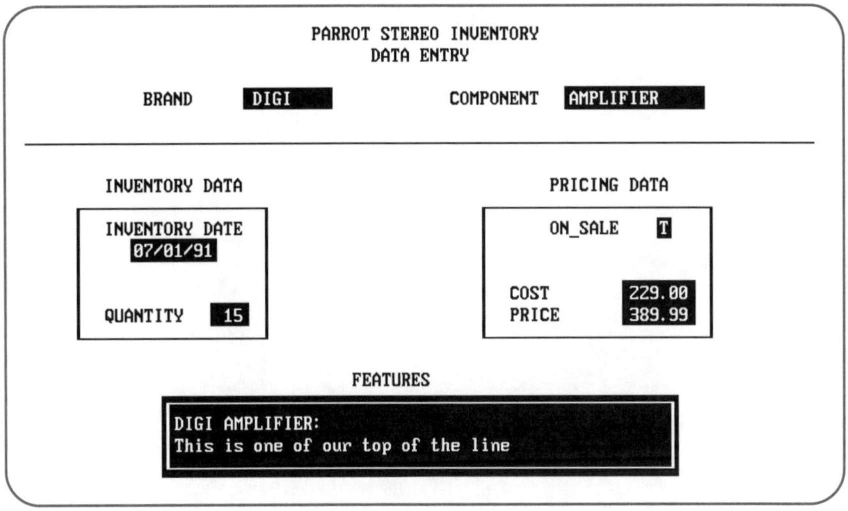

```
PARROT STEREO INVENTORY
DATA ENTRY

BRAND  DIGI          COMPONENT  AMPLIFIER

INVENTORY DATA                 PRICING DATA

INVENTORY DATE                 ON_SALE  T
07/01/91
                               COST     229.00
QUANTITY  15                   PRICE    389.99

FEATURES
DIGI AMPLIFIER:
This is one of our top of the line
```

Figure 15.15. *Our final custom screen*

Summary

By combining data entry with data display and validation, the custom screen form proves to be an invaluable tool for any system. Custom screen creation is now possible for beginning users and faster for the expert. You can create custom screens by using a word processor to construct format files, but it's much more work to type out the format commands than to let dBASE IV automatically generate them. Additionally, without the visual layout advantage of the forms screen, you can't see what your screen will look like until you are actually finished entering all the commands for the design.

chapter 16

Directories

As you use your computer and dBASE IV, you will accumulate many files of all kinds: database files, index files, report form files, label form files, and so on. How do you keep track of all of these files? What did you call the file? Which index goes with which database file? You must know the names of the files you want to use.

The computer's operating system, called DOS (disk operating system), keeps a list of all the files on each disk you are using. These lists are called the disk directories. Each time you create a new file, its filename is added automatically to the disk directory. Both dBASE IV and DOS provide you with access to this list of filenames through their DIR (directory) commands.

As you learned in Chapter 2, dBASE IV also provides you with the means to catalog your dBASE files. dBASE catalogs help you remember which indexes, report forms, and other dBASE files belong to each database file.

Some systems, usually those intended for use on large computers, also employ a data dictionary. A data dictionary contains all the information about all the files on your database file—including the structure for each separate relation. The dictionary is most useful when you have a very complex database file with hundreds of separate relations, reports, and so on. This chapter focuses on the use of directories. It also explains ways for you to organize your disks, making work with your computer a little easier.

The DOS Directory

DOS, your disk operating system, is what actually tells your computer how to run. DOS is the program that operates all you do with your computer, including loading other programs like dBASE IV. This chapter teaches you a little about DOS so that you will understand some of the concepts that actually make using dBASE IV easier and more productive.

DOS maintains a collection of information about each of your disk files. This information includes the filename, the time and date that the file was last changed, the size of the file, and where the file is located on your disk. You can view the first four of these items with the DOS command DIR. A sample directory page is shown in Figure 16.1.

```
INVENTRY DBT      1536   4-30-91  12:30p
ALLITEMS QBE      3795   4-30-91   1:21p
BUILDX   EXE    153216   4-15-91   9:52a
VENDOR   LBL       859   4-30-91   3:36p
VENDOR   LBG      3124   4-30-91   3:36p
ALLITEMS QBO       516   4-30-91   3:36p
REPOVIEW QBE      3858   4-30-91   3:53p
PARROT   CAT      3322   4-31-91   9:17p
VENDRLET FRM      4744   4-30-91   5:06p
VENDRLET FRG     10519   4-30-91   5:06p
CATALOG  CAT       788   4-31-91   9:23p
REPOVIEW QBO       604   4-30-91   8:17p
FONEBOOK DBF       438   4-30-91   7:20a
VENDRLET FRO     11584   4-30-91   8:19p
INVENTOR SCR      2222   4-30-91  10:08p
INVENTOR FMT      2107   4-30-91   6:58a
INVENTOR FMO      1940   4-31-91   9:16p
        75 File(s)   5076992 bytes free

C:\DBASE4>
```

Figure 16.1. *A sample DOS directory page*

DIR normally provides you with a single long list of filenames. If you have more than 22 files on your directory, the first files will scroll upward off the top of the screen, leaving just the last 22 filenames visible on the screen. To view more than 22 filenames at a time, add a /W to the DIR command, as shown in Figure 16.2. This displays the filenames in five columns. With the /W option, you can view 110 filenames on-screen before any filenames scroll up off screen and out of view.

```
C:\DBASE4>DIR/W

 Volume in drive C has no label
 Directory of  C:\DBASE4

.              ..             EMDBP          SQLHOME        GENERIC  PRZ
ASCII    PRZ   HPLAS100 PRZ   FX85_1   PRZ   CONFIG   DB    DBASE1   RES
DBASE2   HLP   LABEL    PRF   DBASE3   OVL   LABEL    GEN   DBASE    EXE
DOCUMENT GEN   DBASE1   OVL   DBLINK   RES   REPORT   PRF   DBASE2   OVL
DBASE3   RES   MENU     GEN   QUICKAPP GEN   PROTECT  OVL   DBASE1   HLP
DCONVERT EXE   DBASE5   OVL   SAMPLES        DBSAMPLE BAT   DBTUTOR
DBTUTOR  BAT   DBSETUP  HLP   DBSETUP  EXE   DBSETUP  OVL   DBSETUP  RES
INVBRAND DBF   UNTITLED CAT   DBASE4   OVL   DBASE2   RES   FORM     GEN
QBE___12 DBT   INVENTRY MDX   CARY1    PRG   INVSORT  QBE   REPORT   GEN
FRED           DB4            DBASE6   OVL   INVCOST  QBE   MENU     PRG
DBLINK   EXE   BUILD    COM   INVENTRY DBF   INVENTRY DBT   ALLITEMS QBE
CARY1    QBO   BUILDX   EXE   VENDOR   LBL   CARY2    QBO   BUILDX   RES
VENDOR   LBG   ALLITEMS QBO   REPOVIEW QBE   PARROT   CAT   VENDRLET FRM
VENDRLET FRG   CATALOG  CAT   REPOVIEW QBO   FONEBOOK DBF   VENDRLET FRO
INVENTOR SCR   INVENTOR FMT   INVENTOR FMO
       75 File(s)    5068800 bytes free

C:\DBASE4>
```

Figure 16.2. *The wide DOS directory*

You can cause the directory display to pause after every full screen of filenames by adding /P to the command.

```
C:\DBASE4> DIR/P
```

A somewhat annoying feature of the directory system is that the filenames are usually presented in the order that the files are actually stored on the disk; they appear in essentially random order. You can get the filenames to appear in alphabetical order; however, you need a special program to do this. SORT.COM comes with your operating system. If SORT.COM is on the subdirectory you are using or in your path (more about that later), you can sort your directory display.

```
C:\DBASE4> DIR | SORT
```

This command doesn't actually sort the directory. It just sorts the directory display. The Norton Utilities, published by Peter Norton, includes a program that you can use to sort your directory.

Subdirectories

In Figure 16.3, several files are displayed with <DIR> following the filename. These are called *subdirectories*. Each subdirectory is a special "compartment" of a disk directory that you can use to hold some of your disk files. Use subdirectories to group files and to avoid cluttering the main directory. In this example, the subdirectory SQLHOME contains all the files belonging to SQL. The subdirectory DBDATA contains all the data files belonging to the database file. The last subdirectory, TUTOR, contains the dBASE IV Tutorial.

```
C:\DBASE4>dir *.

 Volume in drive C has no label
 Directory of  C:\DBASE4

.            <DIR>       7-30-90   7:07a
..           <DIR>       7-30-90   7:07a
EMDBP        <DIR>       3-15-91   6:00p
SQLHOME      <DIR>       3-15-91   6:29p
SAMPLES      <DIR>       3-15-91   6:43p
DBTUTOR      <DIR>       3-15-91   6:45p
FRED         <DIR>       3-20-91   6:16p
DB41.Z       <DIR>       1-10-91   7:56p
        8 File(s)   5060608 bytes free

C:\DBASE4>
```

Figure 16.3. *The DBASE4 subdirectories*

Creating a New Subdirectory

You can create a subdirectory of the subdirectory you are currently using with the DOS command MKDIR (for make directory). To create a subdirectory named CLIENTS, enter:

```
C:\DBASE4> MKDIR CLIENTS
```

Using a Subdirectory

To use a subdirectory, enter the DOS command CD (change directory) from your operating system. To use this new CLIENTS subdirectory, enter:

```
C:\DBASE4> CD CLIENTS
```

The prompt changes to:

```
C:\DBASE4\CLIENTS >
```

The new prompt tells you that you are on the C drive in the directory DBASE4 in the subdirectory CLIENTS. If the prompt displays only the drive, you have to tell DOS to display the directories. Enter:

```
C:> PROMPT $P$G
```

Your directories and subdirectories are now displayed in the prompt. To look at another subdirectory, DBDATA, enter:

```
C:\DBASE4\CLIENTS> CD \DBASE4\DBDATA
```

The backslash (\) tells DOS to start its search from the root directory and not from the present DBASE4 subdirectory. Because you were in another subdirectory (CLIENTS) you had to tell dBASE to follow the tree forward from the root directory.

The subdirectories of DBASE4 are shown in Figure 16.3. As you can see, these subdirectories contain more subdirectories. DOS allows you to organize your disk into smaller subdirectories to make the task of managing your disk files easier. It's a little like having a filing cabinet with an almost unlimited number of drawers and compartments.

All the subdirectories on your disk are automatically arranged into a hierarchy, as shown in Figure 16.4. The top box in this diagram is called the root directory, possibly because the diagram resembles an upside-down tree. The subdirectory has a filename, just like any other disk file. When you first use a disk, you are automatically in its root directory. To use one of the subdirectories, enter the DOS command CD. To move back up the tree when you have finished with the directory, enter CD followed by two dots:

```
CD..
```

This command moves you "up" one level in the directory. To return to the root directory, enter:

```
CD\
```

When you are in a subdirectory, the DIR command shows you the names of the files in that subdirectory only. However, DOS provides a way to use any file in any subdirectory.

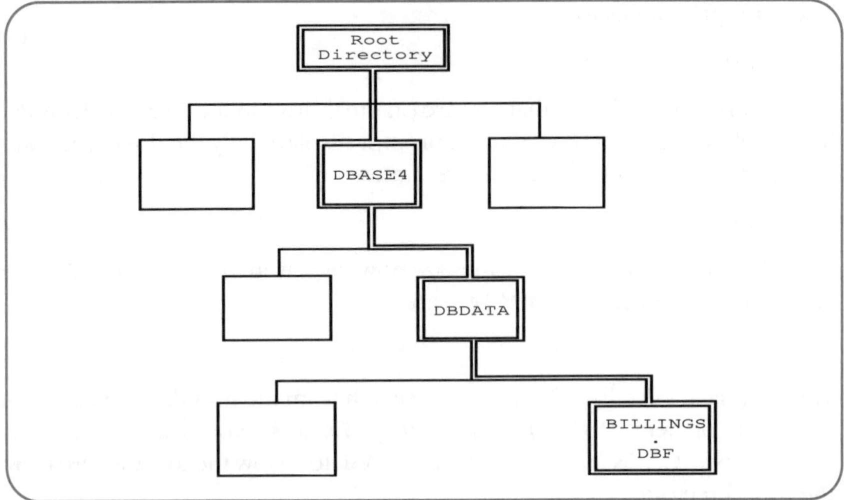

Figure 16.4. Diagram of a directory system

Paths and Pathnames

In Figure 16.4, there is a double black line connecting some of the boxes in the diagram. This line traces a path from the root directory to the file BILLINGS.DBF. The complete name of BILLINGS consists of its filename and the names of all the directories (separated by backslashes) from the root directory to the file:

```
\DBASE4\DBDATA\BILLINGS.DBF
```

This is the absolute pathname of the file BILLINGS.DBF. You can gain access to any file in any subdirectory by using its absolute pathname. For example, you can display all the filenames in the directory DBDATA by means of its absolute pathname:

```
DIR\DBASE4\DBDATA
```

If you trace a path downward from the directory in use, you obtain the relative pathname of a file. For example, if you are using the directory DBASE4, the relative pathname of BILLINGS.DBF is as follows:

```
DBDATA\BILLINGS.DBF
```

The absolute pathname of a file always begins with a backslash (for the root directory). The relative pathname must begin with the name of a subdirectory of the directory that you are currently using.

Subdirectories provide you with a convenient means for organizing the files on a disk. Put the files that belong together into a separate directory. Suppose you have a database file for your department's budget. Along with this budgetary database file, you have many ancillary files—indexes, special screens, report forms, and so on. Put all these files into a subdirectory. This will make it easy to keep track of the files that belong to a particular database file.

Using dBASE IV from a Subdirectory

You can use dBASE IV even though it is not located in the subdirectory you are currently using. Suppose your data is in the subdirectory TOOLS. Ordinarily, you can use only the files in the subdirectory you are currently working in. To use dBASE IV from another subdirectory, enter the DOS command PATH. This tells DOS to search another directory, if what you have asked for (dBASE IV) is not on the current directory. In this case, because dBASE IV is in the DBASE directory, which belongs to the root directory, use the path command as follows:

```
C:\TOOLS>PATH = \DBASE
```

Once you have specified the DOS path, you can switch directories at will. You can always use dBASE IV—no matter which directory you are currently using—by typing `DBASE` after the operating system prompt.

The dBASE Directory

dBASE IV also provides you with a DIR command. You can use it to display the names of the files on your disk from within dBASE IV. The dBASE DIR command is a variation of the DOS DIR command. Used alone, the dBASE DIR command displays specific information about only the database files on your disk in that directory. To display the names of the database files on your hard disk, use the DIR command as shown in Figure 16.5. As you can see, dBASE IV displays the filenames, the number of records, the date that each file was last changed, and the size of each file in bytes.

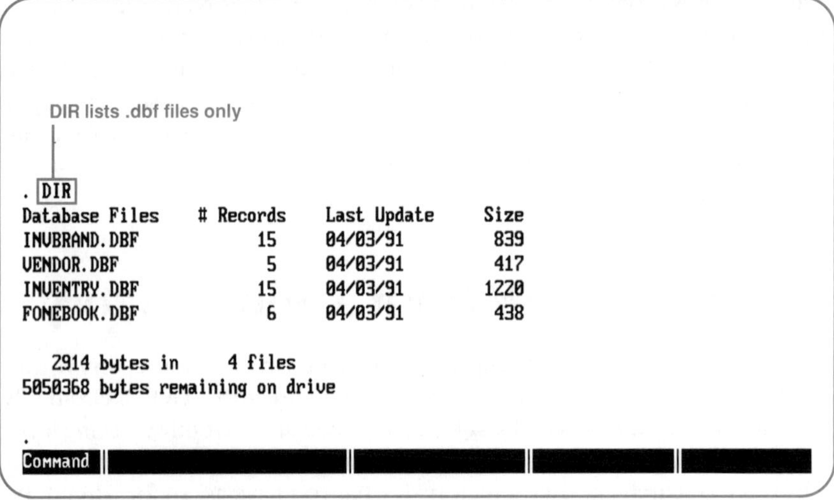

DIR lists .dbf files only
. DIR
Database Files # Records Last Update Size
INVBRAND.DBF 15 04/03/91 839
VENDOR.DBF 5 04/03/91 417
INVENTRY.DBF 15 04/03/91 1220
FONEBOOK.DBF 6 04/03/91 438
2914 bytes in 4 files
5050368 bytes remaining on drive
Command

Figure 16.5. *The dBASE directory command*

Using Wild Cards from dBASE

The basic dBASE IV directory shows only the names of the database files because all your work with dBASE IV revolves around these files. You can view the names of other files on your disk by adding to the basic command. For example, to view the names of all the files on your directory, use the DIR command like this:

```
. DIR *.*
```

Use the asterisk (*) and another wild card character, the question mark (?), to limit this directory display to certain kinds of files, such as report form files, or files that begin with the letter D, and so on.

Here are some examples of restricting the directory display with the use of the asterisk:

. DIR D*.*	Filenames beginning with D
. DIR DB*.*	Filenames beginning with DB
. DIR *.	Filenames without a file extension
. DIR *.FRM	All report form files
. DIR *.LBL	All label form files
. DIR *.MDX	All dBASE IV index files

The question mark substitutes for a particular character position. Suppose you want to display all filenames in which the third character is a D. Or, perhaps, you want to see only those filenames that begin with D but have five or fewer characters. These are cases in which you use the question mark to substitute for individual characters.

. DIR ??D*.*	Files with D as the third character
. DIR ?????.*	Files with 5 or fewer characters
. DIR *.?	Files with a one-character extension
. DIR MENU?.*	Five-character files beginning with MENU

These wild card characters are used to help narrow down the display and to help you locate the files you want from the large number that may be on your disk. The wild card characters are used in the same manner with either the dBASE or the DOS version of DIR. As long as you have only a few files, you won't have much need for many of these commands. But if you make much use of your computer, you will have very many files. You can count on it.

The wild card characters, * and ?, can help you identify which files are indexes, which are report forms, and so on. However, if you have 50 report forms, you will almost certainly end up forgetting which report form belongs to which database file. The same is true with index files and the other services that you use in dBASE IV.

As mentioned before, you can organize your disk into subdirectories. dBASE IV allows you to use files in subdirectories other than the ones you are currently using. For example, suppose you are in the subdirectory DBASE4, and you want to use a particular database file, say INVENTRY, which is in the subdirectory DBDATA. To use this file, simply refer to it by its absolute pathname.

```
. USE \DBASE4\DBDATA\INVENTRY
```

Similarly, you can use files in subdirectories that lie on a path below the directory you are in, by means of the relative pathname. For example, because DBDATA is a subdirectory of DBASE4, if you are in DBASE4 you can use the database file INVENTRY with the command:

```
. USE DBDATA\INVENTRY
```

One small drawback to the dBASE version of DIR is that it does not allow you to see the names of subdirectories. If you need to see subdirectory names, either use the Tools menu of the Control Center (more about that in Chapter 17) or use the RUN command. The RUN command allows you to execute DOS commands and use other programs from within dBASE IV. To use the DOS command DIR as opposed to the dBASE command DIR, enter the command:

```
. RUN DIR
```

You can change directories while using dBASE with:

```
. RUN CD DBDATA
```

dBASE Paths

There is another way to use files from other subdirectories without either changing subdirectories or using pathnames. Simply specify one or more paths for dBASE IV to search. Suppose that you frequently use files from the DBASE4 subdirectory DBDATA, as well as from the subdirectory CLIENTS. You can specify that dBASE is always to look in these subdirectories and the current subdirectory by entering the following command:

```
.SET PATH TO DBDATA, CLIENTS
```

Once you have done this, you can use clients file BILLINGS with this command:

```
. USE BILLINGS
```

dBASE IV first searches the current directory, DBASE4. If BILLINGS is not there, dBASE goes on to search DBDATA. If the file BILLINGS is still not found, the subdirectory CLIENTS is searched.

Another advantage of using subdirectories is that you can have two or more files with the same name—if you don't try to put them in the same subdirectory. You can even use files with the same name at the same time by using an ALIAS. An ALIAS is an alternative name assigned to a work area at the time a database file is opened. Imagine that you have two files named PAYMENTS. One is in the CLIENTS subdirectory and the other is in the DBASE4 subdirectory. To open both PAYMENTS files at the same time, enter:

```
. USE \DBASE4\PAYMENTS ALIAS PAY1

. SELECT 2

. USE \DBASE4\CLIENTS\PAYMENTS ALIAS PAY2
```

In order to do this, you must assign an alias to the first of the two files. If you do not assign an alias to the first file, dBASE IV will not allow you to open the second file of the same name—even if you attempt to assign an alias to the second file.

Summary

This chapter has covered some of the techniques you can use to keep track of your database files and all their supporting files. Some of the tools you can use are provided by your operating system. Although dBASE IV does not require that you know anything about the operating system, it is advised that you learn about disk directories and the operating system commands to view, create, and erase directories. Use subdirectories to help you better organize your data. After all, you probably have uses for your computer besides database file management.

In Chapter 17, you will learn how to interact with DOS through the dBASE IV Tools menu.

chapter

17

Using the dBASE IV Tools Menu

The dBASE IV Tools menu features a wide variety of utility programs to handle such chores as

- Creating keystroke macros
- Importing and exporting data
- Interfacing with DOS
- Creating passwords for your system
- Changing global settings

This chapter focuses on the functions and features of just the dBASE IV Tools menu. Figure 17.1 shows the Tools menu open on the Control Center work surface. The menu has six choices corresponding to the six tasks it can help you accomplish. You'll be concentrating on Macros and DOS utilities in this chapter.

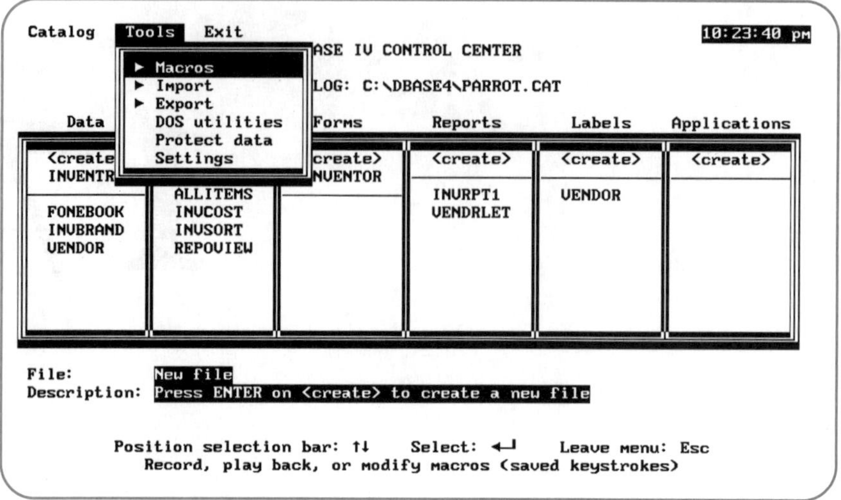

Figure 17.1. *The dBASE IV Tools menu*

Macros

A *macro* is like a computer program because it lets you perform repetitive tasks. However, instead of entering, storing, and running dBASE dot prompt commands, you enter, store, and replay your actual keystrokes. For example, you could store and replay the creation of a database file. This includes all the keys you pressed in the Control Center and in the Database work surface.

dBASE IV creates macros by remembering all your keystrokes and then allowing you to save them. Later you can edit the keystrokes. When you run the macro, your keystrokes are played back in exactly the same sequence in which you entered them.

You may want to use a macro to enter the name of your company automatically. In this book, we used the example of Parrot Stereo Company. Instead of typing this each time, you can save it once as a macro. Each time you want to use it, just press **<Alt>** with the function key you assign to the Parrot macro. dBASE IV plays back those letters onto the screen, just as if you were typing them in.

Other uses for macros could involve creating a database file in the Database work surface, or even creating lines and boxes in a form. If your company has a standard look for reports, you could automatically perform a Quick Layout in the Form work surface and create some standard lines and boxes with a macro. You might even place date and time fields in some standard location along with your company name. Once this is done for you by the macro, you can position your fields on the screen. This could save a lot of time creating standard report forms and ensure that your company standards are being followed.

Creating Macros

There are different ways to create macros. One way is to use the Macros submenu of the Tools menu to create, select, modify, and play your macros.

To create a macro, first tell dBASE that you want to save your keystrokes. Begin by choosing the `Macros` option from the Tools menu. When you choose this, the Macros submenu opens, as shown in Figure 17.2.

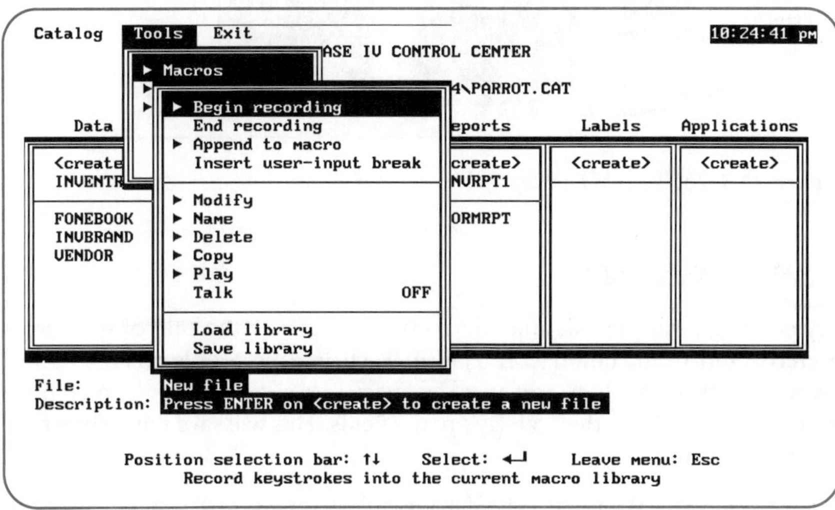

Figure 17.2. *The Macros submenu*

As you can see, this menu has many options divided into three sections. The first section handles the tasks of recording a macro. When you want to begin recording a macro, choose `Begin recording`. After you choose this option, another menu pops up showing you the various keys that you can use to store your macro. When you create a macro, you must assign a function key or letter to press to play back the macro. The Macros Display Table is shown in Figure 17.3. It lists the function keys **<F1>** through **<F10>** and the letters *a* through *z*. **<F10>** is reserved to let you play back the letter macros. In order to play back the function key macros, hold down the **<Alt>** key and press the function key you selected. To play the letter keys, hold down **<Alt>-<F10>** and press the letter of the macro. As you create and name macros, you will see their names and sizes listed in the Macros Display Table.

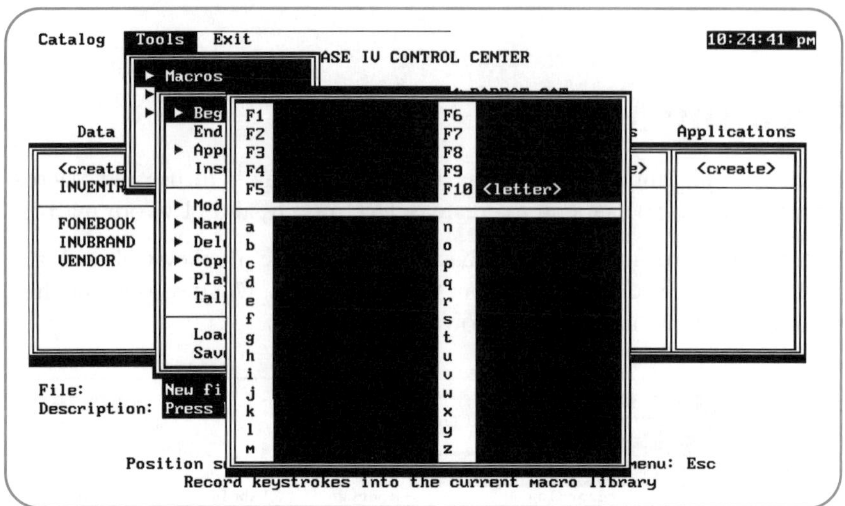

***Figure 17.3.** The Macros Display Table*

A Simple Example

Try creating a simple example macro that will center the title of the Parrot Stereo Company in a new data entry form. Each time the people at Parrot Stereo create a new form, they can use the macro to automatically center their company name. Then they can lay out the fields. This will save time when they create a new form.

Begin by selecting the INVENTRY database file in the Control Center. Move the cursor to the `<create>` marker in the Forms panel. You have now established a starting point for the macro. You will always play the macro you are about to create from this starting point. This is very important. Because you are replaying groups of saved keystrokes, your starting point must make sense for the exact series of keystrokes you have saved. If you haven't started in the right place, your keystrokes will become meaningless at best.

With your cursor on the `<create>` marker in the Forms panel, press **<Alt>-T** to open the Tools menu. Press **<Enter>** twice, first to open the Macros submenu and then to select `Begin recording`. The Macros Display Table opens in front of you, as shown in Figure 17.3.

Type P to create the Parrot macro. Each key you press now will be recorded until you tell dBASE IV to stop recording.

Press **<Enter>** to create a new form. The Form work surface opens, showing you the Layout menu. Press **<Esc>** to close this menu. Now type Parrot Stereo Company on the top line of the form. Next, you must center the title. Press **<Home>** to return to the *P* in Parrot. Press **<F6>** to begin an extended selection, and then press **<End>** to select the entire company name. Press **<Enter>** to complete the selection.

Now that the text is selected, centering the title takes a few more keystrokes. In particular, you must press four keystrokes—**<Alt>-WPC**. The Words menu is opened with **<Alt>-W**. You press P to open the Position menu, and you press C to Center the text.

You have successfully entered the keystrokes necessary to create and center the company title. Now you have to end the macro. Because you can't open the Tools menu from within the Form work surface, you will have to use the Macro shortcut keys. These are:

<Shift>-<F10> — An abbreviated form of the Macros menu; begin and end recording, and play macros

<Alt>-<function key> — To play a function key macro

<Alt>-<F10>-<letter> — To play a letter macro

Press **<Shift>-<F10>** to open the Macros menu. It appears on the work surface, as shown in Figure 17.4. You want to select End recording, so press the E key. That's it! Your macro is complete.

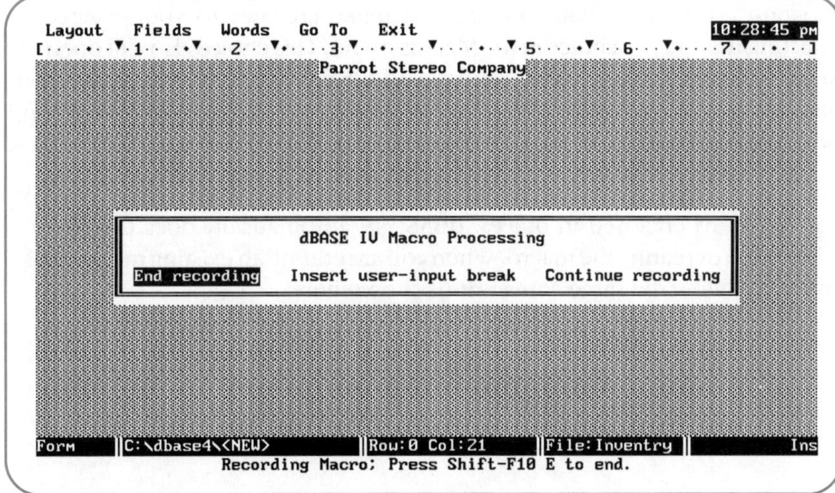

***Figure 17.4.** Ending your macro*

Playing Your Macro

Now that you've created your macro, play it back. Return to the Control Center without saving the screen. Press **<Esc>** twice and abandon the operation. Make sure that the INVENTRY database file is still selected in the Control Center and that the cursor is on the `<create>` marker in the Forms panel.

There are several ways to play the macro. You can open the Macros menu by choosing it from the Tools menu, select `Play`, and choose the `P` macro. The best way to play a macro is to use the **<Alt>**-key combination that selects it directly.

Press **<Alt>-<F10>-P** to select the `P` letter macro. All your keystrokes are instantly played back, and a new form is created with the centered title of Parrot Stereo Company. Once again, press **<Esc>** to return to the Control Center.

Editing Your Macro

There are times when you will make a mistake while entering your keystrokes during the creation of a macro. Even though you created the final product correctly, during playback users see the cursor back up to correct a typing error, or they see a menu open accidentally just to be closed with no action. Another instance in which you want to edit your macro is when certain text information has changed—for example, the name of your company. You don't want to re-create a macro, so you edit it instead.

Like a computer program, a macro is a stored sequence of commands. In the case of a macro, the commands happen to be keystrokes rather than dBASE program commands. You can see and make changes to your macros by selecting the `Modify` choice in the Macros menu. This choice also will open the Macros Display Table. Choose `P` and the dBASE editor opens and displays your macro, as shown in Figure 17.5. You can see that the Parrot macro is made up of very few keystrokes. In the editor you can add, change, or delete keystrokes.

Your keystrokes are made up of special keys, characters, and keystroke combinations enclosed in braces. dBASE IV automatically does this for you when you're creating the macro. When you are editing an existing macro, make sure you follow the same conventions shown here.

```
10:32:10 pm
[····♦···▼1·····♦·▼··2····▼····3··▼·♦····4▼·····♦···▼5·····♦·▼··6····▼····7··▼·♦·····
{Enter}
{Esc}Parrot Stereo Company{Home}{F6}{End}{Enter}
{Alt-w}pc
```

Figure 17.5. *Editing your macro*

Other Macro Menu Items

Figure 17.2, which shows the Macros submenu, contains several other options not yet discussed. You have tried out the `Begin recording` and `End recording` options. Normally, when you begin recording, you are creating a new macro. There may be times, though, when you want to add some new macro commands to the end of an existing macro. Use `Append to macro` to add new macro keystrokes onto the end of an existing macro. When you choose the macro key from the Macro Display Table, it begins recording at the end of the last statement of the old macro instead of creating a new macro. You also can use `Insert user-input break` to stop a macro during execution. The user can then enter some data or even answer a system question or prompt.

The middle section of the Macros menu contains six options that allow you to work with existing macros. These six options and the tasks they perform are shown in Table 17.1.

Table 17.1. *Macros menu options*

Option	*What It Does*
`Modify`	Makes changes to an existing macro
`Name`	Changes the user-entered name of an existing macro

continues

Table 17.1. continued

Option	*What It Does*
`Delete`	Deletes an existing macro
`Copy`	Makes a copy of a macro to a new slot in the macro table
`Play`	Plays a macro
`Talk`	Displays the macro steps in a message line as the macro is executed; you use this to check macros

The bottom of the Macros menu contains two very important options, `Load library` and `Save library`. When you create new macros in your library, they are not saved until you actually save them. They will exist only for the duration of the session until you save them in a library. There is no limit to the number of libraries you can have. Each library will have 35 macro keys. When you save a library, you will be prompted for a library name. You name a library following the same naming conventions as for any other file. When you save the library, you will see no library name. Enter the name `Parrot`, and a new macro file called PARROT.MCR is created. This library now becomes the default library. You can use this unless you have some need to create specialized libraries or you run out of the 35 choices.

Importing and Exporting Files

Importing and exporting files is made easier from the Tools menu. At some time in the future, you may need to move data from one database file to another, or even to move it to an entirely separate software program, such as an electronic spreadsheet or a word processor. For example, you might want to include selected parts of a database file in a memorandum or a report you are preparing for upper management. In this case, you'll want to move data from a database file into a file you can use with the word processing program.

Similarly, you may need to move data from another program into a dBASE database file. Why would you want to do that? You may have obtained data that was entered into disk files using another software program. Different programs often store data in widely varying formats. In the past, one program could not ordinarily make effective use of data stored by another program—there was no software "Rosetta stone." This is no longer the case. Many programs are now capable of reading data stored by at least the most widely used programs, such as dBASE IV and Lotus 1-2-3. Chapter 18 covers the topics of importing and exporting data in depth.

DOS Utilities

dBASE IV provides an access to DOS commands through the Control Center to make it easier to use the DOS commands. With this feature you can execute complex DOS commands easily and visually without leaving dBASE IV.

Once you choose `DOS utilities` from the Tools menu, you'll see the DOS screen, as shown in Figure 17.6. dBASE takes a few seconds to read your directory so it can display your files. The DOS screen itself is another work surface, but it is considered a "foreign" surface because it has nothing directly to do with dBASE. This same work surface could be run from outside of dBASE in DOS, as well as from within dBASE IV.

```
DOS   Files   Sort   Mark   Operations   Exit                        10:36:55 pm
                              C:\DBASE4
   Name/Extension      Size    Date & Time      Attrs     Space Used

   <parent>           <DIR>   Dec 24,1990  1:03p  ****
   SAMPLES            <DIR>   Dec 24,1990  1:09p  ****
   SQLHOME            <DIR>   Dec 24,1990  1:03p  ****
   ALLITEMS QBE       3,895   Dec 25,1990  6:28a  a***          4,096
   ALLITEMS QBO         800   Jan  6,1991  1:43p  a***          2,048
   ASCII    PRZ         680   Oct  4,1988  2:23p  a***          2,048
   BRAND    DBF         839   Dec 25,1990  9:51a  a***          2,048
   BRAND1   DBF         839   Jan  6,1991 10:20a  a***          2,048
   CACHEDB  BAT       1,295   Aug 10,1990 10:43a  a***          2,048
   CATALOG  CAT         439   Jan  6,1991  9:34a  a***          2,048
   CHRTMSTR DBO      43,200   Sep  5,1990 11:53a  a***         45,056

  Total  <marked>          0 (   0 files)                           0
  Total  <displayed> 3,523,063 (  73 files)                  3,606,528

     Files:*.*                                          Sorted by: Name

DOS util  C:\DBASE4
          Position selection bar:↑↓   Mark file:←┘   Directories:F9
```

Figure 17.6. The DOS utilities screen

The DOS screen can help you choose your subdirectories and move about your disk with ease. This option also provides many tools that are simply not available in DOS, such as marking certain files and then performing operations on all the marked (or unmarked) files.

The Purpose of the DOS Screen

The DOS screen gives you access to many of your favorite DOS commands. A series of submenus at the top of the screen lets you perform many DOS operations, including:

- Running any DOS command from within dBASE IV
- Changing the active disk and directory
- Filtering for certain files
- Re-sorting the files by name, extension, date and time, or size
- Deleting, copying, moving, renaming, viewing, or editing one file or groups of files

One of the DOS utilities features is the ability to perform an operation on more than one selected file. You frequently may want to delete a group of files. Through a process known as *marking*, you can select multiple files on which to perform the desired operation (such as deleting).

Examining the DOS Screen

The DOS utilities screen displays up to 11 files or subdirectories per screen. Five distinct types of information are listed for each file. First is the filename and extension or subdirectory name. Next, the size in terms of actual bytes is displayed, then the date and time. The `Attrs` stands for attributes. You can find from zero to four different attributes for each file. Attributes include those shown in Table 17.2.

Table 17.2. File attributes

Attr	*Attribute*	*What it means*
a	Archives	The file has been changed since the last time it was created or backed up
r	Read only	The file cannot be changed
s	System file	Used by DOS
h	Hidden file	Will not be displayed by normal directory commands

The last column on the DOS utilities screen shows the amount of disk space used to store the file. The Space Used column defines the number of characters on the disk that must be used to store the file. This differs from the DOS directory command. The DOS directory command displays the actual space used. DOS, however, actually requires a file size to be rounded up to the nearest sector size. In this author's hard disk, the minimum sector size is 2,048 bytes. Because the minimum sector size is 2,048 bytes, each file is rounded up to the nearest 2,048-byte sector regardless of the actual space used. Thus, a 502-byte file still takes 2,048 bytes. dBASE IV displays this size rather than the actual space used. This is why you may notice that files take up more space than you've noticed before.

At the bottom of the screen is the total number of bytes in the subdirectory. In this example, it is 3,512,798 bytes, which includes 201 files. In case you have marked any files, the total number of marked files and the space that those files occupy are also listed.

Any filter criteria and the type of sort in use are listed below the file box. As indicated by the *.* (wildcard), all the files were selected. The files are presently sorted by name. You can change any of these options by using some of the options in the menus.

Moving About the DOS Screen

You can move one file up or down in the directory by pressing the **<Up arrow>** and **<Down arrow>** keys. You can move a full screen of files at a time with the **<PgUp>** and **<PgDn>** keys.

Viewing Your Directories

There are several options to change your current directory in order to see other files. You also can change directories visually through a directory map that can be called up at any time. Press **<F9> Zoom** to display the directory map shown in Figure 17.7.

At the top of the map is the drive name. The root directory, represented by the backslash (\), is shown just below that. The main directories include those along the far left bar. Some directories like DBASE4 and FW3 have subdirectories; others, such as MOUSE and PE2, do not.

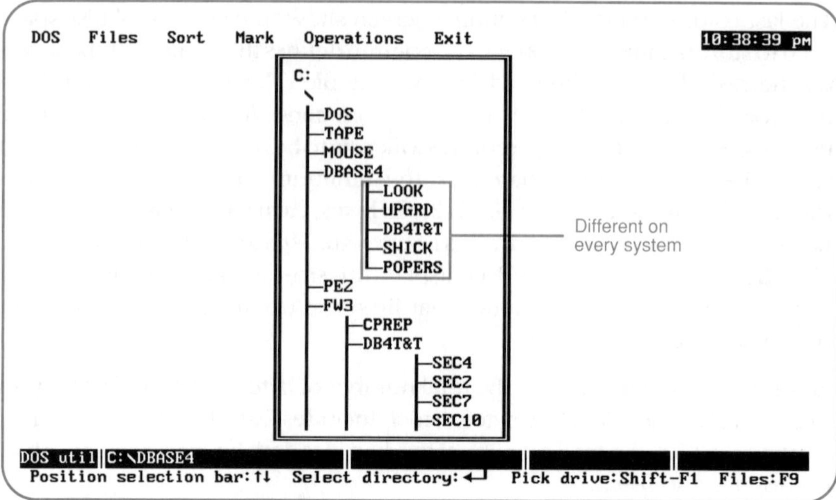

Figure 17.7. *The DOS directory map*

You can move along the directory map by pressing the arrow keys along with the **<PgUp>** and **<PgDn>** keys. Once you have moved the cursor onto the desired directory, you can select it by pressing **<Enter>**.

You can change the active disk drive by pressing **<Shift>-<F1>** and then selecting the desired disk drive. You then see a directory tree for that disk drive.

You can return to the file listing from the directory listing by pressing **<F9>** or the **<Esc>** key.

There is a series of menus at the top of the DOS utilities screen that lets you have access to all the power of DOS from within an easy-to-use work surface. These menus are easy to learn and will help you perform DOS functions.

The DOS Menu

The DOS menu is shown in Figure 17.8. This menu has only a few choices. The first choice, `Perform DOS command`, opens a box into which you can enter any valid DOS command. There is no difference between this and "real" DOS. You can enter such commands as CHKDSK, ASSIGN, BACKUP, or any other DOS command you may want to run. The results of the command will be displayed on the screen. After you finish, press **<Enter>** and the file list will again be displayed.

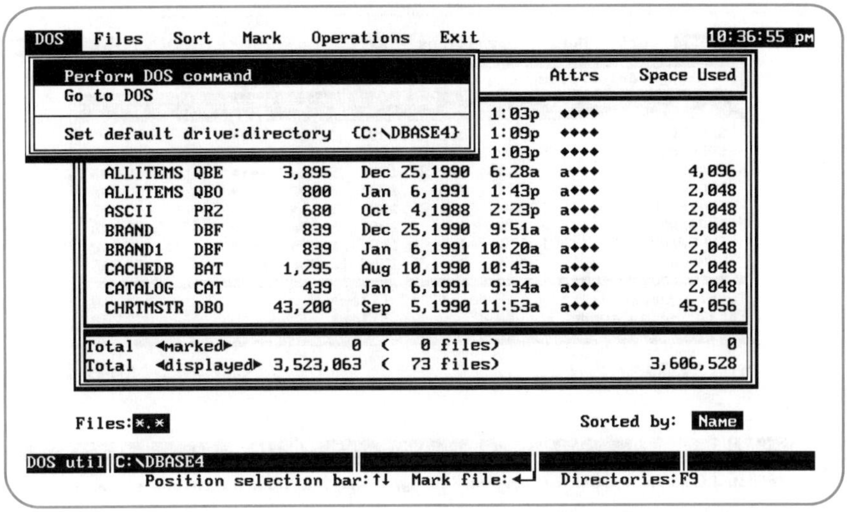

```
DOS   Files   Sort   Mark   Operations   Exit                        10:36:55 pm
 Perform DOS command                          Attrs   Space Used
 Go to DOS
                                   1:03p  ****
 Set default drive:directory {C:\DBASE4}   1:09p  ****
                                   1:03p  ****
  ALLITEMS QBE     3,895  Dec 25,1990  6:28a  a***     4,096
  ALLITEMS QBO       800  Jan  6,1991  1:43p  a***     2,048
  ASCII    PRZ       680  Oct  4,1988  2:23p  a***     2,048
  BRAND    DBF       839  Dec 25,1990  9:51a  a***     2,048
  BRAND1   DBF       839  Jan  6,1991 10:20a  a***     2,048
  CACHEDB  BAT     1,295  Aug 10,1990 10:43a  a***     2,048
  CATALOG  CAT       439  Jan  6,1991  9:34a  a***     2,048
  CHRTMSTR DBO    43,200  Sep  5,1990 11:53a  a***    45,056

 Total  <marked>          0  (  0 files)                     0
 Total  <displayed> 3,523,063 ( 73 files)            3,606,528

  Files:*.*                                   Sorted by: Name
DOS util C:\DBASE4
       Position selection bar:↑↓   Mark file:↵   Directories:F9
```

***Figure 17.8.** The DOS menu*

The next choice, `Go to DOS`, takes you temporarily out of dBASE and into a DOS prompt. When you are through with DOS you can return to dBASE by entering `EXIT` at the DOS prompt. Be careful about marked files—they will no longer be marked when you return from DOS.

The last choice in this menu lets you select the drive and directory in which your files will be stored. This is very different from changing the directory to view the files stored there. Instead, it actually changes the default file that dBASE IV uses to retrieve its data, including programs, catalogs, reports, forms, and database files. Choosing `Set default drive: directory` alters where dBASE IV stores new data and other work surface files.

The Files Menu

Figure 17.9 shows the Files menu. It contains two options. The first lets you change the drive and directory for purposes of viewing your file list. Unlike the option in the DOS menu, it does not affect where data will be stored. Once you choose this option, you can type in a different drive or directory. You also can press **<Shift>-<F1>** to pick from a list of drives and directories.

This accomplishes the same result as choosing **<Shift>-<F1>** from the directory tree to change disk drives, changing the directory from the directory tree, then pressing **<F9> Zoom** to go back to the file list.

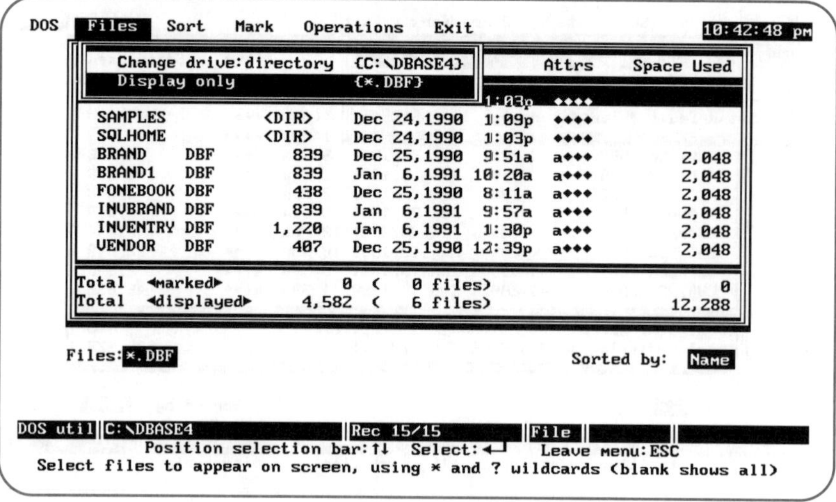

***Figure 17.9.** The Files menu with database files*

The other menu item, `Display only`, lets you designate what files you view. By using the * and ? wildcards, you can "filter" out files you don't want to see. You can use the asterisk (*) and another wildcard character, the question mark (?), to limit the directory display to certain kinds of files, such as report form files or files that begin with the letter D.

Here are some examples of restricting the directory display by the use of the asterisk.

. DIR D*.* — Filenames beginning with D

. DIR DB*.* — Filenames beginning with DB

. DIR *. — Filenames without a file extension

. DIR *.FRM — All report form files

. DIR *.LBL — All label form files

. DIR *.MDX — All dBASE IV index files

The question mark substitutes for a particular character position. Suppose that you want to display all filenames in which the third character is a D. Or, perhaps, you want to see only those filenames that begin with D and have five or fewer characters. These are cases in which you use the question mark to substitute for individual characters.

. DIR ??D*.*	Files with D as the third character
. DIR ?????.*	Files with five or fewer characters
. DIR *.?	Files with a one-character extension
. DIR MENU?.*	Five-character files beginning with MENU

These wildcard characters narrow down the display and help you locate the files from among a large number that are on the disk. As long as you have only a few files, none of this has much value. But if you make much use of your computer, you will have very many files and this selection will be invaluable.

Once you choose this option, you can add any filtering criteria you want to limit the displayed files. These include any characters or numbers, special characters, and the two wildcard symbols. In this screen, `.DBF` is the filtering criterion, and only database files are displayed along with the directories. Notice that the `Total displayed` line is telling you that only six files have been selected.

The Sort Menu

The Sort menu displayed in Figure 17.10 lets you determine how your data files are sorted in the directory.

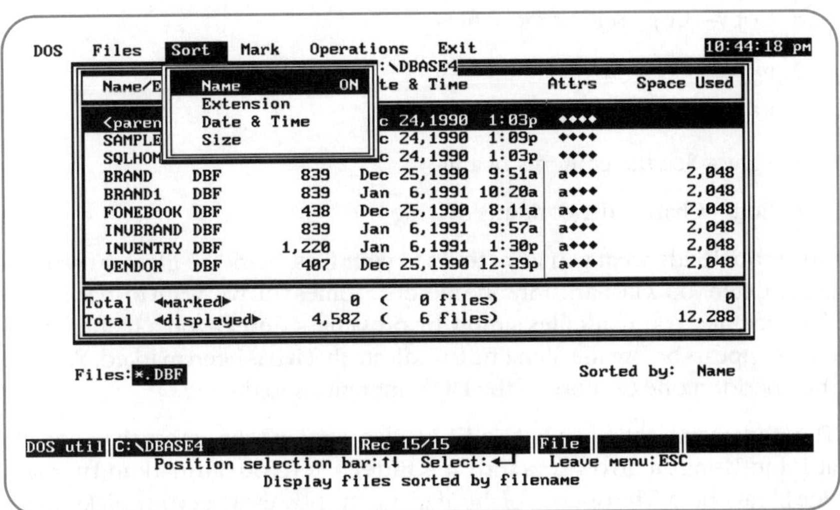

Figure 17.10. *The Sort menu*

There are four choices:

- `Name`
- `Extension`
- `Date & Time`
- `Size`

The default is `Name`, as shown in the menu. If you want to sort your files by `Date & Time`, for example, simply press `D`, or move the cursor to `Date & Time` and press **<Enter>**. The files list is resorted instantly into the new order. These options sort only the directory display. They do not affect the actual contents of your directory. You can choose only one sort method at a time.

Marking Files Using the Mark Menu

So far everything you have done has been strictly to view your files. Now it's time to do something to the files. That something can include many of the normal DOS operations that you do in the course of using your data. These operations include:

- Delete—Delete one or more files
- Copy—Copy one or more files
- Move—Move one or more files
- Rename—Rename one or more files
- View—See the contents of a file
- Edit—Change the contents of a file

Once you decide what you want to do to your files, mark the files you want to affect. Often you will mark only one file, but at times you will want to mark more than one file. You mark files simply by pressing **<Enter>** on a filename. An arrow appears before the filename to indicate that it has been marked. You can then perform one or more of the DOS operations to the file.

The Mark menu, shown in Figure 17.11, also lets you select more than one file at a time. Using the arrow keys and the **<Enter>** key, you can mark and unmark one file at a time. The options of the Mark menu, however, let you quickly mark multiple files.

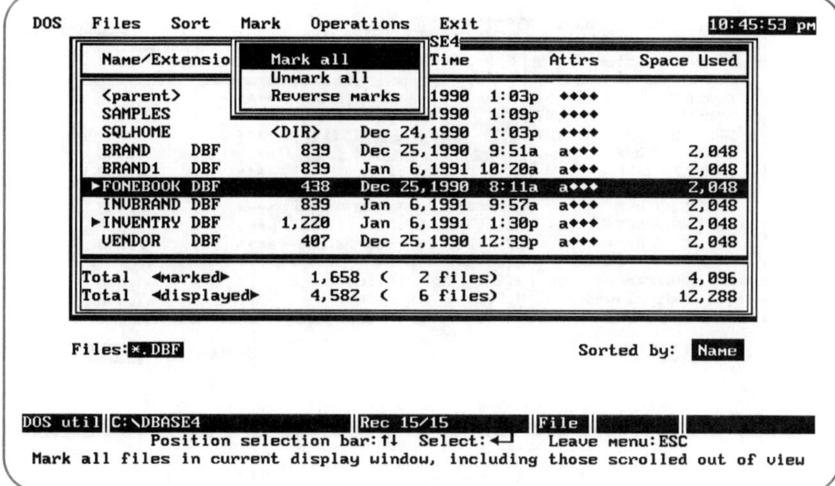

***Figure 17.11.** The Mark menu showing some marked files*

This menu has three choices:

- `Mark all`
- `Unmark all`
- `Reverse marks`

The first option marks all the files in the file box. If you limit the display using the Files menu, you will mark only those files. Once all the files are marked, you can unmark one at a time by highlighting the filename and pressing **<Enter>**. Two of the files are marked in this screen. The ones that are not marked do not have arrows in front of them.

You also can unmark all the files by using the second option.

The third option is the most interesting. Suppose you want to perform an operation on all but a few files. You could mark the files you didn't want to affect and then choose the option `Reverse marks`. All the marked files are then unmarked, and the unmarked files are marked.

The Operations Menu

Once you have marked the target file or files, you can perform an operation using the Operations menu, shown in Figure 17.12. This menu contains several of the most popular DOS operations.

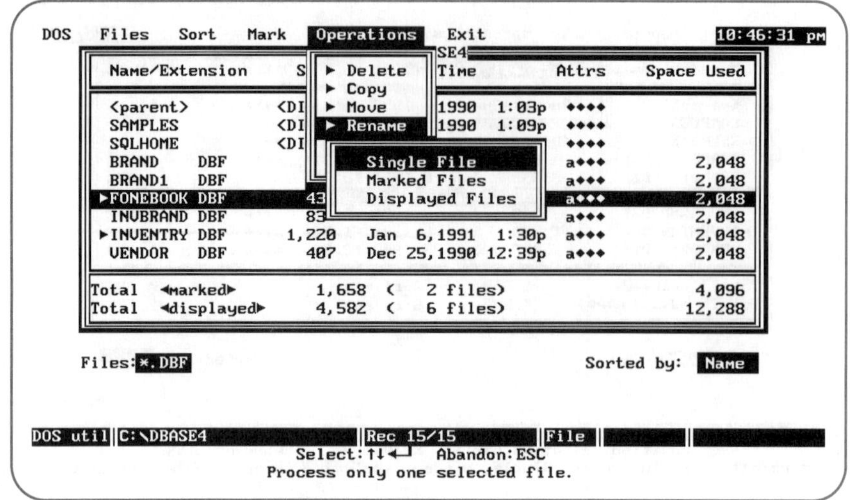

Figure 17.12. The Operations menu

Most of the operations work the way you are accustomed to, but some of them need some special processing. When you select `Delete`, `Copy`, `Move`, or `Rename`, an additional box appears, as shown in Figure 17.12. This box gives you three choices. You can perform the operation on a single file, on all the marked files, or on all the displayed files regardless of markings.

The `Delete` operation lets you specify or confirm the files you are about to delete. You can cancel the operation by pressing **<Esc>** or proceed with the operation by pressing **<Enter>** on the desired selection. You also can choose one of the displayed files to confirm the delete for only that one file. By the way, a more traditional way to delete a single file is simply by pressing **<Del>** when that file is selected.

The `Copy` command duplicates one or more files into another directory. When this option is chosen, a box appears so you can specify the destination disk and directory. If you have marked multiple files, all the marked files will be copied to the new drive and directory. If you are copying multiple files, you are given the option to rename the files during the copy. As an alternative, you can rename the files by placing a wildcard in the filename space in the prompt box.

The `Move` command performs the same operation as `Copy` except that it doesn't leave a copy in the original directory. The original file is deleted after successful completion of the copy.

You also can copy or move one file at a time by selecting the file from the file list and then pressing **<F7> Move** or **<F8> Copy**. The same prompt box appears for you to select the transfer destination drive and directory.

The `Rename` command allows you to give an old file a new name. After you choose `Rename`, a prompt box appears and dBASE IV asks for the new name. Multiple files are renamed only through the use of wildcards.

The `View` command works with only a single file. It displays the file regardless of the type. If the file is not all text, the non-text characters are filtered out. The display pauses after each screen of data.

The last option, `Edit`, lets you change a text file. You are placed into the dBASE IV editor and can make any changes you want to the file.

Remember, in order to use any of these options you must have first marked at least one file.

Summary

The DOS utilities provide a powerful interface to many of the DOS commands. You will find that this work surface, coupled with the ability to execute any DOS command, will give you the full power of DOS without leaving dBASE. Macros provide mini-programs that enable you to store and replay the keystrokes of your frequent dBASE tasks. In the next chapter, you will see how to import and export data from many sources.

chapter 18

Importing and Exporting Data

Sometime when you're using dBASE IV, you will need to move data from one database file to another, or even to move it to an entirely separate software program, such as an electronic spreadsheet or a word processor. For example, you might want to include selected parts of a database file in a memorandum or report that you are preparing for upper management. In this case, you'll want to move data from a database file into a file that you can use with the word processing program.

Similarly, you may need to move data from another program into a dBASE database file. Why would you want to do that? You may have data that was entered into disk files using another software program. Up until now this would have been somewhat of a problem. Different programs often store data in very different formats. One program could not ordinarily make effective use of data stored by another program. This is no longer the case. Many programs are now capable of at least reading data stored by some of the most widely used programs, such as dBASE III PLUS and Lotus 1-2-3.

There are many ways to move data from one database file to another or from one form to another. There are several options in the Control Center and Database work surfaces to facilitate the movement of data. There are also many options in the dot prompt to accomplish this. This chapter looks at many of the ways to move data.

Copying Data from One Database File to Another

You can copy all or part of a database file to a second database file. There are several ways to do this. The first way involves using the Control Center Database work surface.

Figure 18.1 shows the Append menu open on the Database work surface along with the menu for the option `Copy records from non-dBASE file`. The Append menu does three things. It lets you:

- Enter records from the keyboard (BROWSE/EDIT)
- Append records from a dBASE file
- Copy records from a non-dBASE file

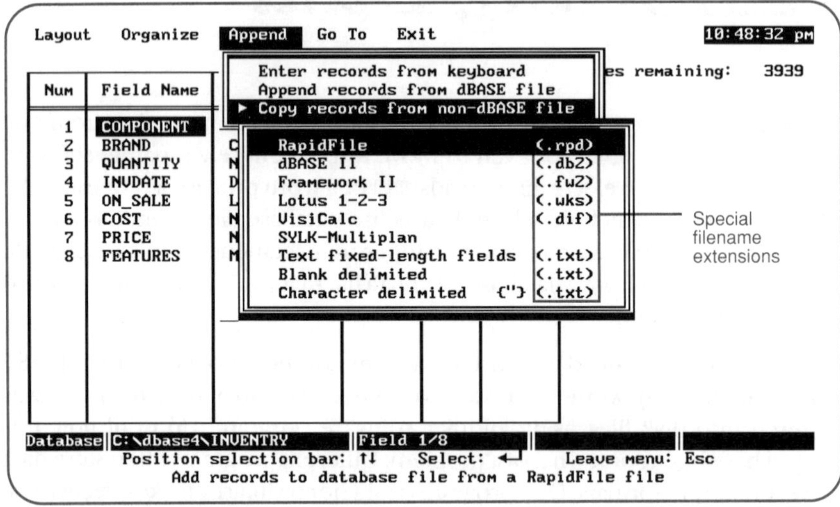

Figure 18.1. The Append menu on the Database work surface

Entering Records from the Keyboard

The first option, `Enter records from keyboard`, which you learned about earlier in this book, simply puts you into the BROWSE or EDIT mode just as if you had pressed **<F2> Data**. It puts you directly into a mode where you can add (append) records to the current database file in the BROWSE or EDIT modes. Of course, you also can review your records, make changes to them, or even delete them. This option simply acts as a "gateway" to the BROWSE and EDIT modes; it doesn't limit what you can do here.

Appending Records from a dBASE File

The next option, `Append records from dBASE file`, lets you add (append) all the records from another dBASE file to the current dBASE file structure. If there are already records in the current database file, the new records are added at the end. dBASE IV will add all the records from the database file you select onto the end of the current database file. However, it copies only those fields from the second database file that have the same name as fields in the first database file. When you are copying data from one dBASE file to another, it is very important that your fields have the same names in both files. If not, the data of those fields having different names will not be copied.

You also must be careful that fields on both files have the same data types, and that the receiving database field sizes are each large enough to receive data from the source database file. Though most data types (character, numeric, date, and logical) can be copied to a character field and will be transformed automatically into a character data type, they will lose the special abilities inherent to their data type. Numeric fields will lose their mathematical abilities, logical fields will contain character *T*'s and *F*'s, and date fields will be just a series of numbers and slashes. If the receiving field size is not large enough, the data will be truncated. Remember to make sure that your two database files are compatible when appending records.

Adding Records from a Non-dBASE File to a dBASE IV File

Besides entering and retrieving data from dBASE files, you also can retrieve data from non-dBASE files. These include files from other database file programs such as PFS:FILE, RapidFile, dBASE II, and even Framework. You also can retrieve data from spreadsheets, including Lotus 1-2-3, MultiPlan, and VisiCalc. Finally, dBASE IV can retrieve data created in text editors or word processors in a variety of formats, including Comma Separated Values (CSV) and Blank Delimited. These are known as text files.

Copying Records from a Non-dBASE File

The last choice on the Append menu, as shown in Figure 18.1, lets you add records to the end of an existing database file using the existing database file's field types and sizes as a template to flow your data into.

Data that is appended from another database package (RapidFile, PFS:FILE, Framework II, or dBASE II, for example) is appended by field name because dBASE IV is able to recognize field names. But data that is appended from spreadsheets and word processors contains no field names. In this case the data must be copied very differently.

Spreadsheet and word processed data is copied by *position*, not by field name. When retrieving data from these non-dBASE files, there is no way of knowing the field names of these foreign files because these products do not have field names. For this reason, the data must be copied by its position in the foreign file, reading from left to right, one row at a time.

When you choose the last option on the Append menu, `Copy records from non-dBASE file`, a list of all the supported file types is displayed. You then select which type of file to copy records from.

Depending on the file type you select, dBASE looks at the data and decides which data belongs to which field in your database file. For some of the file types it's easy. Spreadsheets like Lotus 1-2-3 and MultiPlan contain columns. dBASE IV simply assumes that each column can become a field in the database file. With other file formats, such as Blank Delimited, dBASE IV assumes that the data to be retrieved has a space between the fields and that the fields are in neat little rows. Others, like Comma Separated Values, require certain delimiting symbols like commas between fields, and quotes surrounding character data. Once you select the file type, dBASE IV retrieves the data and adds it to your existing database file column-by-column.

The dBASE database file that you are copying to must have a database file structure capable of accepting the type of data found in the foreign file, and it must have enough fields to accommodate all the data. If not, only the data that fits the field structure will be copied into your dBASE file.

Creating a New dBASE File from a Non-dBASE File

You can import data from foreign files into dBASE IV and automatically create a new dBASE database file. In some respects, this is easier than trying to append records to the end of an existing dBASE file. You don't have to worry about making sure that the dBASE file structure matches the foreign file's field types or sizes. Because a new database file is automatically created based on what dBASE IV finds in the foreign file, it always creates a new dBASE database file that's just the right size. If you still want to append this new file to the end of an existing file, you can examine the new dBASE file and rename the fields to match your old dBASE file after you import the data. You also can change the field types and sizes once the file has been imported.

Importing Files Using the Tools Menu

The menu choice that lets you import data and create a new dBASE file is found in the Control Center Tools menu. As you read in the last chapter, this menu contains an option called `Import`, shown in Figure 18.2. The menu option works very similarly to the Append menu. When you choose `Import`, a list of available foreign file types appears.

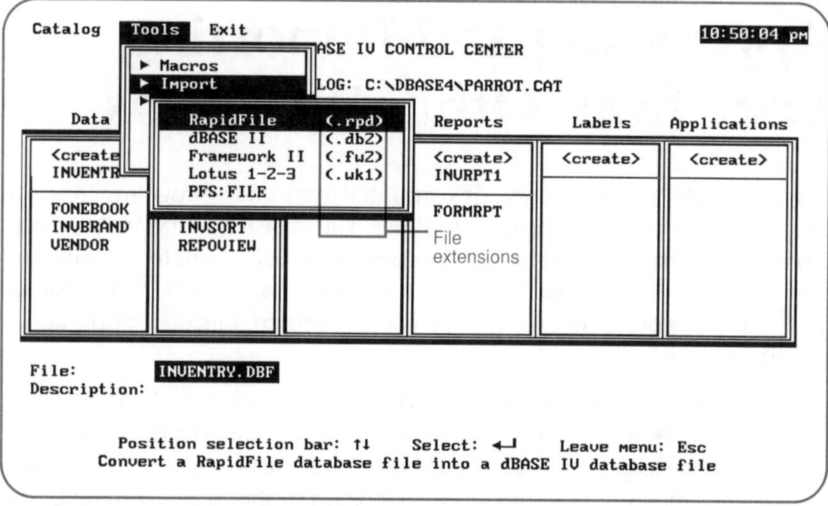

Figure 18.2. The Import submenu of the Tools menu

This menu option offers a more limited selection of foreign file types than can be imported by the Append menu. These include files from other database programs such as PFS:FILE, RapidFile, dBASE II, and Framework II, or the Lotus 1-2-3 spreadsheet. You cannot retrieve data from word processors or other spreadsheets here. This is because it is difficult for dBASE IV to determine the lengths and types of fields that come in unknown conditions (from word processors) or from file types less commonly used (MulitPlan (SYLK) or VisiCalc (DIF)). For this reason, those file types must be imported using the Append menu option and an already-created dBASE database file.

When you create a new database file by importing a foreign database file, dBASE IV uses all the foreign file field names. That is, your new dBASE file will contain the same field names as found in the original foreign file. However, when importing data from Lotus 1-2-3, dBASE IV does not find any field names but simply uses letters from A to Z for the field names.

You also might have noticed a difference in the Lotus 1-2-3 file types. The Append menu option in the Database work surface reads 1-2-3 version 1 and 1a files (.WKS). The `Import` option of the Tools menu reads Lotus 1-2-3 version 2 file (.WK1). Be careful to use the correct menu option depending on the version you have of 1-2-3. If you are using the newer version of Lotus and you want to add some records to an existing dBASE database file, you first must import the data and automatically create a new dBASE database file. Then append the files into an existing dBASE database file, just as you would any dBASE file.

Appending and Importing Data from Other Programs

If you already have data on your computer from other programs, you can probably move that data into dBASE IV files. The same is true if you obtain data from some outside source. dBASE IV provides specific means for moving data from Lotus 1-2-3, RapidFile, Framework, PFS:FILE, MultiPlan (SYLK), VisiCalc (DIF), most word processors, and many standard business applications programs.

In Figure 18.1, the last Append menu option, `Copy records from a non-dBASE file`, allows you to add records to the end of an existing database file from any of the formats listed in Figure 18.1. A dBASE file must be in use when you use this menu option. In Figure 18.2, you saw the `Import` option of the Tools menu that lets you import data from a smaller selection of foreign file types and create a brand-new dBASE database file.

Importing Data from Other Database Files

RapidFile, dBASE II, Framework, and PFS:FILE work the same way because they are databases. A database file in each of these foreign file types contains actual fields, records, and data. This makes it easy for dBASE IV to understand what the data looks like and how it is to be appended or imported.

If you are appending records from one of these formats to an existing dBASE file, first select the dBASE file in the Control Center. Then press **<Shift>-<F2> Design** to get into the Database work surface. Before you choose the Append menu and open the `Copy records from non-dBASE file` menu, make sure that the source file contains data compatible in both type and size with your dBASE file.

Look at both files. Are the field types all the same? Remember that numeric data can become character data, but dBASE IV does not let you import or copy character data into a numeric field. Do you have field types in the dBASE file like logical, date, or memo? Chances are the foreign file does not have these field types, and you will lose the data while copying or importing. Is each field in the dBASE file large enough to handle each field size in the foreign file? If not, the imported data will be truncated. Because dBASE IV recognizes field names in your foreign database files, it will copy by field name. If you have a memo field in dBASE, make sure the same name doesn't exist in a field in the foreign file.

If you can't answer these questions, take a good look at the foreign file. If you are importing a RapidFile data file, start up RapidFile and examine the database file structure. This will tell you all you need to know. If the package doesn't have a database file structure with easy-to-see field types and lengths such as the one found in Framework II, then examine the data. What type of data is found in each field? What is the maximum size of each field?

If you don't know the foreign file structure, or don't have access to it offhand, you can always use the Import menu and read the file into a new dBASE file. Then examine the dBASE file. After you make it compatible with your old dBASE file, append the two sets of dBASE files together.

RapidFile

Try going through a couple of examples. Append data from a RapidFile file to an existing dBASE INVENTRY file. Begin by examining the RapidFile database file, as shown in Figure 18.3. Parrot Stereo has decided to add headphones and VCRs to its product line. Your new buyer used RapidFile to create the database file, and you must get that into a dBASE IV file format.

File Layout Records Write Print 07 24 pm

	COMPONENT	BRAND	QUANTITY	COST	PRICE
1	HEADPHONES	DIGI	15	65	115.99
2	HEADPHONES	HITECH	15	109	225.89
3	VCR	ALLWOOD	10	329	299.99
4	VCR	ONESOUND	10	439	629.99
5	VCR	DIGI	10	589	999.99

TABLE: NEWPROD C:NEWPROD.RPD Selected: 5 of 5

***Figure 18.3.** The RapidFile database*

You can examine this database file and see if the field names are the same in the dBASE database file. If you use RapidFile you know that the basic data type choices are text, numeric, and date. This example contains only text and numeric data.

Go to the Control Center and select the receiving file. In this case, make the INVENTRY file active. Then press **<Shift>-<F2> Design** to go to the Database work surface. Next, open the Append menu and choose `Copy records from non-dBASE file`. The pick list is displayed, as shown in Figure 18.1. Choose `RapidFile (.RPD)`. A file box is displayed with all your RapidFile files listed. If your file is not shown, that is probably because it is not in your dBASE directory. If you move the cursor to `<parent>` in the file list box and press **<Enter>**, a list of your other directories opens. You can then choose the RapidFile directory and see your RapidFile files. Select the source file. dBASE IV automatically imports the data into the INVENTRY database file. When you look at your INVENTRY database file, you find that there are now 20 records with the five RapidFile records added to the bottom of the file.

The dBASE IV data file contains data for only those five records in which the field names were the same. The dBASE file fields not found in the RapidFile file were left blank in the appended records.

Now import the same RapidFile file to create a new database file. Instead of going to the Database work surface, start directly in the Control Center. This time open the Tools menu and select `Import`, as shown in Figure 18.2. The menu opens and reveals just five file types. Again, choose RapidFile and choose the RapidFile file called NEWPROD. The data is automatically retrieved and converted, and a new dBASE file called NEWPROD is created. Data records from the RapidFile file are transformed to the dBASE file format. The fields in your new database file have the same name as the fields in the RapidFile file. You can select this file in the Control Center and BROWSE through it, as shown in Figure 18.4.

Records Fields Go To Exit 9:10:48 pm

COMPONENT	BRAND	QUANTITY	COST	PRICE
HEADPHONES	DIGI	15.00	65.00	115.99
HEADPHONES	HITECH	15.00	109.00	225.89
VCR	ALLWOOD	10.00	329.00	299.99
VCR	ONESOUND	10.00	439.00	629.99
VCR	DIGI	10.00	589.00	999.99

Browse C:\DBASE4\NEWPROD Rec 1/5 File

***Figure 18.4.** The imported data*

You can see that the newly created file has the same names and appears to have the same file types. The only surprise is the QUANTITY field. Because RapidFile stores its data without regard to the number of decimals, dBASE imported this integer as a number with two decimals. You could go into the dBASE structure and simply change the number of decimals to 0.

Framework II

You use the same procedures to import data from Framework. Begin by looking at the new products in a Framework II database file, as shown in Figure 18.5.

The field names are the same in this file as in the dBASE database file. If you use Framework II, you know that there are no special data types. What you enter is what you get. The only way Framework can tell what you entered is by your method of data entry: the **<Spacebar>** or the **<F2>** key. The **<Spacebar>** tells Framework II that the type of data is character; **<F2>** indicates a numeric type field.

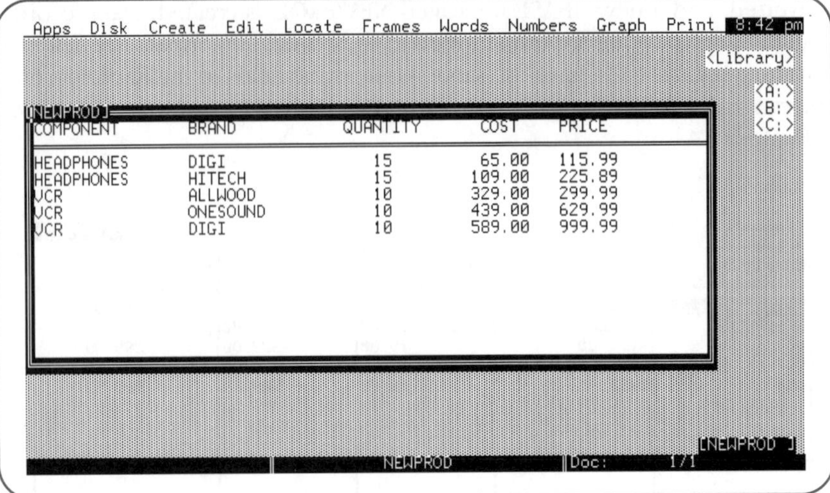

Figure 18.5. *A Framework II database*

Go to the Control Center and select the receiving file. In this case, make the INVENTRY file active. Then press **<Shift>-<F2> Design** to enter the Database work surface. Next, open the Append menu and choose `Copy records from non-dBASE file`. The pick list is displayed, as shown in Figure 18.1, and you can choose `Framework II (.fw2)`. A file box is displayed with all your Framework II files listed. Select the file from the box. dBASE then automatically imports the data into the INVENTRY database file. When you look at your INVENTRY database file, you find that there are now 20 records with the 5 Framework II records added to the bottom of the file.

Now import the same Framework II file to create a new database file. Instead of going to the Database work surface, start in the Control Center. This time, open the Tools menu and select `Import`, as shown in Figure 18.2. The menu opens and reveals just five file types. Again, choose `Framework II`, then choose the file called NEWPROD. The data is automatically retrieved and converted. A new dBASE file called NEWPROD is created. Data records from the Framework file are transformed to a dBASE file format. You have as many fields in your new database file as in the Framework II file. Each record in the Framework II file becomes a record in the database file.

As you can see, there is virtually no difference between appending and importing data from one database file format or another. Because dBASE IV is able to understand the file structures, the format is the same whether you are importing Framework II, RapidFile, PFS:FILE, or data from other versions of the dBASE family of products.

One small note on dBASE II data. When you import dBASE II data, you must first rename the file from .DB2 to .DBF.

Importing Data from Spreadsheets

Spreadsheets like Lotus 1-2-3 v1.0 and 1.A, MultiPlan (SYLK), and VisiCalc (DIF) are, for the most part, appended to an existing dBASE database file. Of these, the Import submenu contains an option for only Lotus 1-2-3 v2.0 files. Spreadsheets are translated by rows and columns and not by field names. Because spreadsheets have no field names, there is no other way dBASE IV can interpret the data. With the exception of Lotus v2.0, all spreadsheets must be appended to an existing dBASE file. You must first create an empty dBASE file with fields that match the data found in the columns of the spreadsheet.

Once you create your dBASE file, you can select the `Copy records from non-dBASE file` option of the Append menu, as shown in Figure 18.1, and choose the spreadsheet you want to copy into a dBASE file. Your dBASE fields can be named anything you want, because the data from the spreadsheet is translated by position, not by field name.

dBASE IV adds data records from the Lotus 1-2-3 .WKS file to the database file you are using. The fields in your receiving database file must be in the same order as the columns in the Lotus file. In the transfer, Column 1 in the Lotus file is added to Field 1 in the dBASE IV file, Column 2 to Field 2, and so on. Each row in the Lotus file becomes a record in the database file. The field width of each dBASE field must be at least as large as the corresponding Lotus column. If not, the data content is truncated during the transfer operation.

Lotus 1-2-3 v2.0

Depending on which version of Lotus 1-2-3 you have, you might need to use the `Import` option of the Tools menu, rather than the Append menu in the Database work surface. Lotus version 2.0 files (.WK1) can be read only by the Import menu. Lotus version 1.0 files (.WKS) can be read only by the Append menu option.

Look at your data as it might have been entered into a Lotus 1-2-3 v2.0 spreadsheet. This is shown in Figure 18.6. Because Lotus 1-2-3 is a spreadsheet, the data is arranged into neat rows and columns.

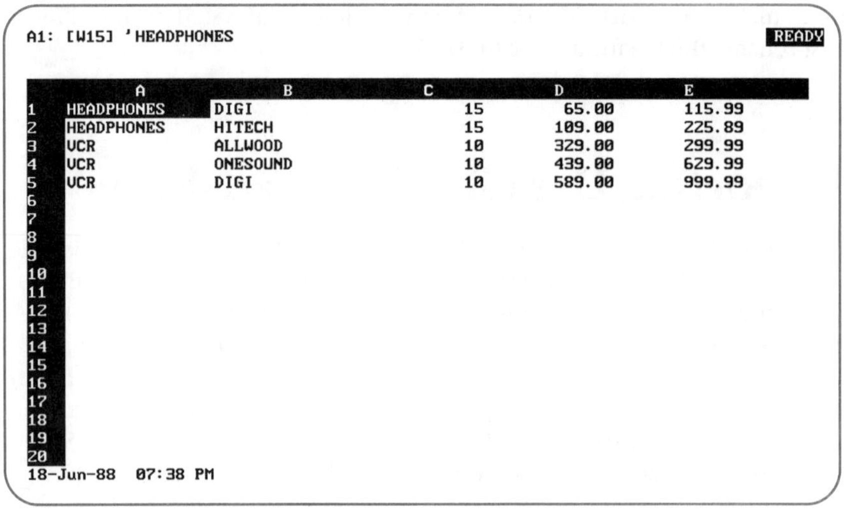

```
A1: [W15] 'HEADPHONES                                                    READY

      A               B                   C          D           E
1   HEADPHONES      DIGI                 15        65.00       115.99
2   HEADPHONES      HITECH               15       109.00       225.89
3   VCR             ALLWOOD              10       329.00       299.99
4   VCR             ONESOUND             10       439.00       629.99
5   VCR             DIGI                 10       589.00       999.99
6
7
8
9
10
11
12
13
14
15
16
17
18
19
20
18-Jun-88  07:38 PM
```

Figure 18.6. The Lotus 1-2-3 database

Lotus v2.0 data is imported, not appended. As shown in Figure 18.2, the Lotus .WK1 is supported only in the `Import` option of the Tools menu. Because you are using the `Import` command, you do not have to have a dBASE file ready to receive the transferred data; dBASE IV will create one for you. After you choose `Lotus 1-2-3 (.wk1)` in the Import menu, a file box opens listing all your 1-2-3 files. If your file is not listed, it is probably because it is not in your dBASE directory. If you move the cursor to `<parent>` in the file list box and press **<Enter>**, a list of your other directories will display. You can then choose the 1-2-3 directory to see your 1-2-3 files. Just select the file. dBASE IV automatically imports the data into a dBASE IV database file with the same name as the Lotus file, except the new file has a DBF file extension.

Because you are importing a file format (spreadsheet) with no field names, dBASE uses the letters of the alphabet as field names. The first column is called A, the second is called B, and so on. Once the data is imported, you can modify the dBASE data structure and change the field names to something more meaningful.

Moving Data from a Word Processor or Any Other Software

There are three special types of data supported by the dBASE IV Append menu. These are:

- Text Fixed-Length Fields, also known as Standard Data Format (SDF)
- Blank Delimited Format, also known as Text Variable-Length Fields
- Character Delimited Format, also known as Comma Separated Value (CSV)

These formats let you read data from virtually any software package in the world. Most software packages support SDF and CSV. These formats have been around since the early days of IBM Personal Computer software. They are very simple and allow for data translation between spreadsheets, databases, and word processors.

Figure 18.7 shows the new products in these three standard formats. Even if you are using programs like Microrim's R:base or Borland/Ansa's Paradox, you can export your data in one of these formats and then append the data to a dBASE IV file.

```
           TEXT FIXED-LENGTH FIELDS (STANDARD DATA FORMAT (SDF))

HEADPHONES     DIGI                       15         65.00         115.99
HEADPHONES     HITECH                     15        109.00         225.89
VCR            ALLWOOD                    10        329.00         299.99
VCR            ONESOUND                   10        439.00         629.99
VCR            DIGI                       10        589.00         999.99

                         BLANK DELIMITED FORMAT

HEADPHONES DIGI 15 65.00 115.99
HEADPHONES HITECH 15 109.00 225.89
VCR ALLWOOD 10 329.00 299.99
VCR ONESOUND 10 439.00 629.99
VCR DIGI 10 589.00 999.99

             CHARACTER DELIMITED (COMMA SEPARATED VALUES (CSV))

"HEADPHONES","DIGI",15,65.00,115.99
"HEADPHONES","HITECH",15,109.00,225.89
"VCR","ALLWOOD",10,329.00,299.99
"VCR","ONESOUND",10,439.00,629.99
"VCR","DIGI",10,589.00,999.99
```

Figure 18.7. *Three common text-file formats*

Standard Data Format

As you can see in Figure 18.7, each data format is a little different from the next. The first format known to dBASE IV as Text-Length Fields is better known as the Standard Data Format. You may also hear it referred to as SDF format. Each row contains one record. Each column is a predefined size. In this figure, each column is 15 characters wide. The character fields have blank spaces to the right of the entry; the numbers have blank spaces to the left. When dBASE IV reads this format, it first figures out the size of the columns and then is able to translate the data.

Blank Delimited Format

The second format is simply known as Blank Delimited Format. This also could be known as Text Variable-Length Fields. Here the data is still in rows but has no column structure. A blank space simply separates one field from another. This data format would not translate correctly to dBASE IV with the HITECH BRAND name because the space in the brand name would confuse dBASE. This format is not widely used.

Character Delimited Format

The most widely used format is the Character Delimited, better known as Comma Separated Values format. Often referred to as CSV, this format is widely used in spreadsheets and databases. As you can see in Figure 18.7, each row contains one record. However, the fields are separated by commas, and character data is enclosed in double quotes. You can use any character to enclose character strings, though the most common is the double quote. This format wastes little space and allows anything to be entered as a character string, including fields with blanks in their values. To move data from a word processor or any program that uses data in any of these formats, you must first create a dBASE file capable of handling the translated data. Choose the Append menu from the Database work surface. Then choose `Copy records from non-dBASE file`. The different choices appear, as shown in Figure 18.1. You can choose any of the text file formats. You will have to rename the source file so the file extension is TXT. Otherwise, dBASE will not recognize the file.

If you are translating from a Character Delimited file, a list of all possible ASCII characters is displayed. The double quote (") is the default. Pick the character you want to use around the character strings, and the translation process continues. Your data is appended to your dBASE IV file.

When you move data from a standard text file such as the ones above, each row becomes a record in the receiving database file. It's sometimes important to know that a row is the text between carriage returns. A row can wrap around on your screen and appear on two or more screen lines. This way you can append data with many fields.

With the tools available to import and append data, you should never have to re-enter data that already exists in some form. Even if your data is in a word processor and not in one of these forms, you can "massage" it to get it into one of these standard data formats and then import it into dBASE IV.

Exporting Data to Other Programs

Importing data is the process of copying the file of another software program and transforming it so that it can be used directly by dBASE IV. Exporting data is exactly the reverse. It is the process of copying data from a dBASE database file and transforming it so that it can be used directly by the other program.

Exporting data is far easier than importing it. For one thing, you know the structure of the file and the data contained within the file, because the data you are copying from is a dBASE IV database file. You will use only one submenu: the Export submenu found in the Tools menu in the Control Center. This menu is shown in Figure 18.8.

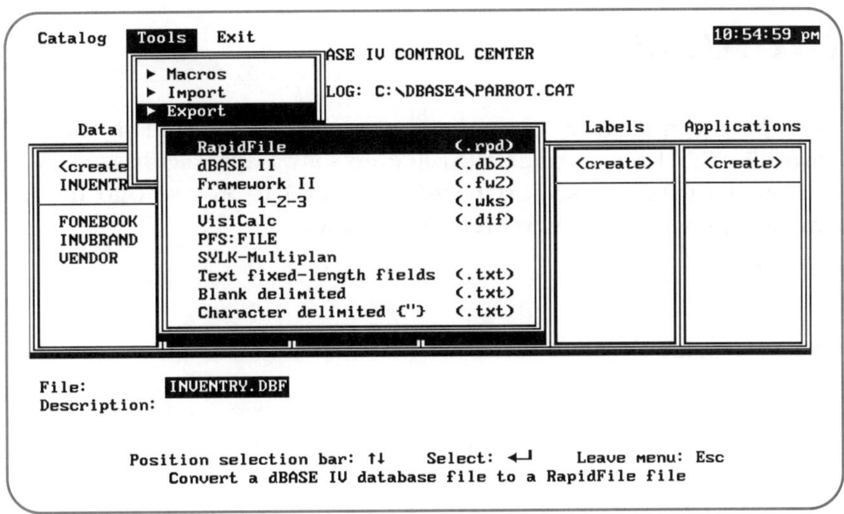

Figure 18.8. *The Export menu*

All the data formats found in the Append menu also are found in the Export submenu. When you export a dBASE file, a new file is created with the correct file extension for the exported file type. The process is identical to importing except that the data flow is from dBASE IV to the foreign file type. To export a dBASE IV file, you first choose `Export` from the Tools menu and select the file type. Next, a file box appears, and you select the dBASE.DBF file to be translated. When you press **<Enter>**, a new file is created in the same directory as the dBASE file. The new file has the same filename and file extension as the extension shown in the Export menu. That's all there is to it.

When you are translating to another database file format, the field names are retained and can be found in the foreign file. When translating to spreadsheets, your dBASE data will be repositioned in rows and columns with the column width adjusted to fit the dBASE field size. If you are exporting to a .TXT file, the data is put in the correct text file format. If you choose `Character delimited`, you have to select the character to be used as a delimiter. Double quotes are the default.

When exporting to Lotus 1-2-3, a version 1 (.WKS) file is created. Lotus v2.0 and 3.0 will automatically translate the .WKS format into .WK1 and .WK3 formats when the file is retrieved.

If you are using Framework III, it will automatically create a .FW3 file when you bring the Framework II file onto the desktop.

Summary

As you have seen, data can be imported or exported quickly and easily into and out of dBASE IV. Remember that virtually every software package has some way of translating the data to some standard format. Even if you have to go through several steps, you should never retype data again.

Section Four

Introduction to Programming and Applications

chapter

19

Programming and Applications

In the early days of computers, everything that went on inside a computer had to be programmed. The computer hardware was useless without intricate instructions from the programmer for each and every function that was to be performed. Each command was initiated by a human being in the form of complex software commands. The operating system, the application programs, and the utility functions were all programs aimed at getting the hardware to perform the proper functions.

Some of the low-level programs, such as routines to put letters on a computer screen, were repetitive and could be used over again in other situations. The differences among the versions of a particular routine were the actual words written on the screen, not the routines themselves. The same applies not only to screen writing but also to screen forms, report writing, disk storage, and other computer functions. These are routine activities. That is, reports differ in content, but the steps for actual report creation, in dBASE IV for example, are always quite similar.

This same philosophy is applied to higher functions within application systems. For example, the only difference between an add function for two different database files is the fields used in the function. The basic function, which is to add a record to the file, is always the same.

Using Work Surfaces in an Application

You have learned how to use many of the various work surfaces that are necessary to create, input, change, view, and report the data you need to satisfy your information requirements. You have worked with the following work surfaces:

• Database	Create new database files
• EDIT and BROWSE	Input and view data
• Query	Create views of your data Select only certain fields and records Create calculated fields Sort, summarize, and group data Link two or more files
• Form	Develop complex data input screens Create custom edit and validation rules
• Report	Develop custom output reports and output forms
• Label	Produce mailing type labels

There is still one panel in the Control Center that you haven't used. This is the Applications panel. It lets you either write custom programs from scratch or use the Applications Generator to create complete applications.

Whether you use the Applications Generator or design custom programs, you will find that the databases, forms, reports, and labels you created in the various work surfaces prove very valuable when made part of a program.

Why You Would Need a Program

Though you have learned most work surfaces and can now create database files, add records, and produce reports, you have only begun to harness the power of a database. The true power of dBASE is its language for the creation of turnkey systems, better known as *applications*.

A turnkey system can be operated by a person totally unfamiliar with the workings of a database system, but who knows the business side of the system. Take, for example, a typical payroll system. With what you have learned, you can create employee files, tax files, and company files. You can enter data to each file and perform simple edit checking. You can even create a report to print the checks.

If you can do all this, why would you need a program? You would need a program to simplify and speed up your work. You can streamline access to files, calculations, complex data transfers, more complex editing, forms and reports, and other operations that are possible in the Control Center work surfaces.

What a dBASE IV Program Is

A program is nothing more than a collection of dBASE dot prompt statements that, when correctly put together in some logical fashion, perform a repetitive task. These program statements also can act as a "taxi driver," taking you from one place in the system to another. Menus are a good example of a type of program. They transport you quickly from a screen to a function. Programs are stored in files with the file extension PRG.

Programs are built around sequences of statements. Most programs are made up of the same commands that you can enter in the dot prompt. However, some programs also use statements that would be meaningless if used at the dot prompt.

Of Mind and Menus

Traditionally, systems interact with human beings through some sort of interface. Menus are the most common type of interface today. dBASE program commands provide tools for all the same type of menus that are used in the dBASE IV Control Center. These include:

- Horizontal bar menus (at the top of the screen)
- Pull-down menus (that can be attached to a bar menu)
- Pop-up menus
- Pick lists (fields, files, values)

A menu is nothing more than a screen that you display from within an application program. This particular type of screen is one in which you give the application user a set of choices or options for the tasks that the application can perform. The user then chooses a function, either by entering a number or letter that corresponds to that function or by moving a highlight with the arrow keys and pressing the **<Enter>** key to choose the highlighted option.

Creating a menu is even easier than producing a screen format. A menu is mostly text information. Once the text is entered and placed on the screen, you need to identify the operation to be performed when an option is chosen. dBASE IV allows you to create different types of menus. For example, you can produce menus that pop up anywhere on the screen, or you can combine a horizontal bar and pop-up menus to simulate a pull-down menu as the dBASE IV Control Center has.

Menus that are easy to use enhance any interactive applications that you create. The first part of the system that a user sees is the main menu. The user will spend most of the time moving from menu to menu in the application system. The menus also represent the hierarchy of the application system, showing the relationships of various system functions.

Why Use a Generator?

There are certain standard routines that can be created and used in almost any circumstance. The procedure for creating a screen format is almost the same from database file to database file. In fact, this is the reason that dBASE IV can present a "standard" screen layout when you create a database file, before you have even coded a program. This same reasoning applies to reports, especially columnar reports.

Some application functions also can be generated. For example, each database file should have an add, change, delete, and display function. These functions are necessary for maintenance, even if you have programs that are responsible for updating the database file. If the program makes a mistake, or an error is entered, these basic functions can be used to make spot corrections and adjustments.

Screen generators and report generators are dependent on entered text and the fields in a particular database file or set of database files. Once you put the text (such as headings and titles) and fields in place, it is an easy matter to generate program code to create the display screen or report page. dBASE IV takes this a step further by creating this format code in a condensed, quickly executed form.

Applications Generators use the same general philosophy to create dBASE code for an application function. For example, the basic format of a dBASE add-record-to-database function is the same, regardless of the data involved.

The code that is generated can be used for any given database file by changing the name of the screen format that is used. Some editing and range checking can be programmed as a part of the screen format. Other application functions can be generated in the same manner. Most functions can be created generically—and they work in a wide variety of situations.

The Difference Between Programs and Applications

A program in dBASE IV terms should be thought of as the individual dBASE statements that perform a certain function. It usually takes many programs working together to make an application. An application is what the many programs are called when placed together to form one logical task.

For example, a payroll system could be an application. The various add, change, delete, display, calculate, and print tasks each could be programs. Additionally, there may be an overall menu system that controls all these programs, which also is a program. Today, with dBASE IV, you no longer have to be concerned with these individual programs. It is the application itself that has become important.

In dBASE II everything you wanted to do had to be programmed. There were few if any tools to assist you in this process. Screens, reports, menus, even data entry processes had to be programmed from the dot prompt. dBASE III introduced screen forms that let you create the form for data input and output. An application generator existed, but it lacked sophistication and didn't allow very customized applications.

The Many Generators of dBASE IV

dBASE IV includes generators to produce menus, data entry screens, reports, labels, and basic application systems. Each separate work surface generates dBASE code that can be modified, merged into custom programs, or used with the Applications Generator. The functions that can be generated automatically are very sophisticated, and they can fulfill the requirements for most application systems. When the generator isn't quite adequate for your needs, it can be modified to varying degrees, from simple additions of a few lines of code to complete changes using the original generated code as a starting point. Figure 19.1 lists these generators.

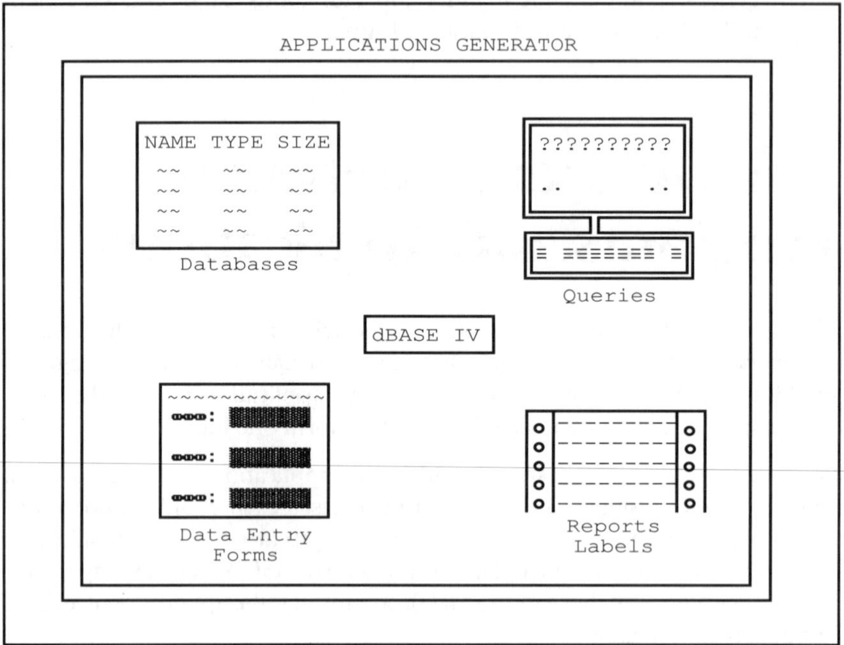

Figure 19.1. The many generators of dBASE IV

As you have learned, the screen generator allows you to position database fields anyplace on the screen, arrange text around the fields, and place headings and borders on the screen to give your applications a professional look. With the use of a generator you do not need to know how to write the program yourself—you can place the fields, text, and borders where you want them and let dBASE IV do the rest.

The dBASE software will generate the code that allows the computer to display your screen exactly as you have designed it. The software also takes care of receiving input data from the screen and performing basic editing functions, such as validating the data type of the input. dBASE IV checks that numeric fields contain only numeric data and that date fields are correct. You also can specify that data in particular fields is within a certain range of values.

The screen generator allows advanced edit validation that you can design yourself to allow only data that meets your most stringent conditions to be accepted by the system. The screen generator lets you design various messages for users when they move the cursor into a data entry field, or when the user makes an error. You can even determine if the field is for display only, or if the user can make any additions or changes.

Producing reports from stored database fields is another process that can be automated easily. Customized report formats are handled the same as a screen format, where text and fields can be placed in any position. Columnar reports display field values along a line or several lines, with headings, footers, totals, and subtotals placed as specified by the entered design. The generated report format can be used to create new calculated fields, produce subtotals and totals, and even format fields for printing, such as placing hyphens in a Social Security number or a telephone number.

Bringing It All Together—The Applications Generator

dBASE IV can help you generate screens, menus, and reports using your database file design or view created in the Queries screen. dBASE also includes an Applications Generator that will help you develop application programs to use for your system.

Applications Generators are programs that help you create your own application programs. General procedures—adding, changing, deleting, and displaying functions—can be created by a program because the only changes between these procedures are the database file and fields that are used. Add to this the fact that you can generate screen formats to use with the database file, and the creation of a generic function is simply a matter of providing the format filenames and the name of the database file.

Although you can generate many parts of an application system using dBASE IV, the generated code likely will not meet all your requirements. dBASE IV allows you to customize the generated code created by the Applications Generator by adding routines to the generated programs. Complete customizing may require that you create your own application programs, but you can still reduce development time and problems by using the dBASE IV Applications Generator as a starting point.

In the next chapter, you will learn how to take all the work surfaces you have created and create an application using the Applications Generator.

chapter 20

Using the dBASE IV Applications Generator

There are two ways to program your designs with dBASE IV. The first is to use the Applications Generator to automatically create most, if not all, of your program. The second, of course, is to do it yourself by typing the actual dBASE programming statements. You can use the Applications Generator to reduce your coding time by generating the basic functions of a system and doing the more complex programming yourself as you get better at it. You can mix your code with the code from the Applications Generator to create a powerful system quickly and easily. This chapter takes you through some examples of programming with the dBASE IV Applications Generator.

The Applications Generator

Most application generators can create several standard functions, including: menus, add routines, change routines, delete routines, display routines, and printing routines. These are the routines needed to maintain and enter the data of any database file. The basic functions are generally the same for all databases. The dBASE IV Applications Generator can do a lot more, such as run your programs in windows on the screen, create Help screens, and even allow batch routines to back up your database file. However, this chapter concentrates on the simple functions.

One of the best uses of the Applications Generator is to create the menus that the terminal operator will use to access your application system. You can build a menu system quickly. The Applications Generator can generate the code for standard functions.

The Idea Behind the Applications Generator

The purpose of the Applications Generator is to allow nonprogrammers to generate application functions quickly. Simply put, an application generator is a program that creates another program, based on some form of input. The input can be in the form of a work surface where you create menus, and it can be based on selections made interactively via a menu, as in the case of the dBASE IV Applications Generator.

The Applications Generator is a system that combines the other facilities of dBASE IV into an application. What the Applications Generator actually does is to provide the "glue" to hold the built-in functions of dBASE together. The existing BROWSE, EDIT, and APPEND features are combined with your screen formats, report forms, and database file layouts or views to form an application.

The glue, in this case, is a series of menu screens that the generator builds for you. You specify a database filename, the type of menu you want, the screen and report formats that you want the application to produce, and even a sign-on screen for your application. The dBASE IV Applications Generator then generates dBASE program code that displays the menus and causes them to perform the functions you specify. Figure 20.1 shows a conceptual view of the generation process.

Programs that perform common database functions are similar in structure. For example, the only difference between the ADD functions for two different database files is the name of the program, the name of the database file accessed, and the names/definitions of the individual fields. These are supplied to the application generator by the programmer, and the changes are made to the stock ADD function from the generator's library of functions.

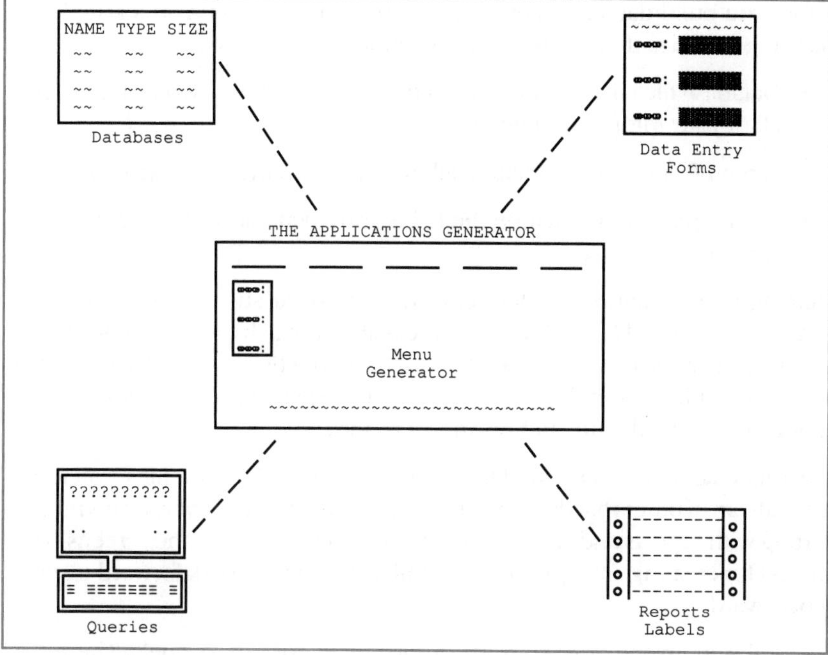

Figure 20.1. *The Applications Generator process*

The Applications Generator creates a basic menu structure for each application. The action to be performed for each choice can be defined as one of the stock functions, or can include custom programs created outside of the Generator. The creation of such a menu is also a stock function, because there are fewer differences between menu programs than between add functions; all that changes are the options on the menu.

Using an application generator is relatively easy. You just fill in the blanks, and the code is generated automatically by the program. You can enter the application quickly, and the programs are available for testing a very short time, usually minutes, after the creation of the database file.

Designing an Application— A Step-by-Step Approach

Before you begin using the Applications Generator, take a few minutes to think about your design. You have already learned that you need to plan a design before you build database files, screen forms, and reports. You learned that planning includes the following considerations:

- Database files have to include all the data that is necessary for any and all of your information needs.
- Screen forms have to include all the data from the database files.
- Each report has to include the fields and calculations that are necessary for the report.

Creating an application is no different. You must make sure that each form you have already created (or will create) is accessible through the menu system you design. Each menu choice you create must have an action assigned to it. Typical actions include: displaying another menu, displaying a data entry form, performing a calculation, and printing a report.

In earlier chapters, you learned that when designing database files, you must know ahead of time what data will be necessary for various reports. This means starting with reports and working backward to database files and screens. The process for creating an application is similar except you work forward instead of backward.

1. Take an inventory of your various forms, reports, and labels. These are what your menu will bring you to. Do you have all that you will need? If not, create them now.
2. Decide which database file or view is the main source of information. Make sure you have built all the views necessary for the retrieval of your information in any form you desire, including indexes and relationships between files.
3. Design your main menu. What type of menu will it be? What choices will it have? What action will each choice cause?
4. Design each submenu (if any).
5. Assign an action to each menu choice.
6. Add custom code to parts of the application.
7. Generate the application.

Actually, most of the steps are done for you before you even begin. You have already designed your database files, screen forms, and reports. All you really need to do is think about your menus; that's your glue to hold the application together. The path to designing an application is shown in Figure 20.2.

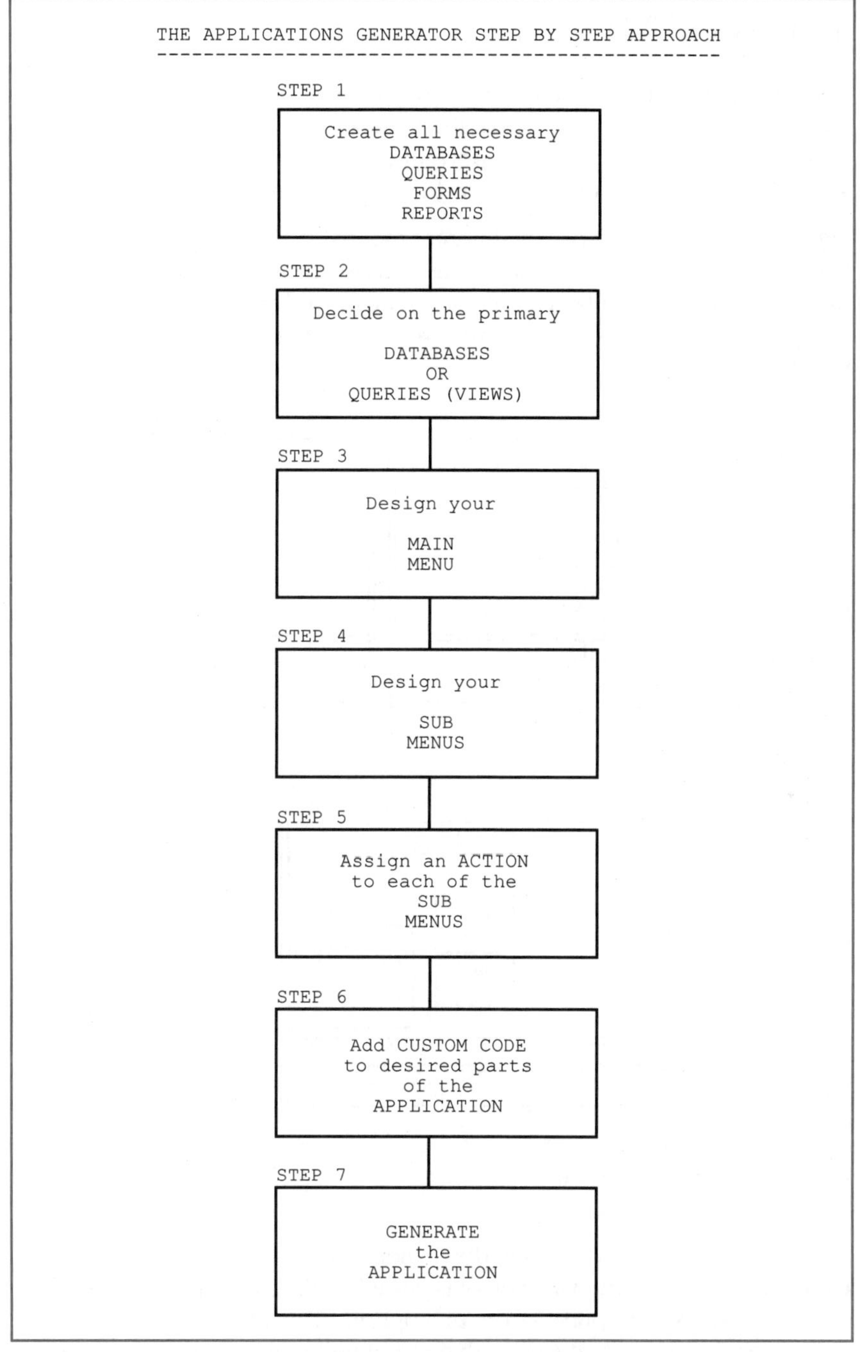
THE APPLICATIONS GENERATOR STEP BY STEP APPROACH
STEP 1
Create all necessary
DATABASES
QUERIES
FORMS
REPORTS
STEP 2
Decide on the primary
DATABASES
OR
QUERIES (VIEWS)
STEP 3
Design your
MAIN
MENU
STEP 4
Design your
SUB
MENUS
STEP 5
Assign an ACTION
to each of the
SUB
MENUS
STEP 6
Add CUSTOM CODE
to desired parts
of the
APPLICATION
STEP 7
GENERATE
the
APPLICATION

Figure 20.2. *The Applications Generator step-by-step approach*

Types of Menus

There are different types of menus, as you learned in the previous chapter. If you are working with only one database file and you want only a few simple functions such as data entry and report generation, it's probably best to use one simple menu rather than a hierarchy in which one menu calls another.

Figure 20.3 shows examples of different menus. At the top of the first screen is a horizontal bar menu. It is called this because the menus run across the top of the screen horizontally. A highlight can be moved from choice to choice by the user. The user can press **<Enter>** on any highlighted item to make a selection.

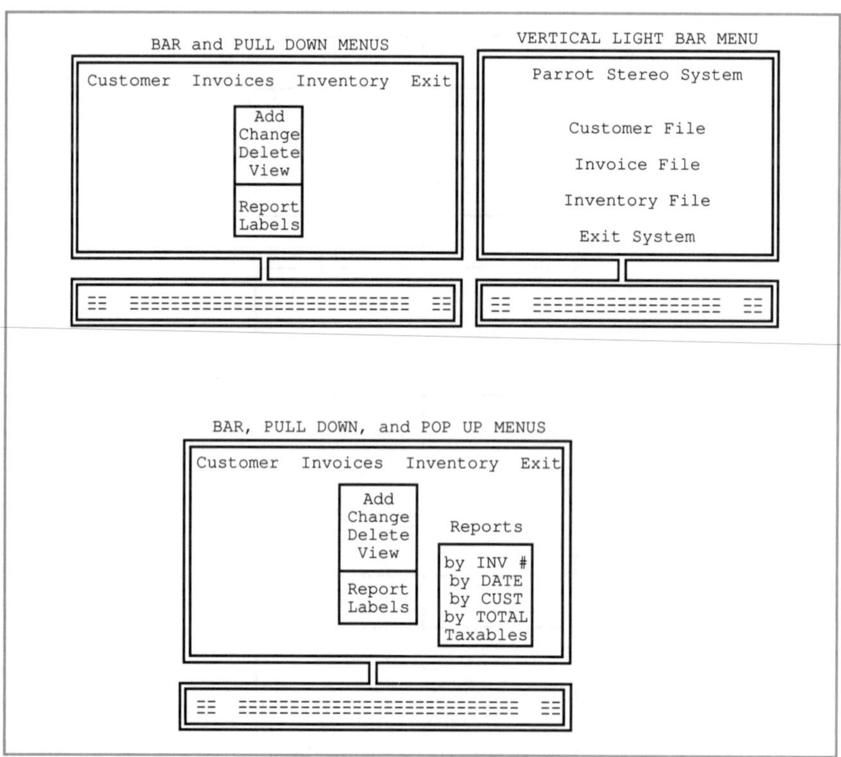

***Figure 20.3.** The different types of menus*

Attached to the bar menu is a pull-down menu. A pull-down menu is displayed either automatically when the cursor is placed on the bar menu option or after the **<Enter>** key is pressed on the option. The dBASE IV Applications Generator allows you to create both types of pull-down menus easily—those that open manually and those that open automatically. (Actually, a *pull-down* menu in dBASE IV is a *pop-up* menu that sits on top of a *menu bar* and appears to pull down from the bar when opened.)

The second screen shows a vertical bar menu in the center of the screen. This is actually a pop-up menu that has been resized and centered on the screen. It is simulating a vertical bar menu.

The final screen shows a series of bar, pop-up, and list menus. This pop-up menu is not attached as a bar menu but rather pops up to the right of the bar menu choice. This is perfectly acceptable. Menus can be placed anywhere on the screen. Bar menus can be placed on the bottom of the screen to open up instead of down. There are four types of pop-up menus. The difference is in their contents. These menu types are:

- **Action List.** A menu that calls other menus or programs, or that executes a command or action
- **Files List.** A list of available files
- **Structure List.** The fields in a database file or view
- **Values List.** Individual field values from records in a database file

Each type of menu will vary in size depending on how many choices there are from the files, fields, or values. You must give the menu some criteria to select its menu contents. Files must be given a list of file extensions to search for, structures must be given the name of a database file, and values must be given the column and database filename.

Beyond Menus—Action Screens

Once you create your menus and give each menu a list of items, you determine an action for each menu item. File, structure, and value lists don't determine actions; rather, they assign the value to a memory variable so you can use the menu items as you desire.

Menu choice actions include, but are not limited to, the following:

- Opening another menu
- Displaying a BROWSE table
- Displaying an EDIT screen
- Printing with a report or label form
- Running a DOS file
- Running a dBASE program
- Running one dBASE command
- Taking no action (the menu choice is for display only)

As you go through the examples in this chapter, you will see the various uses for these menus and actions.

A Design for Parrot Stereo

So far you have created database files, screen forms, and reports. In this section, you will create a simple example application from these input and output tools. In order to do this example, make sure you have both the INVENTRY and VENDOR database files, the ALLITEMS view, the INVENTOR screen form, and the INVRPT1 and INVRPT2 report forms. Before getting started, you can build a VENDOR screen form from inside the Applications Generator, by going from the generator to the Form work surface at the appropriate time. The vendor form will be a simple data entry form. If you don't feel like creating it, you can use the default form when you get to that task. You also need to build a third report using the VENDOR database file. Call the new report VENRPT1. Design it as a simple column layout. If you don't want to build these files for the culmination of our Parrot Stereo example, just sit back and read. The explanation and figures will be sufficient for you to understand the Applications Generator.

You have, basically, two chores in this system—data entry and reporting. You can accomplish both now by using the Control Center or the dot prompt to call up individual records, append new records, or delete unneeded records. You also can print reports from the Control Center or the dot prompt using the forms you have created or the `Quick Report` option.

You need to add a menu around your various forms and to use the generator to add even more functionality to the system. For example, a report form can be used in many different reports. You can determine through a menu which records are selected for a report, and even whether a report is to include summarized data when it prints.

In this example, you will create two separate data entry systems, one for INVENTRY and one for VENDOR. You also will have one report menu that will give you access to several variations of your reports.

Starting the Applications Generator

The Applications Generator can be started (like most work surfaces) from either the dot prompt or the Control Center. Figure 20.4 shows the main

Control Center screen with the <create> choice highlighted in the Applications panel. Choosing this will begin the applications process. dBASE IV will ask you if you want to write a dBASE program using the dBASE editor, or if you want to use the Applications Generator. Because you want to have dBASE IV automatically create your application, choose the `Applications Generator` option.

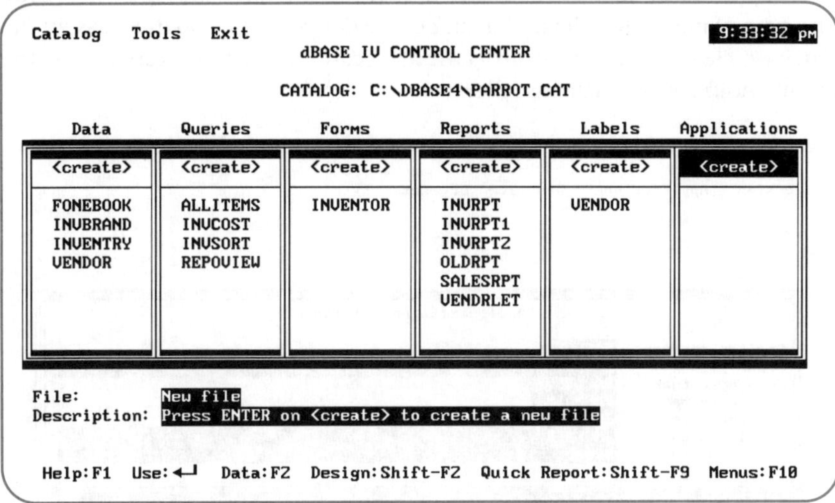

Figure 20.4. *Starting an Applications Generator session*

Objects, Menus, Items, and Actions

As the generator starts, you are placed in a new work surface. This surface has several menus (in fact, they constantly change depending on what you are doing) and several screens behind the menus. Nearly everything you do in this work surface is guided by menus and screens.

The Applications Generator work surface is similar to other work surfaces. In the forms and reports screens you manipulated objects that consisted of the fields, lines, and boxes. In the Applications Generator, the objects you manipulate are menus. You will place on the surface all the menus that will make your system perform its tasks. In this example, you will create one horizontal bar menu and three pull-down menus.

Each menu has a series of options or items. Each menu can have as many choices or items as you want. When you want to work with the entire menu, use the Menu menu at the top of the screen. When you work with an individual item in a menu, use the Item menu. Until you have created your first menu, these two menus won't even appear on the menu bar. You will see the Application choice as you work with the entire application.

Defining the Application

Figure 20.5 shows the Application Definition box open on the work surface. This is the first thing you must fill out upon entering the work surface. If you haven't already given the application a name, this is where you do it. Optionally, you can enter a description for the application that shows up in the catalog. Every application needs a main menu, and you must tell dBASE IV the name and type of menu even if you haven't created it yet. You also must assign the database file or view that controls the application. Later, you can change the menu choices in the database file.

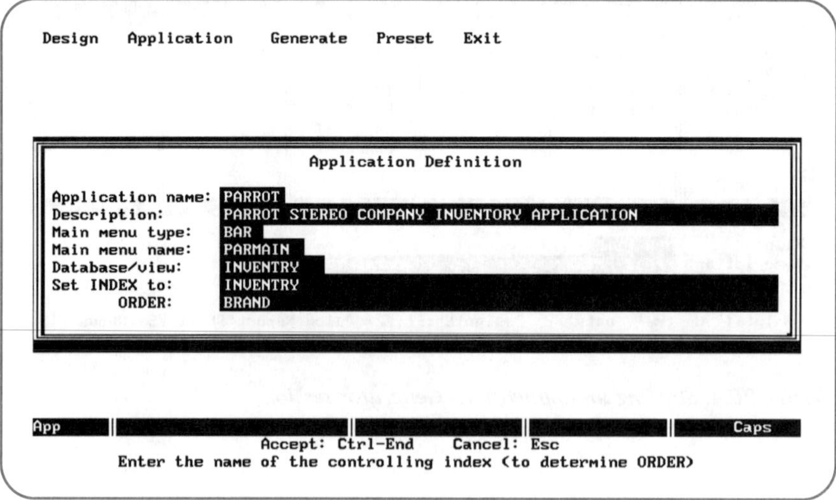

Figure 20.5. *The Application Definition box*

Figure 20.5 has already been filled in. Its content tells you that INVENTRY is the file for this application and that the main menu will be a bar menu named PARMAIN.

It is important to note that objects (menus) are stored separately from the application. This way menus can be shared among applications. You are not limited to the size of an application because you can move these objects on and off the work surface.

Once the initial parameters are defined, an object is automatically placed on the work surface. This is the sign-on banner that the user sees when the application starts. You can control whether the user sees the banner. Initially the banner has predefined text indicating the version of the Applications Generator you are running. Figure 20.6 shows a customized message. You can move the cursor inside the box to delete old text and to add new text.

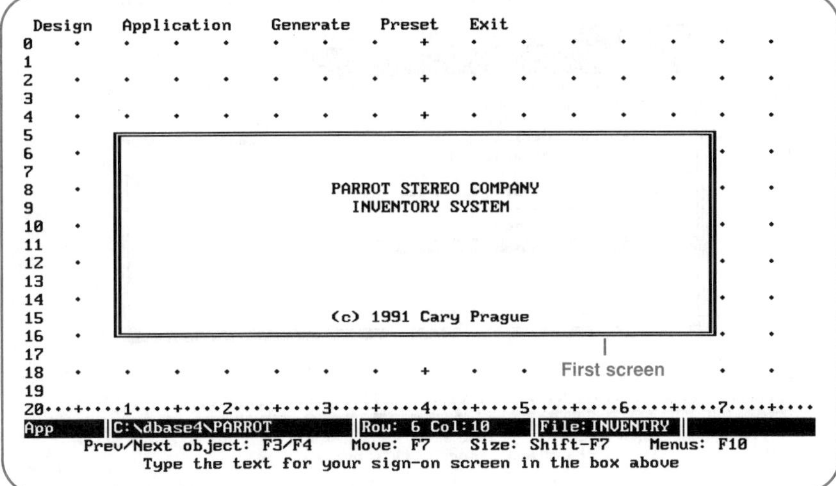

Figure 20.6. *The sign-on banner*

Generating a Quick Application

If you are using only a single database file and want a very quick application, you can use an option that generates a quick application automatically. When you use this option, you are limited to a single database file, screen, and report file. The application is a simple full-screen menu that lets you perform data entry and print your report or label.

Figure 20.7 shows the Application menu opened on the work surface. The choices on this menu affect the entire application. The first two choices let you re-edit the responses you entered when you started the generator. The third choice lets you decide whether the sign-on banner will be displayed when the application is started. The next two choices allow you to change the way code is generated, including the option of adding a header message, such as a copyright, into the generated code, along with changing colors and environment settings.

The important choice here is `Generate quick application`. This lets you generate an entire application without creating menus or assigning actions. If you have one database file, screen format, and report, it can be a big help. When you choose this option, the screen like the one in Figure 20.8 is displayed.

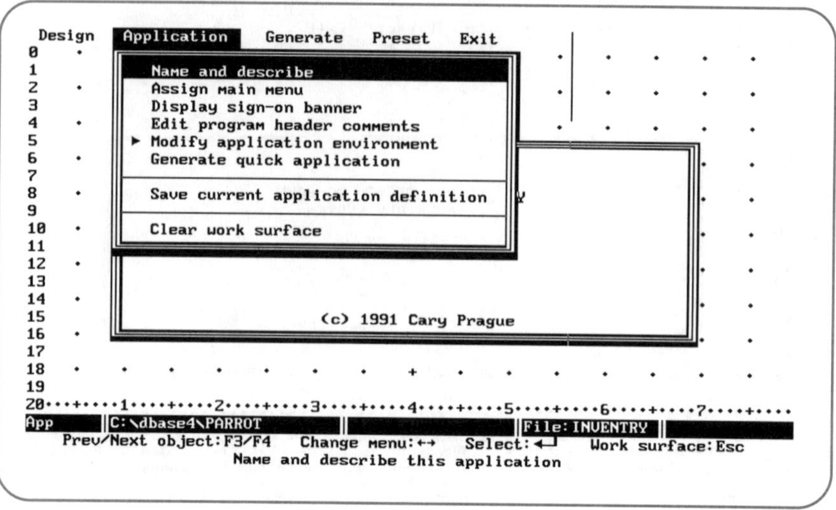

Figure 20.7. The Application menu

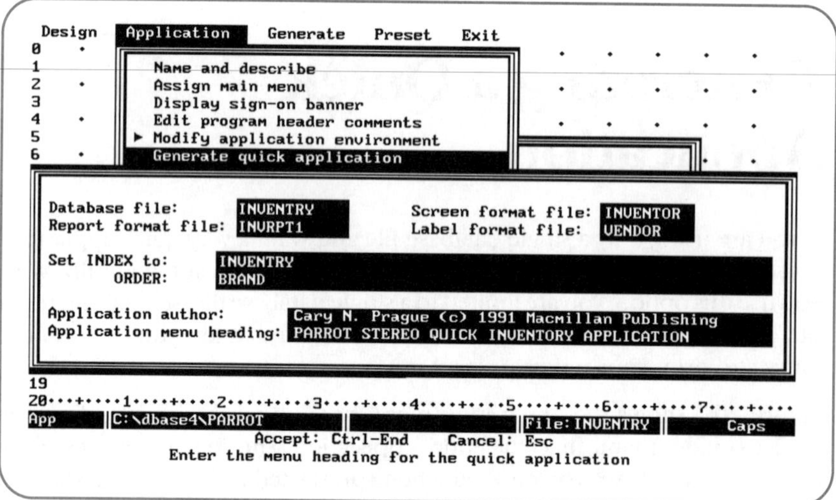

Figure 20.8. Generating a quick application

This screen has eight entry areas. The top half of the screen lets you enter your database, screen format, report format, and label format files. If you have trouble remembering the names of the files you have created, you can always press **<Shift>-<F1>** to open a list of the appropriate files for you to pick from.

The middle part of the screen lets you enter the name of your index file, and in the case of multiple indexes, lets you choose the order in which the data is displayed. The bottom of the screen provides an entry area for documentation that will display on the main menu as a header.

When you have completed the screen, press **<Ctrl>-<End>**. A box appears and asks you to select `Yes` to generate the quick application; `No` to cancel. Select `Yes` to generate the application. You can then run the application from the Control Center by choosing it and pressing **<Enter>**, or by using the dot prompt command DO with the application name. Figure 20.9 shows this application running in dBASE IV.

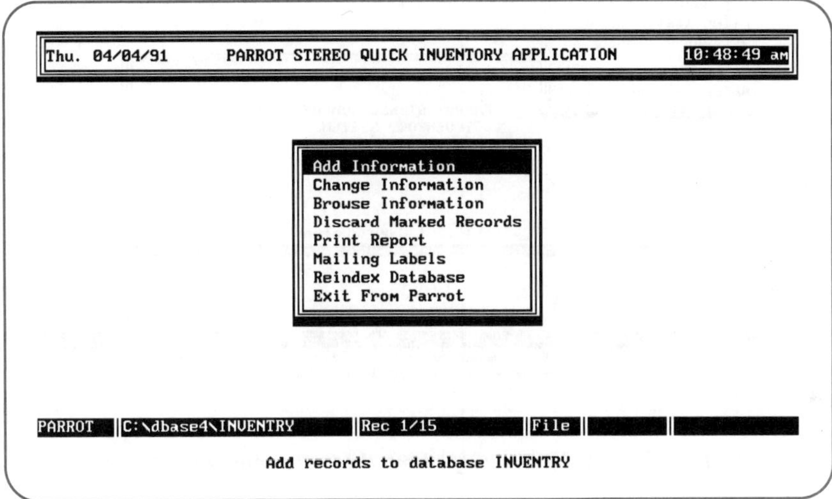

***Figure 20.9.** Running the quick application*

A Complete Application

Creating quick applications is fast and easy, but there will be times when you'll need more control over your application than quick generation can provide. The rest of this chapter is devoted to explaining the basics of generating an entire application.

A complete application can begin with a quick application. You first create the system parameters and the sign-on screen. Once you've accomplished these things, you can turn your attention to building menus.

Creating a Horizontal Main Bar Menu

Begin this application by defining a main menu. In this example, you will use a horizontal bar menu at the top of the screen. The process begins with the Design menu. Figure 20.10 shows the Design menu open on the work surface. This menu has several choices that let you select the type of menu or list. For this example, select the `Horizontal bar menu` choice. A pop-up box opens on the right of the screen.

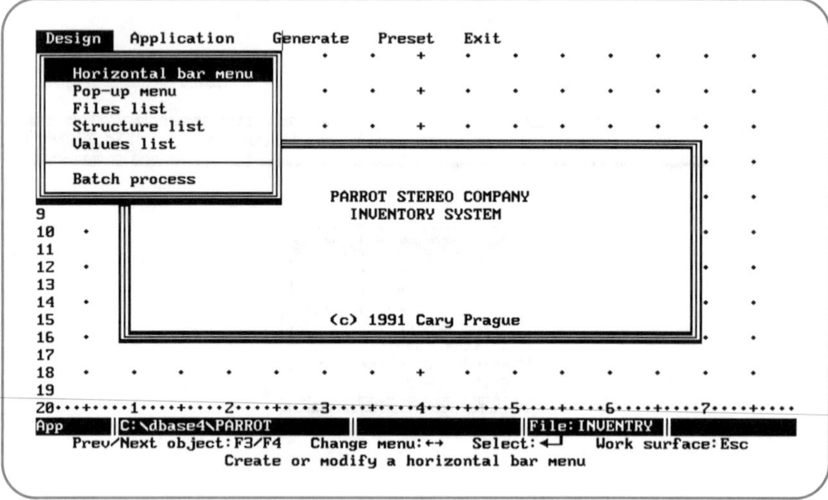

Figure 20.10. Choosing the menu type from the Design menu

A list of all the previously defined bar menus appears along with a `<create>` tag. Choose the `<create>` tag to create a new menu. Another screen appears, as shown in Figure 20.11, with entry areas for the name, description, and message line prompt for the horizontal bar menu.

Once you name this menu box and press **<Ctrl>-<End>**, you can move the empty (or filled in) menu box anywhere on the screen. You can even place it on the bottom of the screen.

The cursor is inside the box waiting for you to enter the items. Define the options in the menu bar by moving the cursor to the place where you want the option to appear, then pressing the **<F5>** function key. Type the option name, and press **<F5>** again when you're finished. This registers the option name, now known as a menu item, to the Applications Generator. After you have entered all the application items you need, you can specify a prompt or message to display when the user chooses that item. Finally, attach an application function to the item.

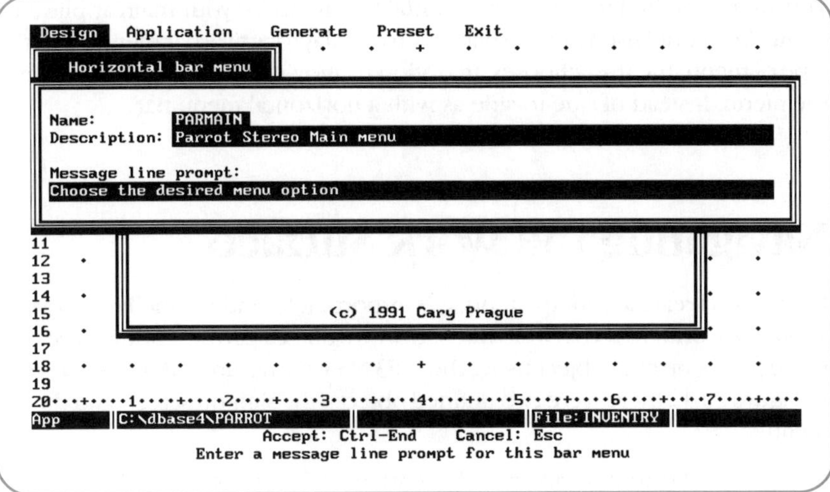

***Figure 20.11.** Creating a horizontal bar menu*

Figure 20.12 shows this menu filled in. Four choices have been created. Each one was created with the **<F5>** key to begin the selection, and with **<F5>** again to end it. This way you can have options with blank spaces between the words.

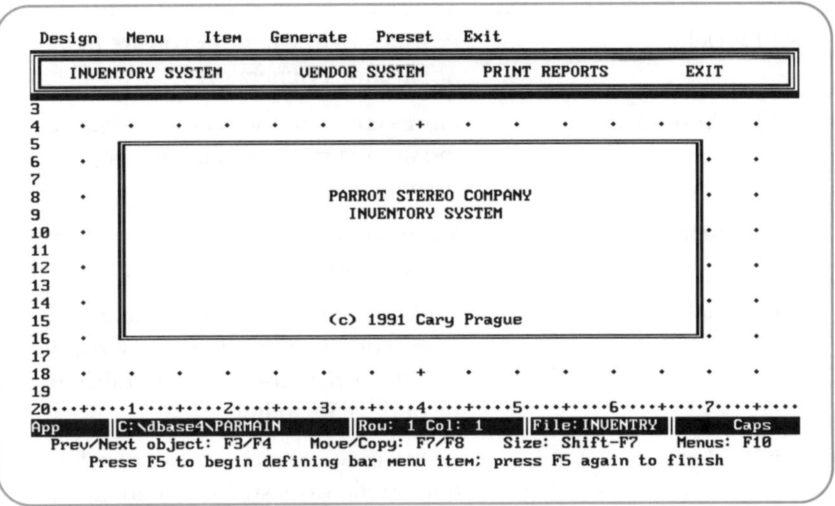

***Figure 20.12.** Press <F5> to begin defining the bar menu choices*

You are not limited to using a horizontal bar menu for your main application menu. You could use a pop-up window to display a vertical bar menu. With this type of menu, the user chooses an option by moving the cursor up and down the menu, instead of side-to-side as with a horizontal menu bar.

Navigating the Work Surface

Before you create a pop-up menu, it is important to understand how to move about the work surface, as well as how to move objects on the work surface. You move from object to object using the **<F3> Previous** and **<F4> Next** keys. In Figure 20.12 there were two defined objects: the sign-on screen and the bar menu.

Objects can be moved around the screen with the use of **<F7>**. This is very important when positioning pop-up menus that will become pull-downs. You also can size the menus to fit the items inside by using the size key, **<Shift>-<F7>**. These important keys are always displayed at the bottom of the screen and are consistent with other work surfaces. A complete list of Applications Generator navigation keys is found in Table 20.1.

Table 20.1. *Applications Generator function and navigation keys*

Function key	*Explanation*
<F1> Help	Provides Help wherever you are in the Applications Generator.
<F3> Previous	Moves cursor to the previous object on the work surface, making that object current.
<F4> Next	Moves cursor to the next object on the work surface, making that object current.
<F5> Field	Marks beginning and end of an item when entering it in a horizontal bar menu (<Enter> may also be used instead of the second <F5> to finish).
<F7> Move	Allows moving an object to a new location on the work surface, or an item and all its attributes to a new location in the object or to a different object of the same type.

Function key	Explanation
<F8> Copy	Allows copying an item to another location in the same object or to a different object of the same type.
<F9> Zoom	Displays or removes the Applications Generator menu bar and information lines, giving a full screen on which to lay out objects.
<F10> Menus	Moves cursor from an object on the work surface to the Applications Generator menu bar. If in a menu, selects the current option.
<Shift>-<F1> Pick	Displays a list when the cursor is on a field that allows a selection.
<Shift>-<F2> Design	From Control Center, displays selected application for modification.
<Shift>-<F7> Size	Allows changing of the length and width of the frames that enclose an object.

Navigation key	Action
<Left arrow>	In an object, editing frame, or dialog box, moves cursor one position to the left. In a menu bar, moves cursor one option to the left and opens and attached pull-down menu. Wraps through options.
<Right arrow>	In an object, editing frame, or dialog box, moves cursor one position to the left. In a menu bar, moves cursor one option to the right and opens an attached pull-down menu. Wraps through options.
<Up arrow>	In an object, editing frame, or dialog box, moves cursor one position up. In a pop-up menu, moves one option up (wraps around in menus).
<Down arrow>	In an object, editing frame, or dialog box, moves cursor one position down. In a pop-up menu, moves one option down.

continues

Table 20.1. Continued

Navigation key	*Action*
<PgUp>	In the item menu, moves cursor to the next item in the menu or batch process. In a list, moves one page down.
<Backspace>	In an object, full-screen editing frame, or dialog box, deletes previous character.
<Del>	Deletes current character.
<Home>	In a dialog box or list, moves to the first field or option, respectively. In a menu or full-screen editing frame, moves to the beginning of the line.
<Ins>	Toggles Insert on and off.
<End>	In a dialog box or list, moves to the last field or option. respectively. In a menu or full-screen editing frame, moves to the end of the line.
<Tab>	In an editing frame, moves to the next tab. In a dialog box, moves to the first character of the next field.
<Shift>-<Tab>	In an editing frame, moves to previous tab. In a dialog box, moves to first character of previous field.
<Enter>	In an Applications Generator menu, executes the currently highlighted option. In a dialog box, confirms choice and moves to the next field. In an object or full-screen editing frame, moves to the beginning of the next line.
<Spacebar>	In a field with choices, cycles through the choices. In an object, editing frame, or dialog box, enters a space at the cursor position.
<Esc>	In an editing frame or dialog box, cancels the changes made and exits. In the Applications Generator menu, exits to the

Navigation key	*Action*
	current object on the work surface. In an Applications Generator submenu, exits to the calling menu. In an object, cancels all unsaved changes made to any object during the current session and asks whether to exit the Applications Generator. Also cancels a move or copy.
<Alt>-key	In combination with the first letter of the desired menu, moves the cursor quickly to an Applications Generator menu.
<Ctrl>-<End>	In a dialog box, editing frame, or multiple-choice list, saves the entries and returns the cursor to the original menu option. In submenus, exits to previous level. In pull-down menus, returns to the work surface. In an object, saves all changes and exits the Applications Generator.
<Ctrl>-H	In a full-screen editing frame, deletes previous character.
<Ctrl>-N	In an object or an editing frame, inserts a line above the line indicated by the cursor.
<Ctrl>-T	Deletes to the end of the current word.
<Ctrl>-W	In a dialog box or full-screen editing frame, saves the entry and returns the cursor to the originating menu option.
<Ctrl>-Y	In an object or an editing frame, deletes the line indicated by the cursor.
<Ctrl>-<Left arrow>	In an editing frame, moves to start of a word.
<Ctrl>-<Right arrow>	In an editing frame, moves to beginning of the next word.

Adding Pop-Up Menus

After you've created the main bar menu, you can create the pop-up menus. This example has three submenus: one for the inventory system, one for the vendor system, and one for reports. The Exit menu choice will allow the user to quit and exit the application.

Pop-ups are created similarly to the way bar menus are created. Use the Design menu to add a pop-up menu to the work surface. Once it is on the work surface, you can add items without pressing any special keys. Just enter the text inside the box as you want it to appear. Each line becomes a separate menu choice.

You can resize the pop-up with the **<Shift>-<F7>** key combination to shrink it or stretch it horizontally or vertically.

Once you have defined the menu, move it to exactly where you want to see it pop up. If it is going to be a pull-down menu, it should reside directly underneath the bar menu choice. Figure 20.13 shows the inventory pop-up menu placed on the work surface. When you press **<F7>** to move the pop-up menu, you are asked if you want to move the entire frame or just an item. If you are moving the entire menu, choose `Entire frame`. If you really want to move your items around without retyping them, choose `Item only`.

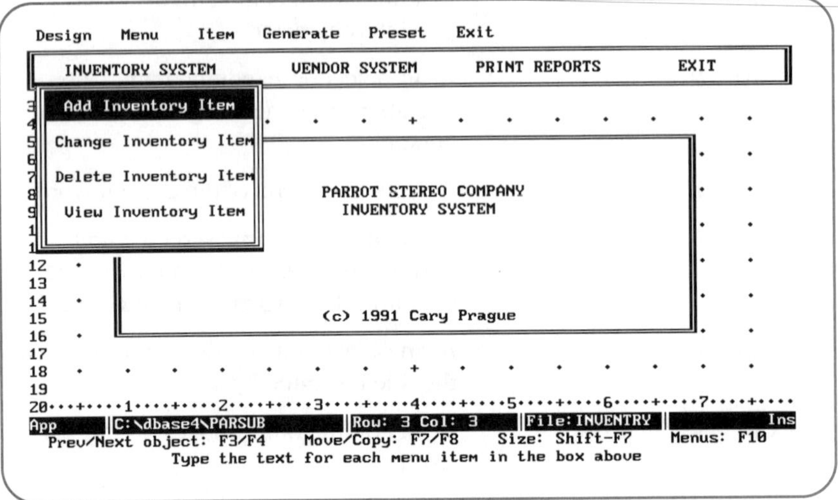

Figure 20.13. *The Inventory pop-up menu*

Making Pull-Down Menus from Pop-Ups

Figure 20.14 shows the Menu menu. This menu name varies depending on the object you are in. Because you are in the bar menu, it is called Menu. If you were in a list, it would be called List and would contain options appropriate for list menus.

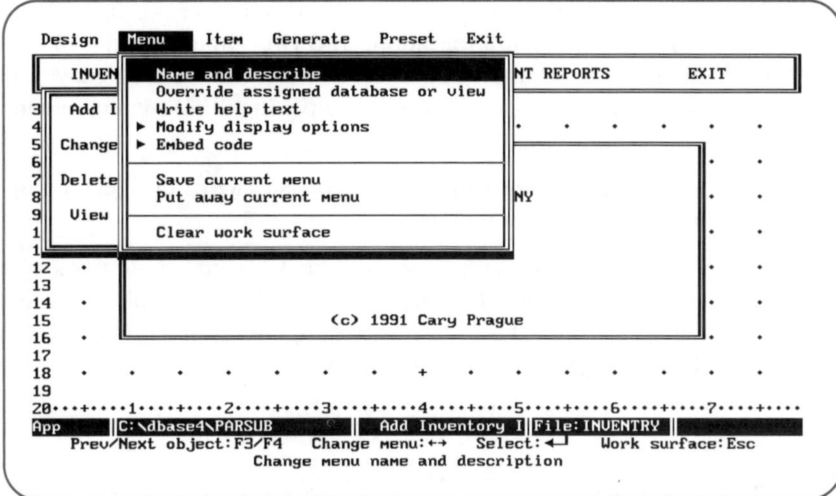

Figure 20.14. The Menu menu

The first option, `Name and describe`, lets you reopen the first screen you saw when you created the bar menu. You can change the name, description, and message line prompt. `Override assigned database or view` lets you change the main database file that controls the application for an individual menu. This option will be discussed further in the next part of this chapter.

`Write help text` lets you create a custom Help screen for the menu. If the user presses **<F1> Help** when in the menu, she or he will see the Help screen that you create here. To create a Help screen, choose this option and enter text anywhere you want in the screen. dBASE IV automatically attaches the Help screen to the menu.

The next item, `Modify display options`, lets you specify the colors and line types for the various objects and menu boxes. Avoid changing colors. Unless you are tracking sales figures for Rainbow Brite, it's a good idea to stick to a couple of basic colors.

`Embed code` lets you place a few lines of dBASE program code either before or after a menu item action.

The last choice in this first part is `Attach pull down menus`. If you choose this and confirm the choice, you will find that, while in the application, if you move the cursor to the menu to which the pull-down is attached, it will automatically open as soon as the cursor touches the menu option. Otherwise, the pull-down doesn't open until the user presses **<Enter>**. Of course, if the action assigned to the bar menu item *isn't* to open a pull-down menu, nothing will happen.

Remember that each menu is a separate entity and can be saved, put away, or retrieved separately from the application. The two choices in the middle section of the Menu menu allow you to save or put away the object you're currently working with. You can retrieve it by opening the Design menu and choosing it.

The last Menu menu choice lets you clear the work surface of all objects except this menu banner or application object.

Figure 20.15 shows all the pop-up menus on the work surface. It may look a little busy right now, but remember, only one menu at a time will open when your application is being used. When you are designing your menus, it's good to see the relative positioning of one to another.

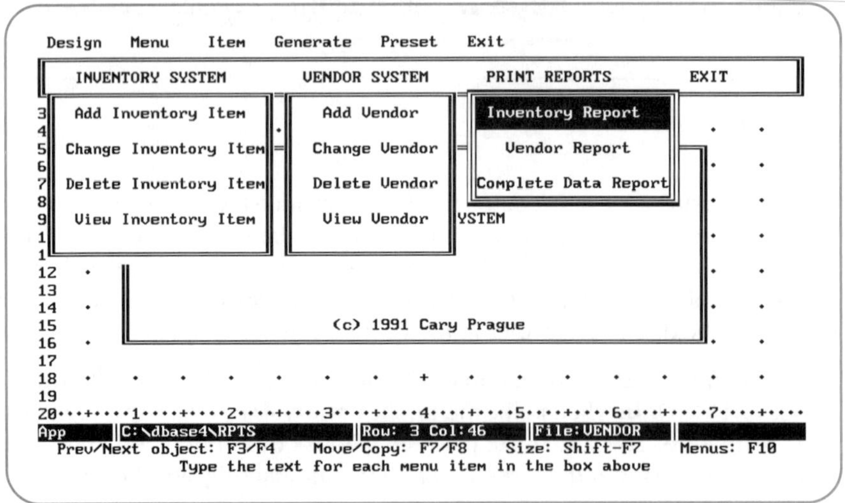

Figure 20.15. *The pop-up menus on the work surface*

Changing Database Files

As it is now, the Vendor menu will not be using the INVENTRY database file. It's set up to use the VENDOR database file for adding, changing, deleting, and viewing records. Therefore, you must change this. You can change database files at the menu or item level. In fact, you will see that the Item menu has many of the same choices as the Menu menu.

To change a database file at the menu level, choose `Override assigned database or view` from the Menu menu, as shown in Figure 20.16.

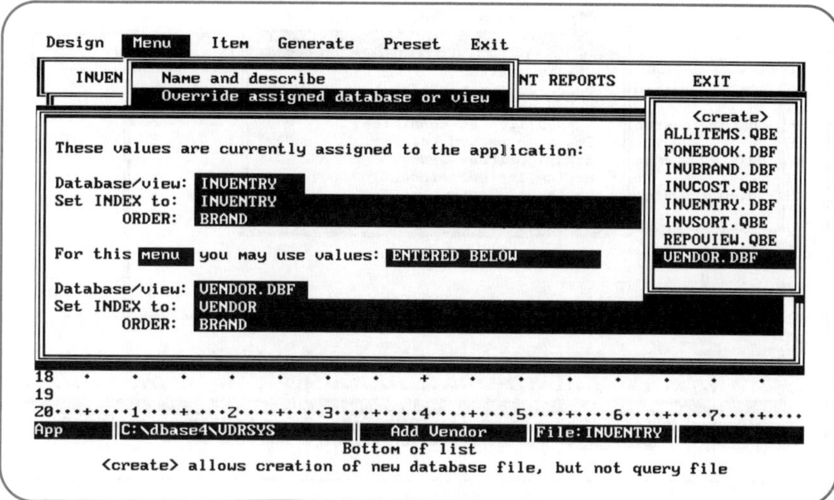

Figure 20.16. *Assigning a different database or view*

The current database/view selection is shown at the top of the box. The bottom of the box has entry areas where you can fill in the database, index, and view you want to use instead. If you can't remember the name of the database file, press **<Shift>-<F1> Pick** to display the pick box of filenames on the far right of the screen. If you choose `<create>` at the top of the box, you could create a new database file without leaving the Applications Generator.

Because you're making this change at the menu level, all items in the VENDOR pop-up also will reflect the change. In the case of your reports, it is probably best for you to make changes at the item level, because some reports use the INVENTRY database file, others use the VENDOR database file, and still others use the ALLITEMS view.

The Item Menu

Figure 20.17 displays the Item menu. This menu has several choices similar to the Menu menu. Remember that the choice you make here deals with the menu item only. Some of the choices include the option to change database files at the item level and to run dBASE code either before or after the action is taken. You can skip the item entirely if a certain condition is met, just as some options in dBASE IV menus work only at certain times. You can position the record pointer to a specific record or change the index order.

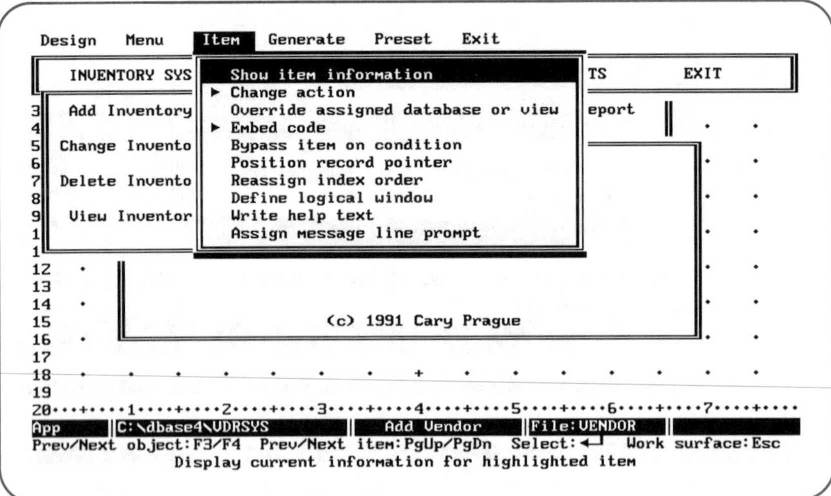

Figure 20.17. *The Item menu*

The third item from the bottom of the menu, `Define logical window`, gives you the ability to define a window. A window is a portion of the screen where the user can run anything, like a BROWSE screen or report output. The window sits on top of the screen, and all output is confined by the borders of the window.

`Write help text` and `Assign message line prompt` are the last two choices you can make at the item level.

Assigning Actions to Menu Items

First, place the cursor on the item you want to assign an action to. If the item you want is in a different object, use the **<F3>** or **<F4>** keys to move to that object. Due to memory restrictions with large applications, you may not be able to have all your objects on the work surface at once. However, you can move an object onto the work surface, assign actions to each item, and then put away the object. When the application is generated, all your objects will be brought together to form the application, regardless of whether you could actually see them all on the work surface at the same time.

Once you've selected the item, you can use the Item menu. First check the current status of a menu item. Choose `Show item information` from the Item menu. Figure 20.18 shows you the results of `Show item information` on the INVENTORY SYSTEM item of the PARMAIN bar menu.

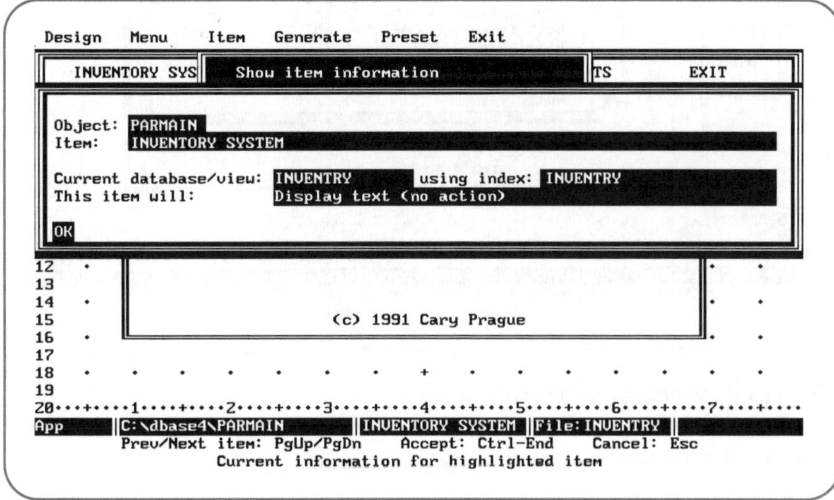

Figure 20.18. *Showing item information*

In this case, the cursor is on the INVENTORY SYSTEM item of the PARMAIN bar menu. The current database and view are displayed. So far, no action has been chosen, so this item will `Display text (no action)`.

This means that the bar menu item is only there for looks. Until you assign an action, it doesn't do anything. To change an action you must press **<Esc>** and choose `Change action` on the Item menu. Figure 20.19 shows the Change action submenu. There are eight basic choices:

- `Text (no action)`
- `Open a menu`
- `Browse (add, delete, edit)`
- `Edit form (add, delete, edit)`

- `Display or print`
- `Perform file operation`
- `Run program`
- `Quit`

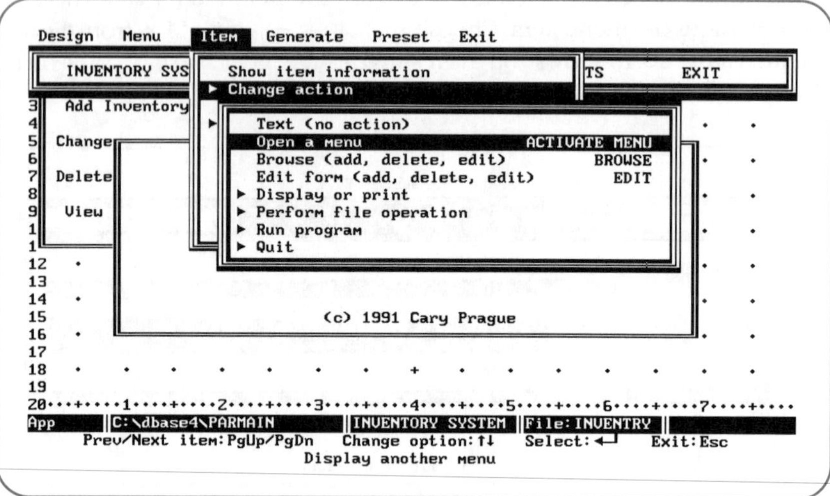

Figure 20.19. Changing the action of a menu item

Opening Menus

The first action you are going to choose is `Open a menu`. This displays another box, as shown in Figure 20.20, which asks you for the menu type and name. Remember that not only is each menu stored separately, but different types of menus have different file extensions.

In Figure 20.20 you can see that the INVENTORY SYSTEM menu will call the pop-up menu INVTACDV. That's all there is to having one menu call another. If you choose `Attach pull-down menus` for the bar menu choice, a pop-up will be displayed as soon as the user moves the cursor to that selection, simulating a pull-down menu. If you don't choose `Attach pull-down menus`, the pop-up won't appear until the operator presses **<Enter>**.

Any type of menu can call other menus or lists. Bar menus can open bar menus, pop-ups can call bar menus, and pop-ups can even open other pop-ups. There is no real limit to the number of menus in a chain. However, if you fill the screen with menus, your user will get lost and confused.

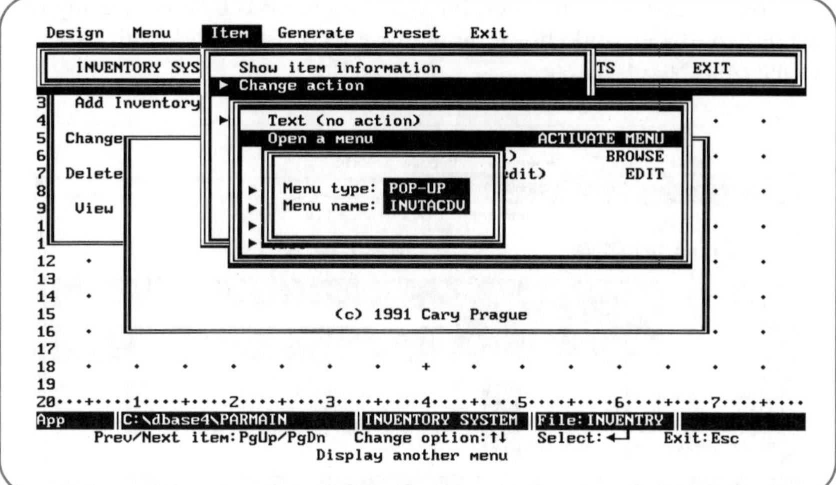

Figure 20.20. Choosing the menu name and type

Adding/Changing/Deleting Records

Data entry is performed by means of the BROWSE or EDIT choices. These are the standard work surfaces you are accustomed to seeing in dBASE IV. The Applications Generator provides you with a series of menus to access all the features of the BROWSE and EDIT screens.

In Figure 20.19, the choice `Edit form (add, delete, edit)` allows user data entry. Your cursor should be on the `Add inventory records` item in the pop-up menu object.

Choosing `Edit form` opens the screen in Figure 20.21. This is the standard EDIT work surface that you are used to by now. You can tell what object and item you are in by looking at the status bar. The item is listed in the center of the status bar, and the object is named in the second field of the status bar.

This screen first asks you for the format file name and if you will be in APPEND mode when adding new records, or EDIT mode when changing existing records. Because this action is on the `Add inventory records` item of the pop-up menu, choose APPEND. The INVENTOR format filename is already entered in the top-left part of the screen. If you hadn't known the name of the format file, or had wanted to create one, you could have pressed **<Shift>-<F1>** to retrieve a list of format files.

The middle half of the EDIT screen lets you select only certain fields and records to work with, just as the Query screen does. This can be especially useful while you're segregating certain records for editing. You can choose which fields will be displayed and in what order, filter desired records by entering any valid dBASE expression, and choose how many records to work with using the SCOPE (ALL, NEXT 20, etc.).

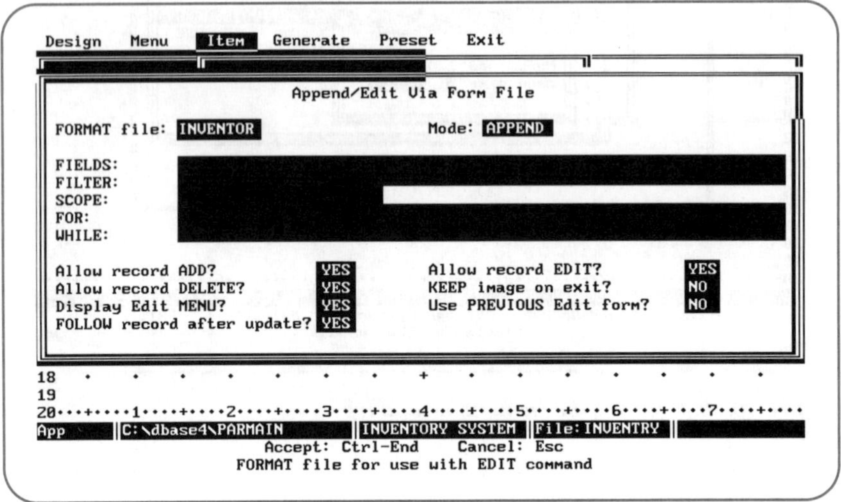

Figure 20.21. The Edit menu screen

The bottom of the screen lets you toggle seven different parameters to determine if certain operations will be allowed. Because this is primarily an add action, make sure there are `YES` indicators to allow records to be added, edited, and deleted. You could, however, limit the action to only additions.

Other toggles let you display the menu at the top of the screen for the operator to use and enable you to affect the way new records are added.

Fill out one of these screens for each item in the pop-up menu. Actually, the design calls for the EDIT screen to be used for adding, changing, and deleting records and the BROWSE screen for viewing the records.

Although you have designed three distinct menu items for adding, editing, and deleting, you can actually treat them the same by allowing the ADD, EDIT, and DELETE toggles for all three. On the other hand, you can allow only new records in the Add item, edited records in the Change item, and the deletion of records in the Delete item. You can accomplish this in the three separate EDIT actions you will create for these items.

Viewing Records

When you've finished assigning each of the first three items to the EDIT screens, assign the BROWSE screen to `View inventory record`. The `Browse` choice, as shown in Figure 20.22, opens the screen where you can enter the parameters for the viewing of more than one record at a time in the BROWSE screen. The design of this application calls for additions, changes, and deletions to be made in the EDIT screen, one record at a time, while viewing of the data will happen all at once in the BROWSE screen.

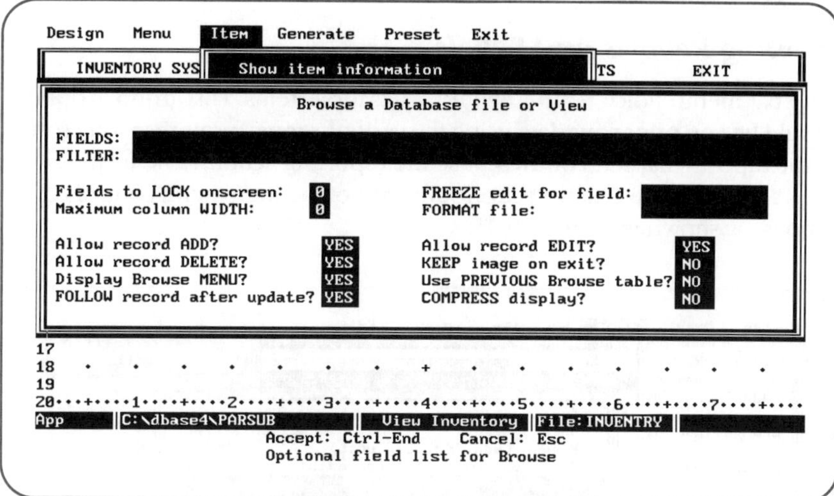

Figure 20.22. *The BROWSE menu screen*

The BROWSE screen is slightly different from the EDIT screen, just as the BROWSE work surfacc is different from the EDIT work surface. The top of the screen lets you decide which fields and records will display. For this example, allow all the records to be displayed.

The middle of the screen features choices from the BROWSE menu normally found at the top of the work surface. You can:

- Lock fields
- Freeze a field for editing
- Determine the maximum column width

You also can perform editing from a format file by using the data validation and display commands from a format file.

The bottom of the screen contains similar option toggles and the EDIT screen. This example calls for the BROWSE screen to be used strictly for display, to not allow additions, changes, or deletions. You also can decide if the BROWSE menu will be displayed at the top of the screen and if the field names will be compressed into the first line of the screen.

Many items in this example need actions assigned to them. In fact, there are 15 separate items in this menu system. The bar menu has four choices, the data entry menus have four each, and the reports menu has three choices. Before going on to the reports menu, complete assigning actions to all the other menus and their items.

Printing Reports and Labels

Your bar menu choice, `Print Reports`, has three items. This group of options should let you print your data using the various report forms that you created in the reports chapter. For these, use the reporting actions. The `Display or print` action in the Change action submenu of the Item menu controls these actions, as shown in Figure 20.23.

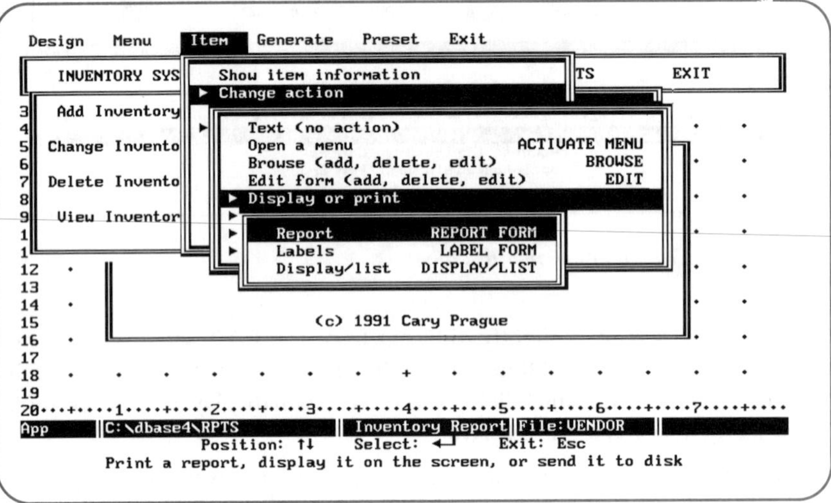

Figure 20.23. *The Display or print submenu*

Make sure you have placed your cursor in the `Inventory Report` item of the `Print Reports` pop-up before choosing the action.

There are three choices for reporting:

- `REPORT FORM`
- `LABEL FORM`
- `DISPLAY/LIST`

The first two choices will let you run a report or label form. The last option will run the LIST or DISPLAY dot prompt commands, after letting you choose the fields and records to be displayed or listed.

In this example, use some of the report forms you created earlier. When you select `Report`, the screen changes, as shown in Figure 20.24.

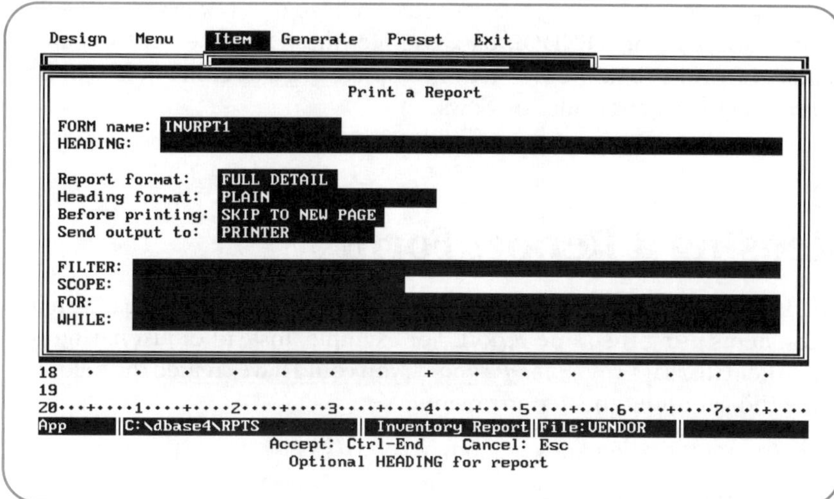

Figure 20.24. *Filling out the Report screen*

This screen gives you access to all the power of the report form. First enter the name of a report form you have already created. If you can't remember the name, press **<Shift>-<F1>** and a pick list of all your report forms will pop open on the left. If you haven't yet created the report you need, you can choose the `<create>` marker and enter the Report work surface. After creating the report form, you will be returned to the Applications Generator so you can finish filling out the screen.

You can enter a heading that will be displayed at the top of the report when it is printed, using the Heading entry area. This doesn't take the place of a heading already in your report form, it simply adds the new heading in front of it. You also can decide if you are going to print all the detail lines in the report or just the summaries, by using the `Report format` toggle. Other toggles let you determine the heading format, whether lines are skipped, if pages are ejected before printing, and where the output should be sent to.

The bottom part of the screen lets you determine which records to process as part of the report. In your example, you will not enter anything into these fields. These are three simple reports, each based on a single database file or view. The first report choice in your menu system, `Inventory Report`, requires simply that you fill out the report screen as illustrated.

The other two menu choices, `Vendor Report`, and `Complete Data Report`, require you to select `Override assigned database or view` first. The `Vendor Report` will use the VENDOR database file; the `Complete Data Report` requires the ALLITEMS view. You can complete this task either before or after overriding the database files or views.

Reusing a Report Form

This last section of the report screen gives you great flexibility in creating many menu items using the same report. For example, instead of just having one menu item that says `Inventory Report`, you could have created the following three choices under the Reports menu:

- `Complete Inventory Report`
- `Turntable Report`
- `Inventory Summary for Past 120 Days`

All three of these reports would use the same report form. The first, `Complete Inventory Report`, would have no special filter parameters. The second might have the filter COMPONENT = 'TURNTABLE', and the last choice might have the filter INVDATE <= DATE()–120 and ask for a summary report.

Though each choice used the same report form, each choice produced a different-looking report including different data. The last report would even have eliminated the detail data and just produced a summary report.

Generating the Application

After you have defined your menus and assigned your actions to each item, you can generate the program that will display these menus and perform the actions by using the `Begin generating` option on the Generate menu, shown in Figure 20.25. Before you begin to generate your application, however, you must tell dBASE IV which template to use for generating the code. A template is a road map for the generator to follow in generating its code based on the work you did on the work surface. A template called MENU.GEN is provided to generate your code. Don't worry about the other templates or custom templates. The MENU.GEN template will do an excellent job generating the code for you. When you choose the `Select template` option on the Generate menu, you will be asked for the template. Enter `MENU.GEN` and then select `Begin generating`.

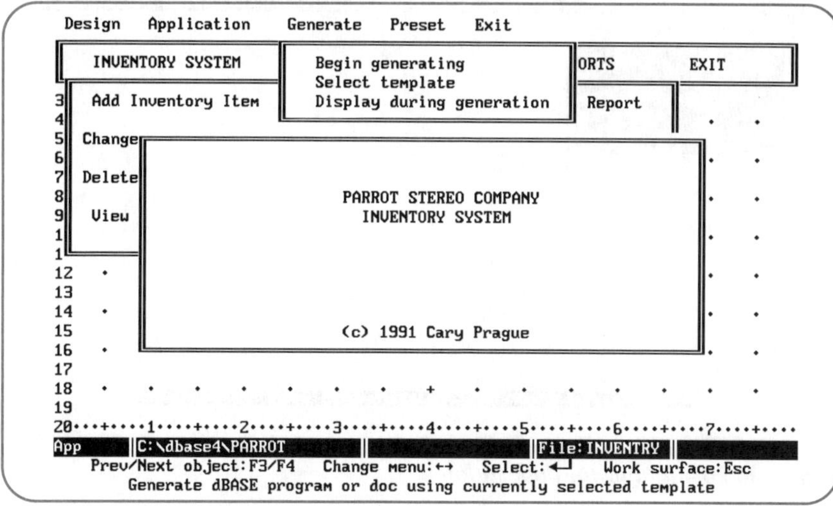

Figure 20.25. *Generating your code*

If `Display during generation` is on, dBASE IV will open a window and show you the dBASE program code as it is generated. This program code is placed in a dBASE.PRG file so that you can execute the application from the dot prompt by using the command DO <*name*>, in which <*name*> is the name you gave to the application. You also can select the PARROT application from the Control Center Applications panel and press **<Enter>** to run the application.

The running application is shown in Figure 20.26. The first menu is open, ready for you to select an item.

Generating Documentation

The dBASE IV Applications Generator also will generate documentation for the programs it generates. The documentation file is a technical overview of each function in the application. You could use the documentation file that is generated as a reference when modifying your application. You also could use the generated documentation, in conjunction with your own documentation design, to create a manual for your application system. You could use such a manual not only for your own reference, but also to train and guide the people who would actually be using the application.

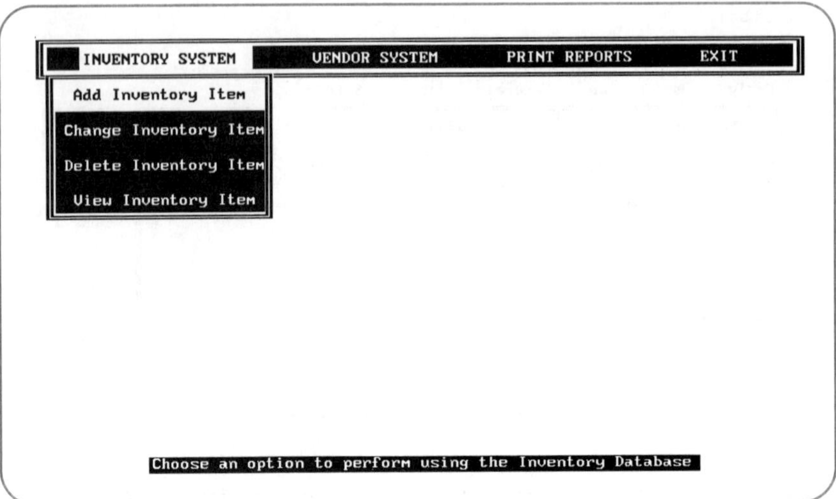

Figure 20.26. Running the application

To generate documentation, return to the Control Center and choose the PARROT application. Press **<Shift>-<F2>** to return to the Applications work surface. Your menus are not on the work surface. Menus are stored separately from the work surface. Open the Generate menu and enter `DOCUMENT.GEN`. This tells dBASE IV to create documentation instead of running a program. When you then choose `Begin generating`, a file called PARROT.DOC is created. You can print the file by going into the dBASE editor and selecting the `print menu` choice. The documentation produced by this file is shown in Figure 20.27.

```
Page: 1  Date: 04-03-91

Application Documentation for System: PARROT.PRG

Application Author: Cary N. Prague
Copyright Notice..: (c) 1991 Macmillan Computer Publishing
dBASE Version.....: 1.1

Display Application Sign-On Banner: Yes

Main Menu to Open : PARMAIN.BAR

Sets for Application:
---------------------
  Bell         ON
  Carry        OFF
  Centry       OFF
  Confirm      OFF
  Delimiters   OFF
```

Figure 20.27. Displaying the documentation file, PARROT.DOC

```
   Display Size 25 lines
   Drive
   Escape       ON
   Path
   Safety       ON

 Starting Colors for Application:
 --------------------------------
  Color Settings:
    Text           : W+/B
    Heading        : W/B
    Highlight      : GR+/BG
    Box            : GR+/BG
    Messages       : W+/N
    Information    : B/W
    Fields         : N/BG

 Database/View: INVENTRY
 Index File(s): INVENTRY
 Index Order: BRAND

================================================================================

 Menu/Picklist definitions follow:
 ---------------------------------

 Page: 2  Date: 04-03-91

 Layout Report for Horizontal Bar Menu: PARMAIN
 ----------------------------------------------

 Screen Image:
     0         10        20        30        40        50        60        70
    >....+....|....+....|....+....|....+....|....+....|....+....|....+....|....+.
 00:
 01:   INVENTORY SYSTEM        VENDOR SYSTEM       PRINT REPORTS       EXIT
 02:
 03:
 04:
 05:
 06:
 07:
 08:
 09:
 10:
 11:
 12:
 13:
 14:
 15:
 16:
 17:
 18:
 19:
 20:
 21:
 22:
 23:
 24:
    >....+....|....+....|....+....|....+....|....+....|....+....|....+....|....+.
 Setup for PARMAIN follows:
 --------------------------

  Description: Parrot Stereo Main menu
  Message Line Prompt for Menu: Choose the desired menu option

 Colors for Menu/Picklist:
 -------------------------
  Color Settings:
    Text           : RB+/N
    Heading        : BG+/N
    Highlight      : G+/N
    Box            : G+/N
    Messages       : RB+/R
    Information    : G+/RB
    Fields         : RB+/R


 Bar actions for Menu PARMAIN follow:
 ------------------------------------
 Bar: 1
  Prompt: INVENTORY SYSTEM
  Action: Open a Popup Menu Named: INVTACDV
 --------------------------------------------------------------------------------
```

Figure 20.27. Continued

```
Page: 3  Date: 04-03-91 12:40p

Bar: 2
 Prompt: VENDOR SYSTEM
 Action: Open a Popup Menu Named: VENDACDV
--------------------------------------------------------------------------------

Bar: 3
 Prompt: PRINT REPORTS
 Action: Open a Popup Menu Named: RPTS
--------------------------------------------------------------------------------

Bar: 4
 Prompt: EXIT
 Action: Return to calling program
--------------------------------------------------------------------------------
Page: 4  Date: 04-03-91

Layout Report for Popup Menu: INVTACDV
-------------------------------------

Screen Image:
   0         10        20        30        40        50        60        70
  >....+....|....+....|....+....|....+....|....+....|....+....|....+....|....+.
00:
01:
02:  ========================
03:  ‖  Add Inventory Item  ‖
04:  ‖ Change Inventory Item‖
05:  ‖ Delete Inventory Item‖
06:  ‖  View Inventory Item ‖
07:  ‖                      ‖
08:  ‖                      ‖
09:  ‖                      ‖
10:  ========================
11:
12:
13:
14:
15:
16:
17:
18:
19:
20:
21:
22:
23:
24:
  >....+....|....+....|....+....|....+....|....+....|....+....|....+....|....+.

Setup for INVTACDV follows:
--------------------------

 Description: The Inventory Add, Change, Delete, View Menu
 Message Line Prompt for Menu: Choose an option to perform using the Inventory D

Colors for Menu/Picklist:
-------------------------
 Color Settings:
   Text           : RB+/N
   Heading        : BG+/N
   Highlight      : G+/N
   Box            : G+/N
   Messages       : RB+/R
   Information    : G+/RB
   Fields         : RB+/R


Bar actions for Menu INVTACDV follow:
-------------------------------------
Bar: 1
 Prompt: Add Inventory Item
 Action: APPEND
 Format File: inventor.fmt
```

Figure 20.27. Continued

```
 Page: 5  Date: 04-03-91 12:40p
--------------------------------------------------------------------------------
Bar: 2
 Prompt: Change Inventory Item
 Action: EDIT
 Format File: inventor.fmt
--------------------------------------------------------------------------------
Bar: 3
 Prompt: Delete Inventory Item
 Action: EDIT
 Command Options:
  NOAPPEND  NOEDIT  NOCLEAR
 Format File: inventor.fmt
--------------------------------------------------------------------------------
Bar: 4
 Prompt: View Inventory Item
 Action: Browse File
--------------------------------------------------------------------------------
 Page: 6  Date: 04-03-91

Layout Report for Popup Menu: VENDACDV
--------------------------------------

Screen Image:
   0         10        20        30        40        50        60        70
  >....+....|....+....|....+....|....+....|....+....|....+....|....+....|....+.
00:
01:
02:
03:                              Add Vendor
04:                             Change Vendor
05:                             Delete Vendor
06:                              View Vendor
07:
08:
09:
10:
11:
12:
13:
14:
15:
16:
17:
18:
19:
20:
21:
22:
23:
24:
  >....+....|....+....|....+....|....+....|....+....|....+....|....+....|....+.
Setup for VENDACDV follows:
---------------------------

 Description: Vendor Add, Change, Delete, View
 Message Line Prompt for Menu: Choose the desired action for the vendor data fil

 Database/View: VENDOR
 Index File(s): VENDOR

Colors for Menu/Picklist:
-------------------------
 Color Settings:
   Text          : RB+/N
   Heading       : BG+/N
   Highlight     : G+/N
   Box           : G+/N
   Messages      : RB+/R
   Information   : G+/RB
   Fields        : RB+/R

Bar actions for Menu VENDACDV follow:
-------------------------------------
Bar: 1
```

Figure 20.27. *Continued*

```
Page: 7  Date: 04-03-91 12:41p

 Prompt: Add Vendor
 Action: APPEND
--------------------------------------------------------------------------------

Bar: 2
 Prompt: Change Vendor
 Action: EDIT
--------------------------------------------------------------------------------

Bar: 3
 Prompt: Delete Vendor
 Action: EDIT
 Command Options:
  NOAPPEND  NOEDIT  NOCLEAR
--------------------------------------------------------------------------------

Bar: 4
 Prompt: View Vendor
 Action: Browse File
--------------------------------------------------------------------------------
Page: 8  Date: 04-03-91

Layout Report for Popup Menu: RPTS
---------------------------------

Screen Image:
   0         10        20        30        40        50        60        70
  >....+....|....+....|....+....|....+....|....+....|....+....|....+....|....+.
00:
01:
02:
03:                                               Inventory Report
04:                                                Vendor Report
05:                                             Complete Data Report
06:
07:
08:
09:
10:
11:
12:
13:
14:
15:
16:
17:
18:
19:
20:
21:
22:
23:
24:
  >....+....|....+....|....+....|....+....|....+....|....+....|....+....|....+.

Setup for RPTS follows:
----------------------


Colors for Menu/Picklist:
------------------------
 Color Settings:
   Text          : RB+/N
   Heading       : BG+/N
   Highlight     : G+/N
   Box           : G+/N
   Messages      : RB+/R
   Information   : G+/RB
   Fields        : RB+/R

Bar actions for Menu RPTS follow:
--------------------------------
Bar: 1
 Prompt: Inventory Report
 Action: Run Report Form INVRPT1.frm
 Print Mode: Send to Default Printer
--------------------------------------------------------------------------------
```

Figure 20.27. *Continued*

```
Page: 9  Date: 04-03-91 12:41p

Bar: 2
 Prompt: Vendor Report
 Action: Run Report Form VENDRLET.frm
 Print Mode: Send to Default Printer
---------------------------------------------------------------------------------

Bar: 3
 Prompt: Complete Data Report
 Action: Run Report Form INVRPT2.frm
 Print Mode: Send to Default Printer
---------------------------------------------------------------------------------

End of Application Documentation
```

Figure 20.27. *Continued*

Summary

Saving development time is especially important when you're starting an application that will require a large data entry effort at the outset. If, for example, a company wanted to computerize its customer list, someone must actually enter all the information on the existing customer list into the computer. Simple data entry functions (add, change, delete, and browse) can be provided quickly with the use of an application generator, because data entry can proceed while the application is still being developed. Manual data entry functions then can be replaced by customized programs or revised to fit the needs of the system.

The dBASE IV Applications Generator is a very advanced application program generator. The program code necessary to create bar and pop-up menus is very complex—but this code is also generic. The program for one horizontal bar menu has to perform the same tasks as any other program that displays a horizontal bar menu. The only differences are the items displayed on the menu and the actions each item initiates.

You provide the names of the items, the associated prompts, their placement on the screen, and the actions to be performed when you create the menu using the Applications Generator. Even such variables as the color of the boxes, bars, and lines can be changed. All these options are plugged into the basic code to produce each type of menu, thus creating an application-specific menu for any situation. This approach is like that of a professional programmer who saves routines for later use when she or he needs a similar routine. The Applications Generator already has the basic programs necessary to produce the menus—you just fill in the blanks!

Although the Applications Generator will not create every system you might want, it can provide the basics for what you want to accomplish. It will give you an excellent foundation for your custom system.

This sophisticated approach to generating applications and documentation makes the dBASE IV Applications Generator a valuable tool. You can increase the speed with which you create prototype applications for review, and decrease the amount of time needed to create a full application system. This process will be a great advantage to you as you create your own dBASE IV application systems.

The last chapter of this book describes systems beyond the Applications Generator and tells you what to read after you finish this book.

chapter

21

From Control Center to Programming— The Next Steps

Beyond the Applications Generator

Though the Applications Generator is an excellent starting point for creating turnkey applications, eventually you will have to write some dBASE program code. The main purpose of the Applications Generator is integration. It allows you to gather all the database files, screens, and reports you have already created and almost effortlessly integrate them behind a menu-driven interface. Giving your users a series of menus to follow helps them become more productive quickly. The problem arises, however, when you want to include a feature in your system that is not available from the Applications Generator menus.

For example, you can compress field titles in the first line of the BROWSE screen, but only with a command you issue from the dot prompt. If you could change the Control Center program, you could add the COMPRESS command as a menu option.

The same is true for systems you will create with the Applications Generator. After you have created all of your database files and screens and have "hooked" them all together with the Applications Generator, you may need some specialized routines. Perhaps you don't like the way a menu works. Maybe you need to embed code more than once during a menu choice.

The Applications Generator gives you enormous flexibility because of its many allowable choices—especially the embed code feature that lets you enter dBASE program code either before or after a menu action. But that is the problem: The code allows you to add more to the process. While developing your application with the generator, you might have told dBASE that when a user selects a certain menu item, a specific action should happen, such as opening a screen for input. By embedding program code, you can also tell dBASE to do something just before and just after the action. Maybe you want to set up some defaults for screen variables before the screen is displayed. Perhaps after the user enters data, you want some additional error checking performed beyond what the screen format files allow. You might want to display a completion or error message depending on what was entered on the screen. These functions are beyond the scope of the Applications Generator. These functions are better known as "process."

Where to Go from Here

In this edition of *Everyman's Database Primer*, you have learned a lot about databases and dBASE IV. However, even with all you have learned, you have just begun to know the power of dBASE IV. Some of the topics covered in the past 20 chapters of this book include:

- Databases and files, records, and fields
- The Control Center
- The dot prompt
- BROWSE and EDIT screens
- Queries
- Reports
- Forms
- The Applications Generator

Working with several sample database files, you have built a respectable system for the Parrot Stereo Company that suits some of the company's information needs very well. The next step is to add to the system's functionality while keeping in mind the goals of simplicity and ease of use.

The main purposes of any system are:

- Getting data into the system
- Getting information out of the system

Everyman's Database Primer has provided information and exercises to improve your understanding of both of these topics. What, then, is left? There are even more complex database designs to learn. There are more complex screens and better-looking reports to create. There will always be more to learn and better things you can do with any software product.

The Power of dBASE IV

You have yet to explore many functions and features in dBASE IV. dBASE power can give you computing ability you may never have thought of. You need sound training to get the most out of any software. Poor training can lead you into expensive and nightmarish situations.

When you design your systems with dBASE IV, remember: Good systems are easy to use and bad systems are not. If you start with a base of simplicity and always sacrifice a little power for ease of use, you will usually end up with a sophisticated and efficient system. Getting there requires a conceptual understanding of the four levels of dBASE IV.

- The Control Center
- The dot prompt
- The Applications Generator
- Programming

Here is an overview of each of these dBASE components, to tie together what you have already learned about each of them.

The Control Center

The Control Center is a gateway to creating many of the pieces that make dBASE work. With it, you can move quickly among the various work surfaces. As you have learned, many of these work surfaces function together. By pressing the **<F2> Data** and **<Shift>-<F2> Design** keys, you can move from one mode to another to use your data or to create new work surface tools. You have learned how to get directly into DOS from the Control Center, and how to use the DOS interface to delete, copy, and rename files. You have also learned how to use Control Center features to create data macros and control system defaults.

Besides acting as a gateway, the Control Center performs one more important task. It lets you manage your dBASE files through its catalog management facility. As you become more expert, you will find this tool increasingly useful. Though all your files reside on the disk with dBASE, you can restrict user access to only certain files by making other files appear not to be in the catalog. This means that you can let other people use your system without worrying about their using files that are not part of your system. Catalogs also help you manage a lot of files without resorting to a number of subdirectories.

The Control Center serves as an interface between you and many dot prompt commands. The dot prompt mode, however, features several other necessary and useful dBASE commands not accessible from the Control Center menus.

The Dot Prompt

You learned about the dot prompt in this book and used it to enter simple dBASE commands. Some of these commands do things that the Control Center doesn't—including the functions DISPLAY and LIST and naming your database files, forms, queries, and reports upon creation instead of as you save them.

The dot prompt gives you another way to create database files, screens, queries, reports, and applications. It gives you a shortcut for running these same work surfaces once they are created. As you have seen throughout this book, the dot prompt provides you with alternative ways of filtering data as you run various screens and reports. The FOR and WHILE commands let you use the data, screens, and reports processes without creating a query. You can save queries, but you can't save the dot prompt filters. However, the filters do provide a quick and easy way to see specific data.

dBASE IV features more than 200 commands. Most of these are available from the dot prompt. As you continue to learn more about dBASE, you will continue to gain an understanding of the power of the dot prompt. You'll learn that knowing how to use both the dot prompt and the Control Center is important for achieving the maximum possible productivity.

Eventually, you will begin to get tired of performing the same repetitive tasks. Once you have defined your database files, screens, queries, and reports, you will want to bring them all together to work as a system. As you learned in the previous chapter, the Applications Generator is the starting place for creating a complete menu-driven system.

The Applications Generator

There are two ways to program system designs with dBASE IV. The first is to use the Applications Generator to create most, if not all, of your program quickly. The second, of course, is to do it yourself by typing out the actual dBASE programming statements. You can use the Applications Generator to reduce your coding time by generating the basic functions of a system, and you can do the more complex programming yourself as you get better at it. You can mix your code and the Applications Generator code to create a powerful system.

The Applications Generator can create many standard functions for you, including menus, add/change/delete/display programs, and even printing routines. These are the programs needed to enter and maintain the data of any file. Beyond this are the programs that can automate your processes. Certainly you now have the expertise to create a data entry screen for the records of all your employees' names and the hours they worked this week. You can even program a report to produce checks and tally deductions. But the intermediate calculations and the accumulation of year-to-date totals must be programmed. This requires programming and utilization of the full power of the dBASE IV programming language.

Programming

dBASE IV allows you to process, store, maintain, query, and report on your data without writing programs at all. The real power of dBASE, however, can be realized only by creating your own customized systems using the dBASE programming language.

The true power of a database is its language for writing *turnkey systems* (applications). A turnkey system can be operated by a person who is completely unfamiliar with the database system but who knows the business side of the system.

It is often said in data processing circles that anything can be programmed. Those of you who have been programming for any length of time know this to be true. dBASE IV runs on the same basic equipment as dBASE II, dBASE III, and dBASE III PLUS. For the most part, dBASE itself is written in languages that were around long before Wayne Ratliff, in the early '80s, wrote the first Vulcan prototype that eventually became dBASE II.

How, then, is all this new power possible if the tools haven't changed? It's like building a new house. You use the same wood, nails, hammers, and saws that have been around for decades. However, through experience and ingenuity, new architectural styles and building methods have evolved. Similarly, new software systems allow programmers to combine ease of use and power for the first time.

Anything can be programmed. It depends only on your imagination and skill. The question then becomes one of gaining this new skill. In the previous few chapters you learned about applications and programming. It is time to discuss the underlying philosophy of what happens when you work in one of the dBASE IV work surfaces and how dBASE program code is automatically produced.

Why dBASE IV Work Surfaces Produce Code

As you become better at using dBASE IV, you will understand more of the tools available to you. In some respects it is better for you to be learning dBASE now, in the early 1990s, than seven or eight years ago, when the language was raw and consisted only of program commands and the dot prompt. Many programmers today still start with a blank screen and program their applications. Even with all the new tools available, they refuse to change, because this is the way they learned. You will find that if you have half the experience of an original dBASE II programmer, you will have greater programming skills.

The last thing you want to do is write large amounts of complicated program code. In fact, you don't want to write large amounts of any type of code. This is why Ashton-Tate created the Applications Generator in dBASE IV. It provides you with a great starting point for incorporating all your work surface efforts with a menu generator that lets you create complete applications.

Every work surface in dBASE IV (except the database) creates dBASE program code. You can view this code and even rename it, modify it, and run it again with changes. This way, you achieve the beginnings of a programmed system before you even start programming. The effort it used to take to create a new system can now be spent customizing the system.

Index

Symbols

B

C

D

G

M

R

S

T

X

Z